When and Where I Enter

ABOUT THE AUTHOR

PAULA GIDDINGS, a graduate of Howard University, worked at Random House before becoming an editor at Howard University Press. Later she was Paris bureau chief for *Encore American and Worldwide News*. Her articles have appeared in *The Washington Post, Jeune Afrique, Amistad 2,* and elsewhere. She received a Ford Foundation grant for the completion of this book. Paula Giddings lives in New York City.

When and Where I Enter

The Impact of Black Women on Race and Sex in America

~ ~

Paula Giddings

106689

BANTAM BOOKS
TORONTO · NEW YORK · LONDON · SYDNEY · AUCKLAND

For Virginia I. Giddings—
my mother, my friend, my support

WHEN AND WHERE I ENTER: THE IMPACT OF BLACK WOMEN ON RACE AND SEX
*A Bantam Book / published by arrangement with
William Morrow and Company, Inc.*

PRINTING HISTORY
William Morrow edition published May 1984
A Book-of-the-Month Club Selection
Bantam edition / October 1985

Library of Congress Cataloging-in-Publication Data

Giddings, Paula.
    When and where I enter.

    Reprint. Originally published: New York: W. Morrow, 1984.
    Bibliography: p.
    Includes index.
    1. Afro-American women—Political activity—
History.   2. Feminism—United States—History.
3. Afro-Americans—Civil Rights.   4. United States—
Race relations.   I. Title.
[E185.86.G49   1985]   973'.0496   85-47761
ISBN 0-553-34225-8

Published simultaneously in the United States and Canada

---

*Bantam Books are published by Bantam Books, Inc. Its trademark, consisting of
the words "Bantam Books" and the portrayal of a rooster, is Registered in U.S.
Patent and Trademark Office and in other countries. Marca Registrada. Bantam
Books, Inc., 666 Fifth Avenue, New York, New York 10103.*

PRINTED IN THE UNITED STATES OF AMERICA

O   0 9 8 7 6 5 4 3 2 1

~ Preface
A History of Our Own ~

On the wall of my mother's bedroom is a large portrait of my great-grandmother. The woman who peers out of the oval frame is fair-skinned, with broad features; her neck is adorned with the high Victorian collar that was popular in the nineteenth century. My great-grandmother's expression is serene, tranquil—perhaps even defiantly so. For if you look closely, there is an almost imperceptible rim of determination that circles her otherwise soft, luminous eyes.

Her mother had been a slave—the daughter of a Virginia master —who had been taught the rudiments of education, fine embroidery, and music, as well as the harsher lessons of being Black and a woman in America. All of those things—and the hopes they inspired—were passed down to my great-grandmother, who, in turn, kept them alive for succeeding generations. But, the story behind those eyes remains largely untold.

That is why for a Black woman to write about Black women is at once a personal and an objective undertaking. It is personal because the women whose blood runs through my veins breathe amidst the statistics. They struggled north during the Great Black Migration, endured separations, were domestics and schoolteachers, became pillars of their community, and remained ordinary folk.

Writing such a book is also an objective enterprise, because one must put such experiences into historical context, find in them a rational meaning so that the forces that shape our own lives may be understood. *When and Where I Enter* attempts to strike a balance between the subjective and the objective. Although it is the product of extensive research, it is not without a point of view or a sense of mission. A mission to tell a story largely untold. For despite the range and significance of our history, we have been perceived as token women in Black texts and as token Blacks in feminist ones. Most of the books that focus on Afro-American women are of the "contributions" type: the achievements of Black women who, despite double discrimination and oppression, were able to duplicate the feats of Black men or White women.

What I learned by reading these texts was important and illuminating. But it wasn't enough. For Black women have a history of their own, one which reflects their distinct concerns, values, and the role they have played as both Afro-Americans and women. And their unique status has had an impact on both racial and feminist values.

So I set out to write a narrative history of Black women, tracing their concerns—and what they did about them—from the seventeenth century to the contemporary period. It is thematic in approach, using a broad canvas to illustrate the nature and meaning of the Black woman's experience. Because there is so little evidence of the *thoughts* and *ideas* of Black women, their own words, wherever possible, were used to record that experience. This meant conducting numerous interviews as well as delving into primary resources: letters, papers, and other materials found in the Library of Congress, Howard University's Moorland-Spingarn Collection, and the Bethune Historical Development Project, in Washington, D.C.; the Schlesinger Library and the Black Woman Oral History Project at Radcliffe College, in Cambridge, Massachusetts; and the Schomberg Center for Research in Black Culture, in New York City, as well as other sources. This method does bring a bias to the book. The women who appear most prominently are those who were articulate and who had a measurable impact on the Black and women's struggle in this country.

In the course of my research, several themes emerged. One of them, clearly exposed through the experience of Black women, is the relationship between sexism and racism. Because both are motivated by similar economic, social, and psychological forces, it is only logical that those who sought to undermine Blacks were also the most virulent antifeminists. The means of oppression differed across race and sex lines, but the wellspring of that oppression was the same. Black women understood this dynamic. White women, by and large, did not. White feminists often acquiesced to racist ideology, undermining their own cause in doing so. For just as there is a relationship between racism and sexism, there is also a connection between the advance of Blacks and that of women. The greatest gains made by women have come in the wake of strident Black demands for their rights.

Of course, Black women could understand the relationship between racism and sexism because they had to strive against both. In doing so they became the linchpin between two of the most important social reform movements in American history: the struggles for Black rights and women's rights. In the course of defying the imposed limitations on race and sex, they loosened the chains around both.

In the racial struggle—in slavery and in freedom—they fought in every way that men did. In the feminist battle they demanded the same protection and proprieties that the "best" White women enjoyed, but at the same time redefined the meaning of what was called "true womanhood." For the Black woman argued that her experience under slavery, her participation in the work force, her political activism, and her sense of independence made her more of a woman, not less of one.

Throughout their history, Black women also understood the relationship between the progress of the race and their own feminism. Women's rights were an empty promise if Afro-Americans were crushed under the heel of a racist power structure. In times of racial militancy, Black women threw their considerable energies into that struggle—even at the expense of their feminist yearnings. However, when militancy faltered, Black women stepped forward to demand the rights of their race from the broader society, and their rights as women from their men. The latter demand was not seen in the context of race *versus* sex, but as one where their rights had to be secured in order to assure Black progress.

Another theme of the book is how Black women transcended double discrimination—and the price they were forced to pay for that achievement. Prejudice against their race and sex forced Black women to work and simultaneously limited the kinds of work they could perform. The only choice Black women had were the professions—where until recently there was less competition from White women—or domestic work. Since education is the key to the more attractive occupations, Black women have a history of striving for education beyond what their gender or their color seemed to prescribe. Black men, on the other hand, have not had the same motivation, historically, because they had a greater range of options —including blue-collar work, which often pays better than the traditional women's professions (teaching, social work, nursing, and so on).

However, men have faced fiercer competition in those areas that White men wanted for themselves. So Black men's consequent unemployment or underemployment, combined with a frequently lower educational attainment, has caused conflict between Black men and women. However, the suggested remedy for the conflict was to slow down women's progress rather than to rectify their men's exclusion from the better-paying occupations. The prevalent attitude that the "overachievement" of Black women rather than the forced under-achievement of Black men was responsible for increasing numbers of family breakups created guilt and ambivalence in the minds of Black women. These feelings crested in the post-World War II years. And although Black women again came to the fore during the civil rights movement of the fifties and early sixties, these self-doubts remained to stultify the kind of feminist activism which had occurred at the turn of the century.

Nevertheless, the present-day crisis of Black families and Black communities; the impact of the women's movement; and the still-unrealized potential of Black leadership demand a reassessment of Black women's roles. That reassessment should reflect lessons of the past as well as realities of the present. For another theme of *When and Where I Enter* is the relevance of historical issues to the challenges we face today.

~ Acknowledgments ~

In the course of writing this book, there were many moments when I had to dig deep inside; and I would like to acknowledge the people I found there. There were my parents: a mother who encouraged me and a father who instilled pride and erased self-doubts by simply asking, "What's your name?" There were also three teachers who had an important influence in my life: Mr. Roger Sorrentino, a high-school teacher who first encouraged me to write; and Howard University professors Arthur P. Davis and Jeanne-Marie Miller, who were models of scholarship and dedication. In my professional life I was fortunate to work for two wise and caring mentors, Charles F. Harris and Ida E. Lewis.

I would also like to extend my appreciation to those who directly aided in the publication of this book. James Finkenstaedt of William Morrow supported my project from its inception. Maya Angelou, Margaret Walker Alexander, J. Saunders Redding, Clay Goss, Anna Arnold Hedgeman, and the late Alfreda M. Duster both inspired and assisted me in the crucial early stages of my work. A grant from the Ford Foundation enabled me to have the time and resources for the research and writing of the book.

When and Where I Enter was immeasurably improved by the insightful comments of those who read it in manuscript. I would like to gratefully acknowledge Bettina Aptheker, Luther P. Jackson, Jervis Anderson, Milly Hawk Daniel, and Benjamin Quarles for their thoughtful criticism.

Last but not least, special thanks are due to my editor, Eunice Riedel, whose skill, enthusiasm, and energy devoted toward this book will never be forgotten.

CONTENTS

Only the BLACK WOMAN can say "when and where I enter, in the quiet, undisputed dignity of my womanhood, without violence and without suing or special patronage, then and there the whole . . . race enters with me "
—ANNA JULIA COOPER, 1892

Part I

INVENTING THEMSELVES

... she had nothing to fall back on; not maleness, not whiteness, not ladyhood, not anything. And out of the profound desolation of her reality she may well have invented herself.

—TONI MORRISON

I

~ "To Sell My Life as Dearly as Possible": Ida B. Wells and the First Antilynching Campaign ~

Before they took his life, they asked Thomas Moss if he had anything to say. "Tell my people to go west," he told his abductors. "There is no justice for them here."[1] With those final words, Thomas Moss and two of his friends, Calvin McDowell and Henry Stewart, were lynched a mile outside of Memphis, Tennessee. A newspaper account of the mob-murder pointed out that the men did not die without a struggle. McDowell had tried to wrestle a gun from the hands of one of the killers. When the Black man's body was recovered, the fingers of his right hand had been shot to pieces; his eyes were gouged out.

The lynching of March 9, 1892, was the climax of ugly events in Memphis. From the time the three Black men had gone into business for themselves, their People's Grocery, as it was called, had been the target of White resentment. The store, which sold food and miscellaneous items and became a gathering place for Memphis Blacks, represented, after all, a desire for economic independence. The start-up capital for the grocery had been provided by Moss, a postman who was the city's first Black to hold a federal position. He worked in the store evenings, while his partners worked there during the day.

For Whites the most galling thing about the People's Grocery was that it took away business from a White store owner who had long been used to a monopoly of Black trade. The White proprietor initiated against the Black businessmen a series of provocations that culminated in an attack of armed thugs sent to raze the grocery. The attack came on a Saturday night, when the store was full of Black men —armed Black men—who repelled the invaders and shot three Whites in the process. In short order Moss, McDowell, and Stewart were arrested along with one hundred other Blacks charged with conspiracy.

The White press in Memphis whipped the community into a frenzy over the incident. The Black men were painted as "brutes" and "criminals" who victimized "innocent" Whites. If the wounded men died, Blacks were warned, there was going to be a bloodletting. The threat hung heavy in the air. Whites were permitted to enter the jail where the Blacks were interned to "look them over." Outside, Blacks stood vigil to discourage the possibility of mob violence.

The vigil ended when it was reported that the Whites would recover from their gunshot wounds—for the Blacks thought their friends would now be safe. They were wrong. In a predawn raid, Moss, McDowell, and Stewart were taken from their cells, put on the switch engine of a train headed out of the city, and lynched. In the angry aftermath of the killing, a judge issued an order for the sheriff to shoot any Black demonstrator who seemed to be "causing trouble," and prohibited the sale of guns to Blacks. Emboldened by the order, and unappeased by the death of the three men, armed Whites converged upon the People's Grocery, helped themselves to food and drink, then destroyed most of what they couldn't consume or steal. Creditors auctioned the brutalized remnants and the store was closed down on an ominous note of finality.

If the incident had occurred in any other time or place, it might have been set down as just another dreary statistic. Lynching (legally defined as murder committed by a mob of three or more persons) of Blacks had been on the rise for the last decade. In 1892, the year of the Memphis murders, there had been 255 lynchings, more than in any previous year.[2] But the deaths of Moss, McDowell, and Stewart would open a new chapter in the racial struggle, for they spurred two women to dedicate their lives to the fight against lynching and the malevolent impulses that underlined it. Two women named Mary Church Terrell and Ida B. Wells.

Terrell was living in Washington, D.C., when she heard the terrible news. Born Mary Church in Memphis, Tennessee, she had been a friend of Thomas Moss since childhood. Terrell had seen him less than a year before in Memphis, at her wedding. That had been such a happy time. She had just returned from two years of study in Europe, and it was so good to see her Memphis friends again—especially Moss. For a wedding present he gave her a set of elegant silver oyster forks.

Moss's death was particularly unsettling for Terrell at this time in her life. She was twenty-nine and, though expecting her first child, had not found peace of mind in domestic tranquility. That she always wanted to work had been a point of contention between Mary and her father since her graduation from Oberlin eight years before. A former slave who became one of the wealthiest Blacks in the country, Robert Church wanted his daughter to live the life of a gentlewoman. Ladies didn't work, he always told her. But Mary continually defied that notion. She taught at Wilberforce University and later at Washington Colored High School, despite her father's threats to disinherit her. In D.C. she met Robert Terrell, principal of the highly touted Black public school. She married him and settled in Washington, where the future of her husband—a Harvard graduate and lawyer bound for a municipal judgeship—was assured. The marriage and difficult pregnancy had almost persuaded Terrell to try to live the life of a "lady," as her father would put it. But then came the news about Thomas Moss.

She sought out an old family friend, the abolitionist Frederick Douglass, and together they secured an appointment with President Benjamin Harrison at the White House. They implored him to condemn lynching in his annual address before Congress. Douglass's plea was especially eloquent, Terrell later wrote, but like every President before Franklin Roosevelt, Harrison refused to take a public stand against lynching.

For Terrell, though, the lynching of her friend, followed not long after by the death of her newborn infant in a segregated, poorly equipped hospital, erased forever any idea of leading the traditional life of a lady. She plunged headlong into work, embarking upon a vibrant activism that would continue until her death, sixty-two years later. In a short span of time, she served as president of the country's most prominent Black cultural organization, the Bethel Literary and Historical Society; was appointed to the Washington, D.C., Board of Education, becoming the first Black woman to serve on a citywide board; and co-founded the Washington Colored Women's League.

The implications of Moss's death were seared into Terrell's memory by an editorial in the Black Memphis newspaper *Free Speech*. "The city of Memphis has demonstrated that neither character nor standing avails the Negro if he dares to protect himself against the white man or become his rival," it said in part.[3] The words were written by Ida B. Wells, columnist and co-owner of the paper. She had been so stunned by the lynching that she had had to force herself to write a cogent editorial for her readers. In her ten years as a journalist, and in the nearly half-century of writing that followed, her columns on the Moss lynching were the most painful. A woman who never made friends easily, Wells considered Thomas Moss and his wife, Betty, her very closest friends. She was godmother to their little girl, Maurine; Betty, she knew, was pregnant with her second child.

As a widely respected journalist, Wells's words were taken to heart by the beleaguered Black community. Her first editorials suggested that Blacks, vulnerable to the whims of White lawlessness, should take Moss's advice to "save our money and leave a town which will neither protect our lives and property, nor give us a fair trial in the courts, but takes us out and murders us in cold blood. . . ."[4] Those residents who could, did just that. Hundreds of Blacks began leaving Memphis for Kansas, Oklahoma, and points west. Ministers escorted whole congregations; entire families began their exodus to unknown territories, taking only what they could carry. Betty Moss stayed in Memphis until her child was born, and then moved to Indiana.

So many Blacks took the advice of Wells that the White business community began to panic. "Business was practically at a standstill," Wells recalled in her autobiography, "for the Negro was famous then, as now, for spending his money for fine clothes, furniture, jewelry, and pianos and other musical instruments, to say nothing of good things to eat. Music houses had more musical instruments, sold on the installment plan, thrown back on their hands than they could find storage for."[5] Wells also helped instigate a Black boycott of the city's trolleys, causing the transportation company to join the list of businesses beginning to teeter on the edge of bankruptcy.

Ida B. Wells didn't believe in the ultimate efficacy of passive resistance, however. She purchased a pistol, determined to "sell my life as dearly as possible," and suggested that other Blacks do the same. "A Winchester rifle should have a place of honor in every home," Wells told her community. "When the white man . . . knows he runs as great a risk of biting the dust every time his Afro-American victim does, he will have greater respect for Afro-American life."[6]

But Wells would go beyond these responses to the Moss lynching. What had occurred in Memphis was only a part of a larger phenomenon that threatened Blacks throughout the country. Her entire life, it seemed, had prepared her not only to understand but to confront the broader issue head on—despite the consequences.

Her life paralleled Mary Church Terrell's in many ways. The two women were born a year apart, and both were daughters of former slaves. Their fathers were sons of their former masters; both were men who filled their daughters with racial pride—and the spirit of defiance. Settling in Memphis after the Civil War, Robert Church was the owner of a saloon which was ransacked in the Memphis riot of 1866. He was shot in the head and left to die, but miraculously survived. The threat of continued violence did not stop him from testifying against the men in a federal inquiry, or from being politically active in the community thereafter. He was a "race man," as one would have been called then.

James Wells, Ida's father, was also a race man, in Holly Springs, Mississippi, where Ida was born. He, too, was a man who refused to be intimidated. A carpenter who worked for the town's leading contractor, Wells refused entreaties to "sell" his newly won vote. The refusal cost him his job, and without hesitation—or regret—he moved his family and went into business for himself. It was a lesson not lost on his oldest daughter. The fathers of both Wells and Terrell married energetic and determined women. Louisa Church established a fashionable hair salon in Memphis which provided the family with their first home and carriage. Elizabeth Wells thrust most of her energies into the rearing of six children, making sure they understood discipline and the need for education, both secular and religious. "Our job," Ida, the firstborn, wrote, "was to learn all we could."[7] Like so many freedmen and women, the Wellses believed deeply in the sanctity of family life. James and Elizabeth were among the many who, though married as slaves, renewed their vows "officially" as persons of free will. Their ideals made the event of 1878 all the more tragic.

That year was a turning point for both families. A yellow fever epidemic raged through the Mississippi Valley leaving death in its wake. Both of Ida's parents were consumed by the disease within twenty-four hours of each other, and their nine-month-old baby died as well. Friends tried to help out, offering to take the children in. But Ida Wells refused to have her five surviving brothers and sisters separated; her parents would "turn over in their graves," she felt, especially since one of her sisters, crippled from a spinal disease, would have been put into an institution. So at the age of sixteen, Wells ended her childhood to become the sole support of her young family. She left Rust College and, lying about her age, got a teaching position in a rural school. For two years Wells maintained a grueling schedule of riding a mule to the school each week and returning on weekends to take care of the domestic needs of her siblings, until at last relatives in Memphis could take the family in.

The epidemic changed the lives of the Churches too, but in another way. Robert Church sent his wife and daughter to New York but remained in Memphis, where residents were deserting their properties or selling them at depressed prices. Church, speculating that the city would eventually recover, bought up all the property he could. The gamble paid off in handsome dividends. Church reputedly became the first Black millionaire in the South.

Both women lived in Memphis in the 1880's. Wells attended LeMoyne Institute and received a license to teach elementary school. During summer vacations she took teachers' training courses at Fisk University. Although never a close friend of the Churches she had brief associations with both Mary and her father. Once, in dire need of funds, Wells wrote Robert Church, asking him for a loan. She was in California and did not have the fare to return to Memphis in time for the opening of the school semester. In the letter Wells assured him that she would repay the loan, with interest, and that she was a woman of reputable character. She wrote to him, Wells said, because he was "the only man of my race I knew could lend me that much money [$150] and wait for me to repay it."[8] Robert Church sent her the needed fare.

Wells also met Mary Church briefly, probably just before the latter went to Oberlin. On Ida Wells, who was serious-minded and disdained social frivolities, the meeting left a lasting impression. Mary Church was "the first woman of my age who is similarly inspired with the same desires, hopes and ambitions," she observed. "I only wish I had known her long ago."[9] At the time, Wells hardly realized that their lives would diverge, only to intersect periodically, sometimes contentiously, for the remainder of their lives. Both had distinct roles in the struggle ahead, roles shaped by the contrasting resonances of their young adult years.

While Mary Church was studying the "Gentleman's Course" at Oberlin—a curriculum that included classical Latin and Greek—Wells underwent a different sort of education. It was 1884, and Ida B. Wells took her accustomed seat in the "Ladies' Coach" of a train bound for Memphis from Woodstock, Tennessee. But by that year, customs in the South were changing. A conductor demanded that Wells leave the first-class section for the smoking car. When she refused, the conductor attempted to force her from her seat—a mistake, he quickly realized when he felt a vicelike bite on the back of his hand. He called more conductors to his aid, and to the standing cheers of the White passengers on the train, the three men dragged the petite Black passenger out of the car.

A humiliated and angry Wells returned to Memphis and immediately engaged the sole Black lawyer in the city to bring suit against the railroad. The attorney seemed to dawdle on the case, and Wells suspected that he had been bought off by the authorities. She got a White lawyer and had her day in court. Before a judge who was an ex-Union officer, the determined Wells won the decision. The case prompted a White paper, the *Daily Appeal,* to write the first of many articles about the city's most controversial resident: A DARKY DAM-SEL OBTAINS A VERDICT FOR DAMAGES AGAINST THE CHESA-PEAKE & OHIO RAILROAD ran its headlines on Christmas Day, 1884.

Needless to say, Wells was ecstatic about the victory. Inaugurating her journalistic career, she wrote an article in a Baptist weekly called the *Living Way.* If Blacks stood up for their rights, she said, those rights, granted in Reconstruction legislation, would be preserved. But what she would come painfully to realize was that Reconstruction, in more ways than one, was in rapid eclipse. What historian Benjamin Quarles calls the South's "counterrevolution," though incomplete, was inexorably moving forward. The institutionalization of "legal" disenfranchisement, segregation, and White terror tactics had not yet congealed, but it was hardening.

The Chesapeake & Ohio Railway appealed to a higher court. Company officials offered Wells more money than the damages previously awarded, if she would agree not to contest the case. Of course she refused the money, on principle, but it was not until much later that she realized the full import of the case. Wells was the first Afro-American to challenge the 1883 nullification of the Civil Rights Bill passed during Reconstruction. Her victory would have set a significant precedent—a fact not lost on the Tennessee Supreme Court, which reversed the lower court's decision.

Wells was devastated. For her, it wasn't just the loss of the case, but the loss of faith that justice would ultimately prevail. "I feel shorn of that belief and utterly discouraged. . . ." she wrote in her diary.[10] In hindsight, her despondency seems naïve, but as late as the 1880's most Blacks still believed that racial injustice was the handiwork of the lowly, an aberration that could be successfully challenged. It was their faith in the "system" that steeled their determination to be worthy citizens despite the bitter experience of slavery and discrimination. With that faith, Afro-Americans—and not just the most privileged ones—were making substantial economic gains after the war. They were attending school in droves: All in all, more than a quarter million Blacks attended more than four thousand schools established by the

Freedmen's Bureau. Afro-Americans were also making extraordinary efforts to organize their family life in the wake of a turbulent slave system. But as the twentieth century drew nearer, that deeply rooted faith in justice began to be shaken.

For Wells, the court decision brought a focus to her brooding concerns, a focus that would be expressed through journalism. She began writing a column for the *Living Way* on a regular basis, and her articles, about everything from compelling national issues to local community ones, became so popular that they were picked up by other Black newspapers throughout the country. The evolution of her career would parallel that of the Black press nationally. In the 1880's almost two hundred Black newspapers were being published every week, and the best of them—including the Detroit *Plaindealer,* the *New York Age,* and the *Indianapolis Freeman*—carried her columns under the pen name of "Iola." Wells's bold style, combined with her physical attractiveness, elicited a great deal of attention—especially from her male colleagues. The editors of the *Washington Bee* described her as a "remarkable and talented schoolmarm, about four and a half feet high, tolerably well proportioned and of ready address."[11]

The careers of Wells and Church continued on divergent paths in the late 1880's and 1890's. In 1889, while Mary Church was studying in Europe, Wells was elected as the first woman secretary of the National Afro-American Press Association. T. Thomas Fortune, editor of the *New York Age,* referring to her election at the association's convention in Washington, D.C., noted:

> She has become famous as one of the few of our women who handles a goose quill with diamond point as handily as any of us men. She is girlish looking in physique with sharp regular features, penetrating eyes, firm set thin lips, and a sweet voice. She stuck to the conference through all the row and gas and seemed to enjoy the experience. If Iola was a man she would be a humming Independent in politics. She has plenty of nerve; she is smart as a steel trap, and she has no sympathy with humbug.[12]

Although Wells, unlike Church, was always strapped for funds, she managed to buy a one-third interest in *Free Speech* that year, and none too soon, it turned out. In 1891, the year that Church married an upwardly mobile young lawyer, Wells was fired from her teaching position as a result of an exposé on the Memphis school system. Her lack of sympathy with "humbug" obviously applied as much to the Black community as to the White. Teaching, frankly, bored her anyway, but the dismissal did pose a financial problem. For all of her fame as a journalist (she was even called "Princess of the Press") it didn't pay the rent. But her new circumstances forced her to turn a passionate avocation into a full-time job. So she took to the road, traveling through Arkansas, Mississippi, and Tennessee to increase the paper's circulation. Within nine months after her school dismissal, *Free Speech* subscriptions increased from 1,500 to 3,500, and within a year she was earning the same income she had as a teacher. Wells was in Natchez on one of those business trips when she heard about the lynching of Thomas Moss.

While Terrell agonized over the incident from afar—in Washington—Wells was forced to return to a Black Memphis community in shock and despair. "I have no power to describe the feeling of horror that possessed every member of the race in Memphis when the truth dawned upon us that protection of the law was no longer ours," she wrote.[13] Wells must have had a sense of *déjà vu* from her own earlier experiences with the railroad. What she had gotten a glimmer of in 1883 was being vented full-force less than a decade later. Beginning with neighboring Mississippi in 1890, all the southern states were in the process of disenfranchising Blacks by legal means; oppressive Black codes replaced their slave antecedents; segregation was becoming the rule, and violence toward Blacks was on the increase.

Still, Blacks in Memphis, perhaps more than those of any other southern city, were convinced that the blood tides would not reach them. True, Memphis had been the scene of one of the worst postwar riots in the country, when forty-six Black men, women, and children were killed and more than $100,000 worth of Black-owned property was destroyed. Black women had been especially victimized by the violence. Federal inquiries revealed that many of them, living alone, were robbed, beaten, and raped. Cynthia Townsend, a Black woman who testified before federal authorities, told of a neighbor who was attacked by "three or four men," all of whom "had connexion [sic] with her in turn around, and then one of them tried to use her mouth." The woman, Townsend told the authorities, "has sometimes become a little deranged since then."[14]

It was widely believed that such racial violence was a perversion, the work of poor Whites who had always resented economic competition from Blacks. But endemic racial violence was a thing of the past, many Blacks believed. In subsequent years, Black businessmen had thrived; Black legislators were elected to state and city government. But the Moss lynching of 1892 dimmed such optimism. And the rude awakening sent Wells and Terrell on a course that changed both their lives. Their approaches were different—symbolized by Wells purchasing a pistol, situated as she was within the belly of the beast, while Terrell, no doubt wearing her accustomed white gloves and expensive strand of pearls, went to the White House. Each would be effective in her own way; but Wells's radical response would have a more immediate impact.

"The Truth About Lynching"

The lynching of Thomas Moss further clarified Wells's perspective: The increasing violence toward Blacks had little to do with their alleged criminal behavior; rather lynching was the tool of the new caste system being imposed by the South. For Thomas Moss, everyone knew, was a good man, a loving husband and father, and a sterling citizen. His only crimes were to succeed at a business of his own, then to defend himself when Whites tried to destroy it. Furthermore, his murder was not at the hands of a few aberrants, but with the entire White establishment as accomplice. "The more I studied the situation," wrote Wells, "the more I was convinced that the Southerner had never gotten over his resentment that the Negro was no longer his plaything, his servant, and his source of income."[15] The resentment was even more intense, she surmised, toward Blacks who were in a position to compete with Whites. Lynching was a direct result of the gains Blacks were making throughout the South.

Thomas Moss was only one of a growing number of Afro-Americans who were planting solid economic stakes into southern soil. At the turn of the century, the National Negro Business League, an organization founded by Booker T. Washington, reported that in a city as small as Montgomery, Alabama, with two thousand Black residents, there were:

> . . . twenty-three Black-owned restaurants, a dry-goods store, thirty shoe-makers, twelve contractors and builders, fifteen blacksmith shops, wood and coal yards, butcher stalls, greengrocers, draymen, insurance and real-estate agents, a lawyer, a dentist, 400 preachers, five physicians, and two undertakers—all doing well.[16]

The same report noted that 187,000 Afro-Americans in the South owned their own farms, several of them more than a thousand acres in size. How such figures could be translated into political power was vividly seen in the Populist movement of the late nineteenth century. The movement was made up of farmers who sought to wrest control from the planter class, and in a number of contests, Blacks held the balance of power in electing Populist candidates in the South. If something weren't done, Blacks could upset the South's long-standing political and economic power base. For Black men now represented a significant portion of the electorate; in some states like Mississippi —whose border lay close to Memphis—there were more Black eligible voters than White. There was no doubt about it: Afro-Americans were a threat and lynching was the means to counteract it.

Of course Whites used a more devious rationale to explain the "strange" dark-skinned "fruit" hanging from southern trees. The "Black peril," authorities like Philip A. Bruce proclaimed, was loosed upon the land of the magnolias.

There was no better candidate to articulate the "danger" for the entire nation than Bruce. He was a trained historian; the son of a plantation owner who had lorded over five hundred slaves; the brother-in-law of writer Thomas Nelson Page; the nephew of the Confederacy's former secretary of war—and a Harvard graduate. Bruce's thesis, formulated in the 1889 publication *The Plantation Negro as a Freeman,* was that Blacks, "cut off from the spirit of White society," had regressed to a primitive and thus criminal state. Bereft of the master's influence, Blacks were now even closer to the "African type" than the slaves had been.

This sudden outbreak of barbarism included a penchant for rape. Black men, he said, "found something strangely alluring and seductive in the appearance of White women."[17] If any poor Black soul thought he could take refuge from the sweeping charges on the basis of his class, he was sorely mistaken. The regression and attendant lust was as true for "the Black legislator, the teacher who graduated from college, and the preacher who studied the Bible as it was for the common laborer," Bruce concluded.[18] In fact, as a *Harper's Weekly* article noted, middle-class Blacks were the *greater* threat. For it was they who were "most likely to aim at social equality and to lose the awe with which in slavey times, Black men had learned to respect the woman of the superior race."[19] The magazine called the phenomenon "The New Negro Crime."

The charge was leveled so consistently against Black men, and came from such impeccable sources, that the whole nation seemed to take it for granted. Not only *Harper's* but other scholarly and reputable magazines and newspapers wrote about the "new crime." The liberal reformer Jane Addams, though opposed to lynching, nevertheless believed that Black men had a proclivity for rape. Even some Blacks began to wonder. Frederick Douglass had begun to believe that "there was an increasing lasciviousness on the part of Negroes," according to Wells.[20] Wells herself had doubts: "Like many another person who had read of lynching in the South," she wrote, "I had accepted the idea meant to be conveyed—that although lynching was irregular and contrary to law and order . . . perhaps the brute deserved death anyhow and the mob was justified in taking his life."[21]

But Moss and his friends were not guilty of any crime, "new" or otherwise. Perhaps others weren't either. Perhaps, as Wells wrote, "lynching was merely an excuse to get rid of Negroes who were acquiring wealth and property and thus keep the race terrorized and 'keep the nigger down.' "[22] Wells set out to find the truth by investigating every lynching she could. For months, she culled newspaper accounts, went to the scene of lynchings, interviewed eyewitnesses. All in all, she researched the circumstances of 728 lynchings that had taken place during the last decade.

The result was a fastidiously documented report. Only a third of the murdered Blacks were even *accused* of rape, much less guilty of it, Wells discovered. Most were killed for crimes like "incendiarism," "race prejudice," "quarreling with Whites," and "making threats." Furthermore, not only men but women and even children were lynched. "So great is Southern hate and prejudice," Wells wrote, "they legally (?) hung poor little thirteen-year-old Mildrey Brown at Columbia, S.C., Oct. 7th on the circumstantial evidence that she poisoned a white infant. If her guilt had been proven unmistakeable, had she been White," Wells concluded, "Mildrey Brown would never have been hung. The country would have been aroused and South Carolina disgraced forever. . . ."[23]

Had Wells been content to publish these findings, she would have been provocative enough. But she tempted fate even further by exposing the rawest nerve in the South's patriarchal bosom. In the course of her investigations, Wells uncovered a significant number of interracial liaisons. She dared to print not only that such relationships existed, but that in many cases White women had actually taken the initiative. Black men were being killed for being "weak enough," in Wells's words, to "accept" White women's favors.

Wells gave an example of a lynch victim who had tried to escape the advances of his boss's daughter, even to the point of quitting his job. The woman pursued him, however, and when they were discovered together, the girl charged rape. In another instance, Wells investigated a case in Indianola, Mississippi, where a man was lynched after allegedly raping an eight-year-old girl. The girl, Wells discovered, was not eight but *eighteen* and had been a frequent visitor to the Black man's cabin. The journalist also documented several cases of White women calmly bearing Black babies; one such woman, to protect her lover, tried to deny that she was White. She had reason. Several Black men had been lynched for the crime of miscegenation.

When two more lynchings occurred while Wells was still conducting her investigations, she wrote the editorial that prompted her permanent banishment from the South. "Nobody in this section of the country believed the threadbare lie that Negro men rape white women," she challenged. "If Southern white men are not careful, they will overreach themselves and public sentiment will have a reaction. A conclusion will then be reached which will be very damaging to the moral reputation of their women."[24]

Fortunately, while the editorial was still being set into type she was on her way to Philadelphia to accept a long-standing invitation from the activist and writer Frances Ellen Harper. From Philadelphia she went to New York, where she was met by T. Thomas Fortune of the *New York Age*. By then, the editorial had come out in Memphis and the backlash had been brutal and immediate. Wells's newspaper office was looted and burned to the ground; her co-owners, barely beating the mob, were run out of town; and Wells herself was warned that she would be hanged from a lamppost if she were to return. There were "agents" posted at the train station, she was told, to watch out for her. Fortune, who was no stranger to the South (he was a Floridian) was troubled by the news from Memphis. Now that she was in New York, he told her, "I'm afraid that you will have to stay."[25]

"The issue was forced," Wells thought after hearing the reaction to her editorial. She would simply have to fight from "exile." On June 5, 1892, the *New York Age* carried her seven-column article on its front page. Touted as the "first inside story of Negro lynching," it included names, dates, places, and circumstances of hundreds of lynchings for alleged rape. The response to the article was sensational and Fortune published ten thousand copies of the issue; one thousand were sold in the streets of Memphis alone.

In the following months, as a paid contributor, Wells continued to write two weekly columns for the paper under the heading "Iola's Southern Field." Always the businesswoman, Wells also purchased a one-fourth interest in the *Age* in exchange for her *Free Speech* subscription list.

Wells next wanted to publish her investigative findings in booklet form. But she faced the ever-present problem of insufficient funds to underwrite such an enterprise. In 1892, Black women came to her aid. They planned a testimonial, both in honor of her courageous stand and to raise funds for her booklet, which would be called "Southern Horror: Lynch Law in All Its Phases."

The testimonial, held October 5 in New York City's Lyric Hall, was a historic event: "the greatest demonstration ever attempted by race women for one of their own number," Wells later wrote.[26] Never before had so many leading women of the race come together. Two hundred and fifty Black women came to honor Wells, and the list was a veritable *Who's Who* of the Black eastern establishment. Present was Boston's Josephine St. Pierre Ruffin, a suffragist, activist, and wife of a prominent legislator and judge. Dr. Susan McKinney from Brooklyn was also there. She was the valedictorian graduate of Long Island Medical College and considered the leading woman physician of the race. Sarah Garnet, the first Black principal of an integrated school in New York, and widow of the famous abolitionist Henry Highland Garnet, also attended, as did the journalist Gertrude Mossell, whose Philadelphia family could trace its activism and wealth to the eighteenth century. The prime organizer for the event was Victoria Earle Matthews of New York, whose White Rose Working Girls Home was a predecessor of the Urban League.

The testimonial had all the earmarks of a grand occasion. Wells's pen name, Iola, was spelled out in electric lights across the dais. The printed programs were miniature prototypes of the Memphis *Free Speech*. Soul-stirring music was interspersed with uplifting speeches. Five hundred dollars was collected for the booklet, which Wells dedicated "To the Afro-American women . . . whose race love, earnest zeal and unselfish effort made possible this publication."

Wells *was* genuinely grateful for the support—if a little surprised by it, especially since it was initiated in New York. The city, she knew, "had the name of being cold-blooded and selfish in its refusal to be interested in anybody or anything who was not to the manner born, whose parents were not known, or who did not belong to their circle."[27] The pistol-toting journalist was many things, but she was not "to the manner born."

But as Wells's investigations had so vividly revealed, all Blacks, regardless of class or achievement, were vulnerable. Also, the nature of Wells's campaign had struck a particular chord in Black women, who had never been thought of as a significant factor in the racial struggle, who remained unprotected, and who were held responsible for the denigration forced upon them. They well knew, as Wells stated publicly, that while Black men were being accused of ravishing White women, "The rape of helpless Negro girls, which began in slavery days, still continues without reproof from church, state or press."[28]

The negative images of Black women had always made them vulnerable to sexual assault, but by the late nineteenth century, that stereotype had even more sweeping consequences. Philip Bruce had included women in his diatribe against the race. They, too, were "morally obtuse" and "openly licentious," he wrote. But because they were women, their regression was seen as much worse than that of men. For it was women who were "responsible" for molding the institution of marriage and a wholesome family life which was the "safeguard against promiscuity." In Bruce's eyes, Black women who saw no "immorality in doing what nature prompts," who did not "foster chastity" among their own daughters, were not only responsible for their own denigration but for that of the *entire race*. Even the Black man's alleged impulse to rape was the Black woman's fault. Historically, the stereotype of the sexually potent Black male was largely based on that of the promiscuous Black female. He would have to be potent, the thinking went, to satisfy such hot-natured women. Now released from the constraints of White masters, the Black man found White women so "alluring" and "seductive" because, according to Bruce, of the "wantonness of the women of his own race."[29]

Wells's campaign, by undermining the stereotype of Black men, also challenged presumptions of the immorality of Black women.[30] And it was the public defense of the integrity of Black women, by Black women, which opened the way for the next stage of their political development. Black women like those at Lyric Hall responded to Ida B. Wells's antilynching campaign as not only a call to arms for the race, but for women specifically as well.

The ideas that drew them into battle were older than the Republic itself—for they were rooted in the European minds that shaped America.

II

~ Casting of the Die: Morality, Slavery, and Resistance ~

> I most sincerely doubt if any other race of women could have brought its fineness up through so devilish a fire.
> —W.E.B. Du Bois

Chattel slavery in the North American colonies preceded the arrival of the first African men and women, who came to Virginia in 1619. Many of the White, mostly poor, indentured servants who came to the colonies found themselves "manipulated in the interests of the [Virginia] Company" and "held in servitude beyond a stipulated term," according to colonial historian James Ballagh. The system of indenture, he added, "tended to pass into a property relation which asserted a control of varying extent over the bodies and liberties of their person during service as if they were things."[1] Henry Spelman knew that; in 1609 he was sold to a group of Native Americans by Captain John Smith. In the same year, Thomas Salvage was traded to Native Americans for one of their own servants.

Furthermore, not all of the approximately quarter-million servants who came to the settlements did so voluntarily. Some were kidnapped, others lured under false pretenses, coerced or entrapped. They came on overcrowded ships, were hoisted onto auction blocks where they were stripped, examined, and sold without regard to the separation of families. They were thought to be contented with their lot, lazy, and immoral. Female servants were sexually exploited by masters. And not all so victimized were adults. Records show the arrival of 1,500 "friendless boyes and girls" who were expropriated to work in the colonies. The authorities were so pleased with their services, they pleaded for more.

A month before African men and women set foot in Virginia, the colony's legislative body, the House of Burgesses, passed a law stating that masters could whip their servants and that female servants could not marry without the master's consent. Another ominous development was that in the same year, 90 "young and incorrupt" English women were sold to the Virginia settlers as wives for 120 pounds of tobacco each.

During the first years of the African presence in North America, Blacks had a higher status than other servants, because the circumstances of their seizure put them under the protection of international law. The first Africans worked as servants for the colonial administrators, and in subsequent years they worked side by side with White servants. Africans worked out their indentures, and several subsequently purchased large parcels of land—and the services of their own servants. Black women and White also shared the same kinds of labor in a society where, as historian Eleanor Flexner points out, little distinction was made among the duties of the indentured servant, the artisan's wife, and the gently born mistress.

Perhaps the historically most important Black woman of the first generation of Africans was Isabell Williams. Her marriage to Anthoney, who had been on the same ship, resulted in the birth of probably the first Black child in America. Baby Williams made his auspicious appearance in 1624. The threesome were not listed as servants on the official register, indicating that they were most likely free persons in the colony.

But all of that would change as the need for labor—more profitable labor—increased. Some would have to be exploited more than others, and that meant creating categories of class and color. The dress rehearsal for slavery and sexual exploitation had already taken place, and the mind-set of the English administrators influenced the casting of the various roles. It was a seventeenth-century mind that had been shaped by the Renaissance, with its cult of individualism and the "moral" right to exploit those weaker than oneself; by the Protestant Reformation's ethic and evangelical piety, which separated body from soul; by the Age of Discovery, which found a continent of people different from the explorers; and by the Commercial Revolution, with its vision of wealth on a global scale. The slow but inexorable change in the status of Blacks and women reflected all these developments.

The 1619 bride sale presupposed that the settlers made a distinction between servants and those "incorrupt" women specifically imported to be wives. After all, it had been accepted as far back as Plato that women fell into three categories: whore, mistress, and wife—the last of whom was expected to organize the household and provide "legitimate" heirs to her husband's material acquisitions.

Of course, acquisition was what this early multinational corporation, later called America, was largely about. And the seventeenth-century outpost of Western civilization offered a tremendous challenge to colonial administrators. Profit had to be wrung out of an erotic wilderness that could make a man forget why he was there in the first place. The challenge became more emotive as the colonies were populated by increasing numbers of Africans, who at once represented the means of wealth and the "dark," sensuous side of the English soul. So, Englishmen had to "remind themselves constantly what it meant to be civilized, Christian, rational, sexually controlled and white," observed historian Ronald Takaki.[2] This need would have a tremendous impact on the history of both women and Blacks in America. Blacks would be victimized by the White impulse to affirm, through Black degradation, "the virtues of self-control and industry";[3] to impute "to people they call 'savages' the instinctual forces they had within themselves," as Takaki observed.[4]

While Blacks were to be degraded for this purpose, White women would be "elevated"—sometimes tyrannically so. In addition to organizing the household, their job was to civilize men, raise them "above the sordid and sensual considerations which hold sway . . . in their intercourse with each other."[5] The Protestant ethic, which delayed gratification in order to accumulate capital, did not abide well with "sordid and sensual considerations." And women who provoked passion rather than warding it off were looked down upon and often punished.

Black women—described by English slave traders as "hot constitution'd ladies," possessed of a "lascivious temper," who had an inclination for White men—would be impaled on the cutting edges of this race/sex dialectic.[6]

Thus it is little wonder that the focus fell on them when colonial administrators began to make this dialectic the law of the land. The first judicial decision that specifically referred to race in the model Virginia colony involved a Black woman. The decision, *Re: Davis*, rendered in 1630, read:

> Hugh Davis to be soundly whipt before an assembly of negroes & others for abusing himself to the dishonor of God and the shame of Christianity by defiling his body in lying with a negro which fault he is to actk [sic] Next sabbath day.[7]

As law historian A. Leon Higginbotham infers, since the race of Davis was not mentioned he was probably White. The rarity of masters' being whipped suggests that Davis was not a member of that class. The tendency of court records to specify the given names of Black men leaves one to assume that the "negro" in question was a woman (and further, that Black women were held in lower regard than Black men). Although all "fornicators" were punished (if caught, that is) Davis's crime evidently contravened not only the law of man, but of God and Christianity as well. That his punishment was to be witnessed by an "assembly of negroes" indicates it was to be an example for the Black community as well as the White.

The implications of the Davis decision became clearer as the number of Africans rose in the colony from a mere twenty-three in 1625 to three hundred by 1640. The increase stimulated the inexorable force that would bind slavery and race inextricably. No African man or woman who set foot in Virginia after 1640 had the benefit of indentures or the hope that their "service" would be anything but lifelong. Other colonies also reflected this trend. In that year a Black servant, John Punch, and two White servants were found guilty of attempting to run away from their master in Maryland. The Whites were sentenced to four additional years of service, but Punch was to serve his master "or his assigns for the time of his natural life, here or elsewhere." For Blacks it was an ominous precedent, although there was still equal-opportunity exploitation: A year later Massachusetts, that bastion of Puritan piety, became the first colony to recognize slavery by statute, but its first victim was a White servant sentenced to slavery for hitting his master. Also in 1641, Virginia authorized the branding of both Black and White servants.

In the same year as the Punch case, a Virginia court again rendered a decision regarding the punishment of a White man who slept with a Black woman, impregnating her. Perhaps reflecting the deterioration of the status of Blacks in the colony, this time the woman was to be whipped for the indiscretion while the man simply did penance before the church.

By 1643, clear evidence that Blacks were seen as less than human came with the plummeting status of Black women that was established by Virginia's new division of labor. In 1629, Virginia administrators had designated "tithable persons" as all those that "worke in the ground of what qualitie or condition soever." In 1643, however, tithable persons included all adult men and in addition *Black* women.[8] This distinction was made twice again before 1660 in Virginia, and Maryland adopted a similar policy in 1664. How the new division of labor reflected upon women of African descent became clear in a 1656 tract written by Virginia's John Hammond. Servant women, he wrote, were to be used in a domestic capacity, rather than the field. "Yet som wenches," he concluded "that are nasty and beastly and not fit to be so employed are put in the ground."[9]

In 1661 Virginia gave official statutory recognition to slavery, and seven years later erased the ambiguity surrounding the status of the Black woman in the colony. Was she "nasty and beastly" because of her color, or because of her status? The question was answered simply. Even free Black women were to be considered tithable, the law stipulated, and they should in no way expect to be "admitted to full fruition of the exemptions and impunities of the English."[10] A year later Virginia passed the most insidious legislation affecting Black women:

> Children got by an Englishman upon a Negro woman shall be bond or free according to the condition of the mother, and if any Christian shall commit fornication with a Negro man or woman, he shall pay double the fines of the former act.[11]

The circle of denigration was virtually complete with this law, which managed to combine racism, sexism, greed, and piety within its tenets. Fornication with a Black woman or man was unchristian and so carried a greater fine than intraracial liaisons. At the same time, children born of a Black woman, no matter who the father was, would inherit *her* status—which was rapidly becoming synonymous with that of a slave. That the status was inherited from the mother was in direct contradiction of the English law—and with reason. Such legislation laid women open to the most vicious exploitation. For a master could save the cost of buying new slaves by impregnating his own slave, or for that matter having anyone impregnate her. Being able to reproduce one's own labor force would be well worth the fine, even in the unlikely event that it would be imposed.

White women were not immune to these legal developments. Virginia administrators were always complaining about "loose" servant women who attempted to gain their freedom by laying "all their bastards to their master." It was no coincidence that in the same year the above legislation was passed, another law said that any servant woman who had a child by her master was subject to two additional years of service. The guilty servant was to be "sold" to the church-wardens, who would employ her in the tobacco fields. The fruits of her labor would be shared by the parish. (Interestingly, men were not punished for their role in the matter.) The preamble of the 1662 law demonstrated the impulse to "raise" White women while denigrating Black women. White servant women were sentenced to the church, to discourage the tendency of "dissolute masters" who had "gotten their maids with child" in order to claim economic benefits.[12] That of course was exactly what the law regarding Black women encouraged.

But in the late seventeenth century it was evident that a loophole was undermining all of this meticulous legislation. White women, and, most disturbingly, free White women, continued to cohabit and produce mulatto children with Black men. Consequently, in 1691 another piece of legislation stipulated that any free Englishwoman who had a "bastard child by a Negro" was to pay a fine of fifteen pounds. Default in payment meant that she would be sold to those mean old churchwardens for five years.[13] But what if they or even White servant women chose to marry their Black partners? Well, that was taken care of too. Another provision of the law showed that the administrators had come to realize that everyone had to be taken into consideration. The provision said that if a White, whether bond or free, intermarried with a Negro, mulatto, or Indian, bond or free, the couple would be banished from the colony forever—a grim punishment in the seventeenth century. Even so, the punishment could have been worse. Banishment may have been chosen by the Virginia lawmakers after hearing of the problems of their sister colony Maryland, which also tried to stop interracial marriages. There they attempted to *enslave, for the lifetime of her husband,* any freeborn Englishwoman who married a Black slave. However, the courts were finally forced to rescind the law. The attitude toward Blacks, the laws of God, and pure White womanhood notwithstanding, so many masters purchased White women for the explicit purpose of marrying them to their Black slaves, "thus making slaves out of them," that it had become a scandal.

By 1705 Virginia had made it patently clear who were slaves and who were not. In that year, the publication of Robert Beverley's *History & Present State of Virginia* carried a note of finality regarding the status of both Blacks in general and Black women in particular. "Slaves are the Negroes" he wrote and:

> Sufficient distinction is also made between the female Servants & Slaves: for a White woman is rarely or never put in the Ground, if she be good for anything else, and to Discourage all Planters from using Women so. Their Law imposes the heaviest Taxes

upon Female-Servants working in the Ground. . . . Whereas on the other hand it is a common thing to work a Woman Slave out of Doors: nor does the law make any Distinction in her Taxes, whether her Work be Abroad or at Home.[14]

So, by the early eighteenth century an incredible social, legal, and racial structure was put in place. Women were firmly stratified in the roles that Plato envisioned. Blacks were chattel, White men could impregnate a Black woman with impunity, and she alone could give birth to a slave. Blacks constituted a permanent labor force and metaphor that were perpetuated through the Black woman's womb. And all of this was done within the context of the Church, the operating laws of capitalism, and the psychological needs of White males. Subsequent history would be a variation on the same theme.

Resistance

In its infancy, slavery was particularly harsh. Physical abuse, dismemberment, and torture were common to an institution that was far from peculiar to its victims. Partly as a result, in the eighteenth century, slave masters did not underestimate the will of their slaves to rebel, even their female slaves. Black women proved especially adept at poisoning their masters, a skill undoubtedly imported from Africa. Incendiarism was another favorite method; it required neither brute physical strength nor direct confrontation. But Black women used every means available to resist slavery—as men did—and if caught were punished as harshly.

In 1681 a slave named Maria and two male companions were tried for attempting to burn down the home of their master in Massachusetts. One of the men was banished from the colony; the other was hanged. In the judgment of the Puritan court however, Maria's crime was more serious than mere arson. The court found that "she did not have the feare of God before her eyes" and that her action was "instigated by the devil."[15] Whether Maria feared God or not is open to speculation, but it is not difficult to imagine the look in that woman's eyes. Maria was burned at the stake, and perhaps as an afterthought the lifeless body of her companion was thrown in to burn with her ashes.

In 1708 a woman was among a small band of slaves who killed seven Whites in Newton, Long Island. Four of the slaves were executed; the men were hanged, the woman burned at the stake.

In 1712, New York City (where the first non-Indian women were Black) was gripped in the panic of a slave revolt. Twenty-three slaves, men and women, had armed themselves with guns and knives and gathered to set fire to a slaveholder's house. They were ultimately subdued, but not before nine Whites had been killed and six injured. Among those arrested was a slave woman, visibly pregnant.

In 1732 the discovery of a slave plot in Louisiana resulted in the hanging of a Black woman and the "breaking on the wheel" of four of her male conspirators. Their heads were stuck onto poles at each end of New Orleans as a warning to others.

In 1741, a slave named Kate and a Black boatswain were convicted of trying to burn down the *entire community* of Charlestown, Massachusetts. Like Maria, Kate was singled out for having a "malicious and evil intent." (The devil, it seems, was very busy in Massachusetts.)

In 1766 a slave woman in Maryland was executed for setting fire to her master's home, tobacco house, and outhouse, burning them all to the ground. The prosecutor in the case noted that there had been two other houses full of tobacco burnt "in the country this winter."[16]

Few attempted revolts struck more fear into the hearts of slaveholders than the one led by Nancy Prosser and her husband, Gabriel, in Virginia, when one thousand slaves met outside of Richmond in 1800 and marched on the city. Though they were routed by the militia, the specter lingered of thousands of slaves—estimated at two thousand to fifty thousand in number—primed for rebellion.

Black women resisted slavery in other ways as well. During the Revolutionary War period for example, the issue of slavery was raised anew as the contradictions sharpened between enslavement of Blacks on the one hand and the colonists' struggle for independence on the other. In this era, slaves like Jenny Slew and Elizabeth Freeman (an eighteenth-century relative of W.E.B. Du Bois) of Massachusetts successfully sued for their freedom on the grounds that the Bill of Rights applied to them as "persons." Freeman's case, heard in 1781, established the legal fact that "a Bill of Rights, in Massachusetts at least, had indeed abolished slavery."[17] The success of Slew and Freeman, among others, largely reflected the fact that the late eighteenth century was a fluid period for Blacks. The underlying philosophy of the war was one reason; the need for Black soldiers to fight it was another. In the beginning, the American commanders were loath to arm Blacks or permit them to fight. However, the need for additional manpower, and the fact that the English Loyalist forces not only welcomed Blacks but promised them freedom for their efforts, made the Americans respond in kind.

An intriguing footnote to this history is that at the height of the war, George Washington invited a Black slave to confer with him at his headquarters. The slave was Phillis Wheatley, a poet who had published a volume of verse and thus become the first Black and the second woman in America to do so. What the country's most famous slaveholder and the country's most famous slave discussed during the half-hour meeting is open to speculation. However, only days later, George Washington issued an order to conscript Blacks into the Continental Army.

The role of Blacks in the Revolutionary War, the discontent of a White working class forced to compete with slave labor, and the infeasibility of slavery at a time of increasing industrialization hastened its abolition in the North by 1830. At the same time, however, slavery became more viable in the South with the invention of the cotton gin and the demands for cotton to feed England's nascent industrial revolution. But after 1830 there were new challenges hurled at the South. The increased number of freedmen and women —there were 100,000 in the South alone by 1810—and the rise of the new abolitionists bent on total and uncompensated abolition, demanded a new southern strategy, one that would suppress the potential for slave revolts such as the Nat Turner rebellion in 1831. And the institution did indeed change.

After 1830 slavery became "domesticated," according to historian Willie Lee Rose. It became "a domestic institution which came to mean slavery idealized, slavery translated into a fundamental and idealized institution, the family."[18] Especially among the wealthier planters, this meant that slave masters adopted a new ethic, and a new image. No longer the cruel and sadistic abusers who kept slaves in submission by beating them half to death, they became "benign," if stern, patriarchs who lorded over their Black "brood." The stick was replaced by the carrot. Masters provided protection, physical necessities, and minimum brutality in return for slave obedience and loyalty. This practice was even reflected in the new Slave Codes, which required that slaves be decently provided for, while prohibiting cruel and unusual punishment.

If the social contract was upheld on both sides, then the slave master and his slaves ideally functioned like an extended "family."

Thus prevailed the resplendent myth of the Big House with the wily mammy, and house slaves—some of whom may have been the master's own progeny. Thus the tranquil picture of the field couples in their cabin surrounded by grinning pickaninnies; of "aunties" and "uncles" with eyes lidded by years of obedience. And what better authority figure than the paternalistic slave master, aristocratic in bearing, bragging that his slaves were better treated than the working classes of Europe? And of course there was the mistress, patronizingly tolerant, and as loyal to Mammy as Mammy was to her.

However operative all this was in practice, the ideal of a Victorian domestic institution had a tremendous effect on slaves and on women. Although the slaves may have been physically better off than before, the psychological effects of the new slavery were potentially devastating. Along with the "benefit" of obedience came the no-holds-barred response to disobedience. The double-sided coin "caused abolitionists to assert that slavery was becoming harsher with each passing year, and enabled southern apologists to state, with equal confidence, that slavery was becoming milder," notes Willie Lee Rose. She continues:

> In fact both sides were right, and both sides were wrong. As physical conditions improved, the slave's essential humanity was being recognized. But new laws restricting chattels' movement and eliminating their education indicate blacks were categorized as a special and different kind of humanity, as lesser humans in a dependency assumed to be perpetual. In earlier, harsher times, they had been seen as luckless, unfortunate barbarians. Now they were to be treated as children never expected to grow up.[19]

The emphasis on family was another dimension of the new slavery. Unlike the slavocracies of South America and the Caribbean, Southerners encouraged organic family units among their slaves. In other countries there were disproportionate numbers of male slaves, illustrating the tendency of those countries primarily to import males to work the plantations. In contrast, by 1840 the ratio of Black men to women in the United States was almost equal. This factor had a number of consequences: Family relationships among American slaves both discouraged rebellion and runaways, and encouraged a self-sustaining reproduction of the labor force.

The Victorian family ideal also carried a specific consequence for women. White southern women found themselves enmeshed in an interracial web in which wives, children, and slaves were *all* expected to obey the patriarchal head of the household, as historian Anne Firor Scott observed. The compliance of White women became inextricably linked to that of the slaves. For, it was believed, "any tendency of one member of the system to assert themselves against the master threatened the whole."[20] As it was often asserted by slavery apologists, any change in the role of women *or* Blacks would contribute to the downfall not only of slavery, but of the family and society as well. Little wonder that the English-born feminist Margaret Fuller held that "There exists in the mind of men a tone of feeling toward women as toward slaves."[21] Little wonder that the earliest White American feminists, Angelina and Sarah Grimké, had been reared in a wealthy slaveholding family. And little wonder, too, that southern women, as a group, were the most reluctant to assert a feminist sensibility.

The Victorian "extended" family also put the "moral" categories of women into sharp relief. The White wife was hoisted on a pedestal so high that she was beyond the sensual reach of her own husband. Black women were consigned to the other end of the scale, as mistresses, whores, or breeders. Thus, in the nineteenth century, Black women's resistance to slavery took on an added dimension. With the diminution of overt rebellion, their resistance became more covert or internalized. The focus of the struggle was no longer against the notion that they were less human, as in Elizabeth Freeman's time, but that they were different kinds of humans. For women this meant spurning their morally inferior roles of mistress, whore, and breeder—though under the "new" slavery they were "rewarded" for acquiescing in them. It was the factor of reward that made this resistance a fundamentally feminist one, for at its base was a rejection of the notion that they were the master's property. So Black women had a double challenge under the new slavery: They had to resist the property relation (which was different in form, if not in nature, to that of White women) and they had to inculcate the same values into succeeding generations.

The narrative of Linda Brent, a South Carolina slave, revealed her struggle against the exchange of sexual favors for material reward. Brent's master, Dr. Flint, didn't try to "rape" Brent by physically overpowering her; he endeavored to make the young slave submit to his will. From the age of fifteen, Flint tried "to people my young mind with unclean images," Brent wrote.[22] He began telling the young girl that she was his property and "must be subject to his will in all things."[23] According to Brent, her master seemed to become obsessed with her "voluntary" submission. He "met me at every turn," she said, "swearing . . . he could compel me to submit to him."[24]

Finally he offered her a cabin on the edge of the plantation if she would accede to his demands. Brent resisted, however, and escaped to the North. Even then, Flint continued to pursue her until a friend purchased her freedom. Although Brent could feel safe for the first time in her adult life, she couldn't help viewing her "purchase" with mixed emotions. "The more my mind had become enlightened," she wrote, "the more difficult it was for me to consider myself an article of property; and to pay money to those who had so grievously oppressed me seemed like taking from my suffering the glory of triumph."[25]

For a slave like Linda Brent to have developed such a consciousness, it was necessary for some authority figure to have given her a sense of self that contradicted the dictates of the new slavery. In her case it was a grandmother, for as Brent wrote, her hatred of her master stemmed from his attempt to destroy the values her grandmother had "inculcated" in her. Slave narratives are replete with examples of mothers attempting to impart such values to their children, often at the price of great emotional anguish. The writer of Sojourner Truth's narrative wrote, for example, that when Truth became a mother, "she would sometimes whip her child when it cried for more bread rather than give it a piece secretly, lest it should learn to take what was not its own."[26] As Truth explained in the narrative, her action was a means of keeping herself and her child from being compromised by the slave system. "The Lord knows how many times I let my children go hungry, rather than take secretly the bread I liked not to ask for," she said.[27]

The efforts of slave mothers to instill values in their children had an effect that was not always positive. The need to be exceedingly harsh or enterprising where their children were concerned often created emotional distance between mother and child. A slave by the name of Aunt Sally recalled how stern her mother was, "rarely talking with her children, but training them to the best of her ability in all industry and honesty. Every moment she could gain from labor," the narrator wrote, "was spent in spinning and knitting and sewing to keep them decently clothed."[28]

The tension was greater, noted the slave Bethany Veney, when the child was a daughter, whose "almost certain doom is to minister to the unbridled lust of the slaveowner."[29] When Veney's daughter was born, she wished that both of them could "die right there and then."[30] Such a wish is commonly expressed in the slave narratives of women, and a number of the rare but not insignificant instances of infanticide can be seen within this context.

It is not difficult to imagine the anxiety of a mother whose daughter had reached the age of puberty in the slave South. According to the narratives, it was that anxiety that created the greatest friction between mother and daughter. "The mother of a slave is very watchful," Brent wrote, especially after she reaches puberty. "This leads to many questions, and this well-meant course has a tendency to drive her from maternal councils."[31]

In Brent's case it caused desperate loneliness, which led to an illicit affair with a White man. When Brent's grandmother discovered Linda's indiscretion, the recrimination was harsh. "I'd rather see you dead," her grandmother told her. "You are a disgrace to your dead mother."[32] The grandmother tore off a wedding ring and silver thimble from Brent's fingers—keepsakes of her deceased mother—and told Brent never to talk to her again.

In the world of the slave mother, there was little room for compassion, because there was no room for weakness. This was especially true when the mother herself had been compromised. A Northerner who settled in Mississippi spoke of mothers who were concubines there: "They had too much pride and self-respect to rear their daughters for such a purpose," he said. "If driven to desperation, she destroyed herself to prevent it, or killed them."[33]

Slave communities also enforced moral codes. Undiscriminating behavior could get a person run out of church; and in some communities a "loose" woman could be the subject of collective recrimination. One slave, Priscilla McCollough, explained that if a woman wasn't acting as she should, her neighbors would adopt an African custom and "play the banjo" on her: make her a subject of a public song that warned her that she "betta change."[34]

Although, as in many African societies, prenuptial intercourse was not necessarily frowned upon, having a baby outside of marriage often was. In spite of the vagaries of the slave system, marriage, fidelity, and an organized family life were important values, combining the ethics of the society, African mores, and resistance to the new slavery.

Perhaps the most dramatic and least known act of resistance was the refusal of slave women to perform their most essential role, producing baby slaves, for which they were rewarded. "Every woman who is pregnant," observed the plantation mistress Frances Kemble, "is relieved of a certain portion of her work in the field. . . . Certain additions of clothing and an additional weekly ration are bestowed upon the family. . . . The more frequently she adds to the number of her master's livestock by bringing new slaves into the world, the more claims she will have upon his consideration and good will."[35]

Even so, a Texas slave by the name of Rose Williams tried to resist a forcible mating. When her master placed a healthy specimen by the name of Rufus in her cabin for this purpose, she chased him out with a three-foot poker. Subsequent visits by Rufus met with the same response. Rose Williams finally relented when the master threateningly reminded her that he had purchased her entire family to save them from being separated. Rose upheld her end of the desperate bargain and bore Rufus two children.[36]

Some slave women, perhaps a significant number, did not bear offspring for the system at all. They used contraceptives and abortives in an attempt to resist the system, and to gain control over their bodies. In 1860 a Tennessee physician, reading a paper before the Rutherford County Medical Society, talked of the wide use of camphor as a contraceptive: "They take it just before or after menstruation, in quantities sufficient to produce a little nervousness for two or three days; when it has effect they consider themselves safe."[37]

When contraception failed, slave women took more extreme measures. "All country practitioners are aware of the frequent complaints of planters about the unnatural tendency in the African female population to destroy her offspring," observed a Georgia physician in 1849. "Whole families of women . . . fail to have any children."[38] Another physician, writing in a Nashville, Tennessee, medical journal, told of a planter who kept between four and six slave women "of the proper age to breed," but in twenty-five years only two children had been born on the plantation. When the slave owner purchased new slaves, every pregnancy miscarried by the fourth month. Finally it was discovered that the women were taking "medicine" supplied by an old slave woman to induce abortions.

At least one slave narrative indicates that the women understood the larger significance of their act. "If all bond women had been of the same mind," wrote the slave Jane Blake, "how soon the institution could have vanished from the earth."[39]

.

Resistance Among the Free

Free Black women in the North also had to struggle with the consequences of being perceived as a "different kind of humanity." Abolition hadn't erased the taint of their alleged immorality, and converging social and economic forces in the 1830's added a new challenge. With the emergence of a self-conscious middle class, Black women had to overcome notions about the relationship of class—as well as color—to morality.

Symbolized by the humming New England textile mills, northern industrialization was reaching new heights in this period. The consequent broader flow of capital created a new middle class striving for upper-class status. For women, the vehicle for these aspirations was what became known as the "cult of the lady" or the "cult of true womanhood." The idea of the lady was not new of course. What had changed was the *cult* idea, its elevation to a status symbol, as feminist historian Gerda Lerner points out. Now a woman had to be true to the cult's cardinal tenets of domesticity, submissiveness, piety, and purity in order to be good enough for society's inner circles. Failing to adhere to any of these tenets—which the overwhelming number of Black women could hardly live up to—made one less than a moral, "true" woman.

Domesticity had a central position in the cult idea. The true woman's exclusive role was as homemaker, mother, housewife, and family tutor of the social and moral graces. Isolated within the home, women "raised" men above lusty temptation while keeping themselves beyond its rapacious grasp. Women's imprisonment in the home virtually guaranteed piety and purity. Submissiveness, too, was assured where housewives depended on male support. When leisure (formerly scorned as idleness) rather than industriousness indicated one's social standing, middle-class women, once contributors to the family economy, became models of "conspicuously unproductive expenditure," as economist Thorstein Veblen noted.[40]

For White men, the cult was convenient. In an increasingly industrial economy, more of them were forced to leave the farms for occupations that middle-class women had enjoyed. Factory owners benefited from the new status symbol as well. During the early rise of the factory system, the main source of labor was proud—if needy—Puritan girls who saw their work as a stopgap until they married. Although the work was strenuous and the wages low, such employment still carried a certain status—and the women showed themselves willing to organize in order to better working conditions and pay. With the coming of the cult idea, however, work outside the home lost its prestige, and women like the Puritan girls were no longer expected to be *in* the labor force but to stay home and *reproduce* the labor force. So when the cult of the lady took hold, they were replaced by poorer immigrant women, a cheaper, more permanent, and more exploitable source of workers. Therefore it was no coincidence, Lerner observed, that "the slogan 'a woman's place is in the home' took on a certain aggressiveness and shrillness precisely at the time when increasing numbers of poorer women *left* their homes to become factory workers."[41] It was also no coincidence, she could have added, that it occurred at a time when the abolition of slavery brought Black women into the wage-labor force. They, however, were excluded from the factories, which for white women had afforded, in the words of the nineteenth-century writer Harriet Martineau, "a most welcome resource to some thousands of young women, unwilling to give themselves to domestic service."[42] The exclusion of Black women from the industrial labor force created a legacy that continued for more than a century.

Nor was it only the factories that excluded them. "There was not a single trade in which Negroes were allowed to work beside white people," a study of northern Blacks revealed. "They were banished to the galleys of menial labor."[43] By 1847 a census revealed that close to half the female Black population of Philadelphia consisted of washerwomen and domestic servants. About 10 percent were needlewomen, and 5 percent involved in trades like hairdressing and dressmaking, jobs that could be performed in their own homes. While the White female labor force was made up primarily of single women, Black women, both married and single, were forced to work, though single women tended to be domestics, while married women, who needed to tend to children and family, were most often washerwomen.

At a time when the former White servant class moved a rung higher, the economic reasons for relegating Black women to the lowest category of labor are obvious. But Black women were also forced to confront a new dimension of racial discrimination in this period, one that emerged as a result of "true womanhood."

As the women's magazines and romance literature of the period suggested, madness, sometimes death, and always tragedy were the fate of a woman who could not fulfill the "attributes" of true womanhood. To be lacking in any of those qualities meant a woman was unnatural, unfeminine, and thus a species of a different—if not lower —female order. Since only women of leisure could even hope to join the pantheon of ladyhood, true women, with all the attendant moral implications, became virtually synonymous with the upper class. So, "Victorian morality," as Gerda Lerner observed "applied to the 'better' classes only. It was taken for granted during the period and well into the 20th century that working-class women—and especially Black women—were freely available for sexual use by upper-class males."[44] The assumption had less to do with real circumstances than with the idea of immutable natural laws that governed morality and femininity. These laws stated that women who worked outside the home, or whose race had a history of sexual exploitation, were outside the realm of "womanhood" and its prerogatives.

Black women activists traversed a tricky and sometimes contradictory path in responding to the challenge. On the one hand they agreed with the fundamental premises of the Victorian ethic. On the other, they opposed its racist and classist implications. At the same time they were conscious of the pressure on free Blacks to prove they could be acculturated into American society. Because of their alleged inability to do so, organizations like the American Colonization Society, which included some of the most influential White liberals in the country, were stepping up efforts to repatriate free Blacks to Africa. For Black women, *acculturation* was translated as their ability to be "ladies"—a burden of proof that carried an inherent class-consciousness.

In part, the proliferation of Black ladies' literary, intelligence, temperance, and moral improvement societies in this period was a reaction to that pressure. But despite their titles, these organizations did more than pursue cultural activities. The Ohio Literary Ladies Society, for example, "probably did more towards the establishment of schools for Black children than any other group of the time in the state," noted the Howard University archivist Dorothy Porter in her study of the Black women's literary societies organized between 1828 and 1846.[45] The societies also helped needy Black women, gave financial aid to Black newspapers, and provided forums for discussion of relevant issues.

In the latter capacity, the Afric-American Female Intelligence Society of Boston did a daring thing. It sponsored a young abolitionist's speech before a mixed audience of men and women in Boston's Franklin Hall. The act was a daring one because the abolitionist was a woman, and a Black woman at that. In 1832 women didn't speak in public, especially on serious issues like civil rights and, most especially, feminism. In June, just four months before her appearance, the most progressive of the abolitionist newspapers, *The Liberator,* counseled: "The voice of woman should not be heard in public debates, but there are other ways in which her influence would be beneficial."[46] But the speaker, Maria Stewart, who had been born free in Connecticut twenty-nine years earlier, would hear none of that. Not only did she speak, thus becoming the first American-born woman to give public speeches and leave extant texts of her addresses,[47] but in speaking about civil and women's rights, she used a chastening tongue. Although her public career was short-lived, lasting barely a year, Stewart articulated the precepts upon which the future activism of Black women would be based. Her ideas reflected both the fundamentals of the Victorian ethic and criticism of its inherent biases. Out of that mix emerged a distinct ethos which underlined Black women's activism for generations to come. And as is evident in Stewart's words, it was an ethos that had its contradictions.

Naturally, Stewart railed against the racism toward Blacks that fueled discrimination in the North and provided a rationale for slavery in the South. Although Stewart had a rudimentary education, her rhetoric often demonstrated knowledge of ancient history. Though "we are looked upon as *things,*" she said, "we sprang from a scientific people."[48] Stewart also spoke of the relegation of Blacks to menial jobs. Continual hard labor "deadens the energies of the soul, and benumbs the faculties of the mind," she said. Orphaned at the age of five and "bound out" to work thereafter, Stewart told her audiences that she had learned the consequences of constant drudgery by bitter experience.

Nevertheless, Stewart castigated free Blacks for not doing enough for their own uplift. She believed they were politically lethargic and ultimately responsible for the continuance of slavery. "Were the American free people of color to turn their attention more assiduously to moral worth and intellectual improvement, this would be the result," she said: "Prejudice would gradually diminish, and the whites would be compelled to say, unloose those fetters!"[49]

In keeping with the Victorian ethic, Stewart believed that Black women had an important part to play in the race's moral and intellectual development. She counseled that Black women excel in "good house-wifery, knowing that prudence and economy are the road to wealth."[50] The role of mothers was essential. "O ye mothers," Stewart implored, "what a responsibility rests on you! It is you that must create in the minds of your little girls and boys a thirst for knowledge, the love of virtue, the abhorrence of vice, and the cultivation of the pure heart."[51] Like most women of the period, Stewart also seemed to subscribe to the doctrine of submissiveness. "My beloved brethren . . . it is upon you that woman depends; she can do little besides using her influence," she concluded.[52]

But in Stewart's view, that influence was undermined by uncultivated women who, in her words, "did not blush at vulgarity." As a woman of her times, Maria Stewart believed in the "cult" notion that only "true women" could exercise the proper moral influence on the family. "Did the daughters of our land [Africa] possess a delicacy of manners, combined with gentleness and dignity; did their pure minds hold vice in abhorrence and contempt, did they frown when their ears were polluted with its vile accents, would not their influence become powerful? Would not our brethren fall in love with their virtues?" she asked.[53] However, Stewart and other Black woman activists challenged the cult idea in a very fundamental way. Though they may have agreed with many of its precepts, they fought against the idea that morality and worth were inherent to a particular class or race. On the contrary, it was external circumstance rather than natural law that determined character, morality, and, in the case of women, "true womanhood." Stewart revealed this perspective in remarks directed toward White women who believed differently:

> O ye fairer sisters whose hands are never soiled, whose nerves and muscles are never strained, go learn by experience! Had we the opportunity that you have had, to improve our moral and mental faculties, what would have hindered our intellects from being as bright, and our manners from being as dignified as yours? Had it been our lot to have been nursed in the lap of affluence and ease, and have basked beneath the smiles and sunshine of fortune, should we not have naturally supposed that we were never made to toil?[54]

Although she felt Blacks could do more on their own behalf, she understood that Whites, including White women, conspired to keep Blacks from "rising above the condition of servants." She had once asked White women "who transact business for themselves" to hire Black girls to work for them, she told her audience, but the women had refused for fear of "losing the public patronage."[55]

Most significantly, Stewart opposed the idea that women, including Black women, were responsible for their own degradation—an attitude which was perhaps the most destructive (and controlling) of any of the cult ideas. Although Stewart criticized the dearth of Black women "who will blush at vulgarity," the primary responsibility lay on America, "who caused the daughters of Africa to commit whoredoms and fornications; . . . upon thee be their curse."[56]

Stewart's assumptions—what would later become known as modernist thinking—gave Black women a freer rein to express and act upon ideas that liberated them from the oppression of both sex and race. The moral urgency of their being Black and female—heightened especially in times when Black men were politically lethargic ("It is of no use for us to wait any longer for a generation of well educated men to arise," Stewart said scornfully)[57]—suffused Black women with a tenacious feminism, which was articulated before that of Whites like Sarah Grimké, who is credited with providing the first rationale for American women's political activism.

For Black women no such rationale was necessary. In their world view, many of the obstacles that White women faced simply didn't apply to their circumstances or beliefs. For example, Black women saw no contradiction between domesticity and political action. So Stewart could talk about dependence on men and excelling in good housewifery, and at the same time make an unmistakably feminist appeal to Black women.

> Do you ask what we can do? Unite and build a store of your own. . . . Do you ask where is the money? We have spent more than enough for nonsense. . . . We have never had an opportunity of displaying our talents; therefore the world thinks we know nothing. . . . Possess the spirit of men, bold and enterprising, fearless and undaunted. Sue for your rights and privileges. Know the reason that you cannot attain them. Weary them [men] with your importunities.[58]

Black women also bypassed the barrier of religious thought that circumscribed even radical White activists until the late 1830's, when abolitionist William Lloyd Garrison introduced a rationale for criticizing organized religion. Again, Black women had been able to justify their activism even earlier. "What if I am a woman?" Stewart declared. "Did [God] not raise up Deborah to be mother, and a judge in Israel? Did not Queen Esther save the lives of the Jews? And Mary Magdalene first declare the resurrection of Christ from the dead?"[59]

A woman who had experienced a religious conversion, Stewart was confident enough to challenge the exhortations of Saint Paul, whose words had long been used to justify slavery and sexism. Stewart, well, simply went over his head.

"Saint Paul declared that it was a shame for a woman to speak in public," she noted, "yet our great High Priest and Advocate did not condemn the woman for a more notorious offence than this. . . ."[60] In any case, Paul's words were of another time, and Stewart was convinced that if he had understood the urgency of these times, his attitude would have been different. "Did Saint Paul but know of our wrongs and deprivations," she said confidently, "I presume he would make no objections to our pleading in public for our rights."[61]

Their perspective also enabled Black women to see a world not of fixed proportions, but of change. Speaking of a past which was bound to become a present again, Stewart talked of women in history who had had a voice in moral, political, and religious affairs. She spoke of women in the pre-Renaissance days who occupied chairs of philosophy and justice, who "harangued" in Latin before the Pope, who were poets as well as nuns. And finally Stewart touched upon an even more ancient history, when nations "imagined that women could look into futurity," when they were seen as "approaching divinity," and when not only non-Western nations but the Germans, Britons, and Scandinavians believed that "the Deity more readily communicates himself to women."[62]

For Stewart, simple logic demanded that in light of the role of women in the past, "God at this eventful period should raise up your females to strive . . . both in public and private, to assist those who are endeavoring to stop the strong current of prejudice that flows so profusely against us at present."[63] Maria Stewart was sure enough of her beliefs to warn others not to doubt the mission of her sex. "No longer ridicule their efforts," she counseled. "It will be counted as sin."[64]

Stewart had little doubt that Black women's prospects were "fair and bright." However, a year after her debut, she announced that her own immediate future in Boston was dim. Citing prejudice among her own people, she announced that she was going to leave the city, perhaps never to return. Her parting thoughts, sanctioned in her mind by God, history, and the need for racial progress, showed that she left undaunted. "Having God for my friend and portion, what have I to fear?" she asked. "As long as it is the will of God, I rejoice that I am as I am; for man, in his best estate, is altogether vanity. Men of eminence have mostly risen from obscurity; nor will I, although a female of darker hue, and far more obscure than they, bend my head or hang my harp upon willows."[65] With that, Maria Stewart left Boston and ended her public career.

The cult of true womanhood left a bitter legacy. For White women, it was used as a means to circumscribe, and make dependent, the very women who had the education and resources to wage an effective battle for their rights. The cult reduced them to an image of frailty and mindless femininity, which in itself became a rationale for their inability to withstand the rigor of the franchise or anything else outside the domestic circle. If the cult caused Black women to prove they were ladies, it forced White ladies to prove that they were women.

If the two had been able to work together to challenge their respective images, there is no telling what could have happened. A glimpse of the potential alliance was seen in 1851 at a women's rights meeting in Akron, Ohio. From the very beginning of the conference, the White women were overwhelmed by the jeers and hoots of men who had come to disrupt the meeting. Their most effective antagonist was a clergyman who used both the gender of Jesus and the helplessness of women to counter their feminist arguments. Present at the meeting was the legendary abolitionist Sojourner Truth, who squelched the heckler with an oft-quoted speech. In the first place, she said, Jesus came from "God and a woman—*man* had nothing to do with it."[66] Secondly, Truth asserted that women were not inherently weak and helpless. Raising herself to her full height of six feet, flexing a muscled arm, and bellowing with a voice one observer likened to the apocalyptic thunders, Truth informed the audience that she could outwork, outeat, and outlast any man. Then she challenged: "Ain't *I* a woman?"[67]

Fearful at first that if Truth spoke, their cause would be associated with "abolitionists and niggers" the White feminists now responded to her remarks with "streaming eyes and hearts beating with gratitude," as one of them wrote.[68] Gratitude did not extend, however, to realizing that Black women had advanced ideas which would help all women. The cult of true womanhood soured potential alliances not only between middle-class White reformers and working-class women, but also among Black women of all classes. This was evident as early as the 1830's, when the first interracial abolitionist societies were organized. A few Black women, whose background of wealth and education exceeded that of most of their White colleagues, were found acceptable to become officers in some of the societies. But the question of Black mass participation in those societies remained more often than not an issue of bitter contention.

It seems ironic that White women abolitionists would discriminate against Black women. For Whites, though, abolitionist activism was primarily a means of releasing their suppressed political energies —energies which they directed toward the goal not of Black liberation, but of their own. White women's discontent "with their position was as much cause as effect of their involvement with the antislavery movement," observed women's historian Ellen Carol Du Bois. "Abolitionism provided them with a way to escape clerical authority, an egalitarian ideology, and a theory of social change, all of which permitted the leaders to transform the insights into . . . the beginning of the women's rights movement."[69]

As both the race and feminist issues intensified in the 1840's and 1850's, it was inevitable that Black and White women abolitionists would come to a parting of the ways. The parting was due not only to White racism, but also to the primacy of race or sex as issues in their respective struggles. All Black women abolitionists (and most of the leading Black male abolitionists) were feminists. But when it came to a question of priorities, race, for most of them, came first. As the words of Stewart revealed, for Black women it was the issue of race that sparked their feminism.

There was something else too. As Sojourner Truth's message implied, Black women had already proven their inherent strengths— both physical and psychological. They had undergone a baptism of fire and emerged intact. Therefore, their convictions concerning the rights of women were deeply rooted in experience as well as theory.

III

~ To Choose Again, Freely ~

The first years of freedom held incredible pathos for Afro-Americans. For Black women especially, the postbellum period was one for critical decisions—concerning their children, their men, their role in the feminist and racial struggles that unfolded so dramatically in these years. Those decisions—and the convictions behind them—often revealed a profound understanding of the relationship between their personal and political strivings.

Among the first and perhaps most important decisions that freedmen and women made was the reestablishment of family ties, as historian Herbert Gutman points out. Even in a world where slavery no longer existed, Blacks faced a variety of obstacles. Postbellum apprenticeship laws, for example, allowed former owners to seize Black children if the courts found that it would be "better for the habits and comfort of the child that it should be bound as an apprentice for some white person."[1] In Maryland alone, an estimated ten thousand children were apprenticed, despite the objections of parents. "Not a day passes," said an officer of the Annapolis Freedmen's Bureau, "but my office is visited by some poor woman who has walked perhaps ten or twenty miles to . . . try to procure the release of her children taken forcibly away from her and held to all intents and purposes in slavery."[2]

The dislocations of war required determined efforts to find spouses—efforts freed Blacks were willing to make, as a Union commander in Mississippi observed. Blacks "whose wives and husbands the rebels had driven off," he said, "firmly refused to form new connections and declared their purpose to keep faith to absent ones."[3] Men and women who found each other, or who were fortunate enough not to have been separated by war and slavery, married or remarried under the official auspices of the Freedmen's Bureau—as in the case of Ida Wells's parents. Observers documented the vivid scene of masses of Blacks coming to the Bureau offices, sometimes seventy couples at a time, to reaffirm their commitment to each other.

To secure their families, freed couples were making every attempt to stabilize their lives. When the abolitionist Frances Ellen Harper toured the South after the War, she reported that the former slaves "were beginning to get homes for themselves . . . and depositing money in the bank. . . . They have hundreds of homes in Kentucky."[4] The Freedmen's Bureau was redistributing land and providing low-interest loans for former slaves. It was overseeing labor contracts between Blacks and White employers. For a moment—and it was just a moment—it seemed that former slaves would be able to lead their lives like other Americans. But in the end such a life would not be possible. For the Black woman had invented herself, and the challenges of the postwar years required the same kind of strength and independence culled in previous times.

History had not instilled in Afro-American women "the spirit of subordination to masculine authority by either economic necessity or tradition," remarked Howard University sociologist E. Franklin Frazier in *The Negro Family in the United States*.[5] This applied to Black women of all classes, in freedom and in slavery.

In slavery, Frazier wrote, "As a worker and free agent, except where the master's will was concerned, [Black women] developed a spirit of independence and a keen sense of personal rights."[6] Of course *every* slave was a worker and a free agent *except* where the master's will was concerned. What Frazier really seems to be saying is that the Black woman exercised independence and personal rights vis-à-vis her Black husband. A more precise statement may be that slave women maintained their authority over the domestic domain— as women have traditionally done—while Black men had no authority over the traditional male spheres of influence. When some figures, such as mammies on the large plantations, were able to extend their domain to the master's house, they often became the "broker" between the slave community and Whites—thus increasing the Black woman's influence. The Black woman's "power," however, still derived from her functionalist roles rather than from influence in the traditional male domains. But it was power nonetheless.

Among free Blacks, male authority was diminished, in many cases, by the inability of a man to support and protect his family. In the North, abolition coincided with the influx of European immigrants, who replaced Black men in occupations they had traditionally held. Consequently, Black wives were forced to work, most of them as washerwomen, whose meager incomes not only saved many families from "utter destruction," in historian Carter T. Woodson's words, but provided capital for struggling Black businessmen in the early nineteenth century. Such economic circumstances made male domination difficult.

Among more affluent Blacks, many of whom were involved in the abolitionist struggle, the woman's social role was more traditional. Many of the activist Black families, like the Fortens, the Pauls, the Remonds, the Purvises, and others, were organized along patriarchal lines. However, their struggle for racial equality sanctioned the nontraditional political activities and education of their wives, sisters, and daughters. Black women like Sarah Remond; Margaretta, Sarah, Harriet, and Charlotte Forten; Susan Paul, and others were well educated and encouraged to participate in abolitionist and other progressive organizations. Men like James Forten, Sr., and his son James Jr. believed that the women's role in the abolitionist struggle was too important for them to be relegated to their homes. In addition to needing all the help they could get, many Black male activists believed in the fundamental equality of the sexes. "Woman is not a mere dependent of man," averred Robert Purvis, son-in-law of the senior Forten. "The relation is perfectly reciprocal. God has given to both man and woman the same intellectual capacities, and made them subject to the same moral argument."[7] It was a stunning position for the early nineteenth century.

There is no question that there was greater acceptance among Black men of women in activist roles than there was in the broader society. This did not mean that sexual equality always prevailed—at home or in the political arena. Black women headed no major community organizations, nor were they regional representatives at national conventions. And although the participation of Black women in those organizations and conventions was more readily accepted than that of their White counterparts—especially after the Seneca Falls Convention of 1848—occasional incidents did occur. In 1849 at a Black convention in Ohio, Black women, led by Jane P. Merritt, threatened to boycott the meetings if they were not given a more substantial voice in the proceedings. At an 1855 convention in Philadelphia, Mary Ann Shadd Cary was admitted only after a spirited debate in which she took part.[8] Both women were active in the Underground Railroad, so one wonders if they were admitted on the strength of their reputations rather than the principle of sexual equality.

The incidents can be seen in the context of the heightened militancy of Blacks in the late forties and fifties. The Fugitive Slave Law, the repeal of the Kansas-Nebraska Act, and the Dred Scott Supreme Court decision had all served to push even the most sanguine activists, such as Frederick Douglass, to call for the violent overthrow of the slave system. In periods of Black radicalism, which always includes a self-conscious quest for manhood, Black men attempt to exercise their male prerogatives more vigorously.

This dynamic was evident in the Revolutionary period, when "manumission fever" was in the air. A petition for freedom presented by male slaves to the Massachusetts legislature in 1773 was especially revealing. The men asked for freedom on the grounds that as slaves they had no authority over their families. "How can a husband leave master and work and cleave to his wife?" the petition read in part. "How can the wife *submit themselves to* [their] *husbands in all things?*"[9] (Emphasis added.)

Male attitudes in the mid-nineteenth century, when Black militancy was at its peak, also reflected a sharpened resolve to take possession of that which had been denied to them. In 1855 a Black convention of male leaders declared that "As a people, we have been denied the ownership of our bodies, our wives, home, children and the products of our own labor." The convention men resolved to "vindicate our manhood, command our respect and claim the attention and admiration of the civilized world."[10]

That vindication included establishing conventional patriarchal relationships, and women were expected to help in this effort. In contrast to the views that Maria Stewart had expressed twenty-four years earlier, a Philadelphia convention resolved:

> . . . we recommend to our mothers and our sisters to use every honorable means to secure for their *sons and brothers* places of profit and trust in stores and other places of business, such as will throw a halo around this proscribed people.[11] (Emphasis added.)

To men's minds, for a woman to work—especially when it wasn't a question of dire necessity—undermined Black manhood and the race as well. "As an evidence of the deep degradation of our race," observed the Black physician and newspaper editor Martin Delany in 1855, "there are among us [women] whose husbands are industrious, able and willing to support them, who voluntarily leave home and become chamber maids, and stewardesses . . . in all probability to enable them to obtain more fine or costly articles of dress or furniture."[12] Delany was convinced that racial progress depended on rectifying that situation. "Until colored men attain to a position above permitting their mothers, sisters, wives and daughters to do the drudgery of . . . other men's wives and daughters," he said, "it is useless, it is nonsense . . . to talk about equality and elevation in society."[13]

Following the Civil War, men attempted to vindicate their manhood largely through asserting their authority over women. For their part, women sometimes welcomed that assertion, sometimes were forced to acquiesce to it, and sometimes resisted it. Influencing the masculine determination was the history of the White man's proprietary "rights" over Black women, and the consequent struggle of Black men to reclaim them. "To the ordinary American or Englishman," said W.E.B. Du Bois, "the race question at bottom is simply a matter of ownership of women; white men want the right to use all women, colored and white, and they resent the intrusion of colored men in this domain."[14] Black men, in turn, resented the accusation that they wanted similar "rights" to White women. "What do we want with their daughters and sisters?" riposted the Black nationalist minister Henry McNeal Turner in 1866. "We have as much beauty as they. All we ask of the White man is to let our ladies alone, and they need not fear us. The difficulty has heretofore been our ladies were not always at our disposal," he concluded.[15]

In the opinion of many Black men, Black women were also responsible for their not being at their men's disposal, as Turner implied. Slave women, he said, had "been insulted or degraded *with or without* their consent."[16] (Emphasis added.) In the opinion of the well-known abolitionist William Wells Brown, most slave women fell into the former category. In his *Clotel,* the first Black novel published in this country (1861), Brown wrote: "Indeed, the greater portion of the colored women, in the days of slavery, had no greater aspiration than that of becoming the finely dressed mistress of some white man."[17] The attitude prevailed long after the 1860's. In writing about the desire of slave women to become mistresses of their masters, E. Franklin Frazier in *The Negro Family* remarked: "The mere prestige of the White race was sufficient to secure compliance with their desires."[18] It was a compliance, he felt, that was voluntary and mutually desired. "The master in his mansion and his colored mistress in her special house nearby represented the final triumph of social ritual in the presence of the deepest feeling of human solidarity," Frazier concluded rapturously.[19] For Black men, the assertion of their claims —which they believed inherent in their freedom—would, like charity, begin at home.

After emancipation, the plantation mistress and writer Frances Kemble observed that Black men were almost as happy to escape from their "domestic tyranny" as from their White slave masters. Others were determined to establish their authority in the household. "Almost immediately after the end of the war," wrote historian Peter Kolchin, "there were signs of a fundamental alteration of the matrifocal structure that had previously prevailed under the slave regime. There was a new determination for men to reassert their position as head of the family."[20] Laura Towne, a northern White woman who taught former slaves in the South Carolina Sea Islands in the 1860's, supported that view. Since the emancipation, "The men wish to rule their wives," she said. Additionally, leaders among the freedmen were urging their brethren "to get the woman into their proper place —never tell them anything of their concerns, etc.; and the notion of being bigger than women generally is now inflating the conceit of the males to an amazing degree."[21]

Some aspects of this new male determination were beneficial in the eyes of their women. The freedmen's desire to exempt their women from field work, for example, served a mutual want and need. The Black woman's obligation to perform double duty in both home and field had dissipated her role as wife and mother, and symbolized the low esteem in which she was held in the society. If men welcomed their escape from domestic tyranny, women welcomed their escape from the fields.

In 1865 a Louisiana plantation owner complained, "The women say that they never mean to do any outdoor work, that White men support their wives and they mean that their husbands shall support them."[22] The planters' problems weren't confined to Louisiana: Similar complaints were heard in Georgia, Alabama, South Carolina, and Mississippi. A Georgia plantation owner confirmed that in his state, "One third of the hands are women who now don't work at all."[23] A southern proprietress noted how negotiations had turned out with a Black field worker and his family: "Gilbert will stay on his own terms," she wrote, "but [he] withdraws Fanny and puts Harry and little Abram in her place."[24] Another mistress said that one of her hired laborers "chose to feed his wife out of his wages rather than get her fed for her services."[25] A Tennessee freedman explained to his employer about exempting his wife from field work: "When I married my wife, I married her to wait on me and she has got all she can do right here for me and the children."[26]

However, attempts to establish a traditional family structure among the masses of Blacks were doomed virtually from the beginning. For when women stayed home, the economy suffered. As a Georgian planter lamented: "You will never see three million bales of cotton raised in the South again until the labor system is improved." What he meant became clear in a report of Boston cotton brokers who inquired into the disastrous cotton crop of 1867–68. The greatest loss, they concluded, resulted from the decision of "growing numbers of Negro women to devote their time to their homes and children."[27] This trend was also evident outside the cotton states. An 1866 census of 563 ex-slave women in Montgomery County, Virginia, showed that less than half of the women with children (47 percent) listed occupations, as compared to about three in four (74 percent) who were either single, or married without children. Throughout the social history of Black women, children are more important than marriage in determining the woman's domestic role.

It would not be long before the decision to work or not to work —whether in the fields or in the cities—would be taken out of Black men's hands. As early as 1863, Black lawyer William J. Watkins noted that "the determination of the white man is to starve us out."[28] As a result, Black women were driven not only back to work, but to take organized action. In 1866, Black washerwomen in Jackson, Mississippi, announced that they were heretofore going to charge a standard rate for their work. They informed Jackson's mayor that anyone in their group who did not insist on the agreed-upon wage was subject to a fine. Their demand was the "first known collective action of free Black workingwomen in American history," and "the first labor organization of Black workers in Mississippi."[29]

By the late sixties and seventies the situation among Blacks had further deteriorated. The Freedmen's Bureau had become a "dead-letter," in the words of W.E.B. Du Bois. Nascent labor unions excluded Blacks from their ranks and from decent employment. "Colored men and women" observed Watkins, "are being driven out of vocation after vocation."[30] The economic struggle was a violent one, and now Black women would not only have to work as they had in slavery, but would again have to take up arms for the defense of the race. Thus when Whites threatened to regain power at the end of

Reconstruction in Charleston, South Carolina, an eyewitness reported seeing Black women "carrying axes or hatchets in their hands hanging down at their sides, their aprons or dresses half-concealing the weapons."[31] In rallying freedmen and women to defend their rights, a Black clergyman of the time could confidently boast of "80,000 black men in the State who can use Winchesters and 200,000 black women who can light a torch and carry a knife."[32]

But the responsibilities of Black women did not diminish their men's demand for dominance—often the demand was heightened. In 1868 the *Mobile Daily Register* noted an alarming increase of wife-beating among Blacks in that city. When the guilty men were arrested, the women "usually begged the mayor to let their husbands off," the paper said. The *Register* could only conclude that "the negro women seem to labor under the impression that their husbands have a perfect right to beat them on every occasion."[33]

Whether or not the article's conclusion was correct, the Mobile reporter wasn't the only one to cite this phenomenon. Two years later, Frances Ellen Harper wrote of her tour of the South that she felt the necessity to counsel the freedmen. "Part of the time," Harper noted, "I am preaching against men ill-treating their wives."[34]

The effort to keep women "in their place" went beyond that of individuals. Such institutions as the Black Church "sought to affirm the man's interest and authority in the family," observed Frazier.[35] The Church attempted to do this in much the same way that Whites had used religion, by putting a new emphasis on the biblical "sanction for male ascendency." The male hierarchy of the Church was also capable of using its formidable social power in this regard. Frances Leigh, daughter of Frances Kemble, reported seeing a Black woman outside a church in the Sea Islands. She was "sitting on the church steps," said Leigh, "rocking herself backwards and forwards in great distress."[36] When asked why she was sitting there, the woman replied that "she refused to obey her husband in a small matter," and so had been expelled from the church. When Leigh intervened on her behalf, she was readmitted to the church, but not before she had made a public apology to the whole congregation.

The Fifteenth Amendment

It was against this background that Black women made the choice whether or not to support the Fifteenth Amendment, which would permit Black men to vote but not women of any race. For the Black female activist, the choice was not so much race *versus* sex, as of finding the best means to secure their own well-being. Thus, women like Sojourner Truth and Frances Ellen Harper held similar views about the rights of Blacks and women, but came to different conclusions about supporting the amendment.

In 1867, Truth delivered her views on the issue before the American Equal Rights Association, an organization founded by Susan B. Anthony, Elizabeth Cady Stanton, and Frederick Douglass. Its purpose was to bring together abolitionists and feminists to agitate for Black and woman suffrage. When it became clear that either, but not both, would be enfranchised, the AERA forums became more heated than ever.

Sojourner Truth took the position of not supporting the amendment. She was fearful that putting more power into the hands of men would add to the oppression of Black women. "There is a great stir about colored men getting their rights, but not a word about the colored women," she said in a famous speech, ". . . and if colored men get their rights, and not colored women theirs, you see the colored men will be masters over the women, and it will be just as bad as it was before."[37] To illustrate her statement she talked about the fate of many Black women who "go out washing, which is about as high as a colored woman gets, and their men go about idle, strutting up and down; and when the women come home, they ask for their money and take it all, and then scold because there is no food."[38]

That perspective was often articulated by White feminists. Earlier that year, before a meeting of Pennsylvania abolitionists, Susan B. Anthony had declared that Black men, trained so well by their Saxon rulers in the ways of "tyranny and despotism," would play the role of the domineering husband with uncommon ease. In the same meeting, Elizabeth Cady Stanton warned that if Black women weren't given the ballot, they would be fated to a "triple bondage that man never knows."[39] She went so far as to conclude, "It would be better to be the slave of an educated white man than of an ignorant black one." Sojourner Truth evidently agreed with this perspective, or at least with the idea that the White feminists were better informed than Black women. "White women are a great deal smarter," she told the AERA delegates, "and know more than the colored women, while colored women do not know scarcely anything."[40]

Frances Ellen Harper was no less aware of Black women's struggles. "I have heard . . . that often during the War men hired out their wives and drew their pay," she had written, describing the situation of some of the Black women she saw in the South.[41] As her writings reveal, she had much more faith in the abilities—and intelligence—of Black women, and Black men, than Sojourner Truth did. As Harper saw it, the greatest obstacle to the progress of Black women was not Black men but White racism, including the racism of her White "sisters." At an 1869 convention, Harper expressed her support for the Fifteenth Amendment. By that year she had reason to believe that if the bill was defeated, Black women would be less, not more, secure.

As an officer of the AERA, Harper may have suspected that the White feminists' sudden (and expedient) concern for Black women was less than genuine. Of the more than fifty national officers and speakers at the association's conventions over a three-year period, only five were Black women. The others besides Harper—Sojourner Truth, the former slave Mattie Griffith, Hattie Purvis, and Sarah Remond—were all nationally known figures in the abolitionist movement. More revealing—and disturbing—was the vicious campaign launched by Anthony and Stanton. Black women like Harper may have had their complaints against Black men, but they must have looked down on White women using them as fodder to further their own selfish ends. That this was Anthony and Stanton's strategy became clear when they allied with a millionaire Democrat, George Train, who financed their feminist newspaper, *The Revolution*. Within its pages was venom of the worst kind. "While the dominant party have with one hand lifted up TWO MILLION BLACK MEN and crowned them with the honor and dignity of citizenship," wrote Anthony, "with the other they have dethroned FIFTEEN MILLION WHITE WOMEN—their own mothers and sisters, their own wives and daughters—and cast them under the heel of the lowest orders of manhood."[42]

Stanton took the theme even further. She wrote of a Black man lynched in Tennessee for allegedly raping a White woman. The point of the story wasn't the awful injustice of lynching, but that giving Black men the vote was virtually a license to rape. "The Republican cry of 'Manhood Suffrage' creates an antagonism between black men and all women that will culminate in fearful outrages on womanhood, especially in the southern states," she railed.[43]

Another disquieting aspect of this campaign was the use of class as well as race as a weapon. In announcing her candidacy for a New York congressional seat in 1866, Stanton introduced the idea that middle-class women should be enfranchised to stave off the poor, the immigrants, and the Blacks. She told her potential constituents:

> In view of the fact that the Freedmen of the South and the millions of foreigners now crowding our shores, most of whom represent neither property, education, nor civilization, are all in the progress of events to be enfranchised, the best interests of the nation demand that we outweigh this incoming pauperism, ignorance and degradation, with the wealth, education, and refinement of the women of the republic.[44]

A logical extension of this concept was "educated suffrage, irregardless [sic] of sex or color," as Stanton advocated. But educational requirements of course would eliminate the vast majority of Blacks and immigrants, both men and women—including Sojourner Truth herself. When Stanton was pressed on how she could advocate a measure that would disenfranchise the women she had said needed the vote most, she was forced to qualify her view. If she had to make a choice, she condescendingly wrote in *The Revolution,* "We prefer Bridget and Dinah at the ballot box to Patrick and Sambo."[45]

The 1869 AERA meeting was a contentious one, resulting in the split of the AERA into two suffrage organizations. Frederick Douglass made an eloquent plea for the greater urgency of Black men's attaining the vote. He said:

> When women, because they are women, are hunted down through the cities of New York and New Orleans, when they are dragged from their houses and hung upon lamp posts; when their children are torn from their arms, and their brains dashed upon the pavement; when they are objects of insult and outrage at every turn; when they are in danger of having their homes burnt down over their heads; when their children are not allowed to enter schools; then they will have an urgency to obtain the ballot equal to our own.[46]

But was this not true for the Black woman? someone asked. "Yes, yes, yes," replied Douglass. "It is true for the Black woman but not because she is a woman but because she is Black!"

As heated words flew back and forth in the session, Douglass also accused Stanton of slandering the freedmen and making negative comparisons between "the daughters of Jefferson and Washington, and the daughters of bootblacks and gardeners." Stanton, Douglass said, was "advancing the cause of women's rights on the backs of defenseless slave women."[47]

Harper supported Douglass on all counts.* "If the nation could handle only one question, she would not have the black women put a single straw in the way," said the authors of the *History of Woman Suffrage.* Harper realized that the White feminists did not make dependable allies. "The white women all go for sex, letting race occupy a minor position," she said. But to her, "Being black means that every white, including every white working-class woman, can discriminate against you."[49]

The support of the Fifteenth Amendment by Black women did not mean that they had less interest in their suffrage, economic independence, education, or any other issue that pertained to them. And their support certainly didn't mean a collective willingness to be oppressed by men, Black or White. But Harper and others understood that the rights of Black men had to be secured before Black women could assert theirs. If the race had no rights, the women's struggle was meaningless. But after the Fifteenth Amendment was assured, Black women continued their own struggle throughout the 1870's with renewed vigor.

By the late 1860's, plans were made to organize a Black union in response to the appalling labor situation. By 1869 the National Colored Labor Union (NCLU), led by Isaac Meyers, had its founding meeting in Washington, D.C., which was attended by both men and women. When in the course of its deliberations it became clear that the specific needs of workingwomen were not being addressed, Black women challenged the proceedings. One delegate from Newport, Rhode Island, exclaimed that she "was much disappointed that in all your deliberations, speeches and resolutions, which were excellent so

---

*The feminist and abolitionist camps weren't neatly divided. Leading White feminists like Lucy Stone and Julia Ward Howe did not believe that the world would come to an end if Black men—whose leadership was sympathetic to woman suffrage and promised to work toward that end—were enfranchised first. On the other hand, in addition to Truth, several prominent Blacks like Charles Remond, Robert Purvis, and his wife, Harriet (Forten), leaned toward enfranchising women in tandem with or even before Black men, despite the political difficulty of accomplishing that goal. "In an hour like this I repudiate the idea of expediency," Remond had said at an earlier AERA meeting. "All I ask for myself I claim for my wife and sister."[48]

far as the men are concerned, the poor women's interests were not mentioned, or referred to." She followed her complaint with an eloquent plea:

> . . . are we to be left out? we who have suffered all the evils of which you justly complain? Are our daughters to be denied the privilege of honestly earning a livelihood by being excluded from the milliner, dressmaker, tailor, or dry good store, in fact every calling that an intelligent, respectable, industrious female may strive to obtain, and this merely because her skin is dusky? These privileges are all denied colored females of Newport. However well they may be fitted for other positions, they are compelled to accept the meanest drudgeries or starve. . . .
>
> Therefore the colored women of Newport would ask your meeting and Convention that is to assemble next Monday to remember us in your deliberations so that when you mount the chariot of equality, in industrial and mechanical pursuits, we may at least be permitted to cling to the wheels.[50]

To the credit of the NCLU, the organization responded by lowering the admission fee of women to the convention, and asked Mary Ann Shadd Cary to address the convention on women's rights and suffrage. Cary, a former abolitionist, certainly was up to the task. She had been the foremost leader of the emigration movement of fifteen thousand Blacks to Canada between 1850 and 1860, and was the first Black woman to publish a newspaper. Her *Provincial Freeman* focused on abolition and women's rights. Described by W.E.B. Du Bois as having penetrating eyes and an "intellectual countenance that looked right through you," she must have made good use of her attributes at the convention.

Following her speech, the NCLU passed a resolution that, "profiting by the mistakes heretofore made by our fellow citizens in omitting women as co-workers," women should now be included in the organization of cooperative societies.[51] This, the NCLU made clear, was as important as any other issue. In the end, the platform of the organization was much stronger regarding women's rights than was that of the White labor unions.

After the passage of the Fifteenth Amendment in 1870, Black men as well as women agitated for the female vote, on both national and state levels. All six of the Black men who served in the Massachusetts House of Representatives supported suffrage legislation, for example, and women like Caroline Remond Putnam of the well-known Salem family, and Josephine St. Pierre Ruffin were active members of the Massachusetts Woman Suffrage Association.

In South Carolina, which boasted the largest number of Black representatives in the Reconstruction period, seven of the eight congressmen supported woman suffrage.[52] Among these was Alonzo J. Ransier, the Black lieutenant governor, who debated in favor of woman suffrage on the House floor. Three especially prominent sisters were involved in the suffrage movement in that state: Frances, Louisa, and Lottie Rollin. The Rollins were from a prewar free Black family in Charleston. Louisa Rollin spoke on the floor of the South Carolina House of Representatives in 1869 to advocate universal suffrage. Two years later, her sister Lottie led a meeting at the state capital to promote woman suffrage. In 1870, Lottie chaired the founding meeting of the South Carolina Women's Rights Association in Columbia. Her address there was apparently the first Black woman-suffrage argument (apart from those of Sojourner Truth) to be published. She said:

> It had been so universally the custom to treat the idea of woman suffrage with ridicule and merriment that it becomes necessary in submitting the subject for earnest deliberation that we assure the gentlemen present that our claim is made honestly and seriously. We ask suffrage not as a favor, nor as a privilege, but as a right based on the ground that we are human beings and as such, entitled to all human rights.[53]

In the District of Columbia, where Black men already had the right to vote, Mary Ann Shadd Cary, who had moved there after the war, tried an extraordinary strategy. By 1870 she was a student at Howard University's Law School. In that year she attended the Woman Suffrage Convention in Washington, where she heard Victoria Woodhull's argument that a suffrage amendment gave women the right to vote on the basis that they were citizens.

Cary subsequently wrote a statement to the Judiciary Committee of the House of Representatives. In it she said that she was a taxpayer and as such had the same obligations as the Black males who paid taxes in the District. Additionally, the Fourteenth and Fifteenth Amendments said that all Blacks were citizens with the right to vote. Although she also reiterated the demand of all women that "male" be taken out of the Constitution, she made a special note of the achievements of Black females who had been exemplary citizens and thus deserved the vote.

In 1871, Cary tested her case and she successfully registered to vote, becoming one of the few women to do so in the period.[54] Along with other women, like her Howard roommate Charlotte Ray, she continued to be active in the suffrage struggle throughout her life. Men as well, including Douglass among others, continued to speak and write and agitate on behalf of woman suffrage and women's rights. Cary's victory and the political alliance that Black women and men were able to forge after 1870 illustrated the efficacy of women's supporting the Fourteenth and Fifteenth Amendments as a prerequisite to achieving their own rights.

Black women also asserted their spirit in social and economic matters—especially when it became clear that the patriarchal family structure was not workable. "Now is the time," remarked Frances Ellen Harper in 1870, "for our women to lift up their heads and plant the roots of progress under the hearth-stone."[55] Many unhesitatingly pulled up roots when it became evident that a writ of emancipation was not synonymous with freedom in the South. Although increased violence and a failing southern economy are most frequently cited as reasons for the western migration—which found seven thousand Blacks moving to Kansas alone in 1879—women's strongest concern seemed to be the protection of their families.

Mary J. Garrett, founder of a committee of five hundred Black New Orleans women in 1878 to support migration, noted that the Black pioneers were compelled to migrate to secure "a home and family."[56] Other Black pioneers spoke of "the want of education and protection for their women." Black women seemed most concerned, as they were in slavery, to protect their daughters from continuing exploitation by White men. One group of Black women pioneers spoke of their desire to "rear their children up—their girls—to lead a virtuous and industrious life."[57] Many added that even if their husbands did not leave, they would.

Whether they stayed in the South or left it, the independence that Black women had internalized in the antebellum years did not dissipate with freedom. With their husbands, Harper observed, they often did "double duty": a "man's share in the field and a woman's part at home." Even if they found themselves without husbands, many managed quite well. Harper wrote of numerous women who successfully worked farms alone or with another woman as partner. "Mrs. Jane Brown and Mrs. Halsey formed a partnership ten years ago," Harper reported in 1878. The women "leased nine acres and a horse and cultivated the land all that time, just the same as the men would have done. They have saved considerable money from year to year, and are living independently."[58] Another woman in Mississippi, though an invalid and with only two women and a boy to assist her, managed to raise six hundred bushels of sweet potatoes, one hundred hogs, thirty dozen chickens, and a large garden of cabbages. She was said to have saved $700 in seven years.

Black women also showed themselves capable of managing other people's large farms. Harper wrote that an employee of the Freedmen's Bureau observed "scores of coloured women in the South working and managing plantations of from 20 to 100 acres. They and their boys and girls doing all the labour, and marketing in the fall from ten to fifty bales of cotton."[59]

That same spirit was evident when it came to managing the lives of their children, especially when it came to education—often a high-priority item. "The women as a class are quite equal to the men in energy and executive ability," Harper stated. "In fact I find by close observation that the mothers are the levers which move in education. The men talk about it, especially about election time, if they want an office for self or their candidate, but the women must work for it. They labour in many ways to support the family, while the children attend school. They make great sacrifices to spare their own children during working hours."[60]

That energy and executive ability were also evident in women who could look beyond family and livelihood toward community activities. Black women had had a long tradition of community activism. In the nineteenth century, for example, organizations such as the Mother Society of New York were largely responsible for the relatively small number of Black women paupers in that city. The first Black newspaper, Freedom's Journal, proudly noted in 1829 that there were ten times fewer Black women than White in this category: 43 and 462 respectively.

During and after the Civil War, numerous Black women's church and civic organizations sent material aid to Black war veterans and their families. Groups like the Kansas Relief Association, organized by Josephine St. Pierre Ruffin, provided funds for Black migrants. In this period, Black women were instrumental in building a number of needed community institutions. Mary Ellen Pleasant, who became wealthy by speculating on the California gold rush and was rumored to have financed John Brown's raid at Harpers Ferry, underwrote the building of the African Methodist Episcopal Church (AME), the AME Zion Church, and the Baptist Church in San Francisco, though she herself was a practicing Catholic. Black women also helped provide for schools, orphanages, and other institutions. "The coloured women have not been backward in promoting charities for their own race and sex," commented Harper during her tour. She further remarked that women of all economic stations participated in the effort. "One of the most efficient helpers," she said, "is a Mrs. Madison, who, although living in a humble and unpretending home, had succeeded in getting up a home for aged coloured women."[61] One of the lesser-known contributions of the great Harriet Tubman was the devotion of her life after the war to a similar project. The woman who personally led three hundred slaves to freedom, who was a spy and "general" for the Union, spent her final years trying to establish the John Brown Home for the Aged. When the government refused to give her a full veteran's pension, the former general sold fruit and had a biography published to raise money for the institution.

On a more personal level, Black women, too, rebelled against domestic tyranny—no matter what color the tyrant. Black mistresses took their white lovers to task, especially in those states where Reconstruction legislation knocked down the prohibitions against interracial marriage. A Black woman in Virginia left her longtime White lover, the father of her child, saying that "she was tired of living that kind of life, and if she could not be his wife she couldn't be anything."[62] According to their son, his father never married again.

Other mistresses of White men demanded that they receive the material support due a wife, whether they were one or not. A northern traveler in Yazoo, Mississippi, reported that Black concubines there went on a "strike" until their financial claims were resolved. They "not only kicked against the pricks, they actually began to wear armor against them," he wrote. The response of the men varied. One "built an elegant new residence" for his mistress; another gave money; yet a third did marry, secretly.[63]

Black women were also making demands of their own men or, at the least, refusing to remain in a relationship where they had responsibilities without privileges. During the Fifteenth Amendment debates, the White feminist Frances Gage, who had done some work in the Freedmen's Bureau, observed that many freedwomen "who had shared equally in the obligations and suffering of slavery, were refusing legal marriage and the submission to men that emancipation seemed to require."[64] This was certainly true of Rose Williams, the slave who had earlier tried to refuse the mate, Rufus, whom her master foisted on her for childbearing purposes. After the emancipation, Rose left Rufus. "I never marries," she explained, " 'cause one 'sperience am 'nough for this nigger. After what I done for de massa," Williams vowed, "I's never wants to truck with any man. De Lawd forgive dis cullud woman, but he have to 'scuse me and look for some others for to 'plenish the earth."[65]

During the 1870's, Whites were commenting on the decline of the entire Black southern population. The Bostonian George Stetson attributed the diminished birthrate to "the root of the cotton plant," "known to all negro women as a powerful emmenagogue, . . . everywhere obtainable . . . [and] extensively used."[66] So it wasn't only "legal" slavery that motivated Black women to exercise control over their bodies.

IV

~ Prelude to a Movement ~

After the end of Reconstruction, Black women were prepared to create organizations and institutions that reflected their feminist concerns. In 1880, Mary Ann Shadd Cary led the way, organizing the Colored Women's Progressive Association. One of the association's goals was to "assert" equal rights for women, including that of suffrage. With the franchise, Cary believed, women would be empowered to help youth, extend the breadth of women's occupations, and more effectively agitate for "independence of thought and action." Underlying Cary's ideas was a tone of feminist contention. The association, she said, was also created "to take an aggressive stand against the assumption that men only begin and conduct industrial and other things." It was to publish a newspaper "conducted by colored women" and to be financed by a joint stock company in which, "while no invidious distinctions may be made, women, having the greatest interest at stake, must be the controlling official power."[1]

It was in the 1880's, Black women's historian Rosalyn Terborg-Penn asserts, that the argument for woman suffrage went beyond the universal-rights concept to address the specific needs of Black women. This trend, seemingly initiated by Cary, resulted in a more broadly based involvement of Black women in the suffrage struggle. As Cary's proposal also signified, Black women were ready to begin institutionalizing their claims to economic, social, and political equality. Beginning in this decade, they were also making unprecedented gains in education and the professions. By the 1880's, the first Black woman had passed the Bar, and Black women became the first female physicians to practice in the South. At the turn of the century, Booker T. Washington's National Business League reported that there were "160 Black female physicians, seven dentists, ten lawyers, 164 ministers, assorted journalists, writers, artists, 1,185 musicians and teachers of music, and 13,525 school instructors."[2]

The progress of Black women became the subject of numerous articles published at the turn of the century. One such article enumerated four thousand women who had graduated from ninety normal schools and universities by 1905.[3] Both the increasing numbers and the political, economic, and social concerns of Black women attending college precipitated the founding of the largest sororities: Alpha Kappa Alpha and Delta Sigma Theta in 1908 and 1913 respectively. In addition to those graduating from Black schools, more were matriculating through institutions like Oberlin, the University of Chicago, Cornell, Radcliffe, Wellesley, and even schools abroad.* Another article, published in 1904, mentioned the increasing economic achievements of Black women. They had accumulated some $700,000 in real property, it said, helped to raise $14 million for the education of children, and educated more than 25,000 teachers of their own race.[4]†

A number of Black women founded their own schools, filling the vacuum left by the Freedmen's Bureau. The daughter of a minister who had purchased his own and his wife's manumission from slavery, Lucy C. Laney, a graduate of the first class at Atlanta University, established Haines Normal and Industrial Institute in Augusta, Georgia, in 1886. Offering courses in liberal arts at a time when Black education in the state was restricted to vocational training and Georgia had no public high schools for Blacks, Laney maintained the school for over a half century. Among the most well known of her protégées were three women who would become school founders themselves: Mary McLeod Bethune, Charlotte Hawkins Brown, and Janie Porter Barrett.

Some of the achievements of Afro-American women reflected those of all women in the postwar period. An increasing number of both groups were able to ride the crest of the nation's economic expansion. Between 1869 and 1899, America's GNP (gross national product) almost tripled, capital investment increased practically sixfold, and the United States replaced Britain as the leading manufacturing nation in the world. In the latter part of the century, that expansion

---

*It is difficult to reconcile figures for educational degrees, particularly as they relate to numbers in the professions. Jeanne Noble, for example, reports 22 women receiving B.A.'s from Black colleges in 1900, and 227 in 1910. Although many women had undoubtedly attained professional status via the standard requirements, some professions (like teaching in elementary schools in certain communities) did not require a B.A., but a normal school degree.

†By 1912 the librarian Monroe Work listed fourteen Black women's colleges, many of which prepared teachers.[5]

spilled over U.S. borders, and Cuba, Hawaii, Puerto Rico, and the Philippines became ripe for imperialist picking. The expansion led to a technological revolution which permitted women to spend more time outside the home. The introduction of gas lighting and domestic plumbing, the commercial production of ice, and the popularization of the sewing machine were welcome additions for any home keeper. Now women could earn wages in the work force without abandoning domestic duties. But there was a negative side to these economic and technological developments. The inequality of the new wealth forced more women to join a wage-labor force that exploited them. Additionally, with the new laborsaving devices, they were still expected to be exclusively responsible for the home.

The new wealth may have allowed more women to enter the recently established women's colleges such as Smith, Vassar, and Wellesley, or schools that were or had recently become coeducational, like Cornell and Boston University, but this development also carried a feminist frustration. Many women found themselves educated to fill a place that did not exist, as historian William O'Neill put it. The situation of the Hull House reformer Jane Addams is illustrative. As was true of half that generation, she didn't marry. Already financially secure, Addams was expected to remain at home and take care of her aging relatives for the rest of her life. Caught between the expectations of two worlds, she literally collapsed under the strain. She had bouts of "nervous prostration" and on one occasion was committed to Dr. S. Weir Mitchell's Hospital of Orthopedic and Nervous Diseases, which specialized in treating women with "nervous complaints." Convulsions, pain, depression, and chronic fatigue were common among Mitchell's patients. Addams had a spine condition that kept her bedridden for six months, and for two years she was encased in a supportive "straight-jacket" composed of whalebone, leather, and steel. But with her establishment of Chicago's Hull House, Addams found relief from her physical and emotional problems. She once described the settlement house as a place for "invalid girls" like herself "to go and help the poor." Addams's activities lessened her sense of "futility and misdirected energy," and she admitted that the settlement house was more "an answer to her personal needs than the needs of those she planned to serve."[6]

If White women were frustrated, Black women were even more so. Although growing numbers of Black women had the opportunity to enter college and the professions, the masses of Black women were still relegated to domestic and menial work. They were excluded from such job categories as clerk and secretary, newly opened to women (who were being hired to replace men at lower wages), because White women wanted them. Orra Longhorne, a writer on race and labor, made it clear in 1886 that "there was a very great need for occupation in which *white* women could support themselves."[7] (Emphasis added.) As has been historically true, discrimination against Black women in the industrial sector resulted in disproportionately high numbers both in the professions—where there is less competition— and in menial occupations. But an even more profoundly disturbing development in the postwar era was the new rapacity of racism and classism that evolved as the economy unfolded.

The late nineteenth century was described by Columbia University historian Richard Hofstadter as a time of "rapid expansion, desperate competition and peremptory rejection of failure."[8] It was a society that pulled the old trip wire of White elevation and Black degradation. But this time there were new forces to contend with: Both Blacks and women had gone pretty far to be pulled down so easily. And now the powers that be would also have to deal with the restiveness of a poor immigrant population (which was beginning to get a hand on the levers of city government), and a White middle class who were becoming increasingly unhappy that seven eighths of the country's wealth was being concentrated in the hands of one eighth of the population.

This time, a rationale backed by "scientific" reason was sorely needed to explain—and justify—why the rich, the poor, Blacks, and women should remain in their allotted places. Although Charles Darwin's conclusions in the *Origin of Species* (1859) were intended to refer to the animal kingdom, his ideas about the survival of the fittest afforded social scientists that rationale. The titans of industry were supposed to be on top because they were superior species, the thinking went. Conversely, the poor deserved to be poor, and if they died from poverty, they deserved that too. Giving them government aid could destroy society, for it would corrupt the natural laws of evolution—the survival of the fittest.

That the captains of industry (only later to be called robber barons) were Anglo-Saxon was both "natural" and necessary to further the evolution of society toward a perfect state. When desperate competition again forced White men to remind themselves what it meant to be civilized, methods were found to rationalize the repression of the "barbarians." A useful tool was the spate of anthropometric theories which determined the degree of "civilization" by measuring brain size and anatomical features. Although these theories dated back to the antebellum years, they took on a new significance when scientists like Dr. Cesare Lombroso, who published *Criminal Man* in 1876 (the year federal troops were removed from the South), "proved" that men with non-Anglo-Saxon features tended to love "idleness and orgies," evil for its own sake, and desired not only to murder but to "mutilate the corpse, tear its flesh and drink its blood."9 Thus, White superiority was further refined into Anglo-Saxon superiority, and the claims of Blacks and Eastern European immigrants (especially Jewish ones) within U.S. borders, and those of darker peoples outside them, were seen to be not only invalid but also dangerous to the society.

As those residing in the South knew all too well, these ideas were most readily absorbed in a region uprooted by defeat and porous with humiliation and fear. Already possessed of a hedonistic state of mind, the White man in the South, noted W. J. Cash, had the "repulsive suspicion . . . that he might be slipping into bestiality."10 White men had good reason for that suspicion. Lynching, always a fixture in the South, had turned more gruesome when, with the end of slavery, the majority of its victims became Black rather than White and the image of Blacks changed from that of children to dangerous animals.* Now there was an evident need to dismember, to castrate, even to fight over body parts to take home for souvenirs.

Racial hostility was especially focused on Afro-Americans who had made substantial economic gains in the postwar period—gains now being checked by the South's counterrevolution, the eclipse of the Freedmen's Bureau, and later the depression of 1893.

Thriving Black communities were congealing into ghettos. Children had few recreational facilities and suffered neglect, as both parents were forced to work at labor that deadened the energies of the soul, as Maria Stewart would say. The situation worsened as Black communities became havens for drugs (cocaine was popular even then), crime, and prostitution—often with the complicity of White authorities. All these things added to the pressures on Black family life which were exacerbated by Black migration to the cities, both southern and northern. Between 1890 and 1910, as many as 200,000

---

*Between 1840 and 1860 there were three hundred recorded victims hanged or burned by mobs. Of that figure, only 10 percent were Black.

Blacks left the soil that had borne so much of their blood and tears. Blacks were beleaguered. The Black family was under siege.

At the same time, Black political power in the state and federal governments had dried up virtually overnight. By 1889, Henry W. Grady, part owner of the *Atlanta Constitution,* the South's largest newspaper, boasted that the "negro as a political force has dropped out of serious consideration." Black men were disenfranchised in the South, and national publications were advocating the repeal of the Fifteenth Amendment. Black leaders, who had been so vociferous just a few years before, were now strangely silent. With the exception of T. Thomas Fortune's Afro-American League, there was no organized Black resistance.

As the status of Blacks deteriorated, that of White women rose. White men needed to transcend sordid considerations, and Social Darwinists talked about a society made perfect by the elimination of lust. From public lecterns, intellectuals cautioned even married couples to copulate only for the purpose of having children. Mainstream women's organizations such as the Women's Christian Temperance Union (WCTU) and the YWCA promoted this idea.

Still, it would be difficult to persuade women to stay at home where they could perform their assigned tasks undistracted. So an array of scientific theories was directed at them too. Gustave Le Bon, the founder of social psychology, pronounced the intelligence of women "closer to savages and children than adult civilized males." Their "incapacity to reason" made educating them "a dangerous chimera," he said, which would create women "utterly useless as mothers and wives."[11] Harvard professor Dr. Edward Clarke went so far as to say that college education could "destroy a woman's productive organs."[12] The propaganda unleashed to keep women out of the impure realms of the classroom, politics, and the labor force was formidable. This was particularly true for White southern women, who were beginning to find the pedestal stultifying.

The Civil War had left a generation of women without men, observed southern historian Ann Firor Scott, and relatively speaking, women had done quite well. Many had shown their resourcefulness when they were forced to manage plantations and their own lives without chivalrous shoulders to lean on. After the war many southern women were forced to work. Others were joining local women's organizations as well as national ones like the WCTU. By 1887 the WCTU supported the women's franchise, and after the unification of two separate woman-suffrage organizations into the National American Women's Suffrage Association (NAWSA) in 1890, southern women were also vigorously courted by that group. All this was happening at a time when men were putting a new "emphasis on the purity and reverence for White women," wrote Cash, so much so that it resulted in "pure gyneolatry."[13] That White southern women were squirming on their postwar pedestals undoubtedly contributed to the rise of lynching in these years, observed southern historian Jacquelyn Dowd Hall. The "pursuit of the black rapist represented a trade-off . . . the right of the southern lady to protection presupposed her obligation to obey."[14]

White northern women were better able to find a way out, or off their pedestals: the ripening crises in the cities. If their sphere was the home, women said, then who better to engage in urban reform than they? After all, the growing problems of the slums and the need for pure-food laws and child-labor reform were really matters of "enlarged housekeeping." Anyway, they knew more than men did about such things. And if women were morally superior, they said, then women were better qualified to clean up the corruption in government. Holding women down, they argued, could retard society's evolution toward perfection. Their rationale enabled them to become more active outside the home while still preserving the probity of "true womanhood."

Although they disagreed with the inherent racist assumptions among Whites, Black women did share some of the attitudes of White women reformers. Black women activists believed that their efforts were essential for reform and progress, and that their moral standing was a steady rock upon which the race could lean. They believed that the Black community was at a crossroads. Abandoned by the federal government, subjected to increasing violence, and shorn of political power, it would either be pushed into oblivion or would mobilize its resources and survive. Standing on the brink of this racial precipice, convinced that they could save the race, Black women saw their role in almost ecclesiastical terms. They were "the fundamental agency under God in the regeneration . . . of the race, as well as the groundwork and starting point of its progress upward," wrote Anna Julia Cooper in her *Voice of the South* (1892), one of the best-written books of the period.[15] It was the Black woman, continued Cooper, who "must stamp weal or woe on the coming history of this people."[16] The responsibility was a tremendous one, for as she had told a group of

Black clergymen six years earlier: "Only the BLACK WOMAN can say 'when and where I enter . . . then and there the whole *Negro race enters with me.*' "17

Despite their "high prerogative," in Cooper's phrase, Black women were checked in fulfilling that vital role. Society failed to see them as a distinct political and social force. At a time when their White peers were riding the wave of moral superiority that sanctioned their activism, Black women were seen as immoral scourges. Despite their achievements, they did not have the benefit "of a discriminating judgment concerning their worth as women," as the Chicago activist Fannie Barrier Williams noted.18 Assumed to have "low and animalistic urges" that cast them outside the pale of the movement for moral reform, Black women were seen as having all the inferior qualities of White women without any of their virtues. Allegations like those in the popular periodical *The Independent* typified the prevailing attitudes toward Black women. Like White women, one writer said, "Black women had the brains of a child, the passions of a woman," but unlike Whites, Black women were "steeped in centuries of ignorance and savagery, and wrapped about with immoral vices."19 In this era the idea of a moral Black woman was incredible. "I sometimes hear of a virtuous Negro woman," wrote a commentator for *The Independent* in 1902, "but the idea is absolutely inconceivable to me. . . . I cannot imagine such a creature as a virtuous Negro woman." Evidently such an idea escaped even the fertile imagination of Gertrude Stein. In her classic *Three Lives* (1909) the character Rose, *despite* being raised by Whites, possessed "the simple, promiscuous immorality of Black people."

There was a more liberal set of opinions about Black women. What distinguished it from the others, however, was not that Black women were less immoral, but that there were legitimate reasons for their low state of mind. For example, a report of the Slater Fund, a foundation that subsidized numerous welfare projects for Blacks, declared:

> The negro women of the South are subject to temptations . . . which come to them from the days of their race enslavement. . . . To meet such temptations the negro woman can only offer the resistance of a low moral standard, an inheritance from the system of slavery, made still lower from a lifelong residence in a one-room cabin 2(

The stereotype of Black women, like that of Black men, applied to all classes, including the middle-class leaders.

Although Afro-American women felt they had a compelling mandate, although more of them than ever had the education and resources to fulfill that mandate, they were frustrated by the negative epithets hurled at them, and by the failure of Black leaders to defend them or the race as a whole. It was against this background that Ida B. Wells's antilynching campaign exploded on the scene. "At the very time when race interest seems at such a low ebb, when our race leaders seem tongue-tied and stupidly inactive in the presence of unchecked lawlessness and violent resistance to Negro advancement, it is especially fortunate and reassuring to see and feel the rallying spirit of our women," pronounced Fannie Barrier Williams. That spirit galvanized a group that was already poised to emerge, with or without the sanction of Black men or Whites generally. Immediately after Wells's testimonial in 1892, Victoria Earle Matthews, Susan McKinney, and Josephine St. Pierre Ruffin announced plans to form Black women's clubs in New York City, Brooklyn (then a separate city), and Boston, respectively. Between 1892 and 1894, clubs proliferated throughout the country, from Omaha to Pittsburgh, Rhode Island to New Orleans, Denver to Jefferson City. The clubs were an idea whose time had come with the Wells campaign. "Ida Wells was creating so much interest in her crusade against lynching, it was a good time to carry out the clubs idea," noted *The Woman's Era,* a Black women's publication edited by Ruffin.[21] Consistent with the Black women's concerns, the clubs were organized not "for race work alone," said Ruffin, "but for work along the lines that make for women's progress."[22]

V

~ Defending Our Name ~

In addition to the practical things that needed to be done to assure progress, Black women had to confront and redefine morality and assess its relationship to "true womanhood." For the prevailing views of the society had not only debased their image, but had also excluded them from the mainstream of the labor force and continued to make them vulnerable to sexual exploitation. All of these had the consequence of blunting their progress both psychologically and materially. Josephine St. Pierre Ruffin announced:

> All over America, there is to be found a large and growing class of earnest, intelligent, progressive colored women, who, if not leading full, useful lives, are only waiting for the opportunity to do so, many of them warped and cramped for lack of opportunity, not only to do more, but be more; and yet, if an estimate of the colored women of America is called for, the inevitable reply, glibly given is, "For the most part ignorant and immoral, some exceptions of course, but these don't count."[1]

One of the first items of business on the Black leaders' agenda was to defend their moral integrity as women. Significantly, this was done not by separating themselves along class lines from other women, but by defending the history of all Black women and redefining the criteria of true womanhood.

The World Columbian Exposition of 1893 presented them with one of the earliest opportunities to address the issue in a public interracial forum. The purpose of the exposition was to display the achievements of the Americas to people here and abroad. Included among the exhibits was one that illuminated the achievements of American women; it was housed in a building designed by a woman architect. A board of "Lady Managers," made up of prominent women, selected participants to address the exposition. Although there was a Haitian exhibit presided over by Frederick Douglass—who had been appointed American minister to the island in 1889—Afro-Americans as a group were not allowed to participate. Black women were told by the board of Lady Managers that only national women's organizations could take part. The few Black women permitted to speak, however, were well aware of the true reasons for that exclusion, and addressed the issue directly.

Their frankness undoubtedly shocked the audiences, since those selected to speak must have been considered "safe" by the Lady Managers: the "exceptions," as Ruffin would say. Fannie Barrier Williams, for example, had been born to a middle-class family in Brockport, New York; was a graduate of the New England Conservatory of Music, the first woman to be appointed to Chicago's Library Board, and one of the few Black members of the Chicago Women's Club. However, she did not hesitate to confront the issue that White women rarely discussed in public.

After a few eloquent statements about the achievements of Black women and the need for interracial unity, Williams went to the heart of the matter. "I regret the necessity of speaking of the moral question of our women," she began, but, "the morality of our home life has been commented on so disparagingly and meanly that we are placed in the unfortunate position of being defenders of our name."[2] Echoing the sentiments of Wells, Williams went on to tell the group that the onus of sexual immorality did not rest on Black women but on the White men who continued to harass them. While many women in the audience were fantasizing about Black rapists, she implied, Black women were actually suffering at the hands of White ones. If White women were so concerned about morality, then they ought to take measures to help protect Black women. "I do not want to disturb the serenity of this conference by suggesting why this protection is needed and the kind of man against whom it is needed," Williams threatened. By implying that White men were the real culprits, Williams attacked not only the myth of Black promiscuity, but the notion that women themselves were wholly responsible for their own victimization.

Even for Black women in Williams's position the issue wasn't an abstract one. Sexual exploitation was so rampant that it compelled thousands of women to leave the South, or to urge their daughters to do so. Speaking before the exposition, Williams already knew what she would write some years later: "It is a significant and shameful fact that I am constantly in receipt of letters from the still unprotected women in the South, begging me to find employment for their daughters . . . to save them from going into the homes of the South as servants as there is nothing to save them from dishonor and degradation."[3]

Williams was also undoubtedly aware of the responsibility that White women bore in the sexual exploitation of their sisters, as a Black writer in *The Independent* noted: "I know of more than one colored woman who was openly importuned by White women to become the mistress of their husbands, on the ground that they, the white wives, were afraid that, if their husbands did not associate with colored women they would certainly do so with outside white women," she wrote. ". . . And the white wives, for reasons which ought to be perfectly obvious, preferred to have all their husbands do wrong with colored women in order to keep their husbands *straight!*"[4] As Williams told the exposition, Black women's "own mothers can't protect them, and White women will not."[5]

Williams's theme was reiterated by another Black speaker at the exposition, the educator Anna Julia Cooper. Born near Raleigh, North Carolina, and a graduate of Oberlin College, Cooper noted that the real struggle wasn't "temptations" as much as it was "the painful, patient, and silent toil of mothers to gain title to the bodies of their daughters."[6] The issue wasn't an abstract one to her either. Her mother had been a slave, and her father, her mother's master. But the pain of that reality was suffered in silence. Her mother, Cooper once wrote, had always been "too shame-faced" to mention him.

Also held against Black women was their experience under slavery; and in speeches and in writings they expressed their own views on the meaning of their history. As Cooper noted, there was "shame" about their experience under an institution that Fannie Barrier Williams had described as depending upon "the degradation of everything human." But Black women may have been the only group in America able to see not only the degradation but the triumph of transcending what the system would make of them. In their minds, the experience of slavery provided evidence of the Black woman's moral strength and resiliency. Despite a system that made the Black woman "submit her body to a cruelty too diverse and appalling to mention," commented clubwoman Addie Hunton, who was subsequently prominent in the YWCA and NAACP, "there is hardly a daughter of a slave mother who has not heard of the . . . heroic soul of some maternal ancestor that went home to God . . . rather than live a life of enforced infamy."[7] This sentiment was more than mere rhetoric. Many of the Black clubwomen, like Cooper, Mary Church Terrell, and Ida B. Wells, were daughters of women who had once been slaves. And common was the feeling that Anna Julia Cooper expressed about her own mother. "She was the finest woman I have ever known," Cooper wrote.[8]

The lesson that the Black women were trying to impart was that color, class, or the experience of slavery did not nullify the moral strength of true womanhood. Echoing Maria Stewart's ideas, expressed more than fifty years earlier, Black activists attempted to push American consciousness beyond the class and race prejudice that marked Victorian thinking, toward modernist ideas and attitudes. "The moral aptitudes of our women," proclaimed Williams in her speech, "are just as strong and just as weak as that of any other American women with like advantages and environment."[9] Some women, like Mary Church Terrell, took their convictions a step further. Terrell had had the experience of living abroad and was in a position to compare poor Black women with Englishwomen of "like advantages and environment." "In none of my travels, either North or South have I ever seen colored women, no matter how ignorant or degraded they were, so devoid of self-respect and natural womanly pride as were some Englishwomen I saw," she said, with a rather backhanded compliment.[10] The women agreed, however, that a new chapter had been reached in history, and despite White opinions of their past, the record of Black women's present achievements could not be denied. "The question of the moral progress of our women," concluded Williams at the exposition, "has force and meaning . . . only so far as it tells the story of how once enslaved women have been struggling . . . to emancipate themselves."[11]

What White feminists hardly realized was that Black women were providing them a means for their own liberation. For inherent in the Black women's defense of their integrity was a challenge to the Victorian ideas that kept all women oppressed. This was clearly evident in a speech delivered by Frances Ellen Harper before the National Council of Women in the early 1890's.

The veteran abolitionist believed in the moral role of women but discounted the idea that morality was the exclusive property of any one race, sex, or class. "More than the changing of institutions we need the development of a national conscience," she said, "and the upbuilding of national character . . . and it is the women of the country who help mould its character." But, she made clear, character and gender were not necessarily the same. ". . . It is not through sex, but through character that the best influence of the women upon the life of the nation must be exerted," she urged.[12] The nation was in deep trouble, she concluded, and needed the "infusion of clearer and cleaner waters." However, as Harper told the predominantly White council, moral superiority did not originate in class and sex alone. "I am not so sure," she said, "that women are so much better than men that they will clear the stream by virtue of their womanhood." Moral superiority came through struggle, Harper told her audience, through the willingness "to grapple with evils which undermine the strength of the nation," through the demand for "justice, simple justice, as the right of every race; to brand with everlasting infamy the lawlessness and brutal cowardice that lynches, burns and tortures your own countrymen."[13]

Instead of the dubious rationale of enlarged housekeeping, Harper and other Black activists offered White women reformers a gauntlet, one they had earlier failed to take up in the abolitionist movement. It was through the Black struggle—past, present, and future—that White women could engage the kind of issue appropriate to their own struggle. But they failed to transcend their racism and classism to be able to grasp the significance of the Black women's perspective, even as it related to their own cause.

Toward a National Organization

For Afro-American women it was the "demand for justice," for the race and for themselves, that propelled them on to the next stage of their political development. And again it was Ida B. Wells who would be a catalyst for the creation of a Black women's organization.

In February 1893, Frederick Douglass invited Wells to speak before Black women activists in Washington, D.C. Mary Church Terrell was present, as was Anna Julia Cooper, principal of the M Street School, and other prominent figures in the city. Two hundred dollars were collected and the meeting ended in a "blaze of glory," in Wells's words. However, the next morning she was shaken by an item in the newspaper. One of the most gruesome lynchings to take place in this period had occurred in Paris, Texas. A Black man, Henry Smith, was accused of raping a five-year-old White girl and had been tortured with red-hot irons, then burned alive. The lynching had taken on the air of a festive event. Schoolchildren had been given a holiday so that they could witness the burning; the railroads ran excursions for people in outlying areas. After the man's body was reduced to ashes, a mob fought over bones, teeth, and buttons for souvenirs in the still-hot rubble.

Wells used the money collected the previous evening to hire a Pinkerton detective, and sent him after objective facts in the case, whose sensational details were picked up by newspapers both here and abroad. In Scotland, two women reformers, Isabelle Mayo and Catherine Impey, read of the incident, and after inquiring as to who could best come to the British Isles to talk about it, issued an invitation to Ida B. Wells. She went on a lecture tour through the isles and returned in time to attend the Columbian Exposition in Chicago.

There, Frederick Douglass, Wells, and her husband-to-be, Ferdinand Barnett—a lawyer, and publisher of Chicago's first Black newspaper, *The Conservator*—wrote and distributed a contentious pamphlet entitled "The Reason Why the Colored American Is Not in the Columbian Exposition." With an introduction in three languages (there wasn't time to translate the rest) the pamphlet was "a clear, plain statement of facts concerning the oppression put upon the Colored people in this land of the free and home of the brave," as Wells characterized it.[14]

Her trip to England and her appearance at the exposition caused Wells to attract national attention. A local antilynching campaign was one thing; an international one was quite another. Many Whites were particularly concerned about English opinion. The views of the British elite carried great prestige in the minds of their American cousins. More importantly, England's role as the leading importer of American cotton gave British views additional weight in American affairs. And here was Wells, arousing the same kind of moral indignation that had proven so useful to American abolitionists in the antebellum days. When Wells was invited a second time to the British Isles, soon after her appearance at the exposition, there was even more reason for White concern.

To British liberals, Wells's assertion that liberal American Whites condoned lynching was just as disturbing as the fact of lynching itself. At first, Britons were incredulous at the charge. What about women like Frances Willard? they asked. Willard, the president of the Women's Christian Temperance Union, was right there in England at the time. She was known as a liberal and had been heralded in the English press as the "Uncrowned Queen of American Democracy." Whatever her claims to royalty, few American women could rival her influence. An ambitious and talented organizer, she was elected secretary of the WCTU at its founding meeting in 1874, and quickly rose through the ranks. Under Willard's stewardship, the WCTU became one of the most formidable women's organizations in the country. There were branches in every state, and it could boast a membership of 200,000. Temperance was not an end in itself to Willard, but a means of politicizing women who considered a direct demand for suffrage too radical. Suffrage, she told her members, was needed if women were to protect their homes from vice. Ironically, her circumventing of the women's rights issue helped make the temperance organization a more effective advocate of the franchise than the suffrage associations were. Under Willard's prodding, the WCTU endorsed suffrage as early as 1887.

Willard's rationale may help to explain the charge that Wells leveled against her. To those who inquired about Willard's position on lynching, Wells said that the temperance leader was not only silent on the issue, but had added fuel to the fire of mob violence. Bringing a copy of a published interview with her to substantiate her charges, Wells told Britons how, on a recent tour of the South, Willard had blamed Blacks for the defeat of temperance legislation there and had cast aspersions on the race. "The colored race multiplies like the locusts of Egypt," she had said, and "the grogshop is its center of power. . . . The safety of women, of childhood, of the home is menaced in a thousand localities."[15]

When Willard and her powerful hostess and counterpart, Lady Somerset, heard Wells's accusations, they were enraged. They said Wells was lying, and Lady Somerset attempted to use her influence to keep all of Wells's future comments out of the press. Wells responded by exposing the fact that despite Willard's abolitionist forebears and Black friends, no Black women were admitted to the WCTU's southern branches. (The record in the North wasn't so great either, although Black women were active in the organization's northern segregated branches. Frances Ellen Harper, who believed in the need for temperance among Blacks and was the only Afro-American to serve on the WCTU's executive committee and board of superintendents, often criticized the racism of the organization's members.)

The dispute between Wells and Willard in England intensified the mean campaign against Wells in the American press.* A Memphis

---

*Wells's confrontation with Willard also reverberated among Blacks. Black clubwoman Josephine Silone Yates defended Willard and the WCTU, saying Wells's criticisms were misleading and unjust. A letter supporting these views was signed by Frederick Douglass and other leaders. However, *The Woman's Era* took Wells's side. "Doubtless Miss Willard is a good friend to colored people, but we have failed to hear paper suggested that she be tied to a stake and branded with an iron. *The New York Times* ran an article insisting that Black men were prone to rape, and that Wells was a "slanderous and nasty-minded mulatress" who was looking for more "income" than "outcome."

The vitriolic assaults from so many directions began to offend the British sense of fair play, Wells wrote. The critical "overkill" proved Wells's contentions better than she herself could. "It is idle for men to say that the conditions which Miss Wells describes do not exist," a British editor wrote. "Whites of America may not think so; British Christianity does and all the scurrility of the American press won't alter the facts."

With help from her detractors, Wells's British tour was a personal triumph, and in the end had a great impact on the antilynching campaign. Before she left, the British Anti-Lynching Committee was formed, and it included such notables as the Duke of Argyll, the Archbishop of Canterbury, members of Parliament, and the editors of *The Manchester Guardian* and other important newspapers. Money was raised for the campaign, and upon her return she had access to White groups that would have been closed to her save for British influence, according to women's historian Bettina Aptheker.

English opinion had also broken the silence of many prominent American leaders. No longer could they afford to ignore "the talented schoolmarm," and such influential people as Richard Gilder, editor of *Century* magazine, Samuel Gompers, the labor leader, and, yes, even Frances Willard eventually lent their names in support of the campaign.

Wells's success also had an even more direct impact. The number of lynchings decreased in 1893—and continued to do so thereafter. The decline in the murders can be directly attributed to the efforts of Ida B. Wells. The effect of Wells's campaign was aptly demonstrated in her home city. Memphis exported more cotton than any other city in the world, and Wells's assertions had been especially damaging to its image. So, as a direct result of her efforts, the city fathers were pressed to take an official stand against lynching—and for the next twenty years there was not another incident of vigilante violence there.[17]

Needless to say, the signs of Ida B. Wells's success left many

---

from her and the WCTU any flat-footed denunciation of lynching and lynchers," it editorialized in 1895.[16]

diehard racists appalled—especially, it seemed, the president of the Missouri Press Association. He was moved to publish an open letter addressed to an Englishwoman "who had manifested a kindly interest in behalf of the American Negro as a result of Miss Ida B. Wells' agitation,"[18] Fannie Barrier Williams reported. As Williams understated it, the letter accused Wells, and all Afro-American women, of "having no sense of virtue and of being altogether without character." The letter proved to be the proverbial last straw. Citing the charge, Josephine St. Pierre Ruffin issued a call for a national convention in Boston. In July 1895 one hundred women from ten states met to formulate plans for a national federation.

Although it was the letter that had precipitated the meeting, the women actually spent little time discussing it. There were many more important things to be done. After three days of meetings, they announced the creation of the National Federation of Afro-American Women, which united thirty-six clubs in twelve states. Elected as president of the organization was Margaret Murray Washington, who had recently become the third wife of Booker T. Washington and was known as the "Lady Principal" of Tuskegee Institute.

Similar efforts to unite the clubs were being made by the National League of Colored Women in Washington, D.C., headed by Mary Church Terrell. By 1896 plans were completed to unite the Federation and the League into the National Association of Colored Women (NACW), and after some debate as to who would head the organization, Terrell became its first president.

The founding meeting in Washington, D.C., was quite a milestone. Appropriately, it was attended by women who personified the struggles of the past as well as of the present. There was Rosetta Sprague, the only daughter of Frederick Douglass, who had been the leading male feminist of his times. Douglass had died a year earlier. Ellen Craft, named after her famous mother, was also there. Her slave parents, Ellen and William Craft, had engineered a spectacular thousand-mile escape, finally settling in England, where they became active in the antislavery movement. What had prompted their flight was Ellen Craft's determination that her children be born on free land.

The abolitionist and suffragist Frances Ellen Harper also attended the meeting. With her "noble head," "bronze color," and "musical voice," Harper had been one of the leading speakers on the antislavery circuit. Just a few years before, Harper, now in her seventies, had become one of the earliest Black women to publish a novel; *Iola LeRoy* chronicled the struggle of a Black woman to maintain her pride, dignity, and racial commitment during the years of slavery and Reconstruction. However, it was Harriet Tubman, Harper's contemporary, who stole the show. The grand old woman, who had led more than two hundred slaves to freedom, had been a Union spy, and had been active in women's organizations after the war, arrived to a standing ovation. In the course of the meeting, she presented the newly born child of Ida Wells-Barnett, Charles Barnett, who was proclaimed "Baby of the Association."

Ida Wells-Barnett should have been pleased. Her antilynching campaign had not only helped to launch the modern civil rights movement, but it had brought Black women into the forefront of the struggle for Black and women's rights.

VI

~ "To Be a Woman, Sublime": The Ideas of the National Black Women's Club Movement (to 1917) ~

Lifting As We Climb

The organization of the NACW was a watershed in the history of Black women. They were not participating in a women's auxiliary of a like-minded men's group, as had happened with the social-uplift and abolitionist associations of the past. "Our woman's movement is a woman's movement in that it is led and directed by women," announced Josephine St. Pierre Ruffin at the Boston national convention. Nor would they be forced to be a minority in White women's groups. "We are not alienating or withdrawing," Ruffin continued. "We are only coming to the front."[1]

This movement was also distinguished by its scope. Even twenty years before, observed Fannie Barrier Williams, few women "beyond the small circles . . . who could read and were public-spirited" would have responded to the call to activism. By contrast, in less than twenty years after its founding, the NACW represented 50,000 women in 28 federations and over 1,000 clubs.

The Black women's club movement did have a number of things in common with the White club movement that preceded it. In some ways, as Fannie Barrier Williams noted, Black women were indeed inspired by the success of the White movement. The two groups were organized in much the same way; the General Federation of Women's Clubs was the White equivalent to the NACW; the membership of both organizations consisted mostly of middle-class educated women who were steeped in the Protestant ethic. Neither group questioned the superiority of middle-class values or way of life, or had any romantic notions of the inherent nobility of the poor, uneducated masses; education and material progress were values that Black and White women shared. Both also believed in the importance of the home and the woman's moral influence within it. Black and White women saw the family as a microcosm and cornerstone of society. In the broadest sense, this idea imbued all female reformers with a new self-awareness and a stronger sense of importance.

"If the fifteenth century discovered America to the Old World," said Frances Ellen Harper, "the nineteenth century is discovering woman herself."[2] To the reformers, that discovery made progress possible in the home, in the country and even beyond: "The world can not move without woman's sharing in the movement,"[3] Harper declared. "China compressed the feet of her women and thereby retarded the steps of her men."[4] The "world needed to hear her voice," concurred the Black educator Anna Julia Cooper. That women were "daring to think and move and speak" was "merely completing the circle of the world's vision," she said.[5] This era, female reformers believed, belonged to them: "We are living," Fannie Barrier Williams concluded, "in what may be called a woman's age."[6] Such convictions inevitably led to feminist ideas. "The old notion that woman was intended by the Almighty to do only those things that men thought they ought to do is fast passing away," Williams said. "In our day and in this country, a woman's sphere is just as large as she can make it and still be true to her finer qualities of soul."[7]

Nevertheless there were distinct differences between the White and Black organizations and the perspective of the women within them. Although there was a mutual concern for the recognition of women as a distinct social and political force, Black women had a more difficult time of it. For them the club movement had become a vehicle for that recognition. "If within thirty-five years [Black women] have become sufficiently important to be studied apart from the general race problem," stated Fannie Barrier Williams, "that fact is gratifying evidence of real progress."[8] Despite the similarity of their roles, Black women felt a special calling. "To be a woman of the race, and to be able to grasp the significance of the possibilities . . . was a heritage . . . unique in the ages," Anna Julia Cooper wrote.[9] That uniqueness made them the "most interesting women in the country," Williams said. It also gave reformers an added sense of exhilaration. "To be alive at such an epoch is a privilege," Cooper believed; "to be a woman, sublime."[10]

High on both organizational agendas were reform, aid to the poor, and fulfilling what psychiatrists call self-actualization. But with these things, too, the difference between the women's organizations was immediately apparent. As early as 1894, Williams stressed: "I believe that it is possible for us to work out, define, and pursue a kind of club work that will be original, peculiarly suitable to our peculiar needs and that will distinguish our work essentially from white women's clubs."[11] Those needs, combined with the beliefs that had molded Black women's thinking, made the mission of Black clubs quite different.

One of the earliest White women's clubs was founded in response to the exclusion of women journalists from the New York Press Club in 1868. After helping to organize a dinner honoring Charles Dickens, the women were put out when they were denied tickets to attend the affair. The consequent founding of the Sorosis Women's Club set a general pattern for these organizations. They were created by women who were frustrated by their exclusion from occupations and other activities for which their education and background had prepared them. They had little concern for women who were forced to work, with the exception of "the middle-class spinster, widow, or woman whose marriage had failed, or was doing teaching, doing office work, or in some instances training herself for a profession," as a feminist historian noted.[12]

It was not that these groups entirely ignored the plight of the poor. There were salutary efforts toward improving living and working conditions for the less fortunate. However those efforts were often motivated by upper-class frustration. For women, helping the poor was one of the few socially sanctioned activities that could be performed outside the home.

Black women, many of them "cramped for lack of opportunity," had frustrations too. But theirs were based on the problems of the race rather than those of their particular class. The Black women activists did not have to be altruistic to have this perspective. The fact was, they understood that their fate was bound with that of the masses. As Mary Church Terrell, one of the wealthiest and best educated Black women of the time, declared: "Self-preservation demands that [Black women] go among the lowly, illiterate and even the vicious, to whom they are bound by ties of race and sex . . . to reclaim them."[13] Unlike the social-uplift organizations of the past, Black women of the late nineteenth century knew that for them, "Progress included a great deal more than what is generally meant by the terms culture, education, and contact," as Fannie Barrier Williams observed.[14] One reason why "progress" meant that much more to them was that all Black women were perceived in the light of those who had the fewest resources and the least opportunity. In commenting on the NACW's motto, "Lifting

As We Climb," Terrell wrote that the club's members "have determined to come into the closest possible touch with the masses of our
women, through whom the womanhood of our people is always
judged."[15]

The differing missions of the Black and White movements were
evident in the people each group chose to serve. "The club movement
among colored women reaches into the sub-social condition of the
entire race," Williams wrote. "Among colored women the club is the
effort of the few competent in behalf of the many incompetent.
. . . Among white women the club is the onward movement of the
already uplifted."[16] The motive for forming the Black women's clubs
was quite "simple and direct," Williams explained. They were organized by women concerned with "how to help and protect some
defenseless and tempted young woman; how to aid some poor boy to
complete a much-coveted education; how to lengthen the short school
term in some impoverished school district; how to instruct deficient
mothers in the difficulties of child training."[17]

Although some among them were concerned about their own
class, the Black clubwomen as a group had a different attitude toward
class and the poor than did the society in general. In many instances,
the lessons of their own lives had taught them that it was opportunity
and environment—not circumstances of birth or previous experience
—that separated them from the masses. Therefore their job was to
help—by word and by deed—to create that opportunity and environment for all Black women. Josephine St. Pierre Ruffin had this in mind
when, in her opening address to the Boston conference, she said that
the movement was not only "created for the sake of fine, cultured
women," but for "the thousands of self-sacrificing young women
teaching and preaching in lonely southern backwoods, for the noble
army of mothers who have given birth to these girls, mothers whose
intelligence is only limited by their opportunity to get at books."[18]

For these Black women, character was judged by where a woman
wanted to go rather than by where she was. "Womanliness is an
attribute and not a condition," *The Woman's Era* counseled. "It is not
supplied or withdrawn by surroundings." The middle-class Black
activists had their elitism, but it was based on "morals first, and then
education, and finally means," in the words of Josephine Bruce, wife
of Blanche K. Bruce, the Reconstruction U.S. senator from Mississippi.[19]

Black women were as deeply concerned about such things as was
the society at large. However, their views about morality, education,

and means also reflected their pragmatic racial concerns. Moral women were the cornerstone of "good" homes, and it was only through the home "that a people can become really good and great," said Mary Church Terrell. "More homes, better homes, purer homes is the text upon which sermons have and will be preached."[20] Olivia Davidson, Booker T. Washington's second wife, who was instrumental in the development of Tuskegee, reiterated Terrell's theme: "We cannot too seriously consider the question of the moral uplifting of our women," she said, "for it is of national importance to us. It is with our women that the purity and safety of our families rest, and what the families are, the race will be."[21] Fannie Barrier Williams extended this idea to the political fortunes of Blacks:

> It took the colored people a long time to realize that . . . to be a citizen of the United States was serious business, and that a seat in Congress was an insecure prominence unless supported by good women, noble mothers, family integrity and pure homes. It was not until the Negro race began to have some consciousness of these primary things that the women of the race became objects of interest and study.[22]

These views were based on some very urgent concerns. Health conditions among large numbers of Blacks was so perilous that an 1899 conference at Atlanta University concluded that if conditions weren't improved, the race could actually be destroyed. "Go into the shanties and hovels in town and country . . . and you have all about you the generators of disease," remarked Olivia Davidson before the Alabama Teacher's Association.[23] She had seen numerous examples of "insufficiency, if not actual want"; families did not eat properly, and were ignorant about health, she said. It was the duty of persons like themselves, she told the teachers, to inspire women to "have better homes and care for their bodies."[24] Much of what has been interpreted as mere imitation of White values among middle-class Black women was a race-conscious mission. They saw themselves not just as messengers but as living examples. "The mother in the home, as the teacher in the schoolroom, and the woman in the church set the standards for the multitude," as Josephine Bruce observed.[25]

The role of mothers was also important, of course. The philosophy of the clubwomen concerning motherhood reflected the new realities they faced in the late nineteenth century. In the 1830's, Maria Stewart told Black mothers it was their duty to "cultivate a pure heart" and the "thirst for knowledge" in their children. By nurturing these noble qualities, Stewart believed, "the hissing and reproach" toward the race would cease. More than half a century later, Black women leaders believed that those same qualities were to be taught so that children could *endure* that inevitable reproach. "We believe," said Terrell, "we can build the foundation of the next generation upon such a rock of morality, intelligence and strength, that the floods of proscription, prejudice and persecution may descend upon it in torrents and yet it will not be moved."[26] Josephine Bruce supported that view: "The Negro home," she said, "is rapidly assuming the position designated for it. It is distinctly becoming the center of social and intellectual life; it is building up strength and righteousness in its sons and daughters, and equipping them for the inevitable battles of life which grow out of the struggle for existence."[27] For these Black women the home was not so much a refuge from the outside world as a bulwark to secure one's passage through it.

Black activists knew, however, that their sisters were under tremendous strain, the kind of strain that made proper child rearing difficult. "Three fourths of the colored women are overworked and underfed," observed Olivia Davidson, "and are suffering to a greater or lesser degree from sheer physical exhaustion."[28] Realizing children "could be made maimed for life . . . because of the treatment received during their helpless infancy," as Terrell noted, they became the focus of club attention.[29] The NACW urged their clubs to establish day nurseries, and many of them set up committees specifically for this purpose. Officers of the NACW raised money to send out a "kindergarten organizer" whose duties were to "arouse the conscience of our women and to establish kindergartens wherever means therefore can be secured."[30]

Although other reformers were also concerned with child care, it was such a compelling issue for Black women that they were especially prominent in this area. In 1898, for example, Anna Evans Murray, who headed the kindergarten committee of the Colored Women's League in Washington, D.C., led a successful lobbying effort to get a $12,000 federal appropriation to establish kindergarten classes in the District's public schools. As always, the actions of the club movement had distinct racial overtones. "The real solution of the race problem lies in the children," Terrell asserted, "both so far as we who are oppressed and those who oppress us are concerned."[31]

The establishment of kindergartens was consistent with the club movement's emphasis on education. Going to school was considered important for both men and women, and essential for the latter. After the Civil War, Anna Julia Cooper said, "our girls as well as our boys flocked in [the schools] and battled for an education."[32] No matter what their thirst for knowledge, it was particularly important for women to get an education because the majority of them had to work. Since their occupations were limited to "teaching in colored schools or domestic service," as Fannie Barrier Williams observed, an education not only had a dramatic impact on their status and quality of life, but often shielded women from the sexual harassment that many of them confronted in White homes. The stark choice between these two occupations was a verity of American life until the World War I years.

The great desire for education, combined with the status of teaching, provided an escape from the limitations that the society imposed on women. As educator Jeanne Noble wrote in her study of Black women's education, "The social system of the Negro rewarded the enterprising, clever, ambitious woman. Later, when attitudes challenging a woman's right to college education emerged, missionaries and earlier college founders were able to overcome these attitudes partly because of the need for teachers to educate masses of ignorant Negroes. Negro women were needed to teach."[33] This attitude provided an additional impetus for Black women, such as Lucy C. Laney, Nannie Helen Burroughs, Charlotte Hawkins Brown, and Mary McLeod Bethune, to found schools. Although the curricula of these schools included academic subjects, there were large doses of industrial arts courses, particularly homemaking, and an environment that enforced codes of morality and thrift. There was a general attitude, says Noble, that "Negro women should be trained to teach in order to uplift the masses."[34]

Of course the training aspect of Black education for women fell in line with the Booker T. Washington philosophy, which was ascendant in this period. Funds for Black schools were easier to come by if one's curricular "buckets" were cast in the Washingtonian mold. But there was also a very pragmatic concern about the relationship among training, the purity of the home, and economic survival. Terrell, for example, saw the "professionalization" of domestic work as doing more "toward solving the labor question than by using any other means it is in our power to employ." She explained that women contributed as much support to the family income as men, and when they were out of a job, the whole family suffered.[35]

Probably the most vociferous on this score was Nannie Helen Burroughs. In 1900 the Washington-born Burroughs became secretary of the Women's Auxiliary of the National Colored Baptist Convention, among the largest of the Black denominations. She was also the founder of the National Training School for Girls in Washington, D.C., whose curriculum included liberal arts courses as well as those which reflected her staunch belief that domestic work should not be disdained but should be made into a science. Mindful of the influx of poor European immigrants in the period, she felt that "the women who earn their living as cooks should take training and become professionals. Household engineers—if you please. The field is still open—but if Negro women do not learn the art, they will surely lose out in another occupation (we have lost several) that, in the world of tomorrow, will be highly paid, standardized professions."[36] Additionally, the domestic arts, as she called them, should be learned to ensure a healthy, wholesome homelife. In her view, lack of such knowledge made women "social and moral liabilities."

Morals and education were also deemed necessary if Blacks were to emerge from the pit of poverty. Rising out of poverty would in turn benefit the entire race. "Race progress is the direct outgrowth of individual success in life," Rosa Bowser wrote in *The Woman's Era*. "The race rises as individuals rise . . . and individuals rise with the race," she concluded.[37] "A man with money can do more for his country, his race, and himself than one without this necessary adjunct," counseled another article in the *Era*. "Get wisdom, but with all our getting get wealth."[38]

Whatever their views about social sanctions, one reason for the emphasis on morality was that lack of it could be impoverishing. Behavior that "menaced the integrity of the home," Addie Hunton warned, was not good for the pocketbook: "Immorality and thrift," she said, "do not mate very well." So, a good part of the philosophy of uplift had to do with lifting the burdens of "ignorance and immorality," Lucy C. Laney wrote, with "true culture and character, linked with—cash."[39]

Booker T. Washington and the Club Movement

The Black club movement coincided with the rise of Booker T. Washington to fame and power. Although Black women leaders were influenced by his formidable presence, they never became captives of the famed Washington machine.

In 1895, Washington, then principal of Tuskegee Institute, delivered one of the opening speeches at the Atlanta Cotton States and International Exposition. His "homespun eloquence," remarked Benjamin Quarles, combined with a message of compromise, drew national acclaim that Washington masterfully transformed into influence. In the subsequent twenty years, the Washington machine dominated Black higher education, business, the press, and political patronage. Booker T. Washington's pipeline to the White House during the Roosevelt, Taft, and McKinley administrations, as well as to such philanthropists as Andrew Carnegie (who gave Tuskegee Institute $600,000 in 1903), assured that dominance until his death in 1915.

From the very beginning of Washington's national acclaim, Black clubwomen expressed conditional praise for his achievement. "How proud we have all felt over the achievement of our great orator, Mr. Booker T. Washington, whose address at the opening of the Cotton States exposition excited more comment than any other of the day," wrote clubwoman Cora Smith for *The Woman's Era.* "Being a typical Negro, his great qualifications cannot be attributed to his Caucasian ancestors," continued Smith, who was herself light-skinned. ". . . Of course some of us do not agree altogether with some of his utterances, but every man has a right to his convictions."[40]

Beyond such reservations, the clubwomen must have had ambivalent attitudes toward Washington. On the one hand, they deeply believed in his philosophy of Black self-help, mutual aid, and racial pride. Many of them, particularly the school founders and educators, were not opposed to Washington's ideas of industrial education. "I believe in industrial education with all my heart," announced Anna Julia Cooper. "We can't all be professional people. We must have a backbone to the race."[41] For school founders like Charlotte Hawkins Brown and Mary McLeod Bethune, the idea of industrial education may have echoed their own convictions, and was certainly essential for the economic survival of their schools. "Before making gifts to Negro colleges," Benjamin Quarles writes, "prospective white donors sought Washington's assurance that their monies would be earmarked for this kind of education. Struggling Black colleges were only too anxious to add trades to the curriculum in order to get badly needed funds."[42] Even projects not directly linked to education but requiring foundation support felt the power of Washington's hand. His silence on a proposal was condemnation enough for a prospective recipient.

Booker T. Washington's National Negro Business League, founded in 1900, was another potential source of the Black leader's power over clubwomen. A number of them, like Madame C. J. Walker, the hairdressing magnate, and Maggie L. Walker (no relation), president of the St. Luke's Bank in Richmond, were businesswomen themselves. By 1915 the league became a Black Chamber of Commerce which had six hundred state and local branches.

Finally, Washington's political pull also had potential significance for many of the club leaders. Terrell and Wells-Barnett had husbands whose political future could be undermined by the "Wizard of Tuskegee," as Washington was called. "I enclose you a list of the principal Negro appointments, and you might ask Booker T. Washington as to their character," ran a memo from President Theodore Roosevelt to a political aide.[43] Actually, most Black federal appointments originated with Booker T. Washington, Quarles reports. Roosevelt, and to a lesser extent Presidents William McKinley and William H. Taft, made him the Black broker both for appointments and for general matters regarding Afro-Americans.

With his views about self-help, and his access to the purse strings as well as the "heart of the white race," as Black sociologist Kelley Miller put it, it is not surprising that there would be links between the machine and the club movement. The connection was personified by Margaret Murray Washington, the Tuskegeean's third wife. From the beginning of the club movement, Mrs. Washington had been a high-ranking officer and served as NACW president from 1912 to 1916. For a number of years she also edited and subsidized the official organ of the NACW, *National Notes,* which took the place of *The Woman's Era* when the Boston group headed by Ruffin could no longer publish it.

These connecting links did not mean that the movement was hostage to the most powerful Black leader in the country. Though in many instances there was accommodation to Washington's ideas—and power—Black women also operated independently of his influence. The educators, for example, believed in industrial education, but they also believed that Blacks should attain the highest academic level possible. One foot was in Booker T. Washington's camp on this issue, the other with W.E.B. Du Bois, who supported the concept of the "talented tenth," a well-educated cadre of Black leaders. Anna Julia

Cooper, for example, may have believed in industrial education with all her heart, but as an educator, and principal of Washington, D.C.'s The M Street School, she was best known for her success in channeling Black students into the most prestigious universities in the country. In fact, her insistence on an academic curriculum drew charges of insubordination from the Washington, D.C., school board, and was probably a reason she was not rehired in 1906. After retiring at the age of sixty-seven, Cooper herself earned a Ph.D. in Latin from the Sorbonne in Paris. Mary Church Terrell may have written wonderful tributes to the accomplishments of Tuskegee, but as a Greek scholar she must have found ironic Booker T. Washington's complaint that the "black boy is studying Greek, while the Greek boy is blacking shoes."[44] Mary McLeod Bethune advocated "domestic science," but she also confronted (successfully) her White board members who wanted to maintain her school's curriculum below university status.

But it was Washington's philosophy of eschewing equal political and social rights that the clubwomen rebelled against most vehemently. Whatever their views on interracial relationships, for example, clubwomen took a stand against the prohibition of interracial marriage. Their position was that such laws made Black women all the more vulnerable to sexual exploitation. Even more an issue of contention was Booker T. Washington's conciliatory attitude when Black rights were violated. Josephine St. Pierre Ruffin must have been disturbed when she and other clubwomen asked for his intervention after she was refused admission to the Milwaukee Convention of the General Federation of Women's Clubs in 1900. Ruffin, who was a member of both a predominantly White women's club and the Black New Era Club, was told that she could participate as a member of the White club, but not as a representative of the Black one. Insisting on being admitted as representative of the New Era Club, she was excluded from the proceedings; and despite numerous appeals, Booker T. Washington refused to use his influence in her behalf or to take any stand on the matter.

Even Washington's closest ally among the NACW's leaders, Mary Church Terrell, finally broke with him, though it took some time for her to do so. Booker T. Washington was responsible for the appointment of her husband, Robert Terrell, to a municipal judgeship in the District of Columbia. When the battle between Washington and W.E.B. Du Bois flared into the open, Mary Church Terrell's loyalties were quite clear. As a member of the Washington, D.C., school board she used her influence to assure the appointment of a "Bookerite" over Du Bois as assistant superintendent of the schools. She was also active in T. Thomas Fortune's Afro-American Council after it had been infiltrated by Washington's men and molded to the Tuskegeean's political viewpoint. Ida Wells-Barnett consequently resigned her post as head of the Council's antilynching bureau, and it was Terrell who took her place.

The Washington-Du Bois rivalry was also probably reflected, at least in part, in the 1899 NACW convention in Chicago where a political struggle ensued over the reelection of Mary Church Terrell as president. The NACW constitution stipulated that a president could serve no more than two terms and Terrell had already been elected twice. She and her allies argued, however, that the first term shouldn't have been counted, since it preceded the writing of the constitution. The battle was a bitter one. Although the convention was held in Chicago, Wells-Barnett's bailiwick, Terrell kept her from having an influential hand in the proceedings. Terrell's forces eventually triumphed, but not without a price. According to Wells-Barnett, the fight "killed" Terrell's influence among the women, and her "selfish ambition" destroyed the opportunity she had once had to lead the organization to even greater heights.

However, Terrell's loyalty to Booker T. Washington perceptibly weakened by 1903—a year in which she spoke at Atlanta University at the behest of W.E.B. Du Bois, and two days later spoke at a luncheon hosted by Washington. But it was the Tuskegeean's stand on the "Brownsville riot" in August of 1906 that strained the relationship with Washington to the breaking point. Brownsville, Texas, was the scene of a bitter race riot involving three companies of the all-Black Twenty-fifth Regiment and the White citizens of the town. Before the shooting stopped, one White was killed, another wounded, and the chief of police injured. The Blacks were accused of shooting up the town, and a full-scale race war was on the verge of boiling over. On the basis of an inspector's report, President Theodore Roosevelt dismissed the entire regiment with a dishonorable discharge and disqualified the soldiers from further military or civil service. Roosevelt's actions, undertaken without the semblance of due process, were attacked even by Whites in Congress. Senator Joseph Foraker of Ohio pushed for a full Senate investigation, which eventually resulted, as one historian observed, in "the most pointed and signal defeat of the Roosevelt administration."[45]

Needless to say, Blacks, especially those who remembered the bravery of Black soldiers commanded by Roosevelt in the Spanish-American War, were beside themselves with outrage.

But Booker T. Washington hedged on the issue. He went so far as to make apologies for Roosevelt's action. It was at this juncture that Mary Church Terrell became so openly critical of Washington that a "Bookerite" recommended to her husband that she be "muzzled."[46] Undeterred, Terrell planned to accept an invitation to the 1909 founding conference of the National Association for the Advancement of Colored People, an organization hostile to Washington and his policies. When Washington got word of Terrell's intentions he wrote her husband that her "embarrassing affiliation" with the NAACP, which was likely to attack the new President, William H. Taft, could make it difficult for him to secure the judge's reappointment to the bench. "Of course I am not seeking to control anyone's actions," Washington told him, "but I simply want to know where we stand."[47]

Mary Church Terrell responded to the threat by becoming a member of the NAACP's executive committee, and organizing a Washington, D.C., branch, of which she was elected vice-president.

Another woman present at the NAACP founding conference was Terrell's adversary, Ida Wells-Barnett. Of course, her politics and those of the Wizard of Tuskegee were as oil is to water. Yet even she had once had good words for him.

In 1890, Wells wrote to Booker T. Washington praising him for an article of his in the Detroit *Plaindealer*. In that uncharacteristic piece, Washington condemned the corruption of the Black clergy, a subject on which the muckraking Wells was an expert. But that would be one of the last good words she would have to say about him. Wells-Barnett became one of the worst banes of Booker T. Washington's conciliatory existence. Wells, especially, fought his tightening control over the Afro-American Council and took every opportunity to proselytize for Du Bois's and her own views concerning education and equality. Washington's penchant for subversion was indicated by his response to Wells-Barnett. A letter to Charles W. Anderson, one of his political henchmen, documented his attempt to remove her husband, Ferdinand Barnett, from his post as assistant state's attorney for Cook County in Illinois. "We must defeat Barnett if possible," Washington wrote in 1904. "He is a regular sneak. During the first two years of the President's campaign he and his wife spent their time and effort in stirring up the colored people and embittering them against the President."[48] In subsequent years, as the Washington machine grew more powerful, Wells-Barnett would also become alienated from the NACW after a failed attempt to change the editorship of *National Notes,* controlled by Margaret Murray Washington, into an elective position. So, despite some of the interlocking cogs of the NACW and the Washington machine, the clubwomen were too diverse and much too independent to be its captive.

Personal Politics

A profile of 108 of the first generation of clubwomen revealed that most had been born in the South between 1860 and 1885 and had moved north before the mass migration of the late nineteenth century.[49] Historian Carter G. Woodson observed that the group of Blacks who left the South in the earlier period were among the most talented. Many of the clubwomen had been reared to respect discipline, thrift, and piety—values that were confirmed by their teachers, in many instances imbued with New England missionary zeal. About 67 percent of the clubwomen were teachers themselves. Other occupations represented were clerk, hairdresser, businesswoman, and there was one bank president. Three quarters of them were married, and almost three quarters of them worked outside the home. Only a fourth of the women had children. The career-oriented clubwomen seemed to have no ambivalence concerning their right to work, whether necessity dictated it or not. Richmond educator Josephine Turpin Washington said that Black women claimed "the right of admission in varied fields of employment."[50] Anna Julia Cooper believed that all married women should earn a livelihood because it "renders woman less dependent on the marriage relation for physical support (which, by the way, does not always accompany it)."[51]

Undoubtedly another reason for the importance to them of self-support was that they believed women should not be forced into traditional roles. In 1894, *The Woman's Era* offered the opinion that "not all women are intended for mothers. Some of us have not the temperament for family life. . . . Clubs will make women think seriously of their future lives, and not make girls think their only alternative is to marry."[52] A woman like Cooper no doubt agreed there were other means of self-actualization. Women, she said, were not "compelled to look to sexual love as the one sensation capable of giving tone and relish, movement and vim to the life she leads. Her horizon is extended."[53]

Nevertheless, their ideas about marital relations could be quite traditional. Although few felt that women should be subservient, Josephine Turpin Washington cautioned that "the true woman takes her place by the side of the man, as his companion, his co-worker, his helpmate, his equal, but she never forgets that she is a woman and not a man."[54] That women should not supersede their men seemed also to be on Olivia Davidson's mind when, in speaking about the need for women to become "stronger intellectually," she demurred, "I would not have you think, especially you, my brother teachers, that we are asking to find out how we can produce more strong-minded women as that term is used in the objectionable sense."[55] Remembering that one was a woman meant being feminine and not forgetting one's priorities. "The progressive woman of today is modest and womanly," observed Josephine Turpin Washington. "She would never neglect home and husband and children to enter professional life or to further any public cause, however worthy."[56]

Perhaps this belief was responsible for the fact that some of the most active and ambitious clubwomen married relatively late in their lives. Mary Church Terrell, for example, was twenty-eight when she tied the wedding knot; Margaret Murray Washington was thirty-one, and Ida Wells-Barnett, thirty-three. All three had had to resolve the conflicts between what they wanted for themselves as women and what middle-class society expected of them as women. Terrell experienced great difficulty on that score. Although education was seen as a laudable ambition for Black women, certain kinds of education were not. "It was held by most people that women were unfitted to do their work in the home if they studied Latin, Greek and higher mathematics," Terrell commented. "Many of my friends tried to dissuade me from studying for an A.B. degree."[57] Terrell's father was also unhappy that she chose to work after graduation. "He felt that he was able to support me," she said. "He disinherited me, refused to write to me for a year because I went to Wilberforce to teach. Further I was ridiculed and told that no man would want to marry a woman who studied higher mathematics. I said I'd take a chance and run the risk."[58] She did marry, of course, and found herself subverting the traditional housewife's role in order to engage in activist pursuits. The choice must have weighed heavily on her mind, especially since she underwent the heart-wrenching experience of losing three babies within days of their birth in a span of five years. Against her doctor's advice, she became pregnant a fourth time. This time she went to New York, where she could receive better medical attention than she could in Washington, and this time a daughter, Phyllis (after the poet Phillis Wheatley), survived. Years later, approaching her fortieth birthday, Terrell adopted the daughter of her half-brother, Thomas. "But absorbing as motherhood was," notes a biographer, "it never became a full-time occupation."[59] In light of Terrell's lecture schedule and organizational work, that seems to be an understatement.

Ida Wells-Barnett also wrestled with the idea of activism versus domestic (specifically maternal) roles. She had her first child just before the founding meeting of the NACW. But 1896 was an election year, and soon after the meeting Wells-Barnett was asked to campaign through Illinois for the Women's State Central Committee, a Republican political organization. She accepted the invitation on the condition that arrangements be made for a nurse for her six-month-old son, Charles. The committee agreed to provide someone to take care of him in all the cities where she was scheduled to lecture. "I honestly believe," Wells-Barnett recalled, "that I am the only woman in the United States who ever traveled throughout the country with a nursing baby to make political speeches."[60]

A year later she was pregnant again. By this time her husband had been appointed assistant state's attorney, and Wells-Barnett decided to sell *The Conservator* (which she had purchased from her husband), resigned from the presidency of the Ida B. Wells Club, and announced that she was retiring from public life to devote time to her family.

The "retirement" lasted about five months. A brutal lynching in South Carolina compelled her to lobby the President and Congress in Washington, D.C. Again she took a nursing infant along. This was followed by her work for the Black soldiers in the Spanish-American War, activities in the Afro-American Council, her continued anti-lynching campaign, and the birth of two more children in 1901 and 1904. After the youngest, Alfreda, was born, Wells-Barnett attempted to "retire" once more. The activist must have felt pulled in several different directions. On the one hand, Black men, resentful of her activism, applied pressure to "keep her in her place." Her election as financial secretary of the council elicited this response from the *Colored American* newspaper:

. . . we are compelled to regard her election . . . as an extremely unfortunate incident. She is a woman of unusual mental powers but the proprieties would have been observed by giving her an assignment more in keeping with the popular idea of women's work and which would not interfere so disastrously with her domestic duties.

The newspaper suggested that Wells-Barnett be made head of a women's auxiliary instead. "The financial secretary of the Afro-American Council," it concluded, "should be a man."[61]

On the other hand, Wells-Barnett knew that her crusade was important, and that few could do as effective a job as she could. The dilemma was noted by the suffragist Susan B. Anthony, whom she had gotten to know over the years. Anthony, who never married, told her:

. . . women like you who have a special call for work [should never marry]. I know of no one in all this country better fitted to do the work you had in hand. Since you've gotten married, agitation seems practically to have ceased. Besides, you're trying to help in the formation of this league and your baby needs your attention at home. You're distracted over the thought that he's not being looked after as he would be if you were there, and that makes for a divided duty.[62]

But Wells-Barnett had married. And although, due to her early experiences with her siblings, she did not have "the longing for children that so many other women have," she was glad that she had them.[63] Not having children, she felt, robbed women "of one of the most glorious advantages in the development of their own womanhood."[64] The dual role of mother and activist may not have been an easy one, but she appeared to strike a balance between the two for the remainder of her life.

For all of the political and social conservatism of Margaret Murray Washington, she, too, had her doubts about the joys of motherhood. Born of an Irish father and a Black mother in Macon, Georgia, she first met Booker T. Washington at Fisk University's commencement ceremonies. She had been a part-time student there for eight years, and boldly approached Washington to ask him to hire her as a teacher at Tuskegee. Margaret Murray was attractive, often described as buxom, and obviously bright. The combination was undoubtedly compelling for the two-time widower and Murray was appointed an

English teacher at the institute. Her abilities were immediately apparent and she soon was promoted to "Lady Principal" or Dean of Women at Tuskegee.

It wasn't long before Margaret Murray and Booker T. Washington began courting, and he proposed to her in 1891. However, she had real doubts about the marriage, and especially about children: Her letters to Washington revealed that she didn't like them. "You do not have much sympathy with me because I feel as I do in regard to little folks," she wrote. "I get annoyed at myself but the feeling is there just the same."[65] Not only did she profess little maternal instinct, but she had a particular dislike for Washington's eight-year-old daughter, Portia. "You have no idea of how I feel because I can not feel toward Portia as I should. And I somehow dread being thrown with her for a lifetime."[66] Telling him that she would understand if he gave her up because of these feelings, she wondered "if it is a wise and Christian thing for me to love you feeling as I do?"[67] Margaret Murray did marry Washington, of course, and in the course of their twenty-three-year-long marriage, she seemed to work out her difficulties with Portia.

Of course, Terrell, Wells-Barnett, Washington, and others who married men prominent in their own right, had the latitude to make decisions without reference to dire economic need, or concern that they might threaten their husbands' self-worth. It was easier to be a co-equal or partner with a man who had himself acquired a certain importance. Clubwomen, at least partially for this reason, counseled both men and women on the virtues of accomplishment. These Black women saw the status of their men as part and parcel of many of the goals they were trying to achieve.

"Colored women will never be properly known and the best of them appreciated, until colored men have become more important in those affairs of life where character and achievements count for more than prejudices and suspicions," wrote Fannie Barrier Williams, who was married to a Chicago attorney. "Every colored man who succeeds in business brings his wife and daughter a little nearer to that sphere of chivalry and protection in which every white woman finds shelter and vindication against hateful presumption. . . . A beautiful home built by a man is a tribute, not only to his own wife and family, but is also a tribute to womanhood everywhere."[68] In a similar vein, Addie Hunton, in writing an obituary of Sarah Garnet, thought it important to mention that her father was the first Black man to build a home for his family in New York.

Marrying men of achievement was also an integral part of their determination to fulfill themselves as women. "The question," said Anna Julia Cooper, who married a minister but was widowed two years later, "is not now with the woman 'How shall I so cramp, stunt, and simplify and nullify myself as to make me eligible to the honor of being swallowed up into some little man?' but the problem . . . rests with the man as to how he can so develop . . . to reach the ideal of a generation of women who demand the noblest, grandest and best achievements of which he is capable."[69]

That demand went beyond men's material achievements to male perceptions about Black women themselves. Many men, they felt, left something to be desired when it came to seeing their women in the proper light and to protecting their virtue—literally as well as figuratively.

"It is absurd," said Anna Julia Cooper, "to quote statistics showing the Negro's bank account and rent rolls, to point to the hundreds of newspapers edited by colored men, and lists of lawyers, doctors, professors, D.D.'s, L.L.D's, etc. etc. etc. while the source from which the life-blood of the race is to flow is subject to the taint and corruption of the enemy's camp." For "a stream," she exhorted, "cannot rise higher than its source."[70] At the turn of the century, Black women still had "no fixt public opinion to which they could appeal," as Fannie Barrier Williams pointed out, "no protection against the libelous attacks on their characters, and no chivalry generous enough to guarantee their safety against man's inhumanity to women."[71] Since she included Black men in this group, Williams challenged: "Is the Colored man brave enough to stand out and say to all the world, 'This far and no farther in your attempt to insult or degrade our women'?"[72] The question was important. Nannie Helen Burroughs asserted: "Whenever the men of any race defiantly stand up for the protection of their women, . . . the women will . . . be saved from the hands of the most vile."[73] That men had not so stood up made the sharp-tongued Burroughs protest: "White men offer more protection to their prostitutes than many Black men offer to their best women."[74]

Apart from their concern about protection from the "vileness" of White men, Black women criticized the attitudes of Black men toward them. In the opinion of the activists, the times demanded that men not treat women as mere quarry. "We need men," Cooper said, "who can let their interest and gallantry extend outside the circle of their aesthetic appreciation; men who can be father, brother, a friend to every weak, struggling, unshielded girl."[75] What Black women craved, above all things, continued Williams, was to "be respected and believed in. This is more important than position and opportunities."[76]

In this period Black women saw their sisters as extremely vulnerable, and men often taking advantage of them. Many young women were on the move, traveling to unfamiliar surroundings to find jobs. Lonely, often naïve, they could be easy prey. "Thousands of women are . . . in the clutches of men of our race," complained Burroughs, perhaps the most sardonic of the commentators, "who are not worth the cost of their existence. They can dress well, and live on the earnings of servant girls."[77]

An anonymous writer for *The Independent* had a more direct complaint: "We poor colored women wage-earners in the South are fighting a terrible battle," she said. "On the one hand we are assailed by White men, and on the other hand we are assailed by Black men, who should be our natural protectors."[78]

The problem, as Fannie Barrier Williams saw it, was a fundamental lack of respect for Black women as a group. "I believe that as a general thing we hold our girls too cheaply," she said. "Too many colored men entertain very careless, if not contemptible opinions of the colored girls."[79] It was not that Black women were so perfect, said Williams. "It is true we have our trifling girls, and in this respect we are thoroughly human."[80] Her complaint was that Black men too often had the same stereotypical notions about Black women that others did: "We have all too many colored men who hold the degrading opinions of ignorant white men, that all colored girls are alike."[81]

The problem wasn't confined to the lower classes. In her autobiography, Ida Wells-Barnett recounted an incident of a minister in Memphis defaming her character because of his prejudice against southern Black women. Wells confronted him with the charges. "I . . . wanted him to know that virtue was not at all a matter of the section in which one lived," she said, "that many a slave woman had fought and died rather than yield to the pressure and temptations to which she was subjected. . . . I wanted him to know . . . at least one southern girl, born and bred, who had tried to keep herself morally clean as my slave mother had taught me."[82]

Williams concluded, "There is something fundamentally wrong

within our social instincts and sentiments, if we fail to recognize the ever enlarging difference between the pure and the impure, the upright and degraded of colored women."[83] Despite the evidence of Black women's efforts during this time, despite the evidences of character and determination, Williams was saying, Black men were "apt to look to other races for their types of beauty and character."[84] "What our girls and women have a right to demand from our best men is that they cease to imitate the artificial standards of other people and create a race standard for their own."[85]

Imitating those standards included color consciousness, Nannie Helen Burroughs charged, in a devastating article entitled "Not Color But Character": "There are men right in our own race, and they are legion, who would rather marry a woman for her color than her character," she said.[86] "The white man who crosses the line and leaves an heir is doing a favor for some black man who would marry the most debased woman, whose only stock in trade is her color, in preference to the most royal queen in ebony."[87]

Black men themselves commented on the phenomenon of their attraction to fair-skinned women. "It is generally the case," said the editor T. Thomas Fortune during a debate about Black identity, "that those Black men who clamor most loudly and persistently for the purity of Negro blood have taken themselves mulatto wives."[88]

However, Burroughs did not confine her criticism to men on this score. She also struck out at women who used skin lighteners and hair straighteners. "What every woman who bleaches and straightens out needs, is not her appearance changed, but her mind changed. . . . If Negro women would use half the time they spend on trying to get white, to get better, the race would move forward apace."[89]

Another problem was the attitude of men who had difficulty accepting the intelligence of women, especially if they were also attractive. The editor of the Black newspaper *Indianapolis Freeman* once chided Ida B. Wells: "Iola makes the mistake of being pretty as well as smart. She should remember that beauty and genius are not always companions. George Eliot, George Sand, Harriet Beecher Stowe and other bright minds were not paragons by any means."[90]

The patronizing attitude was shared by men who had better intentions than the *Freeman* editor. The Black leader Alexander Crummell, for one, wrote a book whose purpose was to praise Black women, because, he said, so few had raised a voice in their behalf. He wrote of Black women's "tenderness," "modesty," "sweetness," "humility," and "warm maternity." But for all the achievements of Black women in this period, the most complimentary conclusion he could draw was: "If there is any other woman on this earth who in native aboriginal qualities is her superior, I know not where she is to be found."[91]

Such an attitude made Anna Julia Cooper remark, "While our men seem thoroughly abreast of the times on every other subject, when they strike the woman question, they drop back into sixteenth-century logic." Cooper was particularly critical when that "logic" extended to discouraging women from attending college. "I fear the majority of colored men do not yet think it worthwhile that women aspire to a higher education,"[92] she charged.

This attitude extended into other intellectual pursuits. As an instance, Black women were excluded from the American Negro Academy, which was organized in 1897 and whose purposes were to bring together leading intellectuals like Reverend Francis Grimké, Reverend Alexander Crummell, and W.E.B. Du Bois—graduates of Princeton, Cambridge, and Harvard respectively—and to promote scholarly work, establish an archive, and encourage promising Black youth. The academy's bylaws stipulated that only men of African descent were to participate. During some of the first organizational discussions, however, George Grisham suggested that women be admitted and that the encouragement of youth also include young women since ". . . in the year of our opening there has been a *higher attainment of scholarship . . . by our women than our men.*" (Emphasis added.) The bylaws were never changed, however, and the academy listed no women on its roster.[93]

Black women were also peeved at the male reluctance to take their political role seriously. It was especially irksome when men seemed so politically ineffectual. In speaking of the NACW, Fannie Barrier Williams cautioned the organization against following the examples of "our colored men, whose innumerable conventions, councils and conferences during the last twenty-five years have all begun with talk and ended in talk."[94] Like Williams, Cooper criticized their men's tendency to "exaggerate the importance of mere political advantage,"[95] so that women weren't accepted as full partners in the racial struggle. Even more disturbing, men often criticized women who took the initiative, as Ida Wells-Barnett discovered. The now familiar accusation of Black women "emasculating" Black men almost discouraged her from going to the scene of a lynching in 1909. "I had been accused," she wrote, "by some of our men of jumping ahead of them and doing work without giving them a chance."[96]

Even T. Thomas Fortune criticized the attitudes of his brethren: "The race could not succeed," he said, "nor build strong citizens, until we have a race of women competent to do more than hear a brood of negative men."[97]

However, many of these conflicts were submerged by the larger racial struggle in which Black men and women worked together effectively. This was evident when the issue of woman suffrage took center stage again after fourteen years of relative inactivity between 1896 and 1910. In that period no new states passed suffrage amendments, but in 1913, Illinois gave the presidential ballot to women; and by the beginning of 1914, five new states and the territory of Alaska had enfranchised them. In these years the debate within the Black and White communities, and the struggle between the communities regarding the women's vote, reached a new level of intensity.

VII

⌁ The Quest for Woman Suffrage (Before World War I) ⌁

Although the Black woman's contribution to the suffrage campaign is rarely written about, Blacks, including Black women, had a more consistent attitude toward the vote than Whites. As Rosalyn Terborg-Penn explains in her study of Blacks and the woman-suffrage struggle, Afro-Americans maintained a political philosophy of universal suffrage, while Whites, including women, advocated a limited, educated suffrage after the Civil War. Additionally, Blacks, including men, had fewer conflicts about woman's voting and thereby challenging her traditional role.

White antisuffragists harped on the theme of true womanhood in its many variations. Entering the political arena could sully their virtuous aprons. "I do not wish to say the day will come when the women of my race in my state shall trail skirts in the muck and mire of partisan politics," went a familiar sentiment expressed by Representative Clark of Florida in 1915. "I prefer to look to the American woman as she always has been, occupying her proud state as queen of the American home, instead of regarding her as a ward politician in the cities."[1] She could exercise much more influence by the hearthstone, anyway, he concluded.

A woman wanting the ballot, another argument went, was an insult to her husband, who traditionally voted in the best interests as head of the family. By voting, women would be sowing the seeds of domestic chaos and divorce. And although a female role in reform was widely accepted, a number of the antisuffragists argued that a woman didn't have to *vote* to achieve better conditions. *"Housewives!"* read a pamphlet distributed in the period. "Why vote for pure food laws, when you can purify your ice box with saleratus [baking soda] water?" Similar arguments were heard from many White women themselves, including those who advocated other means of reform.

By contrast one would be hard pressed to find any Black woman who did not advocate getting the vote. Additionally, Black men as a group, especially those in leadership positions, supported and worked for the enfranchisement of women. There were exceptions of course. Some church leaders like the Reverend R. E. Wall, writing in the *A.M.E. Church Review,* took the position that although "divine law makes no distinction between the sexes," when it came to politics, "it may not be expedient to make them [women] equal."[2] A good number of the Baptist clergy were even more conservative. A series of articles in a Virginia Baptist paper, published near the turn of the century, claimed, according to *The Woman's Era,* "to prove through Bible authority that the only place for women in the church is that of a singer and a prayer and that in teaching or preaching she is acting contrary to divine authority and that the exercise of the right of suffrage would be a deplorable climax to these transgressions." The *Era* responded: "The writer is . . . sadly in need of enlightenment. . . . it is almost useless to hope that he can be reached by any kind of argument."[3]

One of the few nonclerical intellectuals who opposed woman suffrage was the often-controversial Kelly Miller, an educator who became dean at Howard University and was a founding member of the NAACP. Miller advanced the opinion that "there may be some argument for suffrage for unfortunate females, such as widows and hopeless spinsters, but such status is not contemplated as a normal social relation."[4] Perhaps it was Miller whom Mary Church Terrell had in mind when she said, "For an intelligent colored man to oppose suffrage is the most preposterous and ridiculous thing in the world."[5]

There were also indications that some of the male rank and file looked down on women who were involved in political activity. This was made evident to the members of the Alpha Suffrage Club, organized by Ida Wells-Barnett, in Chicago. The club, founded in 1913, was the first Black women's suffrage organization in Illinois. When its members began canvassing the Black community to register and vote, many were met with derision. A number of women were told they should be at home, taking care of babies; others that they were trying to take the place of men and "wear their trousers." Wells-Barnett reported that many of the women, especially those who were relatively inexperienced in such matters, were discouraged by the men's reaction. But these attitudes were the exception rather than the rule; the overwhelming majority of Black men supported woman suffrage and female participation in the political arena, and the majority of women stuck by their convictions concerning the vote.

Major church leaders such as the bishops Henry McNeal Turner and John Mussilin Brown supported women's enfranchisement. W.E.B. Du Bois, who took Frederick Douglass's place as the leading male feminist of his time, recognized the potential advantage of women's attaining the vote with his pithy observation: "Votes for women, means votes for Black women."[6] His view reflected the consensus: Political empowerment of the race required the participation of Black women.

If "White women needed the vote to acquire advantages and protection of their rights," noted Adella Hunt Logan, the leading suffragist of the Tuskegee Woman's Club, "then Black women needed the vote even more so." As was true of White suffragists, Black women saw the franchise as a cure for many of their ills. But for Black women, sexual exploitation headed the list. As Nannie Helen Burroughs noted, when a woman went to the courts "in defense of her virtue, she is looked upon with contempt. She needs the ballot, to reckon with men who place no value upon her virtue, and to mould healthy sentiment in favor of her own protection."[7] Anna H. Jones of New York saw the vote as a means of controlling prostitution, and to "prevent vice and its train of physical and moral evils."[8] On another front, many women suggested that political rights would enable them to vote down the prohibitions against interracial marriage, which they felt were aimed at Black women's degradation and exploitation.

It was also widely perceived that woman suffrage would be a boon to education, as Howard University graduate and onetime dean Lucy Diggs Slowe pointed out. Blacks could improve conditions by having a voter's influence with legislators and school boards. A number of women also stressed that the vote would enable them to work more effectively toward the goal of compulsory education in the South.

Black women were also interested in the vote because the vast majority of them had to work. A spokeswoman for an organization called The House of Ruth said that since the women of the race were largely wage earners, their labor needed the protection of the ballot.

Most immediate of concerns was the loss of the vote by Black men in the South and the charge that they had, in many instances, "sold" those votes to White supremacist politicians. This issue was prevalent enough for both Black and White suffragists to comment upon it. However, when Whites criticized Black men in the South, Black women came to their defense. After all, the pressures on impoverished freedmen to trade their votes for much-needed material things, or even for their lives, were tremendous. Additionally, under such conditions it was not always easy to recognize the value of the vote, especially in a region known for its corruption. As Mary Church Terrell explained before a convention of the National American Women's Suffrage Association in 1904: "Much has been said about the Negro vote. . . . They never sold their vote till they found that it made no difference how they cast them."[9]

Nevertheless, Black women were generally critical of the men who traded away their hard-won rights. As early as 1870, Frances Ellen Harper had prophetically remarked, "Some of this old rebel element . . . are in favor of taking away the colored man's vote and if he loses it now it may be generations before he gets it again. . . . Perhaps the loss of his vote would not be a serious grievance to many, but his children differently educated and trained by circumstances might feel political inferiority rather a bitter cup."[10]

Several decades later, no group found that cup more bitter than did disenfranchised, racially conscious Black women. "If women cannot vote," said Nannie Helen Burroughs at a 1912 National Baptist Convention, "they should make it very uncomfortable for the men who have the ballot but do not know its value."[11] In fact, women had been doing that for quite some time. In 1892, Anna Julia Cooper commented that uneducated Black women in the South "have actually left their husbands and homes and repudiated [their husbands'] support [for] . . . race disloyalty in 'voting away' the privileges of herself and little ones."[12] A year later Frances Ellen Harper made this phenomenon the subject of a poem in her volume *Sketches of a Southern Life,* published in 1893. A stanza from "Deliverance" read:

> Day after day did Milly Green
> Just follow after Joe,
> And told him if he voted wrong
> to take his rags and go.[13]

Underlying these attitudes was the conviction that unlike the masses of Black men, women would never betray the race if they had the power of the vote. Their exalted sense of themselves as a group extended to their feelings about the suffrage issue. "When Black women get the vote," Burroughs wrote in *The Crisis*, "it will find her a tower of strength of which poets have never sung, orators have never spoken and scholars have never written."[14] Anna Julia Cooper was blunter. The Afro-American woman, she said, "is always sound and orthodox on questions affecting the well-being of the race. You do not find the colored woman selling her birthright for a mess of pottage."[15]

The situation in the South provided an additional and compelling rationale for Black women to gain the vote. "The Negro woman needs to get back by the wise use of it, what the Negro man has lost by the *misuse* of it," said Burroughs about the franchise.[16] Black women weren't the only ones to hold this attitude. W.E.B. Du Bois applauded the greater tenacity of Black women as a group: "You can bribe some pauperized Negro laborers with a few dollars at election time," he said, "but you cannot bribe a Negro woman."[17] Evidently this thought also occurred to White supremacists in the South, especially in the states with large Black populations. South Carolina was such a state. It was estimated by 1914 that there were 100,000 more Blacks than Whites in South Carolina, and that Black women were the largest group of voters. With this in mind, South Carolina's Senator Ben "Pitchfork" Tillman responded to an article in the *Maryland Suffrage News* which advocated that all women in the South be enfranchised. Citing the figures of the Black population in his state, Tillman wrote the editor: "A moment's thought will show you that if women were given the ballot, the negro woman would vote as well as the white woman." The consequences would be particularly disturbing because, Tillman wrote, "Experience has taught us that negro women are much more aggressive in asserting the 'rights of the race' than the negro men are. In other words, they have always urged the negro men on in the conflicts we have had in the past between the two races for supremacy."[18] Mississippi Senator J. K. Vardaman agreed. "The negro woman," he said, "will be more offensive, more difficult to handle at the polls than the negro man."

As the Black leaders discovered, it wasn't just racist politicians who put up obstacles to their enfranchisement. White women, including suffragists who should have been their natural allies, often became their most formidable adversaries. For White suffrage leaders either acquiesced to, or took advantage of, the anti-Black sentiment in the period.

In 1890 the two suffrage factions, which had split over the Fifteenth Amendment and over loyalty to the Republican Party in 1869, reunited under the National American Women's Suffrage Association. Under the guiding hand of Susan B. Anthony and Elizabeth Cady Stanton, NAWSA adopted a strategy of "expediency."

The aim of this strategy was to prove that the enfranchisement of White women would further, rather than impede, the power of a White ruling class that was fearful of Black and immigrant domination. In a society laden with class strife, imperialist venture, colonization of the "inferior races," and Afro-American claims to full citizenship, the equality of all men was no longer taken for granted, as suffrage historian Aileen Kraditor noted. And White suffragists accordingly dispensed with the theory of natural rights. Educated suffrage and the preservation of Anglo-Saxon power overwhelmingly influenced the NAWSA call for enfranchisement. "The government is menaced with great danger," observed Carrie Chapman Catt in 1894. "That danger lies in the votes possessed by the males in the slums of the cities, and the ignorant foreign vote." The solution, according to Catt, who would head NAWSA six years later, was to "cut off the vote of the slums and give it to women."[19] In their strategy to delimit the franchise rather than extend it, educated suffrage was a useful tool. An 1893 NAWSA convention declared:

> Resolved, that without expressing any opinion on the proper qualifications for voting, we call attention to the significant facts that in every State there are more women who can read and write than all negro voters; more American women who can read and write than all foreign voters; so that the enfranchisement of such women would settle the vexed question of rule by illiteracy whether of home-grown or foreign-born production.[20]

It would not be long before the women did express their opinion on proper qualifications, suggesting that educational requirements would ensure permanent supremacy for the native-born White portion of the population.

Black women who had access to White forums challenged this concept. In the year of the NAWSA resolution, Frances Ellen Harper, speaking before the World's Congress of Representative Women, struck the familiar Black theme that it was character, and not color, class, or education, that should be the criterion for the vote. "I don't believe in unrestricted and universal suffrage for either men or women," she told her audience. "I do not believe that the most ignorant and brutal man is better prepared to add value to the strength and durability of the government than the most cultured, upright and intelligent woman."

However she didn't believe either that "educated wickedness, violence and fraud should cancel the votes of honest men." The hands of lynchers, she warned, "are too red with blood to determine the political character of government."[21] Harper concluded that just as the ballot in the hands of native White men was no guarantee of justice, neither was granting the ballot to their sisters "a panacea for all ills of our national life."[22]

The old warhorses of the suffrage movement Elizabeth Cady Stanton and Susan B. Anthony did believe in the female franchise as a panacea to the nation's ills. Because of that conviction, Anthony viewed the strategy of expediency—despite its racist and classist implications—as ends justifying the means. However, Anthony personally maintained and often expressed a liberal point of view. She was not, for example, a proponent of educated suffrage. She often invited Blacks to her home and saw to it that they were treated respectfully Ida Wells-Barnett once visited her and had occasion to require the services of Anthony's secretary. The secretary refused. When Anthony asked her to explain, the secretary made it clear that she would not work for Blacks. She was promptly admonished—and fired.

Wells-Barnett and Anthony would have long discussions about the race and women's issues. Once Wells-Barnett commented that when she cited instances of injustice to Blacks, Anthony would always respond, "Well, now, when the women get the ballot, all that will be changed." Wells-Barnett would reply, "Do you really believe that the millennium is going to come when women get the ballot?" Inevitably the answer was yes. Wells-Barnett, Harper, and other Black women disagreed of course, but Anthony's conviction remained unchanged.

By the turn of the century, Anthony and other suffrage veterans were making way for a new generation of activists in NAWSA. Included were southern White women, and others who had not been weaned in the abolitionist or natural-rights tradition. Most possessed no liberal convictions or philosophical ideas about the vote. Carrie Chapman Catt, for example, once remarked that she didn't "know" what the vote was—"a right, a duty, or a privilege." But whatever it was, "the women want it." Expediency in the minds of this generation was not a means to a justice-for-all end. Like White men, they wanted the vote, and they wanted power—exclusively for themselves. In 1906 a Kentucky Democrat, writing to an Ohio Republican (both national leaders in NAWSA), illustrated the real intent. At a time when northern states were passing literacy requirements, and southern states were disenfranchising Blacks through their constitutions, the Kentucky suffragist wrote: "The National [Association] has always recognized the usefulness of woman suffrage as a counterbalance to the foreign vote, and as a means of legally preserving White supremacy in the South. In the campaign in South Carolina we . . . never hesitated to show that the White women's vote would give supremacy to the White race. And we have also freely used the same argument to the foreign-born vote."[23] Thus White suffragists, northern and southern, found common cause for alliance.

The theory of expediency as it applied to Blacks began to show itself clearly by 1894. That year, Susan B. Anthony asked Frederick Douglass not to attend the forthcoming NAWSA convention in Atlanta, Georgia. The meeting was going to be the first NAWSA convention in the South, and Anthony claimed that Douglass's attendance would be an embarrassment for him as well as for the southern suffragists. Douglass, the only man to speak on behalf of suffrage at the Seneca Falls convention in 1848, the man who had persuaded a reluctant Stanton to call for the vote there, had become "inexpedient." At the convention in 1895, Elizabeth Cady Stanton's speech warned against the dangers of enfranchising illiterate women—much to the delight of the southern audience. But hers was an ironic theme, especially in light of previous claims that Black women had a greater need for the vote than anyone else. Although Stanton's views prevailed, Harriet Stanton Blatch, her daughter, and Susan B. Anthony went on record as opposing them.

However, Anthony continued to support other forms of expediency. When a group of Black women asked her to help in organizing a branch of NAWSA, she refused—on the grounds, she said, that it would be inexpedient. Wells-Barnett was incensed by the refusal. Responding to Anthony, Wells-Barnett told her that she may have made gains for woman suffrage, but she also confirmed White women in their attitude of segregation. The truth of Wells-Barnett's observation was illustrated time and again in subsequent years. Anthony dissuaded Helen Pitts, Frederick Douglass's second wife—who was White, and a suffragist in her own right—from addressing the plight of Black women in southern prison camps. At the same meeting, southern delegates began to hammer out a strategy to make woman suffrage "a means to the end of securing white supremacy in the state."[24]

In 1899, at a convention in Grand Rapids, Michigan, a Black delegate, Lottie Wilson Jackson, became involved in a losing and bitter effort to make NAWSA women take a stand against segregated seating on the trains. Jackson offered a resolution: "That colored women ought not to be compelled to ride in smoking cars, and that suitable accommodations should be provided for them." This caused quite a furor, particularly among southern delegates, who claimed such a resolution was an insult to the South and would reawaken regional antagonisms. Other southern delegates noted that the servant girls who traveled with *them* had no problems. Alice Stone Blackwell of Massachusetts replied that such a resolution cast aspersions not as much on the South as on the railroad companies that enforced segregation. But the argument only provided additional grounds for Anthony's refusal to support the resolution. "We women are a helpless disenfranchised class," she said. "Our hands are tied. While we are in this condition it is not for us to go passing resolutions against railroad corporations or anybody else."[25] Her words drew the discussion to a close, and the resolution was defeated. It was at that convention that Anthony helped put NAWSA on record as saying that woman suffrage and the Black question were completely separate causes.

In 1903, again in deference to southern delegates, a NAWSA convention recognized the principle of states' rights by allowing individual state affiliates to determine their own qualifications for membership. As Aileen Kraditor observed, the states' rights concept was very useful for the strategy of expediency, which included attracting to NAWSA's ranks southern White women who could practice racist principles without censure from other suffragists.

A consequence of this strategy was played out when a huge suffrage march was organized in 1913 by NAWSA and by another group that would assume significance in later years: the Congressional Union, headed by Alice Paul. The march was to take place in Washington, D.C., the day before President Woodrow Wilson's inauguration. Mary Church Terrell would lead the Delta Sigma Theta Sorority women of Howard University. And, of course, Ida Wells-Barnett would lead the Alpha Suffrage Club. But in the meeting called to plan the demonstration, she was told that she could not march with the all-White Chicago contingent of suffragists for fear of offending southern women. For the sake of "expediency," the march for suffrage would be segregated—Wells-Barnett and the Alpha Club would have to bring up the rear. But when the parade got under way, she was nowhere to be found. All were surprised when she suddenly appeared from behind the crowd of onlookers as the Chicago delegation made its way past her. She simply slipped into line, between two White women, and marched as she pleased. Nor, at that point, could anyone do anything about it. The incident moved W.E.B. Du Bois to praise Black women who demonstrated the courage of their convictions despite the "apparent reluctance of the local suffrage committee to encourage Black women to participate."[26] The behavior of the White suffragists also, undoubtedly, confirmed a conviction Du Bois had expressed six years earlier: "The Negro race," he said, "has suffered more from the antipathy and narrowness of women both North and South than from any other single source."[27]

Although NAWSA had gone to some lengths to appease its southern delegates, the organization hesitated to support legislative measures that would have put women's enfranchisement under the jurisdiction of the states. To do so would mean exhaustive and extensive state campaigns to assure the vote. But a southern contingent, led by Kate Gordon of Louisiana and Laura Clay of Kentucky, favored the state approach. It was the only way, they reasoned, that southern states would ever support woman suffrage. In 1913, Gordon, vice-president of NAWSA, organized the Southern States Woman Suffrage Conference (SSWSC). Its intent was to pressure southern state legislatures into putting woman-suffrage amendments in their constitutions. If they did not, she warned, women would be forced to work for a federal amendment which would also enfranchise Black women and thus undermine both the Democratic party and White supremacy.

For a while the SSWSC and NAWSA allied on most issues—like the proposed U.S. Election Bill of 1916, which stated that "women citizens who passed qualifications requisite for men to be electors of the more numerous branch of the state legislature were eligible to vote for senators and congressmen." Although the Bill did not please either group entirely, it was still acceptable to NAWSA and SSWSC. For while enfranchising White women, it could yet apply enough control so that Black women would not acquire the vote in numbers sufficient to upset the rule of White supremacy. Still, the alliance between the two groups would unravel in the very same year.

The NAWSA Convention of 1916 was a contentious and climactic one. The group finally endorsed the Elections Bill, but it did so only after heated debate; and the continued discontent within the organization forced NAWSA to make clear its position on a state or federal approach to enfranchisement. After much argument, NAWSA finally endorsed the passage of the Susan B. Anthony Amendment which was first introduced in Congress in 1878. Federal in scope, it stated that "The right of citizens of the United States to vote shall not be denied or abridged by the United States or by any state on account of sex. Congress shall have the power to enforce this article by appropriate legislation."

As a result of NAWSA's endorsement of the Anthony Amendment, Laura Clay and Kate Gordon split from the organization. The parting came not as the result of a disagreement about White supremacy but, as Kraditor notes, over the "relationship" of White supremacy to woman suffrage.

The machinations of NAWSA did not keep Black women from devising their own campaign. As individuals and within organizations they threw their considerable energies into the suffrage movement. In fact the racist attitudes provided additional impetus for their own struggle. "We should never forget," counseled Fannie Barrier Williams, "that the exclusion of colored women and girls from nearly all places of respectable employment is due mostly to the meanness of American women, and every way that we can check this unkindness by the force of the franchise should be religiously done."[28]

With such convictions, Black women in the NACW and other groups went into action. The Black club organization had a special suffrage department, headed by Sarah Garnet, which represented a force of forty thousand Black women. Throughout the country, Black women organized voter-education clubs, gathered and presented petitions, voted in those states where they had the franchise, and were effective in political campaigns.

By the 1900's, Black suffrage clubs were to be found all over the country, including Tuskegee, St. Louis, Los Angeles, Memphis, Boston, Charleston, and New Orleans, and there were state suffrage societies in Delaware, Idaho, Montana, North Dakota, Texas, New York, and Maryland, among others.

Victoria Earle Matthews's Loyal Union in New York took the campaign to Philadelphia and collected more than ten thousand signatures favoring passage of the Blair Amendment, which proposed women's enfranchisement. On behalf of the NACW, Lugenia Burns Hope of Atlanta called for support of woman suffrage before the influential American Missionary Association, presenting them with a resolution bearing the names of Charlotte Hawkins Brown, Lucy C. Laney, Margaret Murray Washington, and Mary McLeod Bethune. A number of women from the club movement worked in the recently created suffrage department of the NAACP.

Harriet Tubman and Frances Ellen Harper continued to address suffrage meetings. So did Mary Church Terrell, who helped organize the Washington Women's Republican League. Among Terrell's speaking engagements was the 1898 NAWSA convention, where she asked the organization to fight specifically for the enfranchisement of Black women.

The Black women suffragists didn't just raise smoke with their campaign—there was some fire too. In New York a Black woman, Anna K. Lewis, was elected vice-chairman of the predominantly White New York Women's Suffrage Party. In that state, where women became enfranchised before the passage of the federal amendment, some seventy-five thousand Black women were registered. They helped to elect Gertrude Curtis and Laura Fisher delegates to the Republican Convention of New York State—the first state to elect women east of the Mississippi. Two unnamed Black women were also selected as delegates.[29]

In Denver, Colorado, a larger percentage of Black women voted in the 1906 election than their White counterparts—largely through the efforts of the Colored Women's Republican Club, established in 1901. Through similar efforts Black women were able to elect at least one juvenile court judge who, they felt, would treat youth more fairly; and in Washington a Black woman became a juror. But perhaps the most tangible success was scored by Chicago's Alpha Suffrage Club. The first Black candidate to seek the club's aid was Oscar DePriest, who in 1914 campaigned for an alderman's seat. With the Alpha Club behind him, DePriest won the primary, and in 1915 he beat two White opponents to become the first Black alderman in Chicago. After his victory, DePriest expressed his gratitude to the women of the club, who contributed some thousand votes toward his election! His successful candidacy showed that despite the problems the Alpha women had had, when a clear-cut issue of electing a Black candidate was put before the community, Black men and women had come together and supported DePriest (who would subsequently be elected to Congress) overwhelmingly. So it was the raising of specific issues within the context of national concerns that encouraged a broad-based activism among Blacks—an activism whose roots were planted by women.

Until 1916, Blacks were involved primarily in their own suffrage campaigns, making few attempts at open confrontation of Whites—particularly those within NAWSA. But after that date, when the Anthony Amendment became the focus of the suffrage struggle, Afro-Americans would do more than just slip into segregated marches or express their views in White suffragist forums. If 3 million Black women were to be enfranchised, three quarters of them in the South, then Black women would have to fight fire with fire—and that is what they did. The Black woman suffrage campaign after the First World War would be one of several flash points at which Black women would squarely confront White women. By that time Black women were confident in their abilities as a group, and they were both prepared and compelled to demand the rights of full citizenship, economically, socially, and politically.

Part II

A WORLD WAR AND AFTER: THE "NEW NEGRO" WOMAN

Now, women forget all those things they don't want to remember, and remember everything they don't want to forget. The dream is the truth. Then they act and do things accordingly.
—ZORA NEALE HURSTON

VIII

~ Cusp of a New Era ~

By 1916 the women of the NACW could point to a long list of achievements. They had defended the race when no one else had. They had defended themselves when their men had not. The NACW had grown to fifty thousand members and it continued to sustain itself, without White largesse, as the first national Black organization (predating the NAACP and the Urban League) to deal with the needs of the race. The accomplishments of its members were formidable.

School founders like Charlotte Hawkins Brown, Lucy C. Laney, and Mary McLeod Bethune left inspiring legacies for generations to come. Scholarship loans for women to attend college had been provided. Aid toward employment included Victoria Earle Matthews's White Rose Mission, which helped thousands of southern Black women who migrated north to find jobs. Mission workers were at the docks in Norfolk and New York to protect the young girls from unscrupulous labor agents. Once they arrived at the White Rose settlement house in New York they were offered the aid of a job-placement and training center and courses in Afro-American history. In 1905 the White Rose center became a part of the New York League for the Protection of Colored Women, an organization eventually absorbed by the Urban League.

In the field of health, clubwoman Lugenia Burns Hope organized the Atlanta Neighborhood Union in 1908. Hope, whose parents had been free Blacks in Mississippi, had grown up in Chicago and, forced to leave school when her father died, had worked there for eight years as a dressmaker and bookkeeper. In 1897, after marrying John Hope —who would become president of Atlanta University—she determined to improve the appalling and neglected conditions of Atlanta's Black community. Organizing Black women, including wives of the university's faculty, she launched a reform campaign. Her Neighborhood Union raised funds for a playground and provided for kindergartens and day nurseries. After conducting a fact-finding investigation, the Union also lobbied successfully to construct a new school building and to raise the salaries of Black teachers. Through the Union's efforts, streets were paved, lights and sewers installed, forty houses repaired, and general improvements made on some twenty streets in the Black areas of the city, according to feminist historian Gerda Lerner. Perhaps the most notable of the union's efforts was the establishment of a health care center to treat tuberculosis and other illnesses. By 1927, this center was examining nearly a thousand children annually, and in subsequent years its medical, dental, and mothers' clinics were utilized by four thousand people.

Such achievements were duplicated on a smaller scale throughout the country, and several NACW projects became models for the NAACP, the National Urban League, and in the case of the NACW's kindergarten program, the entire public school system of Washington, D.C.

The tangible accomplishments of the clubwomen were all the more satisfying because they had been made, for the most part, without compromise of principles. Most notably, the school founders had had to strike a balance between their values and those of White philanthropists who wanted to assert their own ideas about educating Blacks. Even as conservative a leader as Charlotte Hawkins Brown often found herself between a rock and a hard place. "The question in my heart and mind," she wrote to one of her White supporters, "and God only knows how it hurts, is just what are they going to ask me to submit to as a negro woman. . . . In my efforts to get money now, I don't want my friends to tie my hands so I can't speak out when I'm being crushed."[1]

The breakthroughs of the NACW women were also reflected in the artistic and social achievements of Black women generally. It may have been no coincidence that during the same years that Black women began demanding to be recognized as "an integral part of the general womanhood of American civilization" (as Fannie Barrier Williams had insisted), they also began to express the full range of their artistic talents. As the club movement shattered the stereotypes of Black women, so did the women emerge in a new light. By the turn of the century, *The Creole Show* became the first theatrical production to break with the minstrel tradition and the first production to feature attractively costumed, "glamorous" Black women. A subsequent production called *Octoroons* represented an even further departure from the old minstrel shows by featuring women who sang arias from *Faust, Rigoletto,* and other operas. Such developments paved the way for Black stars like Sissiretta Jones, who sang operatic arias in a vaudeville revue named after her, and dancers like Hattie McIntosh and Madah Myers. Most prominent of the female vaudeville stars was Ada Overton, known for her grace as a dancer. As Overton pointed out, the Black woman "no longer lost her dignity when she entered the theater."[2]

Black women were also breaking into the classical music field. Marie Selika, described by James Weldon Johnson as the "first colored singer with both the natural voice and the necessary training" to make a career as an opera singer, had successful engagements in Europe.[3] In the plastic arts, sculptor Meta Vaux Warwick Fuller's skills were second only to Henry O. Tanner's as the "greatest vindicating examples of the American Negroes' conquest of fine arts," according to cultural historian Margaret Just Butcher.[4] Born in Philadelphia, Fuller studied in Paris, where her talent was recognized by the renowned sculptor Auguste Rodin. Fuller received critical acclaim in Europe and her work was exhibited at the famous Paris Salon in 1903.

In a parallel development, Black women were making their mark in literature. *Megda* by Emma Dunham Kelley (1891), *Iola Leroy* by Frances Ellen Harper (1892), and *Aunt Lindy* by Victoria Earle Matthews (1893) were among the earliest novels written by Afro-American women. Poet Alice Dunbar Nelson came out with two volumes of poetry, *Violets and Other Tales* (1894) and *The Goodness of St. Tocque* (1899). In 1900, the novel *Contending Forces* by Pauline Hopkins was described by one critic as the "most powerful protest novel authored by a Black woman [until 1965] with the exception of Ann Petry's *The Street.*"[5]

Although the progress is more difficult to measure, Black women were making gains in controlling their own lives and in their roles as wives and mothers. By the 1900's, Black women were marrying later. "Their grandmothers married at twelve and fifteen," W.E.B. Du Bois observed in *The Gift of Black Folk,* but 1910 found 27 percent still single past the age of fifteen.[6] They were also having fewer children. Half of all married educated Black women had no children at the turn of the century, and, even more revealing, one fourth of *all* Black women—the majority of them rural and uneducated—had no children.[7] For those who did have children, proportionately more were born in wedlock in 1917 than at any time before or since that date.[8]

Such social development, of course, was one of the goals of the club movement.

At its 1916 convention in Baltimore, the NACW launched a campaign to rescue the home of the late Frederick Douglass from default. The house in Anacostia, a suburb of Washington, D.C., represented more than the physical legacy of an important leader and feminist. Since it was in the process of being made into a museum and historical center, its loss would have been tantamount to erasing the evidence of past achievements. Although the home had been willed upon Douglass's death to his second wife, Helen, a legal technicality prevented her from inheriting it outright. She was forced to take a mortgage on it, and to ensure its preservation had incorporated the Frederick Douglass Memorial and Historical Association. Upon her death, the home was willed to the Association's nine trustees, but when they were unable to redeem the remaining $5,000, the NACW took over the enterprise.

The project was of great symbolic importance to the women. First, it was seen as an obligation of what *National Notes* called "race loyalty with which we are charged," and "which is more greatly developed among our women, than our men." Secondly, rescuing the abolitionist's home represented a tribute to their ancestors. For despite all the evidence of their successful acculturation into American society, these clubwomen continued to gauge themselves against the achievements of their forebears who had not been free. "We realize today is the psychological moment for us women to show our true worth and prove that Negro women of today measure up to those sainted women of our race, who passed through the fire of slavery and its galling remembrances."[9] Thus did NACW president Mary Talbert announce the campaign.

After a tireless effort to mobilize all the resources of the association toward this goal, the money to lift the mortgage, and another $30,000 spent to restore the home and its grounds, was raised within two years. Talbert wrote Mary Church Terrell, who couldn't be at the victory celebration, that the clubwomen gave the honor of burning the mortgage note to the woman who had donated the last $500 needed to close the deal. That privilege had gone to Madame C. J. Walker, who by 1917 already headed one of the largest cosmetic empires in the country.

The redemption of the Douglass home was a fitting way to close one chapter of history and prepare for the next one. In 1917 Black women were on the cusp of a new era, one begun by a single event —America's entry into World War I.

The war would have a tremendous impact on a people suffering racial violence and oppression. For Blacks, an already bad situation was made worse by nationwide inflation, and cotton-killing floods and boll weevils in the South. By 1918 the cost-of-living index had risen 69 percent above the level of just four years earlier, while wages were going down. The economic situation put a vicelike grip on Black lives —sometimes literally. The convict lease system, always used as a pool of free southern Black labor, thrived in these years. In a place like Jefferson City, Alabama, for example, it was no coincidence that twice as many Black as White men, and eight times as many Black as White women, were held in its jails.[10]

For Black men and women who managed to stay out of prison, labor conditions worsened. As many Black women workers were replacing Whites who found better-paying jobs in the defense industries, more attention was paid to the plight of Black female workers. The Women's Trade Union League called for their equal treatment in the labor force. The AFL appointed a Black social worker, Mildred Rankin, to head a national office of Colored Women Workers. But lack of funds and the racism of the union kept Rankin's efforts from amounting to anything.

When it became clear that Blacks would have to organize themselves, clubwomen formed the Women Wage-Earners Association in Washington, D.C. Led by Jeanette Carter, Julia F. Coleman, and Mary Church Terrell, the association's purpose was to organize and protect Black workingwomen. Knowing that it would be difficult to bring Black women into the predominantly White unions, the association sought to teach workers how to organize themselves to better working conditions, wages, and housing. In September of 1917 a branch of the Women Wage-Earners Association in Norfolk, Virginia, attempted to organize some six hundred Black women domestics, waitresses, nurses, and tobacco stemmers to demand higher wages and better working conditions. When their demands were not met, the stemmers, who made up about half of the association's membership, voted to strike the American Cigar Company. Domestics also struck, as did the male oyster-shuckers—most of them husbands and brothers of the tobacco stemmers. These actions brought a lot of confusion to the peaceful city of Norfolk. As the White newspaper the Norfolk *Ledger-Dispatch* complained in one of its articles: "Labor unrest among the colored people of Norfolk has been literally brought home to every household in the city."[11] The Black *Norfolk Journal and Guide* took up the women's defense. It compared a list of expenses for the average woman living in Norfolk with their total weekly wages. The *Guide* concluded that there "was justice and reason in the demand of the women."[12]

Of course "justice and reason" had little to do with the treatment of Black workers in this period. And with the country on a war footing, White authorities had an additional weapon at their disposal to suppress Black workers. "Work or Fight" rules, which could be enforced by the federal government, stipulated that those not aiding the war effort—by either working or fighting—could be arrested. Now labor rebellion could be construed as subversion, as undermining the war effort. To be charged as a "slacker" could bring down on one's head both local and federal authorities.

This weapon, especially in the hands of the South, was very effective. As another White paper, the Norfolk *Virginian-Pilot,* ominously reported, a special squad of plainclothesmen was dispatched to deal with the strikes. The squad was instructed, the paper said, "to prevent 'loafing' among the colored men and women. All industrial 'slackers' . . . will find themselves in the position of defendants before the police justice."[13] The police had also asked for a government investigation of the Women Wage-Earners Association to determine if it was "interfering with the war effort." The request brought from the *Journal and Guide* an angry editorial saying that the police had not called for an investigation nor for the arrest of the three thousand *White* male workers who had recently struck the naval yard for higher wages. So why the Black workers? "The women are asking for BREAD," the Black paper concluded. "Why give them STONE?"[14] But it was to no avail. The strikers were arrested as slackers, and appeals to the White unions were futile. The strike was broken, and the Norfolk branch of the association was smashed. But though the battle was lost, the war would continue.

It continued in a place like Pine Bluff, Arkansas, where reminiscent of an earlier period, Black women refused to work in the fields. Unlike in previous times, however, the war had given them an option. Many of the women received money allotments from their menfolk in uniform, and so, fewer women found it necessary to work. Because the plantations depended on Negro women to pick the cotton, their absence was creating "a hardship," according to one White newspaper. The mayor of Pine Bluff, Simon Blum, and the local chamber of commerce attempted to extend the "work or fight" rule to cover what they called the plantation "negresses." When those efforts failed, Blum attempted to manipulate or reduce the allotments "to the extent that enough labor would be available for all the needs of employers." But the attempt created such a storm of protest that it failed too.

The incidents in Pine Bluff were reported by an NAACP field investigator in 1917 and 1918. The author of the documents was a young man who would become the organization's top executive several decades later—Walter White. Another of White's investigations showed that women working in the kitchens of the South could be just as recalcitrant as those working in the fields. In Jackson, Mississippi, a Black woman, one Mrs. Green, quit her position as cook for a White family when her husband, a carpenter, began making enough money to support them both. The day she quit her job, she stepped out on her porch to see a patrol wagon pull up to the front of her house. Two policemen got out and informed her that if she did not return to work, she would be arrested for vagrancy. So Black women, it seems, found themselves being forced to work, even when they didn't have to. Sometimes the actions were more severe, as another of Walter White's reports indicated. In Vicksburg, Mississippi, Ella Brooks and Ethel Barrett were *tarred and feathered* when they quit their jobs.

It is little wonder that when the opportunity presented itself, Black women, as well as men, left the South to find work at decent wages with better opportunities and a greater sense of dignity. When, between 1915 and 1920, the North beckoned, some 500,000 Blacks heeded its call. Afro-Americans were tired of southern exploitation and violence—especially when the demand for their labor was at a premium in the North. The wages offered by labor-short northern industry, working full gear to meet war production needs, were almost too good to be true. Up north a laundress or cook could earn $1.50 to $2 a day *plus* carfare and meals. That came out to a little less than what a woman would earn for an *entire week* in Jackson, Mississippi. And if she was fortunate enough to get an industrial job, she could earn $3 a day, compared to 50 cents for picking cotton. A young unmarried woman in domestic service in the North could earn about $8 a week, approximately twice as much as she could get in Mississippi. Even if you had no clear idea of what you were going to do, the North seemed to offer so much hope in contrast to the South's despair. "From a willen workin woman," ran an ad penned by a Southerner in the Black newspaper *The Chicago Defender,* which encouraged Blacks to come north: "I hope that you will healp me as I want to get out of this land of sufring. I no there is som thing that I can do here. . . . I don't know just whah but I hope the Lord will find a place."[15]

The result was what Emmett J. Scott, longtime secretary to Booker T. Washington and a journalist, called the "northern fever." Scott described the making of an epidemic: "A good citizen would talk with another about the apparent insanity of those Negroes who had contracted 'the northern fever.' . . . Hardly before another day would pass, one of the two would disappear having emulated the recklessness of the very people he had so recklessly condemned."[16] In this way, Scott reported, Jackson, Mississippi, lost "the majority of lower working class Negroes, twenty-five percent of businessmen, and fully one-third of professionals." Two of the largest churches lost some 40 percent of their congregations. Two thirds of the families that remained in Jackson were part-families, some of whose relatives had recently gone north.[17] All in all, Scott estimated that from two thousand to five thousand people left Jackson alone.

Needless to say, the number of Blacks who left the South caused some alarm. Labor agents who came south to entice Black workers were sometimes arrested. There were horrible scenes when Blacks were dragged off trains heading north. Whites, panicked by the sudden scarcity of Black labor, for a short time even alleviated conditions and raised salaries. But the die had been cast.

Working Up North

Census counts in the northern cities during the migration period showed that a greater number of women than men were making the journey from the South. Even if the male population was undercounted, as often happened, still, a large number of women searched for a new life north of the Mason-Dixon Line. "Negro women are leaving the kitchen and laundry for the workshop and factory," wrote William Ashby, executive director of the New Jersey Welfare League, at the peak of the migration.[18] World War I gave Black workingwomen their first opportunity to be employed in jobs other than domestic work or teaching in a "colored school."

In 1918 a Bureau of Labor Statistics report noted that in 150 plants in New York, Pennsylvania, Ohio, Illinois, Michigan, Indiana,

Virginia, West Virginia, and North Carolina, no less than 40 percent of the 28,520 workers were Black women. A 1920 census showed that of all women employed in manufacturing and mechanical industries, 104,983 were Black. This figure represented an increase of 100 percent for Black women, as compared to an increase of less than 1 percent of all women so employed.[19]

For the first time, significant numbers of Black women were earning decent wages in the mainstream of the American labor force. In the metal industries they drilled, polished, punch-pressed, soldered; Black women also upholstered, tinned, and decorated lampshades. In laundries, most did the heavy work, but others used hand and machine irons. In the garment industry, some factories employed only Black women, who were allowed to take any position that needed to be filled. For the first time they were permitted to use machinery, and some even found jobs as clerks, stenographers, and bookkeepers. These new opportunities had salutary effects which went beyond better wages.

Writing of Black women working in Harlem, journalist and teacher Elise McDougald noted that they were finally "free from the cruder handicaps of primitive household hardships and the grosser forms of sex and race subjugation." In the city, McDougald also observed, a Black woman "had considerable opportunity to measure her powers in the intellectual and industrial fields."[20] In the cities, these fields included more than teaching for significant numbers of Black women. Many, "anxious to devote their education and lives to the needs of the submerged masses," were entering social work.[21] Others were becoming correctional and probation officers, policewomen, vocational guides in the schools, and were working in various branches of the public health services. More unusual lines of work were also open to them: chiropody, bacteriology, and pharmacy. That was the good news; there was also the bad.

Although it was true that Black women were leaving the kitchen and laundry, they did so only as fast as White women made their way up the employment ladder. Black women found jobs primarily in those places left vacant by the shifting of Hungarian, Italian, and Jewish girls to the munitions plants, where higher pay was available. Outside of the industries, the pecking order was also visible. For example, in Philadelphia, Black women were hired as live-in domestics rather than dayworkers only when White women, the previous live-ins, found work in the factories.

The satisfaction Black women received working in the mainstream of labor was tempered by their having to perform the dirtiest and most difficult tasks. The historical stereotypes assigned to Black women were largely responsible for this. For example, because they were thought to be able to withstand more heat, they got the most heat-intense jobs in the candy and glass factories. In the bakeries it was Black women who cleaned, greased, and lifted the heavy pans. In the tobacco industry, Black women did the stripping of the tobacco, the lowest-paid and most numbing work.

Because in many instances White women refused to work side by side with Black women, the latter usually had to perform the worst jobs, under segregated and dirty conditions. In a terminal of the Pennsylvania Railroad, three Black women and one White woman were linen counters. The White woman counted the clean linen in an airy, well-lighted room on the ground floor. The Black women sorted the soiled linen in a dark basement.[22] In other places, conditions could be worse. Floors such as those in the crab and tobacco factories where Black women worked were often damp enough to give them rheumatism.

Not only were Black women forced to work in inferior positions and perform the least desirable tasks, but they were paid from 10 to 60 percent less than ill-paid White women. The insult was double in that Black workers in the manufacturing sector were often more highly qualified than Whites. Only the cream of the Black crop was picked, after all. A 1919 study of representative Black women in New York City, published in the *Southern Workman,* revealed that a typical Black workingwoman was young, southern-born, unmarried, with at least a grammar school education. A significant number had been schoolteachers in the South!

In a time of intense union activity among White men and women, Black women encountered the same kind of racial discrimination leveled at Black men. As McDougald observed, "The laissez-faire attitude of practically all trade unions makes the Negro woman an unwilling menace to the cause of labor."[23] This was due not to Black women's reluctance to join unions, but to the racism of the AFL toward all Black workers and the ineffective organizing and low priority accorded their fate by the Women's Trade Union League and the Women's Bureau. These two organizations were established amidst the new gains by women in the labor force, yet they did virtually nothing about the special needs of 2 million Black workingwomen.

Another example of the bad news: Although there had been an

impressive increase in Black women entering industry, their actual numbers were small. Of the 2 million gainfully employed in 1920, nearly a million were still in domestic and personal service. Another group, nearly as large, was in agriculture. Out of 1,930,000 women workers in industry, only 6.7 percent were Black.[24]

The tenuous foothold that Black women had carved out in industry—and thus in all aspects of social and economic progress—began to erode when the war ended in 1918. With the demobilization of more than 4 million soldiers, with immigrants beginning to look to America again, with the slowdown of industry, competition and Negrophobia were again on the march.

Racial strife was exacerbated by the rise of the "new" Ku Klux Klan, which had been organized in Atlanta, Georgia, in 1915. By 1919 its membership reached 100,000, and its loathsome activities spread throughout the country from Maine to California. The huge increase in the Black population north of the Mason-Dixon became so much grist for the Klan's mill. There were 470,000 more Afro-Americans in the North and West in 1920 than there had been in 1910, and their presence inflamed the labor competition in a shrinking job market. The tension reached its peak in the so-called Red Summer of 1919. In that year, more than twenty major racial upheavals occurred in cities from Omaha, Nebraska, to Longview, Texas. The worst riot took place in Chicago, where 37 people were killed, 537 wounded, and hundreds of families left homeless by the burning and destruction of property.

In the contest for jobs, Blacks were the inevitable losers and the impact on Black women was immediately felt. Black women at every level of the labor force dropped a few notches, and those on the bottom were forced out. Elizabeth Ross Haynes, a pioneer social worker and the wife of National Urban League co-founder George Edmund Haynes, concluded from a 1922 study of industrial plants in the East, West, North, and South "that a large number of Negro women have lost their places within the last twelve months."[25] She noted that a large garment factory in the Middle West which had been one of the first to employ Black women had discontinued hiring them. A southern millowner told her that now they hired Black women only "occasionally" for "odd jobs." Even domestic and laundry workers were jeopardized. In places like Detroit, Haynes wrote, 80 to 90 percent of calls for domestic workers specified White women. For those fortunate enough to retain their jobs, wages often dropped in the course of a year from a standard of $15–$20 a week to $8–$12. In other kinds of jobs, such as elevator operator and stock girl, Blacks were no longer called upon at all.

Furthermore, when minimum wages were established in some occupations, even Black women with seniority were displaced. For example, 90 percent of the laundry workers in Washington, D.C., were Black women who had worked at the same job for fourteen to thirty-eight years, Haynes reported. When laundry owners feared that minimum wages would be imposed, they immediately began asking the employment agencies about the possibility of getting White women.

But as long as there was work, even the most exploited women were considered the fortunate ones—for after the war many Black women could find no jobs at all. Hundreds were seen waiting outside employment offices, desperate, and more often turned away than not. In this period, Black women, unorganized, often inexperienced, discriminated against, and sometimes showing less than peak enthusiasm for the most exploitative jobs, were dazed by the rapid and disastrous turn in their fortunes.

Black women in the trades and professions also had their problems. Because of discrimination, Elise McDougald pointed out, they were dependent on finding work in Black-owned businesses—which made up only 20 percent of all businesses in Harlem. Many of these firms were small, and in the economic climate few new ones were established. In the trades, Black women were further hampered by their small representation in hostile unions. They were now also largely excluded from the garment industry, despite their long tradition in dressmaking. The burgeoning fur industry in New York was also difficult to break into, and even where women could find work, such as in food establishments, they were relegated to the most menial jobs.

Black women had begun to make steady inroads into federal civil service jobs in the early twentieth century. But the administration of Woodrow Wilson had broken the momentum. Wilson, who has gone down in history as the man who sent thousands of American men abroad to make the world safe for democracy, who spoke fervently for the right of self-determination, who helped usher in woman suffrage, was also responsible for resegregating the civil service. His administration halted the small progress of Blacks in securing civil service jobs. When it came to them, such tactics as personal interviews and the sending in of application photos undermined the sacred notion of meritocracy. The attitude began to penetrate the country. "The civil service in New York City is no longer free from discrimination," McDougald observed. "The casual personal interview, that tenacious and retrogressive practice introduced in the Federal Administration during the World War, has spread and often nullifies the Negro woman's success in written tests."[26] The writer cited one woman who was turned down three times, in each instance only after an interview.

In many cases women who could not find jobs in the civil service and looked for other kinds of work, such as clerk or saleswoman in a department store, were stymied there too. "Negro girls who might be well-suited to salesmanship are barred from all but the menial positions," noted McDougald. And in places like the telephone and insurance companies, where large numbers of White women were finding work—and which enjoyed the patronage of Black customers —"Negroes [were denied] proportionate employment."[27]

Black women were more successful in the skilled professions that required college training, because there the competition was less. "In these fields," observed McDougald, "the Negro woman is dependent largely upon herself and her race for work."[28] This explains the disproportionate numbers of Black women—even then—in the dental, legal, medical, and nursing professions, where "successful woman practitioners have usually worked their way through college and are 'managing' on the small fees that can be received from an underpaid public."[29] The new interest in sociology, particularly the study of Blacks, also gave rise to a demand for college-trained social scientists. A disproportionate number of these were Black women as well. However, as McDougald pointed out, even in "work among Negroes, the better paying positions are reserved for Whites."[30] Discrimination also existed in the teaching field, McDougald (a teacher herself) noted, but at least there, "The need for teachers is still so strong that little friction exists."[31]

Of course, few women had the resources to enter the professions, and with the discrimination in the semiprofessional and blue-collar occupations, a large number of women had little choice but domestic work. Even Black domestics who could find jobs had to deal with the consequences of a deteriorating situation. In the twenties, inexperienced and sometimes less than efficient "casual workers" willing to work for lower wages were undermining other types of household workers. But the casual workers were also trapped by circumstance. Often such a woman who, because she had children and little assistance at home, had refused the better-paid and more stable residential domestic work. Such a decision was "a last stand in her fight to maintain a semblance of family life," McDougald wrote. "How else can her children, loose all afternoon, be gathered together at nightfall?"[32] Despite the progress of Black women during the war years, in the end the pattern of their employment opportunities remained very much the same as it had been before the war. Virtually barred from the industrial sector, they were relegated to the professions or to domestic service, with little choice in between. Their greater numbers in both areas were due to the same reason: racial discrimination. Although many White women workers were also losing their jobs or being downgraded in the postwar period, the Black women's loss of income was less likely to be made up by the gains of their men.

A less determined people might have returned south after World War I. The North no longer needed most of the Afro-Americans who had answered its call during the war years; and life for many turned bitter. "I'm folding up my little dreams," went a line written by the Black poet Georgia Douglass Johnson in 1918, "Within my heart tonight, / And praying I may soon forget / The torture of their sight."[33]

One of the dreams that seemed most elusive was that of an untrammeled family life. But in a society where the divorce rate for the general population soared from one divorce for every seventeen marriages in 1890 to one in six by the late twenties, Afro-Americans would encounter special problems—most of them economic. In New York City, for example, a combination of low-paying jobs and too-high rents often resulted in Blacks' spending more than double the percentage of their income for rent that White families paid. Like immigrant women, most Black women had to work, but unlike Whites, they were rarely employed in the home or a family business. This meant, as Elise McDougald wrote, that Black women faced "the great problem of leaving home each day and at the same time trying to rear their children in their spare time—this too in neighborhoods where rents are large, standards of dress and recreation high and costly, and social danger on the increase."[34]

The economic situation also put a strain on marital relations. Discrimination made it necessary for Black women to stay longer in school if they were to do other than domestic jobs, and the consequences were often bitter in the cities, where many of their men were excluded from better-paying jobs. Insufficiently paid, insecure about wives who were at least their cultural equals, "The masses of Negro men," stated McDougald, "are engaged in menial occupations throughout the working day. Their baffled and suppressed desires to determine their economic life are manifested in over-bearing domination at home."[35] In a place like Manhattan, seven out of every ten Black families had a father present in the home, but there were sufficient numbers of divorces and separations to give cause for concern. Many fathers had "succumbed to social maladjustment and abandoned their families," noted McDougald.[36]

Brittle male-female relationships were further weakened by the relative numbers of men and women in the cities. Because of the proportionately large number of Black women who were educated and skilled, high percentages of them were drawn to the cities. In New York City for example, there were 105 Black women to every 100 Black men. As one study points out, a scarcity of women encourages a protective, monogamous attitude toward them by men. When there is a scarcity of men, protectiveness dissolves and men become reluctant to make permanent commitments.[37]

Despite the stress that mothers experienced, valiant efforts were made to secure the well-being of their children. Great care must have been taken by women expecting babies. Between 1915 and 1920 the Black infant mortality rate actually dropped. (For states registering 2,000 or more Black births regularly, the death rate of Black babies dropped from 181 per 1,000 births to 102.) Although the mortality rate was still higher than among Whites, the reduction of deaths among Blacks was more than twice that of Whites. In a number of states, like Arkansas (where the Black infant mortality rate was 69 per 1,000), fewer Black babies were dying than White newborns in South Carolina, Tennessee, or West Virginia; and the rate was the same as that of Whites in Maryland and Pennsylvania in 1929. Although the decrease in infant mortality could be attributed to "scientific discoveries" and "improved medical care," said Grace Abbott, chief of the Labor Department's Children's Bureau, "most of the credit goes to the mothers who have . . . utilized more intelligently the knowledge and skill which the doctor has to offer."[38]

As in the past, a significant number of married women had no children at all, according to sociologist Irene Graham. Comparing similar samples of Black families in Chicago and White families in Rochester, New York, she found that almost half the Black couples were childless, compared to less than 25 percent of the Whites. And Black families who did have children had fewer than immigrant or native-born Whites (2.0, 2.8, and 2.1 respectively).[39] That Blacks had fewer children should be taken into account when comparing the divorce and separation rates among Blacks and Whites. Marriages with children were less likely to break up. During the twenties, three quarters of all divorced couples were childless.[40] However, Black marriages with children seemed, in some instances, to be even more resilient than those of their White counterparts.

In the Chicago study, less than two fifths (37.7 percent) of Black children lived in broken homes, compared to three fifths (60.7 percent) of White children. Herbert Gutman's statistical observations of Black families in Manhattan in the twenties seemed to confirm this trend. There, five out of six children under six years of age lived in two-parent families, and only 124 of the total of 50,000 children in the area lived with other than relatives. In Chicago, Graham showed, nine tenths of Black children lived with their own parents; a portion of the remaining tenth lived with relatives.

Children's Bureau Chief Grace Abbott also noted "the eagerness of Negro women to give their children the advantage of every opportunity offered."[41] This often meant economic sacrifices. A Children's Bureau study of Philadelphia mothers found that whatever the family's economic circumstances, the proportion of mothers who worked varied directly with the number of preschool children. As far as older children were concerned, Irene Graham found—just as Frances Ellen Harper did more than a half century earlier—that Black families were reluctant to have them work regardless of the need for extra income. In Chicago, 68 percent of Black families with children fourteen years of age and older showed no income from their children. This was true even in extended families where only half of the other adult relatives provided income—indicating that many were probably dependents, such as aged parents.[42]

To make ends meet, many Black families brought in lodgers. (In 1920 only 2.1 percent of Chicago Blacks owned their property free of mortgage.) But even the decision to take in unrelated persons— usually unattached Black males—was affected by the presence of children in the house. Fewer families with children took in lodgers. It was a decision, Graham noted, between a more adequate income or safer home surroundings for the children—and the majority chose safety.

The choice between being a roomer or maintaining one's own household was also affected by the presence of children. Among Black families who roomed with others, the majority were childless couples. In contrast, the majority of White families who roomed with others were mothers with children but without husbands. The findings again revealed the independent determination of Black women. "With Negro women," Graham concluded, "maintaining a home seems to depend less upon having a husband to provide it, than upon the presence of children who need to have the home."[43]

Perhaps it was the attention accorded to children that accounted for the relatively low rate of juvenile delinquency among Black boys during the twenties. Eighteen courts throughout the country found a significant increase of delinquency among boys; however, in only two of the nine courts that kept separate figures for Black children were there significant increases among Black boys. Although the delinquency rate in general was still higher among Blacks, their rate was going down while the overall rate was going up. These statistics on the status of children were seen by the chief of the Children's Bureau as a barometer of general progress among Blacks who were handicapped by economic, social, and political discrimination.

While many commentators emphasized the positive efforts of Blacks in the cities, this did not mean that they overlooked the real problems. They wrote of increasing illegitimacy, family disorganization, crime, and other maladjustments. But they saw Black family problems as resulting more from economic difficulties than from sociological ones. Graham, for example, discussing the "abnormalities" of Black family life, observed similar dislocations among all migrant groups. McDougald, writing of "sexual irregularities," stressed that these were no less common among Whites of a similar economic class. They were "not a matter of race, but of socio-economic conditions,"[44] she said, reminding her readers that African tribes had very strict sexual codes.

If slavery had had an impact on the disposition of the Black family, it was in the realm of social attitudes, McDougald believed. For example, she observed that Black women had a different attitude toward children born out of wedlock than did their White peers. It wasn't that less of a stigma was attached to unwed mothers in the Black community, McDougald pointed out, but that slavery made Black women "often temper scorn with sympathy for weakness." Consequently, wrote McDougald, "the foundling asylum is seldom sought" for a child born out of wedlock. Instead, married relatives, even the mother of the unwed mother, would take the child as their own. McDougald concluded that so enlightened an attitude should be accepted as a contribution to the social thought of America.[45]

It was present, not past, inequalities which were negatively affecting the lives of Black families, McDougald and others believed; and the postwar years presented new challenges to Blacks and Black women. In order to advance, many felt, it was now necessary to demand social equality. Only that way could political and economic progress be assured.

IX

~ The Radical Interracialists ~

In 1919, Senator Henry Cabot Lodge of Massachusetts took the unusual step of entering a poem written by a Black man into *The Congressional Record.* [1] "If We Must Die" by Claude McKay—which contained such lines as "Though far outnumbered let us show us brave, / And for their thousand blows deal one deathblow!"—was not put in the *Record* for its aesthetic merit. Lodge had been struck by its bitter and defiant tone. It was clear to the senator that its militant spirit went beyond the feelings of a single angry poet. The Chicago riot—which helped to inspire McKay's sonnet—demonstrated that. Although more Blacks than Whites were killed and wounded in the melee, Blacks had fought back with an uncommon ferocity. Whites had been wounded, too, and of the thirty-seven killed during the violence, fifteen were Caucasians.

In fact, the spirit of defiance was infusing nearly every aspect of Black life. Marcus Garvey began rallying working-class Blacks in New York and throughout the country with his appeal to Black pride and economic independence. By the mid-twenties his Universal Negro Improvement Association (UNIA) claimed a million followers. Black college students, too, were in revolt. They were demanding Black administrators, relevant courses, the elimination of ROTC, and an end to the mandatory singing of Negro spirituals to influential Whites who pined for a bygone era. At the largest Black school, Howard University, the question of academic self-determination was even more controversial because of Howard's financial dependence on Congress. On one occasion, the school's White president, J. Stanley Durkee, was tongue-lashed by Congress for having a book in its library advocating socialism. Durkee was forced to apologize, explaining that the volume was neither taught nor recommended. Commenting on the incident, a young Black student echoed the underclassmen's views: The president "should have informed the body that we could teach what we liked and if the money was withheld, we would have the satisfaction of being untrammeled."[2] The student would become a well-known and controversial writer in subsequent years. Her name was Zora Neale Hurston and her article was published in a magazine called *The Messenger,* one of the most militant Black journals of the period. Its socialist editors, A. Philip Randolph and Chandler Owen, were among the most articulate spokesmen of the new militancy. "The social aims of the New Negro are decidedly different than those of the Old Negro," they pronounced in a 1920 editorial. "The New Negro stands for absolute and unequivocal social equality."

The gauntlet was also thrown down by women activists. The needs of Black women were greater than the NACW, with its limited resources, could satisfy. It was now essential for Black women to become an integral part of the mainstream. On the labor front, the lead was taken by Mary Church Terrell, who was continuing to channel her efforts toward the unionization of Black women workers. In the late twenties, Black representation in the unions was very small. The AFL-affiliated unions had approximately forty thousand Black members, and about twelve thousand more were in independent unions. Of this small total, the number of Black women was negligible.

A great deal of attention was paid to the status of all working women after the war, and Terrell was among those who attempted to extend that focus to the needs of Black women. When the Women's Bureau of the Department of Labor was established on a permanent basis, Mary Church Terrell campaigned, unsuccessfully, for a Colored Women's Division within the bureau. And when, in 1919, the First International Congress of Working Women met in Washington, D.C., she and others attempted to make its program more relevant to Black workingwomen. The program of the congress included equal pay for equal work, inclusion in areas reserved for men, a forty-four-hour week, social insurance, maternity benefits, and job training. But Black women, not to mention their special needs, were excluded. However, the congress did receive a message signed by "Representative Negro Women of the United States in behalf of Negro Women Laborers of the United States." The signatories included Terrell, Nannie Helen Burroughs, Elizabeth C. Carter, and Elizabeth Ross Haynes, and they stated their position plainly. First, they chastised the congress for ignoring the plight of Black workingwomen. Second, they emphasized the urgent need for unionization. That issue was low in the priorities of the congress, which was more concerned about the few workers on the higher rungs of the occupational ladder than about the majority who were in lower-status jobs and in desperate need of protection.

But for Black women, unionization was the essential issue, as their message illustrated. "We, a group of Negro women," it read in part, "representing those two million of Negro wage-earners, respectfully ask for your active cooperation in organizing the Negro women workers of the United States into unions, that they may have a share in bringing about industrial democracy and social order in the world."[3] As labor historian Philip Foner pointed out, the only time that the issue of unionization was even brought up at the congress was in the Black women's message.

The Y

The concern for workingwomen also attracted Black women to the YWCA. In 1920 the Y went on record as advocating collective bargaining, the rights of workers, and economic justice. More important, its industrial departments became vigorously engaged in preparing women for the service sector. "Calls are coming in for positions all along the lines previously held by men, be it business manager, elevator operator or errand boy," noted its annual report of 1917. Because of its tremendous resources, it was obvious that the Y could be a boon to Black women and girls, whose own organizations were comparatively limited in their capacities. The record of the Y on racial matters was, however, spotty.

In 1893 the first segregated Black YWCA was chartered in Dayton, Ohio. After that, segregated locals proliferated throughout the country. When the organization went national in 1906, there were no Black branches in the South. This policy was challenged by the White reformer Grace Dodge, whose efforts resulted in the Y's broaching the race issue at an Asheville, North Carolina, student conference. However, in deference to its White southern members and its own reluctance to have Blacks participate on a policy-making level, the National Board voted to set up segregated Black branches which would be "subsidiaries" to local White branches. In 1913 the YWCA appointed its first Colored Secretary, Eva Bowles, on an "experimental basis." Two years later the organization held its first interracial conference in the South, with the avowed purpose of laying the foundation for more Black participation. But at the national convention, held in the same year, there was only one Black representative, and she left with the impression that the Y was a "spiritual farce" rather than a "spiritual force."[4]

There were some positive signs after the outbreak of World War I. The Y's War Work Council, which provided recreational facilities for soldiers and aid for women working in the war industries, extended its program to Blacks. In 1917 the organization appropriated $200,000 for a Colored Department headed by Eva Bowles. With a small staff, Bowles accomplished as much as anyone could have hoped. Within two years, the Colored War Council established recreational and industrial centers in forty-five communities. Growing Black interest and participation resulted in an increase of Black professional workers in the Y, from nine in 1915 to eighty-six in 1919. In the same span of time, the number of Black branches rose from sixteen to forty-nine, and the number of national secretaries from one to twelve. By 1919, twelve thousand Black girls were enrolled in the YWCA. Bowles, with reason, was pleased by the results. The war, she wrote, "has given opportunity to the colored woman to prove her ability for leadership. She had her chance and made good."[5]

Perhaps too good. At the end of 1919, Bowles's enthusiasm about the progress of Black participation in the Y turned into despair. Her Colored War Council was dismantled by the National Board, and nothing was offered to take its place. When Black women attempted to build on the achievements of the War Council, it became evident that the internal structure of the Y had to be challenged; the issue came to a head when Lugenia Burns Hope attempted to organize a Black YWCA group in Atlanta.

Hope's Neighborhood Union had been the hub of the Women's War Council in Atlanta. Under her leadership, the council not only provided the usual services but also led, in the city where the "new" Klan was founded, public protests against the harassment of Black soldiers and civilians by police officers. Hope was subsequently appointed to the position of Special War Work Secretary, and put in charge of training hostess-houseworkers at Camp Upton, New Jersey. Among other things, she managed to raise $1,800 to build a YMCA for Black soldiers and their families. After the war she returned to Atlanta to organize a Black YWCA, choosing as its site the place where the Y could do the most good: the Black ghetto.

Hope's plans for the Phillis Wheatley branch of the Y were immediately criticized by the field supervisor of colored work in the South, Adelle Ruffin. She accused Hope of attempting to use the organization to "save immoral Alley Girls," instead of helping aspiring middle-class women." The issue was larger than the site of a proposed Y. It precipitated a struggle that encompassed all the racial tensions that had been building for some time. Whom would the Y serve? And who would make the policy decisions concerning Black women, especially in the South? How would the National Board handle the new, more militant demands of Black women activists in their relationship to the organization?

Lugenia Burns Hope and her Black Y allies, including Lucy C. Laney and Mary Jackson McCrorey, responded to Ruffin's charge by raising objections to her leadership. Even before this episode, Hope and other Black women, including Eva Bowles on the National Board, took exception to White women—and southern White women at that—making all the policy decisions for Blacks. A Black branch could not even be organized until local White women gave their okay. "You can have no Association but you may become a branch if the white women in your community will permit," complained Black women in a position paper. "This is true in Little Rock. The Colored women there are waiting for the white women to have a change of heart. . . . Is this fair—is this Christian? Is this as Christ would have it?"[6]

In January 1920, Bowles wrote a letter to Hope, telling her of the response to her request that no White woman be appointed as secretary for "colored" student work. "I found out to my disappointment," Bowles wrote, "that our white women do not properly appreciate the strength of our colored women throughout the country. . . Another thing—our colored secretaries from headquarters must no longer be excluded from Southern soil."[7]

The increasing demands of Black women prompted the southern White field staff, headquartered in Richmond, to use all their authority to bolster Ruffin's position, and, according to a historian, "prevent the black secretaries of the National Board, with their aggressive northern ways, from setting foot on 'southern soil.'"[8] Whites also launched a campaign to remove the Black national student secretary, Catherine Lealtad. Lealtad had always been a thorn in their side. She demanded equal accommodations for Black staff members at national conventions, and had once refused to work under a southern White woman. The Richmond staff proposed that Lealtad be replaced by a southern White woman "who was really sincere and just in her attitudes toward colored people."[9]

This turn of events provoked Hope, McCrorey, and Laney to raise the first public demand that the Y be reorganized on a basis of full equality. On April 6, 1920, Hope called for a meeting of the Black caucus to clarify the principles they thought necessary for Y work in the South. "Northern women," Hope told them, "thought they knew more about it than Southern women. Colored women believed they knew more than both and that's why they wanted to represent themselves."[10] The Black group objected to the fact that program development was proceeding only as fast as "the Southern White would permit"; that young women who needed it most were being excluded; and that Black national secretaries were kept from working in the South. The group drew up a petition asking for Ruffin's replacement, and requesting that "in all work affecting our people, full recognition of leadership should be given Negro women."[11] The Black caucus also suggested that Blacks be allowed to establish independent branches.

Lugenia Hope, Lucy C. Laney, and Mary Jackson McCrorey presented the petition to the YWCA national convention in Cleveland. But the convention refused to take any direct action as a body, and instead left it in the hands of the southern field staff, which incited McCrorey to conclude that "the whole policy is to keep us strictly subordinated."[12] And in fact that was exactly what was happening. Another meeting with the southern field staff was also fruitless. Not only were the efforts of the Black women ignored at the meeting, but the official minutes sent to the National Board "mysteriously" excluded any record of their demands. As we will see, this was an oft-used tactic in interracial confrontations between women.

The persistence of the caucus did bring some, if only token, results. A "Conference on Colored Work" adopted a few general resolutions, and Charlotte Hawkins Brown was appointed to the newly created position of member-at-large of the southern field staff. It turned out, though, that the position included no budgetary allowance for Brown to attend meetings, nor was she asked to attend any. Lugenia Hope was distressed—and disappointed—but not sorry. "I have no regrets for the stand I took . . . even if I had to be misrepresented and rather cruelly treated because of it," she said.[13] But for the time being, there was little hope for any progress on the part of the Young Women's Christian Association.*

---

*In 1924, Elizabeth Ross Haynes became the first Black woman elected to the Y's National Board. Not until 1946, however, did the national convention vote on an "Interracial Charter" and commit the organization to full integration of Black women into the "mainstream of association life."

The Suffrage Campaign

The most encompassing issue for Black women in the postwar years was the suffrage campaign. For them, as for Whites, the vote represented the key to their empowerment. For Black women, suffrage was both a feminist and a racial demand for equality. By 1917 the tide had begun to swell again toward the passage of the Anthony Amendment. In January of that year, six additional states enfranchised women for presidential elections. In New York, the city's political machine, Tammany Hall, made it clear that it would not oppose the federal amendment.

Echoes of the 1860's were heard when White suffragists, including Carrie Chapman Catt, made efforts to woo Black female support. NAWSA even went to the extraordinary length of taking a stand against lynching in 1917. In the same year, Congresswoman Jeanette Rankin of Montana assured the Alpha Kappa Alpha Sorority at Howard University that she supported suffrage for all women, regardless of race.

Black women were understandably wary of this renewed courtship. White suffragists had shown little support for Black women's enfranchisement in the past, even when racial hostility undermined the White suffragists' own position. In 1902, for example, in order to eliminate the voice of Black women, the state of Kentucky had revoked the rights of *all* women to vote in school board elections.[14] In 1914, White suffragists had not challenged the efforts of the Illinois state legislature to eliminate Black women from the voting rolls after it had enfranchised women in the state.

The Black women's suspicions were verified by 1918, the year the Anthony Amendment, with the support of President Wilson, passed the House with the exact two-thirds majority required. Now the suffrage bill had to get through the southern-dominated Senate. At this point, the pretense of racial solidarity was dropped. Immediately after the House vote, the southern racists came out of the woodwork, and White suffragists hoisted their tattered flag of "expediency." Beginning in 1918, several congressmen, including Mississippi's senior senator, John Sharpe Williams, proposed amendments to the suffrage bill so that only White women would be allowed to vote. In the same year, Black women were refused the right to register in Texas. In 1919, Mary Church Terrell informed Walter White, then assistant executive secretary of the NAACP, that White suffragists in

Florida were discriminating against Black women in their attempts to recruit for the suffrage campaign; and that Alice Paul, head of the Woman's Party, was reported to have allayed White fears in South Carolina by scoffing at the idea that woman suffrage meant Black woman suffrage in the state. According to an interview in the *New York World*, published February 18, Paul, who represented the most militant faction of White suffragists, said, "Negro men cannot vote in South Carolina and therefore negro women could not if women were to vote in the nation. We are organizing white women in the South," asserted the New Jersey Quaker, who was a veteran of England's suffrage movement, "but have heard of no activity or anxiety among the negresses."[15]

All these events raised the specter of White suffragists' allying with racists to pass an amendment that would eliminate Blacks from the polls. This prompted Black women, in league with the NAACP, to take the offensive. The civil rights organization informed Alice Paul that they had passed a resolution against her statement, and then sent her a copy of the March 30 *Branch Bulletin* which bitterly criticized her stance. Paul responded not by denying that she made the statement but by writing the *Bulletin*'s editor that she and other women felt "a sincere regret that the negro, whose enfranchisement women helped to win, should now that his own enfranchisement has been obtained speak with sarcasm . . . for the franchise which women are still conducting."[16]

Walter White himself met with Paul and later conveyed his impressions of the meeting to Mary Church Terrell. "Just as you say," he wrote her, "all of them [White suffragists] are mortally afraid of the South and if they could get the Suffrage Amendment through without enfranchising colored women, they would do it in a moment."[17]

Of immediate concern at the time was the proposed Jones amendment, named after the chairman of the Suffrage Committee. The amendment was a compromise measure which altered the original enforcement clause of the Susan B. Anthony Amendment so that it was more acceptable to Southerners.* In response, an NAACP law-

---

*The original Susan B. Anthony Amendment's enforcement clause read: "Congress shall have power, by appropriate legislation to enforce the provisions of this article." Under the Jones amendment this was changed to: "That the several states shall have the authority to enforce this article by necessary legislation, but if any state shall enforce or enact any law in conflict therewith then Congress shall not be excluded from enacting appropriate legislation to enforce it."

yer, John Shillady, canvassed a number of attorneys to get their assessment of the altered amendment. Though most believed that technically the Jones legislation would not prohibit Black women from voting, they agreed with the view of the well-known attorney and first president of the NAACP, Moorfield Storey. Warning of the "ingeniousness of southern legislators to secure rights for Whites and not Blacks," Storey felt any wording that could be subject to interpretation would inevitably present problems.[18] The *New York World,* perhaps with inside information, had a less ambiguous opinion of the amendment's potential impact. Under it, the paper said, "such States as desire could enact enforcement laws under which negro women would be prevented from exercising the right to vote. It would, for that reason, be satisfactory to the Southern Senators."[19]

Although Republicans prevented a vote on the Jones amendment, Black suffragists regarded it as an ominous sign. They took measures to prevent NAWSA and the Woman's Party from supporting such legislation, tacitly or otherwise. The women of the NACW decided on a tactic which struck fear in the hearts of White suffragists who were ardently wooing the South. In 1919, the NACW's Northeastern Federation of Women's Clubs, representing six thousand Blacks, applied for cooperative membership in NAWSA.

The White suffragist organization was dumbstruck. They begged the federation to withdraw their application, temporarily, until the suffrage amendment was passed. NAWSA officers did not try to explain why Black women would want to become a part of their organization *after* the amendment was passed, but they did attempt everything in their power to discourage Black women from applying for membership.

NAWSA president Carrie Chapman Catt dispatched Ida Husted Harper to write Terrell and the federation's president, Elizabeth C. Carter. Harper began the letter by reminding the women of her own liberal credentials. Her parents were abolitionists, she said, and their "doors were always opened to colored people." The suffragist also informed them that Susan B. Anthony had authorized her to write her biography because of her sympathy with *"all that she stood for"*—a reference, one assumes, to Anthony's personal principles of racial fairness. While writing the biography in Anthony's home, the two women entertained several "colored" guests, like Booker T. Washington and Ida Wells-Barnett, Harper noted.

So much for Harper's credentials. Now she went to the heart of the matter. It was a critical time for the fate of the Anthony Amendment, she wrote, and if the moment was lost, "there will not be universal suffrage in your lifetime." She went on: "Every Southern State Suffrage Association now supports the Federal Amendment." Furthermore, Democratic votes from a number of the industrial northern states were needed, and eight congressmen from six states represented by the Northeastern Federation of Women's Clubs were unalterably opposed to the amendment. Finally of course, the specter of Black enfranchisement was the greatest potential monkey wrench in any bill that needed southern support. "Many of the Southern members," wrote Harper, "are now willing to surrender their beloved doctrine of States' rights and their only obstacle is fear of the colored women's vote, in the States where it is likely to equal or exceed the white women's vote. It has been the policy of the leaders of the National Association [NAWSA] to meet this foreboding with silence," the writer admitted. However, NAWSA stood for the original amendment and had refused "to assist in any way the effort of the women of any state for a white women's franchise."[20] Harper concluded that if the Black women proceeded with their application, the entire struggle could be defeated. Couldn't they "sacrifice" the "immediate gratification" by applying at a later time?

The letter was an incredible testimony to patronizing arrogance, and Elizabeth C. Carter made it clear that Harper had missed the point of the application entirely. First, Carter reminded Harper, "I do not believe that one's past treatment of colored people is determining. The question is how one stands today." Then Carter revealed the real motives behind the federation's application.

> The National Association of Colored Women is concerned most that women shall have the vote and that the word, women, shall include colored women without question or equivocation. *I would be willing to recommend to our Federation that they withhold their application . . . provided, and provided only, that [NAWSA] or any other organization into which it has been merged shall stand unequivocally for the Susan B. Anthony Amendment as originally drawn,* in which the enforcement of the amendment shall be given to Congress and not to the states, either directly or by concurrent jurisdiction.[21] (Emphasis added.)

The heated exchanges between the NAACP, the NACW, and the White suffragists did nothing if not clarify the latter's position on Black women's enfranchisement. White women simply were willing to let Black women go down the proverbial drain to get the vote for themselves. This became even more evident when, after the exchange of letters, the NAACP asked Carrie Chapman Catt to state plainly NAWSA's position on the Jones amendment. "NAWSA had never endorsed any amendment to the federal constitution which dealt with qualifications of the voter," Catt replied. "It is well understood that that is a question assigned to the states. We stand for the removal of the sex restriction, nothing more, nothing less."[22]

Somewhat earlier, Alice Paul was also asked by the NAACP to clarify her organization's position. In a letter to the NAACP *Branch Bulletin* editor, she stated that the Jones amendment was just a parliamentary procedure and that it in no way changed "the substance of the original amendment." Curiously, however, in a letter written on the same day to the NAACP's board chairman, Mary White Ovington —a White woman—she took a more forthright, and less patronizing position. After gratuitously observing that the Fifteenth Amendment had already settled the race question, she stated:

> The National Woman's Party has only one object—the passage of an amendment to the National Constitution removing the sex qualification from the franchise regulations. We take no stand whatever on any other subject. This amendment to the Constitution would not, of course, interfere with the states making any restrictions they desire on the franchise, provided such restrictions were not forbidden by the National Constitution. All that our amendment would do would be to see that the franchise conditions for every state were the same for women as for men.[23]

The Jones amendment, if not its principle, became academic with the close of the Sixty-fifth Congress. In the next session, the original Anthony Amendment was repassed in the House and, in June 1919, passed by the Senate. The next and no less difficult chapter in the suffrage struggle was set to begin: ratification by two thirds of the states.

Ratification turned out to be a grueling campaign between suffragists and the considerable forces arrayed against them: the liquor lobby, big business, unconvinced women—many of them of the upper middle class—and state legislatures, including a few which had already passed statewide suffrage amendments.

As the battle waged on throughout the country, it came down, finally, to a clincher. One more state was needed to ratify the amendment, and only Tennessee seemed a possibility. By the summer of 1920, every conceivable interest group swooped down on the state. Of course Catt and company were there. Kate Gordon and Laura Clay were there with their familiar Negrophobia litany. Men representing railroad, liquor, and manufacturing interests went to fight against passage. (Although race loomed large in the suffrage struggle, vested interests against Prohibition, and capitalists who were exploiting women workers in southern mills and other places, had their own fears about *any* woman getting the vote.) The drama played out in the legislature was a tense one. Sometimes it looked as if the vote would go one way, and then it started leaning the other way. Bargains were struck, deals made, trade-offs negotiated. But in the end the state legislature was disbanded without resolving the issue. The nation could hardly withstand a deadlock in Tennessee which would make or break woman suffrage, so President Wilson appealed to the state legislature to convene a special session. In the interim, none other than Alice Paul appealed to none other than the NAACP for help.

"You could not find a more impossible time to appeal to anyone interested in the Negro to help women in their fight for suffrage in Tennessee," replied Mary White Ovington to Paul's entreaty. Ovington explained that at the 1920 Republican National Convention, Robert Church, half-brother to Mary Church Terrell and a major political figure in his own right, had been unseated as a delegate. The action against Church was precipitated by Tennessee White women who did not want to sit "with a Negro from their state," Ovington wrote. The behavior of the White women "has ruined any chance for their receiving support from the colored people in the suffrage fight. I know it has been the determined policy of the suffragists to ignore the colored question in the South. The consequence," Ovington concluded, "is such a happening as that at Chicago."[24]

Of course the suffrage Amendment was finally ratified by two thirds of the states, making this country the twenty-second nation to enfranchise women. But Black women understood that for them, the struggle to be able to cast their votes was just beginning—particularly in the South. And they would discover that even *after* women of NAWSA and the Woman's Party had attained their goal, their racism hardly diminished.

Susan B. Anthony had always asserted that when women got the vote, problems, including the race question, would just disappear. But during the years after the Nineteenth Amendment was passed, it was Anthony's Black critics who proved to be correct.

Nevertheless, the early 1920's provided an auspicious beginning for Black women voters. W.E.B. Du Bois observed in *The Crisis* that Black women were registering in large numbers in the South, especially in Georgia and Louisiana. In the former state the number of Black registrants caused State Representative Thomas Bell to predict that the Amendment could destroy White supremacy in his state! His fears were increased when he was informed of the voting registration pattern in Virginia. Bell implored the White women of Georgia to register and counteract the Black vote before it was too late.[25]

But the South was poised, as it had been for Black men, to use any means to neutralize the Black women's vote. Southern Black women encountered particularly intense opposition in Virginia and the Carolinas. In Columbia, South Carolina, they were forced to wait on long lines until White women registered—in one instance for more than twelve hours. In other states, tax and property requirements were imposed on Black women exclusively. White lawyers harassed Black women and gave them "educational tests."

The once-enthusiastic Du Bois declared: "The South proposes to keep colored women from voting in exactly the same way in which it had disenfranchised colored men. Can it do it? Are we going to let it do it?"[26] It wasn't that Black women weren't trying, persisting against tremendous odds. Their efforts inspired a Black female poet with the pen-name Anise to write about the Black women's experience at Jim Crow polls. On the first day that Black women went to the polls, the poem said, they were humiliated and kept in line for hours, "but still the colored women kept on coming!" On the second day they were given exams and disqualified on technicalities, "but the colored women kept on coming!" And then on the third day, the sheriff threatened physical violence, "but the colored women kept on coming!" The poem ends with the "rumors" that the judge was going to throw the women's ballots out.

> For fear those colored women
> Might really come
> To believe
> That representative government
> Exists
> In America![27]

Black women fought the efforts to render their vote meaningless, not only at the polls but through the Suffrage Department of the NAACP and the NACW. In the former, women like Terrell, Addie Hunton, and Verina Morton Jones conducted voter-education programs, documented instances of discrimination, countered false propaganda that Black women were uninterested in voting, and testified before congressional investigating committees. An attempt was also made to engage White suffrage leaders to help eliminate discrimination throughout the South.

The efforts of Black women to put their case before the League of Women Voters (formerly NAWSA) at its national convention in 1921 embroiled the organization in controversy. Southern delegates threatened a walkout. Though Black women were allowed to speak before the convention, little action was subsequently taken by the League. Even this less-than-warm reception was not accorded Black women by the Woman's Party, headed by Alice Paul.

The Woman's Party remained the most vibrant feminist group among White women after the passage of the Nineteenth Amendment. It launched a campaign for an Equal Rights Amendment. The campaign for the ERA, which was opposed by those supporting workingwomen's interests, would be particularly bitter. But the most pressing concern of Black women voters in this period was to gain the support of Paul and the Woman's Party for Black women voters in the South.

Black women knew that Paul's position was that discrimination at the polls was not a "woman's issue" as such but a "race issue," and therefore irrelevant to the Woman's Party. Black women again attempted to put across the idea that issues of race and sex could not be mutually exclusive. The following exchange between Black women attempting to bring the race issue before the Woman's Party national convention in February 1921 and Alice Paul, who attempted to thwart them, illustrates much about the attitudes—and will—of both sides. In late January 1921 the Black women made their first foray. During the Woman's Party's Advisory Council meeting, a motion was made that the party actively lobby to secure an investigation of voting violations. The motion, made by Mrs. W. Spencer Murray, stated:

That this meeting of the Advisory Council recommend to the Convention that a permanent special committee be appointed if the Party reorganizes to bring pressure to bear on Congress for the appointment of a Special Congressional Committee to investigate the violation of the intent and purposes of the Nineteenth Amendment.[28]

The motion, as expected, was defeated. Now Black women began the second stage of their operation to bring the issue before the Convention.

In a letter to A. H. Grimké of the NAACP, Addie Hunton, now field secretary of the organization, revealed the strategy:

Miss Ovington and I have just returned from the meeting in Washington of the Advisory Council of the Woman's Party. . . . The plan agreed upon this morning is as follows: To have this deputation ask for a hearing during the convention and at the same time have groups picketing the convention the entire time it is in session. We feel that this offers a possibility for a very positive challenge to the Woman's Party to uphold the principles upon which it is founded and to give publicity to the wrongs inflicted upon the colored women of the South in the recent election.

Of course we realize that the whole matter would have to be worked out very secretly in order not to spoil the effect of it.[29]

From the following letter, it seems evident that Paul attempted to deflect the impending imbroglio by asking Hallie Q. Brown, a veteran clubwoman, to simply read a resolution on the convention floor. This precipitated Hunton's letter to Brown:

Miss Paul, I fear, is not a bit interested in the question of suffrage as it relates to the colored women, and I am afraid she has given us the opportunity of having you before the Resolution Committee, because she knows that it will be a nice burying ground for anything that we want to do. However, we will have the deputation wait on Miss Paul Saturday morning. I feel confident that you will do whatever you think wise when you come. . . . You can count on me to stand close beside you in any effort you make for the rights of our women.[30]

On the same day, Hunton gave a progress report on the matter to the executive secretary of the NAACP, James Weldon Johnson:

Miss Paul and I had a sharp contest of words . . . when I tried to set an hour for her to receive a delegation of colored women.

... We have the National Woman's Party in a corner. They are talking night and day, I understand, about this onslaught that is to be made upon them by colored women, and are begging off. Personally, I feel merciless and want this to be a success.[31]

Hunton went ahead with her plans. One of the first orders of business was to enter the defeated motion of Mrs. Murray into the minutes of the Advisory Council meeting. Somehow, it had been overlooked. On February 11, the NAACP received a letter from the WP explaining that the motion had been omitted "by error." Next came the confrontation with Paul, and the report of how it went is found in a letter from Hunton to Johnson:

I think I have never been in quite so difficult a position before. ... After ten days of effort, working day and night, sixty women waited on Miss Paul Saturday at 12:30. ... Women came from Brooklyn, New York City, Pittsburgh, Philadelphia, Baltimore, Wilmington, Jersey City, Detroit, Richmond, Falls Church, California, Minnesota, Ohio, Georgia, and ... the District [including] five girls from Howard University and a goodly number from the College Women's Club. Miss Paul, although thoroughly hostile to the delegation, said it was the most intelligent group of women who ever attacked her.[32]

Hunton went on to talk of Paul's hostility and attempt to wear them down by making the Black women wait "until she had time" to see them. After the meeting, Hunton wrote, "we left, with every movie camera in town centered upon us as we went immediately to the Y to plan for future work."

Evidently fearful of the bad impression the Woman's Party was making, a number of the organization's officers came to talk with Hunton, apologized for Paul's behavior, and begged her and the Black delegation not to bring their resolution to the convention floor. The party didn't want to go on record as defeating the Black women's resolution. They attempted to forge a compromise, but Hunton refused.

Although the NAACP leader undoubtedly put on a confident face during the confrontation, she had apprehensions about certain members of her own delegation. Evidently, some of the Black women were kind of a fifth column, and Hunton was afraid they could be manipulated into a compromise. "My greatest fear," she told Johnson, was "that *some more women* might be *bought* by the Party."[33] For that reason she elected to stay and see the matter through, rather than return to New York before the vote.

Hunton's fears were soon allayed, however, as the Black women's resolution was brought up on the floor. It read, in part:

> We have come here as members of various organizations and from different sections representing five million colored women of this country. We are deeply appreciative of the heroic devotion of the National Woman's Party to the Woman's Suffrage Movement and of the tremendous sacrifice made under your leadership in securing the passage of the Nineteenth Amendment. . . .
>
> [Black women] have also come today to call your attention to the flagrant violations of the intent and purposes of the Susan B. Anthony Amendment in the elections of 1920. . . .
>
> Complete evidence of violations of the 19th Amendment could be obtained only by Federal Investigation. There is, however, sufficient evidence available to justify a demand for such an inquiry. . . .
>
> We cannot . . . believe that you will permit this Amendment to be so distorted in its interpretation that it shall lose its full power and effectiveness. Five million women in the United States can not be denied their rights without all the women of the United States feeling the effect of that denial. No women are free until all women are free.
>
> Therefore, we are assembled to ask that you will use your influence to have the convention of the National Woman's Party appoint a Special Committee to ask Congress for an investigation of the violations of the intent and purposes of the Susan B. Anthony Amendment in the elections of 1920.[34]

Needless to say, the resolution was not passed by the convention. But in a letter to a colleague, Maggie L. Walker (who was the first Afro-American woman to be president of a bank), Hunton nevertheless expressed her satisfaction about the outcome. "While we were not successful in getting our resolution accepted by the Convention, we did two important things: First, in succeeding in getting it on the floor of the Convention, which they did not wish to do, and putting them on record as refusing. Second, having a large deputation of colored women prove that they were alert to the situation."[35]

* * *

The experience of Black women in the suffrage movement offered a number of lessons. The foremost perhaps was that if Black women still had any doubt about the wisdom of Frederick Douglass and Frances Ellen Harper concerning sex or race as the more important factor in their struggle, it should have been resolved. Also, although the White suffragists asked them to defer their demand for rights on the grounds of "expediency," it became very clear that they would continue to be discriminated against even after the battle was won. Susan B. Anthony may have been right on many issues, but regarding the coming of the millennium when women got the vote, she was sorely mistaken.

Another lesson was that Black and White women activists, although they shared common goals, would always have a difficult time working together. For as long as the "race problem" existed they would pursue those goals with different purposes, sometimes even cross-purposes, in mind.

Finally, although Black women showed the same enthusiasm as Whites, and even more, for many women's issues, conflicts such as the one detailed above were very discouraging. This was evident when, during the NAACP's effort to recruit women to attend the Woman's Party conference, Mary White Ovington wrote to a longtime Black activist, Coralie Cook, who was a veteran of the Colored Women's League founded in 1892. Cook had been a close friend of Susan B. Anthony's, and at the celebration of Anthony's eightieth birthday spoke in praise of her and of the need for interracial cooperation. But events in later years caused Cook to doubt the efficacy of working with White activists. In her answer to Ovington, Cook wrote:

> I have never been able to join the National Woman's Party. [I am] heartily in sympathy with its object, [but] I do not subscribe to its methods. I regret also to have to say that I am not an "active" suffragist. The old Nat'l W.S.A. of which I was once an ardent supporter and member, turned its back on the woman of color . . . so I have not been "active" although I was born a suffragist.[36]

X

～ A New Era: Toward Interracial Cooperation ～

In the 1920's an activist coterie of southern White women began to understand what many of their peers in other parts of the country had not: the need to ally with Black women activists on issues of common concern. The realization on the White women's part reflected a sea change in racial attitudes within the country—at least among a significant minority. At the end of the war the diehards may have remained firmly attached to racial bitterness, but liberals and social scientists began to talk about interracial cooperation—having, undoubtedly, become more enlightened on racial matters. Nevertheless there was also a more pressing reason to draw out the poison of racial antagonism: the economy. As Ralph Ellison contended: "Social science, under the pressure of war production needs, was devoted to proving that Negroes were not so inferior as a few decades before."[1]

Racism, and the willingness of Blacks to protest against it, did not make for good capitalistic development. In the South, racial antipathy drove the labor force away, endangered property, and encouraged general lawlessness. But after the death of Booker T. Washington in 1915, and the militancy of Blacks after the war, a new means of racial accommodation had to be found. And by 1920 the perceptible presence of a Black middle class provided a vehicle for that accommodation. Now there was a class of educated Negroes whom Whites could talk to, and who, presumably, could represent the race as a whole.

The White advocates of interracial cooperation did not have "integration" in mind, or even "separate but equal." But Blacks, many believed, would have to be more *nearly* equal if race relations were to be ameliorated. Such was the impetus behind the Council for Interracial Cooperation (CIC). Founded in Atlanta in 1920, it was directed by Will Alexander, a Methodist minister with a well-known liberal reputation. Alexander's denomination was as important as his politics. The Southern Methodists, especially their Woman's Home

Missionary Society, had a history of helping Blacks through settlement house projects and aid to Black education. The CIC, amply financed by the Phelps Stokes Fund, the Rosenwald Foundation, the Laura Spellman Memorial Fund, the Carnegie Foundation, and other sources, became the organizational vehicle for a new era of interracial cooperation.

At first there was a reluctance to bring women into the interracial organization. Could southern Black and White women work together? Would the specter of "social intermingling" between White women and Black men sabotage the whole "experiment"? But the exclusion of enfranchised women who had well-heeled associations of their own (especially those within the Methodist organization) could do more harm than good in the long run. The new thrust toward interracial cooperation would have to take women into account.

When Will Alexander told Lugenia Hope of the plan, it couldn't have come at a better time. At the April Black caucus meeting concerning the Y, the women had also discussed the notion that "the time was ripe [to] go beyond the YWCA . . . and reach a few outstanding White and Negro women, Christian and with a well-balanced judgement and not afraid."[2] The CIC, with its principle of cooperation, seemed to be tailor-made for this idea. Black women were even more encouraged by the resolution of the Methodist Women's Missionary Council to create a commission "to study the whole question of race relationships, the needs of Negro women and children, and methods of cooperation by which better conditions can be brought about."[3] In July 1920, Hope arranged for two leaders of the council, Sara Estelle Haskins and Carrie Parks Johnson, to attend the biennial meeting of the NACW at Tuskegee Institute.

As described by historian Jacquelyn Dowd Hall, the meeting was an emotional and dramatic one. Haskins and Johnson got their first surprise at the initial session of the meeting, when they found themselves "treated simply as members of a group rather than as honored white guests."[4] No doubt they were also startled by the thinly veiled distrust of Black women, who had dealt with these southern types before. From the Black women's past experience, White women's concerns about "Negro betterment" sometimes translated only into finding "better" servants. "I am glad you have not any Negro servants," Charlotte Hawkins Brown thought to herself, "and I am not going to help you get any."[5] Finally, Johnson and Haskins experienced what was for them a shock of recognition that "a race has grown up in our very midst that we do not know."[6] Not only were the NACW women just as sophisticated and educated as themselves, but their achievements had surpassed those of the White reformers. "In contrast with white interracial leaders, whose influence was for the most part limited to local communities or channeled through the southern church," Hall wrote, "many of the southern clubwomen present had gained national recognition as members of a rising middle class."[7]

The White and Black women did find a common meeting ground: their religious orientation. It was a prayer session that provided the bridge across a centuries-old racial gap, and Lugenia Burns Hope was the first to traverse it. "We have just emerged from a world war that cost the lives of thousands of our boys fighting to make the world safe for democracy—For whom? . . . Women, we can achieve nothing today unless you . . . who have met us are willing to help us find a place in American life where we can be unashamed and unafraid." By the end of the meeting Carrie Parks Johnson realized that she saw in "the hearts of those Negro women . . . all the aspirations for their homes and their children that I have for mine." For the times, it was quite a revelation. Whites knew only Black servants and the "criminal in the daily papers," Johnson said, "but the masses of the best people of my race do not know the best of the Negro race."[8]

For the Black women's part, they believed that the contribution of women, both Black and White, was essential to racial harmony. In May 1920, Charlotte Hawkins Brown, addressing the (White) North Carolina Federation of Women's Clubs, asserted, "One of the chief causes of unrest in the South today is the attitude of the women of both races towards each other."[9]

The CIC women reformers set out to form their own organization within the CIC, and in October 1920 a South-wide women's conference was planned in Memphis, Tennessee. There, ninety-one women, representing the Protestant denominations, the women's clubs, and the Y, came together. On the program three Black clubwomen—Margaret Murray Washington, Elizabeth Ross Haynes, and Charlotte Hawkins Brown—spoke from their varied perspectives.

Washington spoke of social achievements, especially among the Black rural folk in the South. She talked of Tuskegee's efforts to further the values of an organized family life, such as legal marriages and having children within wedlock. Washington also cited, to the distress of the other Black speakers, the debt of Blacks in the South to southern White women.

Elizabeth Ross Haynes, who was born in Lowndes County, Alabama, to former slaves, in circumstances similar to Washington's, expressed another point of view. Haynes, like Washington, was a graduate of Fisk University. She had gone on to get a graduate degree from Columbia University, had worked with the Women's Bureau of the Department of Labor, and was to become the first elected Black national secretary of the Y. A sociologist herself, she married one of the leading sociologists of the time, George E. Haynes, a founder of the National Urban League. Her address to the conference was low-key, a mixture of the analytical and the dramatic, drawing on the example of Sojourner Truth and the humiliating experiences of living in a segregated society.

But it was Charlotte Hawkins Brown who struck the most responsive chord. Brown's personal history invested almost anything she said with a special drama. Born in Henderson, North Carolina, as one of nineteen children, she moved to Cambridge, Massachusetts, with her mother and siblings after her father deserted the family. She finished high school with little hope for college, until the fateful day she met Alice Freeman Palmer, president of Wellesley College. As the story goes, Brown was walking down the street in Cambridge, pushing a baby carriage with one hand and reading Vergil from the other. The curious image caught the attention of Palmer, who stopped Brown on the street to talk and ended up inviting the young girl to attend Wellesley. Later, with the founding of the Palmer Memorial Institute, the college president proved a valuable friend.

Charlotte Hawkins Brown was a dynamic and cultivated speaker, and very emotional. At the CIC meeting she was even more high-strung than usual. On her way there she had been ordered to ride in a Jim Crow car, and when she refused, she was pulled out of her Pullman berth by White conductors. Brown was allegedly so enraged that when she got to Memphis the Whites postponed her speech to the last day, hoping that by then she would have calmed down. Nevertheless, her speech electrified the audience.

Brown began by explaining to the CIC White women that Margaret Murray Washington represented "the most conservative type of Negro woman." Black women may have been indebted to White southern women, Brown implied, but not quite in the way that Washington had meant. "The Negro women of the South lay everything that happens to the members of her race at the door of the Southern white woman," she said.[10] That responsibility included everything from "racial unrest" to the continuing charges of Black immorality. The failure to address Black women as "Mrs.," for example, implied a lack of respect ordinarily reserved for immoral women. This in turn, said Brown, made Black women vulnerable to sexual exploitation. She ended her speech with a warning steeped in evangelical tones. In the final analysis, she said, the Christian women would reach out for the same hand as she did. But "I know that the dear Lord will not receive it if you are crushing me beneath your feet." In response to her words, the audience rose, bowed their heads, and sang a hymn of Christian fellowship. That fellowship was more difficult to sustain, however, when events took a political turn.

In preparation for the Memphis meeting, Lugenia Burns Hope and her Black allies had prepared a position paper, focusing on the issues they felt the CIC women's group should address. Among those issues were: working conditions for domestic servants, education, the image of Blacks and their coverage in the press, child welfare, Jim Crow seating on public transportation, the right to vote, and lynching. But before Carrie Parks Johnson read the statement to the Memphis conference she altered the Black women's position paper without even consulting them. Johnson omitted suffrage altogether. She excluded the position paper's preamble, which demanded that Black women have "all the privileges and rights granted to American womanhood," and she added to Hope's unequivocal statement against lynching that "any action on the part of Negro men which excites the mob spirit should be condemned."[11]

Though Black delegates were appalled, some seemed willing at first to take the conciliatory approach of Margaret Murray Washington. "Let us stand shoulder to shoulder with the two white women [Carrie Johnson and Sara Haskins] and their followers," Washington counseled. "This Mrs. Johnson, in my mind, is a sincere southern white woman and certainly will need our cooperation and sympathy. . . . We are expected to mark time."[12] However, when Johnson decided to publish the altered statement in a widely disseminated pamphlet, Hope put her foot down. She wrote to the like-minded Charlotte Hawkins Brown: "Mrs. Johnson refuses to . . . believe that we are ready for suffrage and . . . are trained in all activities of American life."[13] Hope demanded that Johnson delay the publication of the paper, then called a Black caucus meeting to solidify their own position on the matter. A series of letters and hard negotiations between the White and Black women followed, and months later a compromise statement was hammered out. Before it was submitted to the Black women for approval, however, Parks announced that no pamphlet would be printed after all. Lugenia Burns Hope must have had a frustrating sense of *déjà vu;* the CIC women were not much better, in the long run, than those of the Y.

Even so, White women were able to take one step further than they had before. Johnson was among the few who broached the issue of the double standard for Black and White men. "The race problem can never be solved as long as the white man goes unpunished, and loses no social standing, while the Negro is burned at the stake," she said.[14] Johnson and others took a stance against the degradation of all women and the lack of respect and protection accorded Black women. But even these statements carried an underlying motive, perceptible in the use of the code words "racial integrity." For many Southern White women, sexual exploitation raised the specter of race amalgamation. Many of them were actually more concerned about maintaining racial purity—on "both sides," as they generously stated—than with the vulnerability of Black women.

This attitude, combined with overt racial slights (the wife of North Carolina's governor once introduced Charlotte Hawkins Brown as a woman fine as her beloved "Negro mammy"), sent the CIC meetings precipitously downhill by the mid-twenties. Even if White women could summon up the courage to take a controversial stand regarding race relations, few would pursue any issue to which "publicity is attached," as Johnson herself admitted.

One reason for Black women's heightened expectations of the White activists was mentioned in Charlotte Hawkins Brown's Memphis speech. Black women seemed to assume that they and the White reformers had the same degree of influence and independence of action regarding the political course of their race. That belief was a theme that would emerge again and again in subsequent years. In an era of interracial cooperation, Blacks saw the refusal of White women to exercise that influence, or even to recognize it, as a bitter bone of contention.

Needless to say, that also included the White women's taking a stand supporting a federal antilynching bill, an issue that would force them to go beyond sympathetic rhetoric.

Antilynching Revisited

The racial atmosphere of the early twenties made it a possible for Blacks to take the initiative on a number of political fronts. The most important was the attempt to get a federal antilynching bill through

Congress. James Weldon Johnson, executive secretary of the NAACP, persuaded Representative L. C. Dyer, whose St. Louis district was predominantly Black, to introduce the bill in 1921. The Dyer bill passed by a two-to-one margin in the House, only to be bottlenecked in the southern-dominated Senate. It was time for a renewed antilynching campaign, this time directed toward federal legislation.

For many reasons, lynching was as much of a women's issue as a Black issue, so it was only appropriate that women, headed by Mary Talbert, an educator and the sixth president of the NACW, should play a leading part. In 1922, Black women organized the Anti-Lynching Crusaders, which would spearhead the effort of the NAACP to enlist 1 million women and raise $1 million.

Within three months the Crusaders grew in number from sixteen volunteers to nine hundred. They assigned directors in each state, and appointed "key" women in towns and cities to act as coordinators. Among those the Crusaders attempted to proselytize were White women. "This is the first time in the history of colored women that they have turned to their sister white organizations and asked for moral and financial support," Talbert emphasized. "We have never failed you in any cause that has come to US, we do not believe that YOU will fail us now."[15] About nine hundred White women reformers did lend their names to the cause, but Black women would soon see that their "sister" organizations could go only so far and no farther. Little substantive support ever materialized for it from White female reformers.

This did not stop the Crusaders' efforts, however. Though they fell short of their fund-raising and numerical goals, they made a credible showing. An NAACP field secretary, William Pickens, characterized the Crusaders' campaign as the greatest effort of Negro womanhood in this generation. Although the ultimate goal of an antilynching bill was not achieved, the publicity and ideas generated by the Black women may have been partly responsible for the decrease in lynchings from 301 between 1919 and 1923 to 100 between 1924 and 1928.

Still, Black women maintained the belief that White female support was needed to erase racism and its violent manifestations. As Charlotte Hawkins Brown had told the White reformers at the CIC conference in Memphis in 1920: "We all feel that you can control your men . . . that so far as lynching is concerned . . . if the white woman would take hold of the situation . . . lynching would be stopped."[16] Before the end of the decade, White women would be nudged once again on this issue by Black reformers.

Though the CIC experience of the early twenties had revealed the limitations of White women reformers, it had also uncovered some disturbing developments in the thinking of Black women reformers. There were signs that some middle-class Black women began perceiving themselves as Whites perceived them: a group distinct from the masses of Blacks whose fate was no longer bound to the poorer classes. Some members of the new generation of Black women leaders ceased to extol, or even defend, their slave history but sought to separate themselves from it. Charlotte Hawkins Brown epitomized this kind of attitude. At an interracial meeting, she criticized Whites who did not differentiate between that "class of women who were prostituted years ago to save the women of the white race" and those, like herself, who had been acculturated "through fifty years of training and service."[17]

Brown was an extreme example of carrying ladyhood to ridiculous lengths. For her, the challenge that "burnt its way into my very soul" was none other than her grandmother's admonition that "if there be anything like a colored lady, I want you to be one." For women like Brown, the underlying reasons for achieving gentility seemed to have little to do with preserving family life or ensuring race progress and survival, as it had in the past. Her motives were more superficial. "The proper grooming, the gentle and cultivated speaking voice, the kindly courteous air," she often said (and taught in her school), "will carry one further than money."

Efforts to erase the past may also have affected Brown's own self-perception. She was proud of her White ancestry, which seemed to include the bloodlines of the Englishman John Hawkins. This did not mean that she wanted to be White, but her views did indicate a certain color-consciousness. When this was combined with her penchant for sharp-tongued barbs against White arrogance, the result could be quite startling. Addressing a White audience at Berea College in Kentucky, Brown once announced that "The Negro did not want to be white," and did not desire intermarriage, because "slavery had produced a sufficient supply of mulattoes for their children's children if they want light-colored mates."[18]

Most significant about this new attitude of some Black leaders was their belief that their role now was merely to "represent" the Black masses, not to work directly with them. Several of the Black participants at the Memphis CIC conference, for example, noted that one reason White women carried such a heavy racial responsibility was because Black leaders themselves had little contact with the masses of Black women. Therefore it was up to Whites who employed them as servants to "uplift" them. This notion represented quite a turnabout from earlier years.

Perhaps this evolution in thinking was partially responsible for a greater tendency of Black CIC reformers to compromise their principles, as illustrated by their even considering the placating attitude of Margaret Murray Washington over the position-paper issue. More revealing: After the matter had been dropped by Carrie Parks Johnson, Black women published the paper through the Southeastern Federation of Colored Women's Clubs—in an altered form. Under the title *Southern Negro Women and Race Co-operation,* the pamphlet retained their position on suffrage but omitted the preamble containing the statement about their rights, and took a more conciliatory stance on lynching![19]

Although the Black reformers believed that such compromises were necessary for progress, the activities of two veteran Black leaders in this period revealed that the World War I years were no time to retreat on racial matters.

In 1921, the year the Dyer antilynching bill was proposed, Mary Church Terrell threatened to resign from the executive board of the International League for Peace and Freedom, headed by Jane Addams. At issue was a petition sponsored by the league, calling for the removal from Germany of Black soldiers, who were alleged to be committing "terrible crimes against German women." The timeworn charge moved Terrell to write a steaming rebuke to Addams.

As a member of a race that had been assaulted by men of all races, Terrell told Addams, she naturally sympathized with the German women. However, she made it plain that she felt a double standard was being imposed in this situation. "Charges are always preferred against soldiers of all races who are quartered in the land they have conquered," Terrell declared, and no evidence existed that Black soldiers were behaving any worse than the Whites. In fact, she informed Addams, a report from Carrie Chapman Catt herself indicated that Blacks "had conducted themselves with more courtesy than the other men stationed abroad." What made Terrell even angrier about such a petition, she told Addams, was that no fuss was made about White soldiers whose recent occupation of Haiti had resulted in the unconscionable slaughter of almost three thousand Haitians—most of them unarmed. As for the Haitian women, not only were there reports of mass rapes, but many had been murdered. This petition asking for the removal of *Black* soldiers from Germany, Terrell concluded, was "a direct appeal to prejudice."[20] She would refuse to sign it, and tendered her resignation from the board.

Also in this period, Ida Wells-Barnett continued her radical, disputatious ways. She had been very busy in the riot-torn postwar years. In 1917 she held a memorial service for nineteen Black soldiers who, for shooting a number of Whites in self-defense, were hanged after a summary court-martial in East St. Louis. Soon afterward, the Secret Service threatened to arrest her for treason if she continued to generate publicity about this issue. If it was "treason" to criticize the government, she told the Secret Service men, "then you will have to make the most of it."[21] Following an East St. Louis riot in which Blacks were arrested, Wells-Barnett's series of articles in *The Chicago Defender* mobilized so much public sentiment that one Black who had been sentenced to life imprisonment was pardoned and several others were released with only partial service of their prison terms. Her protests and firsthand investigations of the Arkansas riot of 1917—where hundreds of Blacks had been jailed, tortured, and many murdered by vigilantes—were largely responsible for the Supreme Court decision to free the prisoners after years on death row. During the bloody Chicago riot in 1919 she organized a Protective Association for Black citizens. In the same year she was chosen to represent Marcus Garvey's UNIA at the Paris Peace Conference.

By 1924, Ida Wells-Barnett had managed to run afoul of almost everyone with her strident independence and refusal to compromise her principles. The list included: Frances Willard, Booker T. Washington and his wife, Mary Church Terrell, and the United States Secret Service, which, in an intelligence report on Marcus Garvey, mentioned that his association with her was evidence of *his* radicalism.

It even included Du Bois and the NAACP. When she heard the weak antilynching plank proposed at the NAACP's founding meeting, she was said to have stood up and declared: "Our White friends have betrayed us again!" Previously she had criticized Du Bois, the only Black at the preliminary meetings, for dropping her name from the list of the organization's founding forty members. Her name was eventually restored to the list, but Wells-Barnett and the NAACP leadership remained quarrelsome bedfellows. In her autobiography, Wells-Barnett stated that keeping Mary White Ovington as chairman of the executive committee had a deleterious effect on the organization. "She has basked in the sunlight of the adoration of the few college-bred Negroes who have surrounded her," Wells-Barnett charged, "but has made little effort to know the soul of the Black woman; and to that extent she has fallen far short of helping a race which has suffered as no white woman has ever been called upon to suffer or to understand."[22]

And she must have been less than happy at the drift of many of the NACW leaders in the twenties. In 1924 she ran for president of the NACW in an attempt to resuscitate the dynamism of past years. But she had made too many enemies along the way, and lost the election to a woman who was as diplomatic as Wells-Barnett was uncompromising. The victory of Wells-Barnett's opponent, Mary McLeod Bethune, would have a tremendous impact on women's organizations in the future. Wells-Barnett would go on to run, unsuccessfully, for a state senate seat in Illinois as an independent in 1928. Three years later, at the age of sixty-four, she would be dead. Although the course of her life had brought her virtually no close friends —and many enemies—a eulogy in the NACW publication showed that she was both understood and respected by her peers: "She was often criticized, misjudged, and misunderstood," because she fought for justice, the eulogy said, "as God gave her vision."[23]

XI

~ A Search for Self ~

As Afro-Americans discovered in the years following World War I, the goal of social equality evokes more questions than answers. What should *equality* mean? The right to acculturate into American society? Or the right to express one's own distinct cultural values without being penalized for it? The questions brought the "two-ness" or "double-consciousness" dilemma that Du Bois wrote about in *Souls of Black Folk* into sharp relief. Blacks found postwar America a hall of mirrors, where they saw their reflection first from one angle, then from another.

The image of Afro-American women was refracted by two developments in the period: the rise and subsequent decline of Black militancy, and the decline of feminist consciousness after passage of the Nineteenth Amendment gave women the right to vote. In the twenties, two major issues were being promoted by White feminists: the passage of an Equal Rights Amendment which would eliminate protective legislation for women; and the birth control movement which, though legalizing contraception in this country, and launched with the idea of eradicating poverty, degenerated into a campaign to "keep the unfit from reproducing themselves with all its Social Darwinist implications."[1] Both were anathema to the interests of Black women. In any case, for them, racial concerns overwhelmed those of sex.

This was evident in an essay by Elise McDougald, when she wrote that Black women's "feminist efforts are directed chiefly toward the realization of the equality of the races, the sex struggle assuming a subordinate place."[2] Her statement is reminiscent of Frances Ellen Harper's more than half a century earlier. Both women made their pronouncements in periods of heightened militancy, when race overshadows sex as the more important issue. Black women were concentrating their activist energies in the antilynching campaign, which this time was being directed by the male-led NAACP. In fact, since World

War I most initiatives had been spearheaded by men—and women welcomed the development. A letter to *The Crisis,* the magazine of the NAACP, revealed the pride a Black woman felt when Black men fought back in the racial riots of 1919.

> The Washington riot gave me the thrill that comes once in a lifetime. . . . At last our men had stood like men, struck back, were no longer dumb driven cattle. When I could no longer read for my streaming tears, I stood up, alone in my room, held my hands high over my head and exclaimed aloud: "Oh I thank God, thank God!"
>
> . . . a woman loves a strong man, she delights to feel that her man can protect her, fight for her if necessary, save her. . . . Some of us have been thinking our men cowards, but thank God for Washington colored men! . . . They put new hope, a new vision into their despairing women.
>
> God grant that our men everywhere refrain from strife, provoke no quarrel, but that they protect their women and homes at any cost.[3]

Black militancy was also demonstrated by male intolerance of traditional views accorded to Black women. Still extant were the "grotesque Aunt Jemimas of the streetcar advertisements that proclaimed only an ability to serve," Elise McDougald wrote. But demand for absolute social equality, as *The Messenger* had announced, included dispelling that image. This was vividly illustrated when the Daughters of the Confederacy publicized their request to Congress to erect a statue in Washington, D.C., in memory of "Black Mammies." To this rather untimely suggestion Chandler Owen, co-editor of *The Messenger,* angrily responded:

> We favor erecting a monument to the Negro women who have risen above insult, assault, debauchery, prostitution, and abuse *to which these unfortunate "black mammies" were subjected.* . . . Let this "mammy" statue go. Let it fade away. . . . Let its white shaft point like a lofty mountain peak to a *New Negro mother,* no longer a *"white man's woman,"* no longer the sex-enslaved *"black mammy"* of Dixie—but the apotheosis of triumphant Negro womanhood.[4]

In this period Black women would be appreciated not only for their strengths but for their feminine attributes as well.

Femininity, not feminism, was the talk of the twenties. *Feminism* had "even become a term of opprobrium among the young women, conjuring up images of aggressive, man-hating frumps in nondescript tweeds," as one commentator put it.[5] The marriage rate shot up, the number of professional women went down, and sexual freedom was a subject of greater concern than sexual liberation.

The emphasis was on glamour, so much so that it was this decade that "put a beauty parlor in nearly every small town, saw cosmetics grow from a minor business into one with a turnover worth $500 million a year, and created a whole new career for young women, that of the beautician," wrote Geoffrey Perrett.[6]

Particularly in the cities, Black women embraced the beauty ethos of the times. It must have been exhilarating to display their "multiformed charms," in McDougald's phrase, to break out of the hard-edged chrysalis of a stereotyped past. Both men and women celebrated the transformation from drudge to butterfly—in all its variations. McDougald wrote about the "colorful pageant of individuals" in Harlem, "each differently endowed . . . with traces of the race's history left in physical and mental outline on each."[7] All the major periodicals, including *Opportunity, The Crisis,* and *The Messenger,* featured attractive Black women on their covers. The January 1924 issue of *The Messenger* reflected the general thinking when it announced that from then on it would "show in pictures as well as writing, Negro women who are unique, accomplished, beautiful, intelligent, industrious, talented and successful."

The eclipse of Victorian standards in the era also encouraged men to appreciate, and respect, a wider spectrum of women. In their verse and fiction Black men touted Black women from all walks of life —from the dignified matron to the prostitute who possessed *inner* beauty and innocence, noted cultural historian Jervis Anderson.[8] Novels like Jean Toomer's *Cane* described all kinds of women with poetic rapture. His and other works likened feminine beauty to the ultimate pleasures of the senses. Complexions were compared to ginger, honey, cinnamon, dusky sunsets, and the like. No wonder that Black women wanted to fill Black men's eyes with their beauty.

They also celebrated their men's celebration of them. The young poet Helene Johnson wrote contemporary-sounding verses, like: "Gee, Brown boy / I loves you all over," and "Take my hand and I will read you poetry, / Chromatic words, / Seraphic symphonies, / Fill up your throat with laughter and your heart with song."[9]

Even such simple mutual rapture has its complicated side for a people seeking to strike a balance between two opposing cultures. That many of the products used by Black women to enhance their beauty were skin lighteners and hair straighteners drew comment on the irony of wanting to approximate White standards of beauty in such a race-conscious era. Nannie Helen Burroughs continued to put down such tendencies; Amy Jacques Garvey, wife of Marcus Garvey, believed that the glamour fad was dangerously imitative of a White society in the process of decay. Even *The New York Times,* reporting on the use of such products as "Black-No-More," questioned the sincerity of racial pride and concluded that Blacks were really ashamed of their race.

There is little question that a color-consciousness of the self-hate variety was at work here. But it wasn't the only thing at work. Because of historical circumstances as much as attitude, fair complexions were associated with the upper classes. Blacks with White forebears usually had more educational and economic opportunities, were more easily accepted, and thus made up a disproportionate number of achievers. Of the 131 men and 8 women listed in W.E.B. Du Bois's *Who's Who of Colored Americans,* published in 1916, for example, 124 of the men and all of the women were of mixed heritage.

In any case, the color question wasn't as simple as it appeared on the surface. Women featured on the magazine covers were of all hues, although most had Anglicized features. And some of the comments of *Half-Century* magazine revealed interesting variations on the "Black is beautiful" theme. Subtitled "A Colored Magazine for the Home and Homemaker," *Half-Century* was probably the most "bourgeois" and glamour-conscious of all the publications. Even so, its editors seemed to recognize that Black beauty did not have to correspond with conventional standards. "Don't hesitate to send in your picture because you don't consider yourself unusually good-looking," the magazine counseled in its September 1921 edition. "There are many types of colored beauty. Not all of them appeal to every individual."

At the same time, *Half-Century* editorialized that brown skin was not only more beautiful to them but, if the truth be told, more appealing to Whites as well. In the spring of 1922 it took note of the numbers of European women taking henna baths in Europe to darken their skin. "Whiteness to them is monotonous," the magazine concluded. "Blondes were only admired because of their rarity. A beautiful brown face in an assembly of white ones could not but attract attention."

Actually, many of the products that flooded the Black market were designed not really to lighten the complexion but rather to clear dark discolorations of the skin. Jervis Anderson points out that several of them, like the popular Wonder Creme, were really cold creams, the same sort of product that White women used. Though products promising to approximate Caucasian standards of beauty were in wide use, their application carried a certain note of defiance—if a sometimes misdirected one. Following reports that a Black woman had died after using a bleach manufactured by a White company, *Half-Century* magazine told its readers to buy only from Black companies. Whites, it declared, not only didn't care about Black people, but could even be malicious. "They do not wish us to be beautiful and fair," it said in its December 1921 issue. "They do not wish our women to rival their beauty, color, or texture of skin and hair."

Madame Walker

For many Black women, problems with their hair were likened to a crown of thorns. The concern about hair was responsible for the rise of one of the most riveting figures of the period: Madame C. J. Walker.

Born Sarah Breedlove in Louisiana's Delta, in 1867, to former slaves, Walker was orphaned at five, married at fourteen, a mother by twenty, and a widow soon after. She supported herself and her daughter, A'Lelia, by working as a washerwoman in Louisiana, in Vicksburg, Mississippi, and subsequently in St. Louis, Missouri. The force of Walker's determination not to spend her life as washerwoman for wealthy Whites and, in addition, to do something about her own hair (which was falling out), resulted in a dream that served a dual purpose. According to Walker, she had a vision of an old man who told her "what to mix up for my hair." She sent for the products, some of which were from Africa, and tried the formula on herself. In a few weeks, she recalled, "My hair was coming in faster than it had ever fallen out. I tried it on my friends; it helped them. I made up my mind that I would begin to sell it."[10]

Though she began by offering her formula door to door, Walker understood that that was not the way fortunes were made. She established a chain of beauty parlors throughout the country, the Caribbean, and South America. She had her own factories and laboratories, said to be the most advanced of their kind. Walker set up training schools in hair culture, and employed Black woman agents to sell the products—including hair growers, salves for psoriasis, and oils—on a commission basis. By 1910 the Walker company had employed some five thousand Black female agents around the world, and averaged revenues of about $1,000 a day, seven days a week.[11] The effectiveness of her product, her indefatigable energy, and her uncanny talent for business made Madame C. J. Walker the first Black woman millionaire. Although she did not deny herself the luxuries such wealth could bring—an electric car, a thirty-four-room custom-built mansion, and exquisitely appointed adjoining Harlem brownstones—she was also known for her generous contributions to Black educational and welfare institutions, especially those that directly benefited women. Upon her death in 1919, her will stipulated that two thirds of her fortune go to various charities, and that her company always be controlled by a woman.

On the surface, Walker's success could be attributed (and was by some) to her clients' desire for straight, Caucasian-type hair. Although Walker's treatments included the use of the hot comb—a European invention which she redesigned for Black women's hair—imitating White women was not the key to her achievement. "Many people have referred to Madame Walker's representatives as 'hair straighteners.' This is however a grave error. They are not 'hair straighteners' but hair culturists and scalp specialists." The observation was made in 1918 by none other than George Schuyler, well known for his scathing parodies of Blacks who wanted to be White.

In a number of interviews, Walker herself denied that the ultimate purpose of her product was to straighten the hair. Her concern was for Black women who had problems with hair and scalp—which tend to be drier than those of Caucasians. If left alone, the dryness of the scalp caused skin problems and hair breakage. The greatest attraction of Walker's product was that it made the scalp healthier. Her "system of growing hair is conducive to a natural growth and consists of dressing the hair to bring out its fine natural texture," Schuyler commented.[12]

This was consistent with Madame Walker's own view of why her business was so successful. Her company's 1924 yearbook and almanac noted that Walker's product "cured scalps when they were in a frightful condition." Consequently, "many persons who had less than a finger's length of hair when they began using it, their hair grew sixteen inches in less than three years." And finally, Walker's preparation "improved the scalps of persons . . . whose hair was short and stubby all their lives."[13]

For many women, especially those with tightly kinked hair (which always tends to be drier), Walker's preparation was the first they had used that actually had curative powers. This would be particularly important for women who were not of "mixed ancestry." Schuyler concluded:

> What a boon it was for one of their own race to stand upon the pinnacle and exhort the womanhood of her race to come forth, lift up their heads and beautify and improve their looks. . . . The psychological effect of Madame Walker's great activity has been of great importance and can hardly be overestimated. Besides giving dignified employment to thousands of women who would otherwise have had to make their living in domestic service, she stimulated a great deal of interest generally in the care of the hair.[14]

One could safely assume not only that Madame Walker was directly responsible for employing so many women, but that her treatment also helped others get jobs as a result of their improved appearance.

Of course, women's reasons for "beautifying" themselves were not necessarily any deeper than just wanting to look good. Black women were no different from other women in their concern about their looks, or in wanting an opportunity to approximate the glamorous feminine images they had seen and read about. And the hard fact of it was that one had a better chance of meeting the "right" man, and of marrying one of good standing, when one looked attractive. The very small leisure group of women in Harlem, "the wives and daughters of men who are in business, in the professions and in a few well-paid personal service occupations," as McDougald observed, ". . . is picked for outward beauty by Negro men with much the same feelings as other Americans of the same economic class."[15]

Nevertheless there were many questions still to be answered. Afro-Americans may have come to some consensus about their physical selves, but the deeper questions of identity still remained. In a way the answer was even more elusive in a time when Victorian morality was on the wane, when cultural relativism said everybody was all right, when the "simplicity" and the *"joie de vivre"* of Black folk were extolled.

"How grand it was to be valued not for what one might become . . . but for what was thought to be one's essential self," remarked Nathaniel Huggins in *The Harlem Renaissance.* Although most agreed with novelist and *Crisis* literary editor Jessie Fauset that Blacks should develop a racial pride that would enable them "to find our own beautiful and praiseworthy selves, an intense chauvinism that is content with its own types,"[16] there was less consensus on which of those selves or types should be displayed to the rest of the world. Blacks didn't have the luxury of broadcasting more than one message to White society. So what should it be? That given the same opportunities, Afro-Americans were no different from Whites? Or should Black Americans celebrate their differences—differences derived from a vibrant folk culture and African heritage? Or, perhaps, there was something in between the two extremes? Should Blacks explore the interior of their "Afro-Americanness," a melange of two cultures?

It was particularly important that Black women answer the questions, for their image affected how they were perceived—and treated —by the society and by their men. In artistic terms, the cultural renaissance of the twenties offered a whole range of choices. There were the sensually hard-driving blues of Bessie Smith and the fine operatic arias of Caterina Jarboro. There were the sanguine portraits of Laura Wheeler Waring and the "street urchins" of sculptor Augusta Savage. On stage were the exotic excitement of Josephine Baker and the classical concert dance of Edna Guy. In fiction three women writers asked themselves where the essence of their identity as Blacks and as women lay—and arrived at three different answers.

Jessie Fauset, who wrote four novels between 1924 and 1933, shared the perspective of the second generation of clubwomen. Born to a prominent Philadelphia family in 1885, educated at Cornell, the University of Pennsylvania, and the Sorbonne, she believed in emphasizing the ability of Blacks to become a part of (upper-class) American society. This theme is evident in the introduction to her second novel, *The Chinaberry Tree:* "It seems strange," she wrote, "to affirm as news for many that there is in America a great group of Negroes of education and substance who are living lives of genteel interests and pursuits." Fauset's object was to spread that news, to record "a class in order to praise a race," in the words of critic Sterling Brown.[17] Her characters belong to well-to-do families who are concerned about race but at the same time yearn to transcend its limitations. A passage in *There Is Confusion,* her first novel, is illustrative. When a friend exhorts her to "build up *Negro* art," the protagonist, Joanna Marshall, replies: "Why I am . . . You don't think I want to forsake *us* . . . not at all. But I want to show us to the world. I am colored of course, but American first. Why shouldn't I speak to all America?"[18] Joanna Marshall is determined to be successful, and to make her fiancé successful as well. When he becomes discouraged by discrimination, Marshall tells him not to let the petty prejudices of Whites get in the way. For she believes that if one keeps on trying, and is well prepared to meet the world head on, the "confusion" of racism can be transcended.

Nella Larsen's protagonists are far less sure of themselves. Larsen, born in 1893 to a Danish mother and a Black father from the Virgin Islands, wrote two novels in the late twenties: *Quicksand* (1928) and *Passing* (1929). The life of Helga Crane, the protagonist in her earlier and more intriguing novel, seems to reflect much of Larsen's own. The exploration of Crane's interior search for identity creates—with the possible exception of the character Kabnis in Jean Toomer's *Cane*—"the most intriguing and complex character in Renaissance fiction," according to critic Arthur P. Davis.[19]

Helga, the product of an interracial liaison, was born out of wedlock. The circumstances of her birth present a double-edged identity crisis. Where does she belong? The novel opens with her working at a Tuskegee-like institution in the South. She is repulsed by the social and cultural limitations intrinsic to the school's philosophy, yet feels that her own "illegitimate" origins belie her pretensions to the life of an acculturated "lady" like Joanna Marshall. She leaves the South to visit White relatives in Chicago. Embarrassed by her dark presence, they spurn her—but give her money to visit her Danish kin in Denmark.

In Scandinavia she is received warmly and becomes popular in social circles. One of the country's leading artists even proposes to her. But Helga soon realizes that rather than being appreciated for herself, she is seen as an exotic sensual curio because of her Black ancestry. This makes her yearn to be among her own people again, and she returns to Harlem.

But are they really her people? She feels alienated even from "Negro society," which, while professing racial pride and disdain for Whites, still imitates White values. She is left cold and unfulfilled by the Black bourgeoisie, and when the man she loves marries a woman of that social set, Helga is plunged into despair. Still searching for her place, she goes to a fundamentalist Black church where she is swept by the tide of unsuppressed emotion and libidinal release. She meets the rural Black minister who has tapped these primordial feelings within her and, concluding there is no place else for her, consents to marry him and live in a southern rural community. The book, one of the few by a Black woman that confronts the sexual implications in the search for identity, ends with Helga trapped by the provinciality of the town, her husband, and yearly pregnancies. When she finally decides to try to escape her fate, she discovers that she is pregnant with her fifth child.

There is a part of Helga in all of the worlds she has confronted, but she belongs to none of them. And the reader assumes that she will live the rest of her life in mental anguish.

If Fauset emphasized the universality of Blacks, and Larsen the tragedy of their double consciousness, Zora Neale Hurston plunged her characters into the unselfconscious world of Black rural folk. Born in the all-Black town of Eatonville, Florida, educated at Howard University and Columbia—where she studied under the anthropologist Franz Boas—Hurston wrote about a world of juke joints and folkways, fundamentalist religion and human frailty. She wrote three novels between 1934 and 1948 which, though dated after the Renaissance period, shared that era's ethos. Her most famous novel, *Their Eyes Were Watching God,* explores the search for identity of its protagonist, Janie. In a rural Florida town reminiscent of Eatonville, Janie's circumstances couldn't be more different from those of Joanna Marshall.

Reared by her grandmother, who is fearful of her granddaughter's fate when she can no longer protect her, Janie is forced to marry an aging, domineering farmer. Though he offers Janie security, he attempts to suppress the spirit within her—a spirit that conveys the possibility of a better future than as the beleaguered wife of a man trapped in the soil. That possibility becomes embodied in Joe Starks, a man of vitality and vision who is determined to create a bona fide town out of a settlement on the coast of Florida. She runs away with Starks and marries him. But Janie becomes more and more dissatisfied with the marriage when Joe becomes mayor of his town. He wants to put Janie on a pedestal, isolated and "above" the rest of the community, a role he feels appropriate for the "Mayor's wife." Suffocating under his demands, she engages in a bitter test of wills with him until his death years later. It is only when she meets Tea Cake, a man many years younger than she, that Janie feels her "soul crawl out of its hiding place." Though her friends are surprised that she would take up with a man who seems to have little to offer, Janie finds in Tea Cake someone who loves her for herself, not for what she represents to him. This is more important than material security or social status, for it allows her sense of self to be freed at last. Her identity is finally able to take shape, critic Mary Helen Washington observed, because she is able to "throw off the false images which have been thrust upon her."[20]

Hurston's work was controversial because she neither romanticized Black folk life nor condemned it, thus falling between two schools of cultural thought. But *Their Eyes Were Watching God* was one of the purest pieces of fiction published in the period because of its lack of self-consciousness. It was also the most feminist novel. The key to both the novel's integrity and its woman-centeredness was the protagonist's search for identity through her relationship with the Black community rather than White society.[21]

By the late twenties, when militancy was on the wane, Hurston's perspective began to permeate the political thinking of Black women. It is at such times that Black feminism is vented full force—as was evidenced by the developments within the most radical Black organization of the period, The Universal Negro Improvement Association, led by Marcus Garvey.

During the heyday of the Garvey movement, the charismatic leader had captured the imagination of working-class Blacks whom he invested with a sense of self-worth, racial dignity, and a dream of a new society in Africa. Garvey understood the needs of the dispossessed—and their attraction to pomp and pageantry. His followers donned plumed hats, marched in street parades replete with martial bands, received medals and titles of nobility. His African Orthodox Church featured icons of a Virgin Mother who was black—and a Satan who was white.

From the beginning of the UNIA, women were an integral part of the organization. Its constitution guaranteed women's rights; there were Black Cross Nurses, "Lady Presidents" who headed women's auxiliaries, and influential female national officers. A few, like Henrietta Vinton Davis and M.L.T. DeMena wielded much authority as international officers; Davis was a director of the UNIA's Black Star Shipping Company and secretary general of the organization. Amy

Jacques Garvey, second wife of the leader, was also active in the organization. While she held no specific office, it would have been hard to find anyone with greater influence in the UNIA, save for Marcus Garvey himself. Among her myriad activities was the editorship of the Women's Page in the UNIA newspaper, *Negro World.*

Amy Jacques Garvey's views were surprisingly close to those of clubwomen who emerged at the turn of the century, though the movements they represented could not have had less in common. The UNIA was a grass-roots organization which drew working-class Blacks into its ranks. It had a reputation for looking askance at lightskinned Negroes and spurned integration and its advocates. Amy Jacques Garvey's columns praised socialist movements throughout the world, especially as they affected the development of women. Yet she shared an intraracial point of view with the first generation of clubwomen, a common perspective despite political differences. For example, Amy Jacques Garvey believed that women were a "humanizing" force and "the center of the present and future of civilization."[22] She asked Black women to contribute their ideas to her column so that they could show "the world the worth and ability of Negro women, and gain the appreciation of our own men whose lives are guided by our influences and who get inspiration from us."[23]

For Amy Jacques Garvey the "New Negro Woman" was very much the same as the old one. She was to: "(1) Work on a par with men in the office and the platform; (2) Practice thrift and economy; (3) Teach constructive race doctrine to children; (4) Demand absolute respect of the race from all men; (5) Teach the young to love race first."[24]

As earlier Black women activists had discovered, such ideas bring out an inherent feminism. It was again true in the mid-twenties, when the UNIA began to fall apart and frustrated men felt more secure if women were kept in their place. At a UNIA convention in this period, M.L.T. DeMena complained: "Women were given to understand that they were to remain in their places, which meant nothing more than a Black Cross Nurse or a general secretary of a division."[25] But it was Amy Jacques Garvey who delivered the most scathing criticism:

> If the United States Senate and Congress can open their doors to White women, we serve notice on our men that Negro women will demand equal opportunity to fill any position in the Universal Negro Improvement Association or anywhere else without

discrimination because of sex. We are very sorry if it hurts your old-fashioned tyrannical feelings, and we not only make the demand but we intend to enforce it.[26]

If there was any doubt as to Amy Jacques's militant feminism, it was erased by another editorial which had echoes not only of the clubwomen's impatience, but also of a speech that Maria Stewart had delivered almost a century before. Castigating the "cowardice" and "want of energy" of the free Black population in Boston, Stewart concluded, "It is of no use for us to wait any longer for a generation of well educated men to arise. We have slumbered and slept too long already."[27] In 1925, when the UNIA's militancy began to wane, Amy Jacques Garvey warned:

> We are tired of hearing Negro men say, "There is a better day coming" while they do nothing to usher in the day. We are becoming so impatient that we are getting in the front ranks and serve notice that we will brush aside the halting, cowardly Negro leaders, and with prayer on our lips and arms prepared for any fray, we will press on and on until victory is ours.
>
> Africa must be for Africans, and Negroes everywhere must be independent, God being our helper and guide. Mr. Black Man watch your step! Ethiopia's queens will reign again and her Amazons protect her shores and people. Strengthen your shaking knees and move forward, or we will displace you and lead on to victory and glory.[28]

On the social and economic fronts, women were becoming restive too—despite the acclamation of men. "Yes, she has arrived," proclaimed *The Messenger* in 1923:

> Like her white sister she is the product of profound and vital changes in our economic mechanism . . . the New Negro woman has affected a revolutionary orientation. . . . Upon her shoulder rests the big task to create and keep alive, in the breast of Black men, a holy and consuming passion to break with the slave traditions of the past to . . . overcome the . . . insidious inferiority complex of the present which . . . bobs up . . . to arrest the progress of the New Manhood Movement.[29]

But by mid-decade the New Negro Manhood Movement had declined and the New Negro Woman found herself confronted with age-old problems. Though her "white sisters" were spurning the professions and education, discrimination against Black women continued to propel them forward. By 1921 the first Ph.D.'s were conferred upon Black women: Sadie T.M. Alexander (University of Pennsylvania), Georgianna Rosa Simpson (University of Chicago), and Eva B. Dykes (Radcliffe College). In 1920 two out of every ten graduates from Black universities were women, and the trend was upward. The problems between Black men and women, rooted in their different attainment levels, were aggravated. Elise McDougald commented: "The growing independence of Negro working women is causing her to rebel against the domineering attitude of the cruder working-class Negro man." Although McDougald held out hope that younger generations of Black men would be more progressive, she observed that "conditions change slowly. Working mothers are unable to instill different ideals in their sons. True sex equality," she concluded, "has not been approximated."[30]

In 1920, the percentage of Black women working was 38.9, compared to 17.2 percent of White women. By the mid-twenties it was increasingly clear that Black women of virtually every class would have to continue working. But many, especially in nonprofessional jobs, had yet to see work as a lifetime commitment. This was especially true of Black mothers, who left their jobs, when possible, to take care of their children. Such Black intellectuals as Sadie T.M. Alexander, the first Black woman to serve as city solicitor of Philadelphia, understood that such an attitude would keep Black women—who needed jobs more than anyone—on the fringes of industry. Black women, Alexander noted in 1930, "are constantly expecting when children get out of the way, or their husbands obtain better jobs, that they will stop work."[31] Consequently, women were less tenacious of their jobs, particularly low-status ones. But Alexander counseled women to hang on to them, even if they were working on a low entry level. Eventually, she felt, they would get better jobs, if only because employers did not want to lose their investment in longtime workers.

Alexander believed that women should work not only because of immediate needs but for their future well-being. In an increasingly industrialized society, where the work of the housewife was rated by men as "valueless consumption," she wrote that women had to "place themselves again among the producers of the world," and be involved in work "that resulted in the production of goods that have a price value." In this way women would both meet the challenge of the new economy and be happier in their marital relations. "The satisfaction which comes to the woman in realizing that she is a producer makes for peace and happiness, the chief requisites in any home," Alexander concluded.[32] Just as forward-thinking was Alexander's view about a woman's working if she had children: "The derogatory effects of the mother being out of the home are overbalanced by the increased family income, which makes possible the securing of at least the necessities of life, and perhaps a few luxuries."[33]

No matter how she characterized it, the Black woman's response to her historical circumstances made a certain feminist sensibility inevitable. In 1924, W.E.B. Du Bois concluded: "Negro women more than the women of any other group in America are the protagonists in the fight for an economically independent womanhood in modern countries. . . . The matter of economic independence is, of course, the central fact in the struggle of women for equality."[34]

Du Bois, however, also understood the harsh price paid for women's economic independence in a society whose "ideal harks back to the sheltered harem with the mother emerging at first as nurse and homemaker, while the man remains the sole breadwinner."[35] What is the inevitable result of the clash of such ideals? he asked in 1920. "Broken families," he concluded. Nevertheless, Du Bois felt, as many Black women did in the 1920's, that "we cannot abolish the new economic freedom of women";[36] and that "the future woman must have a life work and economic independence."[37] No woman would better personify or work more vigorously toward those goals than Mary McLeod Bethune, whose presence would dominate Black women's history in the decades to come.

XII

~ Enter Mary McLeod Bethune ~

In 1927, Mary McLeod Bethune was aboard an ocean liner bound for Europe. At the age of fifty-two she was about to take her first trip outside of the country, and one of the few vacations in her entire life. Friends who felt she needed the well-deserved rest had contributed money toward her expenses. After the excited farewells at the pier, Bethune had little to distract her except the limitless rim of the ocean. For perhaps the first time in her adult life, she had the time to sit down and just think—about the future, about the hard-earned achievements of her past. On the edge of the Depression, Bethune would begin to draw on her own history to outline the future direction of Blacks, and Black women.

Her history was one of almost ceaseless activity—and responsibility—over the last half century. Born in Mayesville, South Carolina, she was the fifteenth of the McLeods' seventeen children to be born and the one chosen to go to school and teach the others the three *R*'s. With the aid of a determined mother, a keen mind, and timely scholarships, Bethune attended Scotia Seminary and the Moody Bible Institute. Subsequently she taught at Kindell Institute, a mission school; Lucy C. Laney's Haines Institute; and the Presbyterian Mission School in Florida, where she served as director. By the time she had moved to Florida she was married and had had a child, Albertus.

The idea of "mission" had imbued Bethune's early thinking. Since leaving school she had professed a desire to do missionary work in Africa. The desire was inspired both by religion and by a special feeling regarding her heritage: She had often expressed pride that pure African blood flowed in her veins and that her mother had come from a matriarchal tribe and royal African ancestry.

After a number of unsuccessful attempts to go to Africa, however, it dawned on Mary McLeod Bethune that her primary mission was in America. Further inspired by the growing number of Blacks going to Florida during the migration, Bethune decided to concentrate her energies on establishing a school for girls in Daytona. Only the sheerest faith could have convinced her that $1.50, the total amount of her investment capital, would suffice to start a school. The money was used as a down payment on a former garbage-dump site; the rest of the money was raised first by selling pies and cakes, and later by pleading her case for the school to philanthropists, industrialists, and the National Association of Colored Women.

It was during one of her fund-raising trips in the Northeast that she decided to make a detour to attend the 1909 NACW conference in Hampton, Virginia. Bethune asked for permission to address the group, and if she felt self-conscious about coming from a less privileged background than most of the delegates, or by her dark skin and Negroid features, she certainly didn't show it. Bethune spoke with such impassioned eloquence that at the end of her speech Margaret Murray Washington offered to take up a collection for the school. Madame C. J. Walker volunteered to help direct a fund-raising campaign, and Mary Church Terrell prophesied that Bethune would someday head the organization.

By 1924, Terrell's prediction had proven correct. Bethune, who had joined the NACW and subsequently headed the Southeastern Federation of Women's Clubs—one of the most active in the club movement—beat out Ida Wells-Barnett in the election for the NACW presidency. As president, she honed her natural talents for organizational leadership. Bethune knew how to cajole, praise, apply the right pressure here and there, to move toward a group consensus. Unlike Wells-Barnett, who would undoubtedly have attempted to push the organization in a more radical direction, Bethune brought to the NACW the same philosophy that had traditionally sparked its activism. "Our field is no longer circumscribed," she announced in one of her first statements as president, "and the quality of our service is still distinctly our own." With "minds and souls, chastened and refined by a forbearance born of the pain and turmoil which have been the burden and glory of our sex," Bethune believed, Black women were to carry "the steadying, uplifting and cleansing influence" to the struggle.[1]

Under her administration the NACW's programs also reflected the developments of the period: the federal antilynching bill, help for rural women and those in industry, the training of clerks and typists, and the status of women in the Philippines, Puerto Rico, Haiti, and

Africa. Bethune's most tangible accomplishment as president was initiating a successful drive for funds to purchase the NACW's first national headquarters in Washington, D.C. Of course the achievement was a high point in the organization's history, but in the long run the NACW would never fully recover from the depletion of energy and resources expended in the campaign.

But in 1927 it was not her tenure as NACW president that was foremost in her mind. Assessing her achievements and those of other Black women, Bethune believed that the founding of schools was the most significant.

In 1915 the first class of five students graduated from Daytona School for Girls, and by the time Bethune was on her way to Europe, the school had merged with a men's college, Cookman Institute— where future Black leaders like A. Philip Randolph had been educated. Despite bitter fights with many of her most influential White board members who wanted the school to maintain a nonacademic curriculum, by 1927 it was on its way to becoming a fully accredited liberal arts college. In relatively few years, the school founded on a garbage dump boasted buildings and property worth over $1 million. Probably due in part to the voyage, Bethune was more philosophical about such things than she ordinarily was. In that year she wrote an unusually revealing letter to Charlotte Hawkins Brown:

> I think of you and Lucy Laney and myself as being in the most sacrificing class in our group of women. I think the work that we have produced will warrant love or consideration or appreciation or confidence that the general public may see fit to bestow on us. I have unselfishly given my best, and I thank God that I have lived long enough to see the fruits from it.[2]

The last sentence of the letter may have been prompted by the recent death of one of her best friends and staunchest supporters, Margaret Murray Washington. On that occasion, Bethune had written to Terrell: "The sad intelligence of Mrs. Washington's death has just reached me. We all bow in submission to God's will. . . . Everytime one of us drops out it seems to me that it is necessary for us to get closer and closer together. . . . I feel very sad . . . I cannot write you much just now."[3]

Something else happened in 1927 that made her reflective. She was invited to a meeting of the National Council of Women as a representative of the NACW—which had been affiliated with the council as early as 1899. This luncheon meeting was held at the home of New York's Governor Franklin D. Roosevelt and was hosted by his wife, Eleanor. When it came time to sit around the table, a perceptible tension filled the room. Who would sit next to Mary Bethune? Before the anxiety could thicken into an embarrassing incident, Sara Delano Roosevelt, mother of Franklin, took Bethune by the arm and beseeched the NACW leader to sit by her. It would be not unlike Bethune to smile to herself over the incident. When it came to Whites, it was so much easier to get along with the Sara Roosevelts of this world, or the Vanderbilts and Rockefellers who had helped her with the school, or the Gambles (of Procter & Gamble) who had served on the college's board. In any case, Sara Roosevelt's gesture was the beginning of a friendship between the two women that eventually included her daughter-in-law, who in the near future would become as important an ally as Bethune ever had.

The following year Mary Bethune was invited to participate in a White House Conference on Child Welfare. The two experiences helped shape an idea that Bethune would make public in 1929, when she announced plans to create a new Black women's organization—a superorganization which, like the National Council of Women, would act as a cohesive umbrella for women's groups already in existence. As a *New York Age* article quoted her, this women's group would be "a medium . . . through which women may make such progress as would be impossible for any national organization working alone." As Bethune may have realized from the White House Conference, such a superorganization would have greater access to federal dispensation of funds. About a month after the *Age* article, Bethune invited a number of leading women to come to her Florida campus to discuss the organization's formation. In a letter to Terrell, she explained that she had been thinking about such an organization for the last three years. The NACW's representation on the National Council of Women was insufficient, Bethune wrote, to "work out . . . the many problems which face us as a group."[4] In a subsequent letter to Terrell, Bethune stressed: "The result of such an organization will, I believe, make for unity of opinion among Negro women who must do some thinking on public questions; it will insure greater cooperation among women in varied lines of endeavor: and it will lift the ideals not only of the individual organizations, but of the organizations as a group."[5]

In March 1930, Bethune convened the meeting. Among those

present were such women as Maggie L. Walker, the bank president; Mrs. George Williams, Republican national committeewoman; and Mrs. Robert Russa Moton, the wife of Washington's successor at Tuskegee Institute. All in all, women from twelve national organizations—as well as state, fraternal, and educational leaders—answered Bethune's call. But several were conspicuously absent, including the leading lights of the NACW. It soon occurred to Bethune that the NACW would present the greatest obstacle to her plans.[6] And, in fact, it would take another five years of lobbying to convince them of the need for what became the National Council of Negro Women.

It did seem an inauspicious time for a new Black women's organization. The country was in a depression. A number of Black organizations already existed. The Urban League and the NAACP were in full swing, and many activist women were deeply involved in their programs. And, largely due to the Depression, there were new indications of a resuscitated interracial effort which made a new all-Black organization seem, to some at least, behind the times. Moreover, though it was never stated for the record, one could assume that the leaders of the NACW may have felt their power threatened by a new organization, which by its very nature would overshadow the leaders of other groups.

However, a number of events between 1930 and 1935 would vindicate the idea for an organization like the one Bethune proposed. There is a story that when Bethune was born, her eyes were wide open. The midwife who delivered her is said to have told Bethune's mother that Mary would always see things before they happened. Whether or not the story, and the prediction, were accurate, events proved that Bethune did have prophetic tendencies. But before the National Council of Negro Women became a reality, a number of scenarios were to be played out.

As a former president of the NACW, Bethune was as aware as anyone that the organization had by 1930 become an anachronism. The civil rights and welfare organizations that in some ways it had helped to spawn were by then doing many of the things that the NACW had done in the past—and with the financial support of Whites, were doing them more efficiently. Consequently, the NACW would make drastic cuts, it announced in 1930. Instead of thirty-eight departments it would have two, and its focus would be primarily on the home. As "mothers, wives, sisters and daughters of the men of the race," *National Notes* observed, the NACW "should narrow its functions to combating the source of the evils that give the race the unenviable place it holds in the United States." This, of course, was a traditional program of the clubwomen's organization, but in the light of the new developments of the twenties, a dated one.

How dated was evident in a *National Notes* column written in 1929 by the NACW president, Sallie Stewart. In 1929, when the stock market crashed, making families anxious about their future, Stewart counseled: "We want the mothers to take the children's wearing apparel out of boxes and trunks where they are stored, and allow the children to wear them. We want the families that have table linen to use it. We want those who have silver packed in boxes, saving it for the occasional guest, to get this silver out and use it and give their children the right attitude of life and to help them in the formation of their characters in the formative period of their lives. . . . One general difference between the Negro race and the race with which it is most often compared is the problem of home life and general appearances."[7]

In any case, fewer women saw themselves as only "wives, sisters, and daughters" of the men of the race. They saw themselves as workers—workers who were being laid off and downgraded in increasing numbers. The most poignant symbol of the lowered status of all Black women workers was the phenomenon known as the "slave market" in New York City. Magazines such as *The Crisis* ran articles about how domestic workers lined up on empty lots in the Bronx each day, regardless of the weather, to wait for prospective employers who bargained for their day's services. The Whites, often lower-middle-class women who would not be able to afford domestic help in normal circumstances, would ascertain the lowest wage a woman would accept for that day, thereby forcing the Black women to try to underbid one another. As if that situation wasn't bad enough in itself, horror stories abounded of the hours and kinds of work to which these women were required to acquiesce. Many of them received less than the wage they were promised or did not get paid at all. There were also stories of these Black women workers being asked to sell not only domestic services but their sexual services as well.

Because the downgrading of Black women workers coincided more and more with the unemployment of their men, increasing numbers of these women became by necessity the sole support for themselves and their families. With their men gone or out of work, the situation was perilous. Bethune told an audience of the Chicago Women's Federation in 1933: "In recent years it has become increasingly the case . . . the mother is the sole dependence of the home, while the father submits unwillingly to enforced idleness and unavoidable unemployment."[8] As usual, Nannie Helen Burroughs assessed the situation more graphically: "Black men sing too much 'I Can't Give You Anything But Love, Baby,' " she wrote in the *Louisiana Weekly* in the same year. "The women can't build homes, rear families off love alone. . . . The Negro mother is doing it all."[9]

But as has been true throughout the economic history of Black women, while those with the least resources were sinking lower, those with a foot in the proverbial door were making gains—even during this difficult period. By 1930 four out of every ten graduates from Black colleges were women and their numbers were increasing. Although the number of professional workers was still small in 1930 (63,000), it represented an increase of more than 100 percent since 1910, and similar statistics applied to clerical workers. Though Bethune was aware of the divergent paths that poor and middle-class women were treading, it was the upwardly mobile women who captured her political imagination. By 1930 they were dispersed throughout numerous professional, educational, and social organizations such as the Delta Sigma Theta, Alpha Kappa Alpha, and Sigma Gamma Rho sororities; the National Business and Professional Women's Clubs, and the National Association of Colored Graduate Nurses. Bethune wanted to mobilize their potential power within an all-embracing association. These women, she had said in the 1929 *New York Age* article, were not only "more numerous and diversified and more keenly alive to the group" than Black men on the same level, but were in a "better position to make use of the Negro's purchasing power as an effective instrument to keep open the doors that have remained closed." It was Black women, Bethune contended, who "held the pursestrings."[10]

With such ideas, Bethune belonged to the circle of Black activists who saw racial progress through the lens of newly acquired economic power. Larger numbers of Blacks were earning wages from the industrial sector, giving them discretionary income and potential power as consumers. By the early thirties W.E.B. Du Bois was writing about consumer cooperatives and economic boycotts in the NAACP's *Crisis,* asserting that some 22 million Blacks in the Caribbean and the United

States were spending at least $10 million a year as consumers. This perspective, which focused on the collective power of Blacks, would eventually set Bethune and Du Bois against the rising tide of interracialism.

That tide swelled under the gravity of the Depression and the consequent rise of lynching. The lynching of twenty Black men in 1930 amounted to nowhere near the numbers at the turn of the century, or even in the immediate aftermath of World War I. But the news reports of the horrible crimes were made more vivid by the technological advances in communication and photography, and the sensationalism of yellow journalism.

In any case, lynching in 1930 seemed more reprehensible to the White establishment than it had in the past. The reason was, again, economics. The crime was a vivid symbol of the intransigence of a region that threatened the nation's economic survival. The Depression and the problem of national recovery, remarked Ralph Ellison, challenged the assumption of northern capitalists that the social isolation of the South offered "the broadest possibility for business exploitation."[11] Thus, "Northern capital could no longer turn its head while the southern ruling group went its regressive way."[12] As Franklin D. Roosevelt would later remark, the South was the nation's number one economic problem—and this at a time when the southern textile industry was surpassing that of the Northeast, and when southern cities were growing at a faster rate than those in other parts of the country. But lynch law was retarding the South's progress and, as a result, that of the entire nation.

The beginning of the decade was a good time to challenge the "regressive" ways of the southern ruling group. The political force of the KKK was virtually spent. And just as important, southern White women were prepared as never before to confront the sexist notions implicit in the southern lynching mentality. The thirties saw the rise of middle-class urban White women in the South—a group making both economic and educational gains. They were having fewer children. Increasingly sophisticated and independent, they were more aware that southern male chivalry, in its distilled form, was largely a means of control and repression. And they began to realize as well that lynching was an extension of that control, as much over White women as over Blacks. The restiveness of White women was encouraged by the spate of scholarly commentary on the lynching phenomenon. In

1932, Arthur Raper's *The Tragedy of Lynching*, underwritten by the Council of Interracial Cooperation, appeared as one of the earliest scientific analyses of southern mob violence, and other social scientists followed suit. Psychoanalysts like Helene Deutsch also scrutinized the lynching phenomenon. It was Deutsch's opinion that false rape charges reflected the masochistic fantasies of White women. Additionally, the most sophisticated southern White women activists recognized the negative economic impact of violence on the region. For these activists, awareness culminated in a new feminist determination. Those in the Council of Interracial Cooperation, for example, were becoming increasingly dissatisfied with their auxiliary roles in the organization and were anxious to strike out on their own. Lynching provided the issue upon which to stake their claims.

Bethune, also a member of the CIC, was always good at recognizing an opening when she saw one. In 1930 she informed Will Alexander, head of the organization, that she intended to issue a press statement demanding that southern White women assume responsibility for halting the rise of racial violence.[13] Whatever Bethune's motives for this move, it was an unmistakable cue to White women activists, particularly to Jessie Daniel Ames, one of the most dynamic of the southern women.

A Texan by birth, Ames had been named the first woman CIC executive director of the state's interracial committee. She also became a CIC salaried field representative for the entire Southwest. A month after Bethune's announcement, Ames issued a call for White women activists to meet in Atlanta to discuss the lynching issue. Born out of that meeting was the Association of Southern Women for the Prevention of Lynching (ASWPL). They were determined that they would "no longer . . . remain silent in the face of this crime done in their name."[14] The ASWPL organizers stumped the South with their message, which was threefold. First, they talked and wrote about lynching as a feminist issue. Behind the guise of chivalry, said Ames, was the axiom "White men hold that White women are their property [and] so are Negro women."[15] Second, they took note of rape's use as an excuse to subordinate Blacks. "Public opinion has accepted too easily the claim of lynchers and mobsters that they were acting *solely in the defense of womanhood,*" they declared. As the writer Lillian Smith described the ASWPL stand, women understood that they were being used as a shield for White men's "race-economic exploitation." Smith concluded that they were not afraid of being raped: "As for their sacredness, they could take care of it themselves, they did not need the chivalry of lynching to protect them and they did not want it."[16] For the third part of the message, Ames took Smith's economic analysis a bit further. "For the South to be industrialized," she said, "there was a need to assimilate 'the New Negro, into the New Southland."[17] Technology, she stated, "had left no room in the economy for twelve million servants."

For the next few years, the ASWPL could claim a number of successes. They galvanized the support, in the form of endorsements, of over 35,000 White southern women by 1936. Their inherent moral authority on the lynching issue had made governors and other officials take note, and even take public stands against mob violence. After 1933, the incidence of mob violence had significantly declined. Black women were enthusiastic about the new political development. They had always held that White women could be the most effective force in putting a stop to lynching—and all that that violent act implied. A Black paper, the Atlanta *World,* observed of the ASWPL: "The greatest gain of the anti-lynching [fight] is to be found in the support now being given by the white women of the South."[18] Even the irrepressible Nannie Helen Burroughs was impressed. The ASWPL was "the most important anti-lynching group in the country," she pronounced in her *Pittsburgh Courier* column.[19]

This was not to say that Black women were unaware of the inherent limitations of the White antilynching organization and its leader. The ASWPL's fundamental philosophy mirrored that of the CIC, which was that racial harmony rather than equality was the primary goal. For example, although one of Ames's most notable accomplishments was helping to achieve better housing conditions for Dallas's Black community, her motivation was not so much racial fairness as it was "to prevent encroachments into White neighborhoods" by middle-class Blacks who were dissatisfied with housing in the Black community. The ASWPL and its leader also exhibited a patronizing attitude toward Blacks who were expected to be passive participants in the interracial process. Only White women were invited into the antilynching organization.

Furthermore, the organization had been painfully silent about the highly publicized Scottsboro case in 1931, when nine Black men were accused of raping several White women on a train. Ames never considered the ASWPL capable of sustaining political battles over such issues. She patronizingly assumed that the women in her organization were not ideologically prepared to deal with politics. They were "sentimental" and "inexperienced," Ames believed, and hence ill-suited to sustained political activism. These shortcomings made the affiliation with the ASWPL untenable for Black women by 1935—the year the Costigan-Wagner Act was introduced in the Congress.

The measure called for federal intervention in lynching cases where local authorities refused to act. Its proposal would reveal within the liberal movement a number of crosscurrents that would tear increasingly uneasy alliances asunder.

The introduction of the Costigan-Wagner Act precipitated a flurry of activity. The NAACP, headed by its executive secretary, Walter White, led an intense lobbying effort for its passage. A close association was established with the CIC, which had unanimously approved active support of the bill. The Southern Methodist Women's Council, whose members made up a major part of the CIC and the ASWPL, also advocated the measure. The First Lady, Eleanor Roosevelt, took a personal interest in passage of the legislation, and of course Black women activists were solidly behind it. However, Jessie Daniel Ames cast a dissenting vote. She felt that federal legislation would do little more in the end than anger Southerners and, rather than ending mob violence, would simply push it underground. Besides, Ames was offended by anything that undermined the sacred southern concept of states' rights, and despite pleas from the other liberals, including Eleanor Roosevelt and a large group within the ASWPL, she stood steadfast in her position. Black women, thoroughly disgusted by Ames's stance, called a meeting with her and some of her supporters, in Atlanta in 1935.

Daisy Lampkin, who had been involved in the confrontation with the National Woman's Party and who was now a field secretary for the NAACP, began the discussion. The ASWPL's silence, she said, was strengthening the position of congressional opponents of the bill. They "take new courage and they use it to their advantage when they can stand on the floor and say that the . . . southern white women did not endorse the Costigan-Wagner Bill."[20]

Charlotte Hawkins Brown observed that since Southerners virtually ruled the Congress, southern White women could do more "to bring about . . . freedom for the Negro race than a million from the North." Brown, whose perspective had shifted from the moral to the political, concluded, "I would not have expected you to do it . . . if the South was not in the saddle, but I feel you missed a step."[21]

Poor Lugenia Burns Hope was probably the most emotional about the situation. "My heart is so sick and weak," she said, ". . . that I don't know if I can say anything. . . . You may not think so, but it will hold back our interracial work and everything else in the South."[22] If Hope was the most disappointed, Nannie Helen Burroughs was the least surprised about the outcome of it all. "I am sorry," she said, "but I am not disappointed. . . . I did not think this organization was going to endorse the . . . bill. . . . There isn't any use in my telling you in tears that I am so disappointed, because I did not expect you to do it."[23]

Of the entire group, Bethune was the most conciliatory. She would of course have been happy if the ASWPL had endorsed the bill, she told Ames and the others. "But I think you have been cautious and wisely so. . . . My heart is full of appreciation . . . for the step you have taken and the awakening you have given to the courageous because of the daring stand taken by this group of women."[24]

Bethune may have been utterly sincere in her words to Ames, with no ulterior motive whatever. Perhaps she could be sincere because, like Nannie Helen Burroughs, she had understood the political shortcomings of the ASWPL and southern White women from the beginning. As a White delegate to the meeting said, "Our women can go only so far until they have converted the men."[25]

However, Bethune was also capable of suppressing her own personal feelings for political advantage. She admitted this in so many words: "I am diplomatic about certain things," she once said. "I let people infer a great many things, but I am careful about what I say because I want to do certain things."[26] So it may have been no coincidence that in the same year that Bethune expressed patience and understanding of the limitations of an all-White women's group, the all-Black National Council of Negro Women would hold its founding meeting. The failure of the ASWPL served Bethune's own interests.

The year 1935 marked a critical juncture in the direction Black activists would take in the racial struggle. Should their energies be channeled toward interracialism or toward the strengthening of their own institutions? The opposing views among Blacks were dramatically illustrated within the ranks of the NAACP when, in 1935, W.E.B. Du Bois resigned from the organization and from the editorship of *The Crisis.* His repeated confrontations with Walter White, the executive secretary, reflected the debate within the larger Black leadership community. In his *Crisis* editorials Du Bois had counseled that racial segregation and racial discrimination were two different issues. Integration for its own sake was both meaningless and demeaning. "Never in the world should we fight against association with ourselves," he exhorted. Undoubtedly referring to the patronizing nature of interracial cooperation, Du Bois requested that Blacks not "submit to discrimination simply because it does not involve actual and open segregation."[27] He felt that Blacks should be devoting their efforts to building their own institutions instead of integrating White ones. "It must be remembered," Du Bois said, "that in the last quarter of a century, the advance of the colored people has been mainly in the lines where they themselves, working by and for themselves, have accomplished the greater advance."[28]

The implications of Du Bois's position flew in the face of the policies of the NAACP, which throughout the twenties and thirties had fought for integration. Much effort had been directed toward school integration and eliminating restrictive housing covenants, yet here was Du Bois saying there was nothing wrong with living in Black neighborhoods or going to Black schools under the right conditions. Walter White and his high-ranking cohort Roy Wilkins bitterly disagreed with Du Bois. The debate reached its climax when White decided to throw the NAACP's resources behind the interracial effort to lobby for passage of the Costigan-Wagner Act. White had decided to cast his lot with "the rising tide of liberalism in the South and in national politics" in the belief that it "offered an unprecedented opportunity for striking a final blow at terrorism."[29]

Bethune's outlook seemed to fall somewhere between the two camps. Though she publicly supported interracial efforts, many of her actions corresponded to the Du Bois position. For example, Bethune had supported the withdrawal of the NACW from the predominantly White National Council of Women, although a Black clubwoman had recently been named a council vice-president. In July 1935 the NACW president, Mary Waring, criticized Bethune's action before an NACW meeting. She told the membership:

Affiliation with the National Council of Women means more than you realize. We regret very much the calamity of losing our foothold on that which was gained after much constructive work by our presidents, from Mrs. Mary Church Terrell down to the present, culminating in Mrs. Sallie Stewart being a vice-president.

We lost this standing, not by any fault of theirs, but by one of our own women suggesting it go to some other organization. My dear friends, *now* and *ever* let me admonish you not to burn the bridges over which you pass that those who come after may not cross."[30]

By December, Waring had made her views public, revealing that she opposed not only the withdrawal of the NACW from the National Council of Women, but the idea of forming an all-Black women's organization as well. The debate over interracialism also echoed among the ranks of Black women activists. In a *New York Age* article published in December 1935, Waring's letter to the editor warned that Black women should "beware of forming organizations which discriminated on the basis of race," and that "Negroes should not segregate themselves." She also wrote that there were already enough Black women's organizations, and Black women "should build on what they already had." Waring went on to relate that when, on November 30, Bethune had held a dinner for women to discuss the National Council of Negro Women (NCNW) at the Waldorf-Astoria, the famous hotel had at first refused to serve them. Bethune created a furor, demanding to be served. Waring thought Bethune's demand that the hotel be integrated was inconsistent with plans to form an all-Black organization.[31]

Bethune responded by observing that the National Council of Women had "forty-three organizations with only one Negro organization and we have no specific place on their program." She sidestepped the more controversial implications of her views, simply noting, "We need an organization to open new doors for our young women [which] when [it] speaks, its power will be felt."[32] Whether or not one agreed with Bethune's logic, her growing prestige had become virtually irresistible, at least in political terms. In addition to her stature as a college president and a leader of the CIC, she received the prestigious Spingarn Medal from the NAACP in 1935. In a congratulatory note, Reverend Adam Clayton Powell, Sr., wrote Bethune: "It is a long way from the rice and cotton fields of South Carolina to this distinguished recognition, but you have made it in such a short span of years that I am afraid you are going to be arrested for breaking the speed limit."[33] Also in 1935, after attending a White House meeting Bethune had been asked to become a special consultant to the Advisory Board of the National Youth Administration. As her participation in the Roosevelt administration subsequently revealed, Bethune would use the administration's alleged commitment to civil rights as a means to further her own goals and those of the NCNW.

From the inception of her superorganization idea, Bethune had lobbied the Black women leaders, even sending her own representatives to meetings and asking the various groups to report on their feelings about the proposed organization. By the end of 1935 her entreaties were difficult to deny, Mary Waring notwithstanding. On December 5 she held the founding meeting of the NCNW at the 137th Street branch of the YWCA in Harlem. Not surprisingly, Mary Church Terrell came to the meeting, though she had claimed to be "too busy" to attend the planning conferences. She thought the NCNW "worthwhile," but, she admitted: "Reluctantly, I did not believe in the idea. . . . I can't see how this organization can help. . . . I don't think this Council will be any more successful than other organizations."[34]

Charlotte Hawkins Brown, also in attendance, was another leader hesitant to give full endorsement. There were already too many organizations, she felt. "There is a need for a Council or Conference but none for an organization. Such a council could be used as a clearinghouse for all organizations."[35]

Other women, representing fourteen women's organizations, were fortunately more enthusiastic about Bethune's idea, but the misgivings of her old allies must have been disturbing. Still, a historian of the NCNW observed, one of Bethune's greatest assets was her ability to "neutralize her critics" and get a consensus. Bethune moved to make Terrell and Brown fourth and first vice-presidents respectively, and to incorporate the clearinghouse idea in the NCNW's statement of purpose.* In the end Brown and Terrell not only accepted the idea, but the latter formally moved that a unanimous ballot elect Bethune president.

Her achievement was due to more than Bethune's political acumen, or even her influence. For the most part, Black activist women had always supported one another in the final analysis. This was partic-

---

*(1) To unite national organizations into a National Council of Negro Women;

(2) To educate, encourage and effect the participation of Negro women in civic, political, economic and educational activities and institutions;

(3) To serve as a clearing house for the dissemination of activities concerning women;

(4) To plan, initiate and carry out projects which develop, benefit and integrate the Negro and the nation.

ularly true of the early generations in the club movement. Not that they didn't have their differences: A bitter fight over Terrell's quest for a third term as NACW president in 1899 had caused Fannie Barrier Williams to admonish women about potentially destructive battles over leadership. Black women had varying political perspectives (one could hardly imagine Margaret Murray Washington and Ida Wells-Barnett even in the same room), degrees of radicalism, and political loyalties. Terrell was a dyed-in-the-wool Republican, Bethune maintained a close relationship with the Democrats, and others considered neutrality the best means of achieving their goals.

Deep differences existed even in the way they perceived their "Afro-Americanness." Bethune was as proud of her pure African blood as her friend Charlotte Brown was of her English ancestry. Additionally, there were disparities in social background. Still, differences among Black women rarely resulted in the fragmentation or utter alienation of their organizations. William Pickens, field secretary of the NAACP, noticed this, as a letter to Charlotte Hawkins Brown revealed:

> In my own judgment, the colored women are better supplied with eligible leaders than are colored men. And the women are more direct and informal, seemingly more honest than the men, certainly less technical, in carrying out their programs, after choosing their leaders. A woman leader is not so apt to be a "political" choice. I mean a choice of intrigue merely. . . . What a grand line of Negro queens their list of presidents of their national organizations over the last quarter-century makes.[36]

In any case, Black women always found common cause in a vision of the future. And there was no more articulate visionary than Mary McLeod Bethune. "Most people think I am a dreamer," she told the women at the founding meeting of the NCNW. "Through dreams many things have come true. I am interested in women and I believe in their possibilities. . . . We need vision for larger things, for the unfolding and reviewing of worthwhile things."[37] Bethune recognized that the world had widened significantly in the last fifteen years. A growing interest in international affairs had prompted women to see their work in a worldwide context. There was increased awareness that drastic changes had to be made in the political, economic, and social position of Afro-Americans, and that Black intellectuals themselves were capable of drawing up a blueprint for such changes. And yet, as Bethune implied, Black women's organizations had become narrower in their concerns, more involved with the singular special interest of their particular group. It was time for a "larger vision." For despite their achievements, the world, Bethune noted, "has not been willing to accept the contributions that women have made." It was time now for them to pool their resources in order to make an impact on the public policies of the nation. Their vehicle was to be the National Council of Negro Women.

Within a year Mary McLeod Bethune, at the age of sixty-one, was wearing three hats. She was the president of the NCNW, the president of Bethune-Cookman College, and an appointee to the National Youth Administration agency. She was in a position to forward her four passions: race, women, education, and youth. It was her deft maneuvering in the FDR administration that helped to place those passions on the national agenda for the first time in the history of Black Americans.

XIII

~ Black Braintruster: Mary McLeod Bethune and the Roosevelt Administration ~

The election of Franklin Delano Roosevelt in 1932 gave Black leaders no cause for celebration. Roosevelt, member of a political party dominated by Southerners, gave little evidence that his own racial views were any more enlightened. Perhaps recalling the uproar that his cousin Teddy Roosevelt unleashed when he invited Booker T. Washington to a White House dinner, Franklin boasted as late as 1929 that he had never lunched with an Afro-American.[1] As governor of New York, FDR had ignored civil rights legislation and had appointed no Blacks to his administration. As assistant secretary of the Navy in the segregationist administration of Woodrow Wilson, FDR had never protested Jim Crow policies in the armed forces, or anywhere else for that matter. Of course, no ambitious Democrat could afford to take a strong stand regarding civil rights, but FDR gave no indication of being even a closet liberal. After the 1919 race riot in Washington, D.C., the then assistant secretary of the navy had written to a southern associate: "With your experience in handling Africans in Arkansas, I think you had better come up here and take care of the Police Force."[2]

Roosevelt's attitudes seemed scarcely to have changed by the time he won the Democratic nomination. He had ignored repeated NAACP requests to support a civil rights platform; and in the early years of his first term, some of the Black leaders' worst fears were realized. Roosevelt filled his Cabinet with men like Cordell Hull, whom Blacks characterized as an "impenetrable fortress" for upholding Jim Crow in the armed forces; or people like Harry Hopkins and Frances Perkins, who had liberal histories but refused to act on their convictions.

Not surprisingly, the administration made a bad situation worse for Blacks who were ravaged by the Depression. The Federal Emergency Relief Administration of the Department of Labor virtually ignored Black needs. Legislation like the Wagner-Lewis Social Security Bill excluded farmers and domestics, two groups that made up 65 percent of Black workers. Inequities were rife, particularly in those departments where Southerners had a direct say in policy. The Department of Agriculture dispensed relief on the principle that Black families needed less income than White families to live on, and so needed less relief than Whites. The Federal Housing Administration consistently refused to guarantee mortgages for Blacks buying homes in White neighborhoods. And in all the agencies, federal administrators gave local southern officials free rein in distributing federal funds as they saw fit, resulting in tremendous disparities.

Ironically, the administration's policies toward Blacks provided the very spur that resulted in more liberal policies. The Depression, combined with unequal relief aid, brought on a recurrence of "northern fever." During the thirties, 400,000 Blacks left the South to populate northern cities. Before 1935, only one northern city had in excess of 100,000 Afro-Americans, but by the end of that year eleven cities had at least that number.

In the 1930's, the Black migration had deeper implications than ever before. Now, in a time of bloc votes and increasing urban power, Blacks represented a significant political factor. This was seen clearly in the Democratic party's Tammany Hall in New York City. By 1930 there were two Black judges in the system; in 1934, Herbert Bruce became the first Black district leader; and two years later, Tammany appointed two Black state legislators, two aldermen, two assistant district attorneys, and a civil service commissioner. On the eve of the 1936 presidential election, Democrats were openly soliciting the Black vote on an unprecedented scale.

If the Democrats catered to the emerging significance of Blacks, the Republicans remained smugly assured that their "Party of Lincoln" rhetoric was sufficient to win the needed number of Black votes. The Republican attitude was vividly illustrated when Mary Church Terrell offered her services to the Republican National Committee for the upcoming election. Terrell had always been an active Republican. Throughout the twenties and early thirties she either worked for the party by proselytizing Black voters or campaigned for individual candidates, like the Illinois Senate hopeful Ruth Hanna McCormick. As late as 1932 she had been an adviser to the RNC, working among Blacks and women, for Herbert Hoover.

For the 1936 presidential election, however, a high-ranking RNC adviser told her there was no place for her. Terrell then appealed to a more sympathetic committeewoman, who in turn wrote to the RNC's vice-chairman and general counsel on her behalf. The committeewoman's letter, found in Terrell's files, underscores the patronizing and ambivalent attitude of the GOP in the mid-thirties: "I have checked up what she says among her own people and discovered that she has been twice-over the National President of the best colored society in the country, that they all love and respect her. . . . Mrs. Terrell's brother, whose name I have forgotten, is the best Boss among the men of his race in this country." The letter went on to say that since the RNC had some disagreement over the "unimportance of the colored vote," the writer took "courage" in forwarding Terrell's résumé; if it was still "impossible" for Terrell to work on the Committee, perhaps she could "work on the side for a time . . . thus giving her the opportunity of showing what she could do in a preliminary canter."[3]

While Republicans were talking about preliminary canters, the Democrats were heading into a full gallop. As early as 1934, Eleanor Roosevelt began taking an active stand on racial issues. Although she was not naïve about political realities, her actions seemed to be motivated by genuine racial concern. During the early thirties her association with Walter White and Mary McLeod Bethune helped to open her eyes to the racial problem in a way that her background never had. During these years the First Lady also confronted her own personal prejudices, according to her biographer Joseph P. Lash:

> Eleanor worked with [Bethune] closely, but her reluctance to peck her on the cheek, as she did other friends, showed her the residue of racial feeling in herself, what the Negro resented and the White had to overcome. Not until she kissed Mrs. Bethune without thinking of it, she told her daughter Anna, did she feel she had at last overcome the racial prejudice within herself.[4]

Eleanor Roosevelt's empathy for the Black cause had repercussions within the administration. It gave courage to many administrators in the cabinet, especially those with a liberal bent. Blacks began receiving appointments to the relief agencies, and there was a greater consciousness concerning equitable relief dispensation. Eleanor Roosevelt's public support for such legislation as the Wagner-Costigan Bill (a stand her husband refused to take openly) and her increasing association with Black leaders and organizations gave the civil rights movement a kind of crucial visibility and sanction it had never had before. Her personal impact, added to increasing Black political strength and the urgency of national recovery, promised a more sympathetic attitude toward Black leaders in Roosevelt's second term.

The Black rank and file had their own reasons for supporting the Democratic ticket, as Nannie Helen Burroughs contended. For them the concerns were more fundamental than those of civil rights or even physical protection. "I don't think any Negro outside of the asylum voted that ticket thinking the Democratic party was going to bring in the millennium," she said. "It was an economic question with the colored people just as it was with the White people." Black people "were not thinking of getting killed," Burroughs said, "but rather of being filled."[5]

Whatever the priorities, the Black community gave a resounding 76 percent of the vote to Roosevelt. And Roosevelt—appointing Blacks to the administration in unprecedented numbers—responded in kind. Afro-Americans such as Robert Weaver, Henry Hunt, William Hastie, Lawrence Oxley, and Frank Horne were called upon to serve as advisers, assistants, and directors of Negro affairs in the New Deal relief and recovery agencies and in the majority of Cabinet divisions of government.[6] Destined to stand out among the "Black Cabinet" or the "Black Braintrusters," as they were called, was Mary McLeod Bethune.

As a Roosevelt appointee, Bethune had a less than auspicious beginning. Appointed to an obscure position in an equally obscure agency, Bethune became director of the Negro Division of the National Youth Administration (NYA), whose general function was to find employment for young people between the ages of sixteen and twenty-four in private industry, work-relief, and vocational training projects.[7] But at the time of her appointment, the sluggish wheels of the Washington bureaucracy had yet to catch up with Bethune's job description: The Civil Service Commission still had not officially recognized a *Negro Division* within the NYA, much less Bethune as its director.

Resolving that little problem was largely a matter of shuffling papers in the appropriate "in" and "out" boxes. What may have been more disturbing to Bethune was that although she occupied the first federal position created for a Black woman—as she described it—neither the Black press nor the other Braintrusters (all men) seemed to recognize the significance of the appointment. It was not in Bethune's nature to be ignored for long, though, and she went to work. However obscure her position was, Bethune knew what to do with it. She forged tight alliances with Aubrey Williams, the NYA administrator, and Eleanor Roosevelt. She charted the formidable tasks that faced the NYA and started mobilizing all available resources to accomplish those objectives. And, recognizing that the "Black Cabinet" was racked by internal dissension, Bethune organized them into the Federal Council on Negro Affairs, whose purpose was to hammer out a consensus so that they could present a united front on policy.

Within months of her appointment, both the Black press and the Braintrusters had come around to recognizing her as a formidable presence. "Mrs. Bethune has gathered everything and everybody under her very ample wing since her arrival here last June," reported Edward Lawson, Washington correspondent for the Associated Negro Press. Commenting upon the Braintrusters' late recognition of her abilities, Lawson wrote: "Either they were unaware of her tremendous energy and grasp of things or they underestimated the potential power of her position. At any rate, they were unprepared for the manner in which she took the whole situation under control." As far as the other Black appointees were concerned, noted Lawson, before Bethune's organizing efforts, they had been unable "to get together and agree upon any logical program for [Roosevelt's] consideration." Lawson concluded: "With the possible exception of Congressman Arthur Mitchell, she occupies undoubtedly the most strategic position in the administration."[8] It was a position enhanced by Bethune's style of leadership and her keen recognition of what could be done at such a point in history.

Historian B. Joyce Ross has explained that the New Deal's attitude toward Blacks was different from that of other administrations that sought to influence civil rights, such as the administrations of the post-Civil War era or the 1960's. The objective of the Roosevelt administration was not to bring Blacks into the mainstream of American life and institutions but to provide a "separate equality." Thus, as Ross notes, "the greatest shortcoming of the New Deal was its failure to link inextricably the principle of federal auspices of racial equality with the concept of a desegregated society."[9] Yet despite its inherent limitations, the New Deal program of providing opportunities for all non-WASPs, including Blacks, made an indelible mark on American politics. For although the administration did not address itself to Blacks, or even to the poor, as historian Henry Fairlie pointed out, it did achieve a greater empowerment of these groups.

It was within this context, remarked historian Elaine M. Smith, that Bethune established clear goals, then worked persistently but patiently for their realization. Bethune's overall goal was equalizing opportunities for Blacks. In her view this did not necessarily include integrating them into the mainstream. "In places where there is no need for a separate program, for Negro and White groups, we most heartily recommend the one program," Bethune stated before the National Advisory Committee in 1936. "And in fields where it is necessary for us to have a separate program, we most heartily recommend a separate program, taking, of course, under advisement the necessity of the proper leadership and guidance."[10]

Thus, Bethune's perspective drew from several schools of Black thought. Certainly Booker T. Washington's ideas were implicit in her thinking, though unlike him, she was not willing to forgo the concept of equality or rights for Blacks. Nor did she preach racial separateness; she was merely willing to accept its inevitability in the thirties, as long as Blacks had power over their sector. On another occasion she told the Advisory Committee: "May I advise the committee that it does not matter how equipped your white supervision might be or your white leadership, it is impossible for you to enter as sympathetically and understandingly into the program of the Negro, as the Negro can do."[11]

Bethune also believed, like Du Bois, that there were advantages to voluntary separation, though he would hardly have condoned some of the self-deprecating humor that Bethune was capable of expressing in order to get her point across. And of course Du Bois would have felt that using the federal government as a point of departure for this philosophy would be futile from the beginning. Although the NAACP would not agree with Bethune's explicit acceptance of separate but equal, in reality they were conducting their own activities along the same lines. Ross points out that the NAACP, unable to dent the armor of southern school desegregation, was forced to concentrate its energies on demanding equal salaries and Black school facilities, hoping that desegregation would be crushed by its own financial burden.

However, Bethune's philosophy was effective in attaining her goals of providing opportunities for youth, Blacks, and women from her linchpin position at the NYA.

The NYA was first and foremost about youth, of course, and Bethune set to work to give Black youngsters their due. "The drums in Africa beat in my heart," she was fond of saying. "I cannot rest while there is a single Negro boy or girl lacking a chance to prove his worth." Well, there wouldn't be much chance to rest for this wily woman, who was now in her sixties. In the first year of her appointment, she traveled forty thousand miles through twenty-one states to assess the situation, documenting the fact that although Blacks constituted about 13 percent of the youth population, they represented 15 percent of all young people on relief. Additionally, they carried the burdensome legacies of inferior education and other forms of discrimination, including unequal relief grants.

The first order of business was to bring Blacks into the NYA in policy-making positions, which would have a dual purpose. First was the question of empowering individual Blacks who, in turn, would be more sensitive to Black needs. Second, Black appointments were an integral part of a philosophy of the right of Blacks to make decisions about their own. "The White man has been thinking for us too long," she pronounced on one occasion. "We want him to think with us instead of for us." Since the prevailing philosophy of the NYA (and other agencies) was that the local communities knew best how to utilize relief funds, Bethune worked to ensure that Blacks had a hand in dispensing those funds to their own communities.

As early as 1935, when Bethune was an adviser to the NYA before her appointment as director of Negro Affairs, she had advocated that Blacks be named to policy-making positions on all state committees. By the time of her appointment, fourteen had been so named, but the South, not surprisingly, lagged behind. If Southerners had any Blacks at all on their committees, there was rarely more than one.

Although federal NYA officials had advocated a policy of integrated state committees, they had backed down in the face of southern intransigence. In 1935 they had failed to press one of the leaders of the Texas state committee, a man by the name of Lyndon Baines Johnson, after he insisted that Whites would object to an integrated Texas committee. So, one of Bethune's first orders of business was to penetrate the South, beginning with her home state of Florida.

Through her political deftness the Negro Affairs director managed to get two Blacks appointed to Florida's Advisory Committee. By the time she was finished, she had gotten twenty-seven Blacks appointed to state commissions, including representatives in every southern state except Mississippi.

Within her own office, Bethune hired a Black specialist, as they were called, and on her own small staff she had four Black assistants, including the poet (and uncle of Lena Horne) Frank Horne and the sociologist T. Arnold Hill of the National Urban League. Her right hand was a dynamic and capable Black woman, Arabella Denniston. She was also able to hire six Afro-Americans, four of whom were women, in "professional" jobs outside the agency itself.

Bethune had less success in translating her determination into money for Black youth relief. But even here she scored some impressive victories: for example, the implementation of a special fund for Black youth going to college. Black students had greater need, she argued, not less, and often had higher expenses, since many had to attend schools away from their segregated home states. Though the percentage of total expenditure for Black students remained small, under Bethune's stewardship it rose, from Black students' receiving 2.5 percent of higher education aid during the fund's first year to 7.4 percent in the following year. During the seven years of the fund's existence, 4,118 students received a total of $609,930. From a beginning of $75,060 in 1936–37, the monies available for Black student aid increased to $111,105 in 1940–41.[12]

Bethune also involved many of the Black universities in various training programs under NYA auspices, most notably in establishing resident training programs on or near Black college campuses. By 1937, programs were under way in twenty-five southern communities, and by 1941 some 63,622 students were engaged in these projects, which included industrial training, manpower training for war industries, and mechanical and construction work. Other categories included a project to make one hundred librarians available to Black universities that needed such library science personnel in order to become accredited. In addition, Bethune influenced the agency to train high school teachers for Black rural schools in Mississippi, where so few high schools admitted Blacks that scarcely any youths were able to take advantage of NYA student-aid funds. And through her efforts, six Black schools took part in the agency's Civilian Pilot Training Program, which became "the major avenue through which Blacks entered aviation and paved the way for Black pilots in the military."[13] The first Black aviators in World War II were trained at Tuskegee.

Bethune also made her presence felt outside her own agency. She lobbied the White House for Black political appointments not only in areas of specific Black concern but in general areas as well. Although it is not easy to assess her direct impact, a number of her recommendations—such as the appointment of William Hastie to be the first federal judge (of the U.S. Third Circuit Court of Appeals)—were carried out. Bethune also took every possible opportunity to open doors to Blacks. She demanded, for example, White House credentials for the Atlanta *World* to attend presidential press conferences, and it became the first Black newspaper to be so accredited. When she took ill and had to go to Johns Hopkins Hospital, her demand for Black doctors resulted in the admittance of the first Black practitioners to the famous hospital. At the same time, she led the NCNW in securing Black nurses to enlarge the facilities of Howard University's Freedmen's Hospital.

On a larger scale, Bethune also used her influence first to get, then to ensure, federal funding for needed facilities in the Black community. A famous story about a Black housing project in Daytona Beach, Florida, serves as an example. According to the story, when funds for the project got mired in bureaucratic red tape, an SOS went out to Bethune, who simply called Eleanor Roosevelt on the phone. Mrs. Roosevelt, in turn, called the head of the Federal Housing Authority, and in no time funding for the project was approved.

The minutes of an NCNW meeting in 1938 reveal the political push and pull behind the approval, and give a glimpse into the role that Bethune played in it:

We have been able in Daytona Beach to get a $500,000 slum clearance for Negroes there [she told the group]. When they went after that money, we in Washington, knowing the department heads, worked earnestly to help get the money for our people. The moment the money was given, the newspapers in Daytona Beach came out saying that the first $500,000 would be used for White people. Then, because we had some influence in Washington, we went back and got a pin pushed into that money and announced that it would not be released unless the authorities agreed to stand up for their promise and do that work for the Negro people. They found they couldn't get the money unless they did it, and they did. Now we are going to have that $500,000 for Negroes, and on top of that, after they saw the influence we could wield in Daytona Beach, [they] voted me membership on the housing committee . . . the first time in the history of the city that they have permitted a Negro to be on any of the municipal setups of the city. It simply demonstrates that where we have a little influence and where we have press, we will get something done. That is what we have to do in all our communities.[14]

At a time when the federal government was overtaking self-help and White philanthropy as the primary source of funding for Black institutions and welfare needs, it was essential that leaders like Bethune be plugged into the bureaucracy. Perhaps more than any other of the Black Braintrusters, Bethune understood the dimensions of her role as a representative or plenipotentiary for the race.

One of her "sacred duties," as she said, was to "interpret the dreams and the hopes and the problems of my long-suffering people" to White officials who could do something about them.[15] During an NCNW meeting she explained the importance of this function:

> There are a few people who can get a chance to sit down sometimes and talk. I mean just talk to people so that they can get the tones of your voices and vibrations of your souls at the injustices that are being meted out to us in these several fields, and continue to beg and work until something is done about it. I am actually dying on my feet because I am giving every moment, almost night and day—every little crevice I can get into, every opportunity I can get to whisper into the ear of an upper official, I am trying to breathe my soul, a spiritual something into the needs of our people.[16]

This attitude and her silver tongue were very effective weapons for Bethune. When she was just an adviser, she had virtually talked her way into the appointment at the NYA after giving an impassioned speech about the needs of Black youth. Bethune had certainly made a believer of Eleanor Roosevelt, and the First Lady had become one of her staunchest allies. When Roosevelt had made plans to cut NYA funds, another one of her impassioned talks persuaded FDR to restore them to the budget. And certainly her articulation of the need for Black participation in financial decision-making was responsible for many Black appointments in her agency and elsewhere.

Bethune was also more than capable of using her repertoire of race-deprecating humor and homespun homilies to get her point across to White groups. According to historian B. Joyce Ross, once, when Bethune was appealing for Black appointments, she told the predominantly White National Advisory Committee that she wanted to see "more of those darkies dotting around here." At the close of the same meeting, Bethune was said to have commented: "After being down in Harlem, I'm glad to have the opportunity of being up here in the Waldorf-Astoria with you White folks. I wish more of my people could share this opportunity."[17]

Still, Bethune refused to be humiliated by Whites in public. In 1938, when the CIC was reinvigorated and became the Southern Conference for Human Welfare (SCHW), she refused to go along with segregated seating. The meetings had taken place in Birmingham, where the segregation ordinance was strictly upheld by a sheriff whose name would be more familiar in later years: Eugene (Bull) Connor. To emphasize her point, she invited the First Lady and Aubrey Williams to one of the meetings, and they too rejected the segregated arrangement. In one of those meetings, when Bethune was addressed by her first name she retorted that she wasn't going to go down in history as "Mary from Florida," and demanded that the minutes be changed to show she had been properly addressed. On another occasion she was asked to ride on a freight elevator in a southern hotel, and indignantly took the long flight of stairs, although she suffered from chronic asthma. (When she got to the hotel room she had an attack and a doctor had to be called.) Bethune was also undaunted by physical danger, and even stood down the Ku Klux Klan's attempted interference with Black voter registration in Florida.

While she made grand public gestures, however, Bethune could be devastatingly subtle. Once when a White House guard addressed her as "Auntie," she stopped, looked at him intently for a few moments, and in her sweetest and most earnest voice asked him, "Which one of my brother's children are you?"

Bethune understood that public relations was only one aspect of her role. At times, as in the Daytona Beach housing project incident, it was necessary to roll up the cuffs and slosh in the mud. She saw herself not so much in individual terms as playing a part essential to the race as a whole. Not that Bethune had any lack of ego, but as one of the few race representatives she viewed her work in a broader perspective. This was evident at an NCNW meeting, when she spoke of the death of Henry Hunt, who had worked in the Farm Credit Bureau:

> Our strongest man on the field died the other day. . . . We lost Henry Hunt. We must take a moment for Henry Hunt and James Weldon Johnson, and [Arthur] Schomberg. We must take a minute before we go for those people who gave themselves. Henry Hunt called me up just a few minutes before the nightfall came, tired and weary from tramping America in behalf of opening these banks and getting loans, getting something for his people. . . . We can't give up; we have got to continue to do it. . . . We

are not here to hold a position or to be the head of this, or that, or the other; we are here to mass our power and our thinking and our souls to see what we can do to make it better for that mass that can't speak out there. That is why we are here. I have no right to be here, but it is too much to give up. We can't give up! We must keep on.[18]

Bethune's perception of her role made her an effective advocate of Black unity, as was apparent in her organizing of the Federal Council on Negro Affairs. She was always conscientious about giving credit to others, and made sure that other civil rights organizations saw her own National Council of Negro Women as a complement to their efforts rather than as a competitor. "The program of the National Council will not replace or usurp specialized programs of the individual organizations," noted an NCNW press release in 1937, "but acting in a similar relationship to that of the federal government and the states, will represent the coordinated actions and unified front of Negro womanhood at a time when cooperation is most necessary and most fruitful of results."

Cooperation, for Bethune, was not limited to the quest for Black goals but encompassed the strivings of other minority groups who encountered discrimination. When the Nuremberg Laws legalized the persecution of Jews in Germany, the NCNW drafted a telegram to Franklin Roosevelt stating that the U.S. government should support the Jewish struggle. At a 1938 meeting, Mary Jackson McCrorey, a veteran of the Y struggles, passed a motion to "let our President [Roosevelt] know that we heartily recommend the action of our government toward the rehabilitation of the suffering Jews of the world, assuring him at the same time that our approach is one more sympathetic than could come from any other group in this country because of our experience in this country." Seconding the motion, another council member added that the NCNW should state that "we can sympathize because Hitler is endeavoring to reduce the status of Jews in Germany to that of the Negro in New York."[19]

Every aspect of Bethune's philosophy of leadership came into play when she acted as advocate for Black women. She articulated her faith in them with a passion that no other Black woman leader has expressed since. She was adamant about the unheralded achievements of women, always encouraging them to "go to the front and take our rightful place; fight our battles and claim our victories."[20] She believed in women's "possibilities" and their place on this earth. "Next to God," she once said, "we are indebted to women, first for life itself, and then for making it worth having."[21] Of course she had great hopes for the NCNW as a vehicle for realizing the potential of women, and hoped to associate the NCNW with the government, thereby giving Black women visibility on a national scale. When Black women were ignored, as they were in 1941 when the War Department failed to invite them to a conference on organizing women for the war effort, Bethune was quick to show displeasure. She wrote to Secretary of War Henry L. Stimson:

> We cannot accept any excuse that the exclusion of Negro representation was an oversight. We are anxious for you to know that we want to be, and insist upon being considered a part of our American democracy, not something apart from it. We know from experience that our interests are too often neglected, ignored or scuttled unless we have effective representation in the formative stages of these projects and proposals. We are not blind to what is happening. We are not humiliated. We are incensed.[22]

But rather than simply complaining about being left out, Bethune and her NCNW strove to put Black women into the position of directing those projects and proposals. Bethune's organization of White House conferences—one of them in direct cooperation with the NCNW—was a conscious effort to gain sanction for the ideas and presence of Black women on national policy-making levels. "I had to go to Mrs. Roosevelt," she told NCNW women, "about two months ahead of time and sit and talk with her for an hour on the importance of this [conference] so as to bring it there under government surroundings and shrouded in a governmental setting to give prestige and history to it." The result was inspiring, according to Bethune. "Very definite things came out of the White House conference," she said in an NCNW meeting:

> It certainly was history-making. . . . Sixty-seven Negro women marching to the White House in their own right, standing on their feet expressing what they thought concerning their own people and the participation they should have had in the general affairs of the country. I know that you will be happy to know that in that group I think we have five Negro women lawyers. We presented the very best we had because this country, you know,

only knows a few of us, just a few. [Some] wanted to know if these were the people of Booker T. Washington. They don't know any Black man except Booker T. Washington. . . . We want people to understand that there are myriads of prepared Negro women. . . . I was glad to sit aside them and see them stand on their feet fearlessly preparing themselves and their thoughts, not coming as beggars but coming as women wanting to participate in the administration of a human problem. . . .

The pressure we have been making, the intercessions . . . they are finding their way. A door has been sealed up for two hundred years. You can't open it overnight but little crevices are coming. . . . Sixty-seven women sitting down at the White House —the first time in the history of the world . . .

I think we are getting somewhere. . . . The position I hold now—I give you that as an example. The first time in history that a Negro woman filled a national, federal position with the lee-way, the opportunity . . . the contacts. Because one got in there, sixty-seven got in one day and many others are getting in here and there and there and there.[23]

Bethune had her shortcomings. Her acceptance of the separate-but-equal policy often resulted in separateness without the equality, as Ross remarked. She probably had too much faith in the idea that visibility and competence would open doors, more than they ever really could. She was very much a team player in the administration, perhaps too much so, particularly in the forties when Roosevelt retreated from past civil rights policies. And Bethune seemed not to delegate authority easily. Throughout the thirties and forties she must have stretched her own resources thin, as head of her division in the NYA, the NCNW, and Bethune-Cookman College.

Still, the contributions of Mary McLeod Bethune in the Roosevelt era are undeniable. And her unflagging concern for Black women achieved an earlier goal: Because of her efforts, women were counted among the new groups with legitimate demands that had to be taken into account on the national agenda. As a result, Blacks, both men and women, were better prepared to go beyond "separate but equal" to demand integration into the nation's mainstream—a demand that would be pressed as the nation entered upon a second world war.

XIV

~ A Second World War and After ~

The Depression affected people in two ways. The great majority
reacted by thinking money is the most important thing in the world.
Get yours. And get it for your children. Nothing else matters. And
there was a small number of people who felt that the whole system
was lousy. You have to change it.
—VIRGINIA DURR

Before the United States entered the Second World War, married
women who worked made less than single women—if they could
work at all. A National Education Association survey found that 77
percent of 1,500 school systems refused to hire married women, and
63 percent actually dismissed them. Additionally, some 43 percent of
the country's public utilities, and 13 percent of its department stores,
restricted the hiring of wives.[1] Legislative measures like the Federal
Economy Act, and similar laws on the state level, required that one
spouse resign if the other was gainfully employed. Needless to say, in
the overwhelming majority of cases it was the wife who resigned.
Economic need was not the criterion here; being married was.

Nevertheless, in the face of economic need, policy makers may
have been able to make some married women feel guilty about working (Secretary of Labor Frances Perkins called women who worked
for pin money a "menace to society") but they could not quell their
rush into the labor force. Even in the woman-idealizing South, seven
out of eight married women were working by 1940; the national
proportion of such workers was six out of seven.[2] The Women's
Bureau under Mary Anderson conducted studies which showed that
the great majority of women who worked in factories contributed at
least 50 percent to their families' income. Furthermore, more than
half of all married women were employed in domestic and personal
service or low-paying factory work. There was only one conclusion to

draw: Married women were not working for pin money but because their husbands were earning insufficient wages.

If the general female population was in such straits, Black women were even more pressed. By 1940 one Black woman in three over the age of fourteen was in the work force, compared to one in five for Whites. Sixty percent of the former were in service and domestic occupations, with another large percentage in agriculture. White families needed the income of wives; for Black families it was essential. Not surprisingly, Black men were more severely punished by the Depression than Whites. Thus, educator Marion Cuthbert pointed out, "The loss of work opportunities by Negro women [was] not compensated by work gains on the part of Negro men."[3] Nevertheless, Black women remained in "the most marginal position of all classes of labor," wrote sociologist Charles S. Johnson, and the blame for their status was placed squarely on their own shoulders.[4] Mary Anderson, who was so sympathetic to the plight of White working-women, believed that Black women still had "to prove themselves capable of developing skills and ready work habits" and to show themselves "worthy of advancement."[5]

Of course it was difficult to develop skills when relegated to unskilled work, or ready work habits when one was the last hired and the first fired. But this did not mean that Black women felt *themselves* unworthy of advancement. In fact, their difficult and desperate road made them all the more determined. Echoing the earlier sentiments of Sadie T.M. Alexander, Marion Cuthbert reflected: "Here then is the truth that gives direction to the course the Negro woman must pursue. . . . She is a worker. She must throw her lot with workers . . . if her children are to have even the half chance of life that this dual toil of parents makes possible."[6]

Just months after Anderson's statement about Black women workers at an interracial conference in 1933, a number of successful job actions were initiated. In St. Louis, Missouri, nine hundred Black women employed in seven pecan factories owned by the same proprietor walked out, demanding higher pay, better working conditions, and the elimination of differentials between Black and White women workers. The determination of Connie Smith, a middle-aged Black woman who led the walkout, brought cooperation from the community, her fellow White workers, and such organizations as the Unemployed Councils. The owner of the factories tried to divide the women, offering Whites an increase in wages if they returned to work. The answer was returned by 1,500 women of both races marching on

City Hall, and the proprietor gave in. Wages were increased (one Black woman who had worked there for eighteen years was pleased when she received $9 per week instead of $3); conditions improved, and White and Black women got equal pay and working conditions. The successful resolution of the strike spurred the formation of eleven locals of the Food Workers Industrial Union by 1,400 members, the majority of them Black.

Just a few months later, Black women joined Whites in the International Ladies' Garment Workers' Union (ILGWU) strikes in New Jersey, New York, and Connecticut, helping to guarantee their success. And throughout the thirties, the Domestic Workers Union had made strides in organizing Black women in the Bronx slave market and in other cities. Black women led the organization of workers in the laundries, and in cleaning and dyeing establishments. With help from the National Negro Congress, Black women, through the women's auxiliaries, became important allies in organizing the steel industry. A White colleague noted

> the swiftness with which Negro women have taken the leadership in our chapters. There is not one auxiliary where the staying power of those courageous women has not carried the organization over some critical period, especially in the first days of unseen and unsung organizing drudgery before the body took form. They were undaunted and gave great moral strength with their persistence.[7]

Black women were especially proving their worth in the tobacco industry, where they made up a large percentage of the workers and where they were relegated to the lowest-paying and most numbing work. In 1937, four hundred Black women walked out of the I. N. Vaughn Company in Richmond, protesting wages and working conditions. Previous appeals to the AFL had been met with the response that the women were "unorganizable." But with help from the Negro Congress and the Southern Negro Youth Congress, an independent union was set up, and the women were able to negotiate contracts resulting in $300,000 in pay increases, in addition to rates for overtime and holiday pay. The union eventually joined with the CIO. Emerging as a leader was Mamma Harris, a tobacco stemmer, who became known as "Missus CIO in Richmond." In the following year she led a strike of Vaughn workers in the Export Department—some seven hundred of them. The women, aided by the ILGWU and other unions, won their goals in eighteen days.

In 1943 it was Reynolds Tobacco Company's turn. In that year, a Black worker fell dead in the Winston-Salem plant after a supervisor had refused him permission to leave work and go home. Black women workers led a spontaneous sit-down which led to a strike involving ten thousand employees; they succeeded in shutting down the plant, and organizing Local 22 of the CIO's Food, Tobacco, Agricultural and Allied Workers of America (FTA). Eventually the workers won a more amenable contract regarding pay, working conditions, and benefits. When the contract expired four years later, another round was fought. This time Reynolds was able to get help from the government, more specifically from the House Un-American Activities Committee (HUAC), which sought to make an example of Local 22. Led by young Congressman Richard Milhous Nixon, HUAC investigated the local on the grounds that it was a "Communist-dominated union." Nixon eyed the investigation as a possible first case involving the anti-Communist provisions of the Taft-Hartley Bill, which required trade union officials to sign an anti-Communist oath. Although the strike received broad-based support from the White liberal and Black communities, the UAW, and notable figures such as Paul Robeson, who spoke at a mass rally of twelve thousand people, the strikers did not get the kind of contract they wanted. However, as labor historian Philip Foner notes, what they did get—a 12-cent-per-hour pay raise, maternity leave, wage and job classifications—was a testament to the women's strength and determination.

In 1949, Moranda Smith became the FTA's southern regional director, the first woman to serve in that capacity for an international union in the South. She organized CIO unions throughout the region, and political activities in Winston-Salem, which resulted in the election of the first Black alderman in the South since the turn of the century. But the constant traveling, confrontations, and continuing harassment took its toll. In 1950, at the age of thirty-five, Moranda Smith was dead. The cause, a colleague charged, was the "strain of her activities."

But the forward march of Blacks in the labor movement was braked by a number of factors: Unions continued largely to exclude both Blacks and women. So, in addition to racial discrimination, Black women had to deal with the sexist attitudes of such organizations as the AFL. Even during the years of war mobilization, the union was characterized by Mary Anderson as the greatest obstacle to women in the labor force. Additionally, civil rights leaders—with the exception of labor leader A. Philip Randolph—were often ambivalent about throwing their weight behind Black participation in the union movement. Much of the funding and personnel of the civil rights organizations, after all, came from the ranks of big business. In any case, the only union that sought Black participation was the CIO, and its leftist affiliations alienated many Black leaders who were offended by its ideology and fearful of harassment. The overall situation made a conservative Black intellectual like Kelly Miller argue: "Logic aligns the Negro with labor, but good sense arrays him with capital."[8]

Clearly the greatest opportunity for the Black worker was the defense industries.

Women and War

The year 1941 marked not only a day of infamy, but also the beginning of a dramatic shift in attitude toward women, married or not, joining the work force. Unemployed and working men alike were called into battle, American industry tooled up, and suddenly it was more than desirable for women to work—it was their patriotic duty. The employment of both married and single women would "help speed the day of victory," as more than one poster from the Government Printing Office beamed. Anything less, the country was warned, could mean the specter of American women yielding to the evil whims of the enemy.

Women heeded their nation's call. By 1940 and 1945 the number of women in the work force increased from less than 14 million to 20 million. By 1945, they constituted 38 percent of the work force. Not only were more of them working, but they were employed in jobs that had previously been the exclusive domain of men. Women were working in the naval yards, weapons factories, communication equipment lines. The image of a smiling Rosie the Riveter was etched into the American consciousness. But the great employment wave withered to a trickle when it came to Black workers in general and Black women in particular.

There were still 5 million unemployed Whites to be absorbed in the economy before Blacks would even get a nod. Even when they did, the attitude of employers was typified by the president of North American Aviation, who frankly stated: "While we are in complete sympathy with the Negro, it is against company policy to employ them as aircraft workers or mechanics . . . regardless of their training. . . . There will be some jobs as janitors."[9] The new sociology, it seemed, may have brought Black Americans more sympathy but little in the way of employment opportunity.

The situation enraged Blacks. Discrimination was a hard enough pill to swallow in times of general unemployment, but for Whites to be called back to work while Blacks were left without jobs was outrageous. The humiliation was all the more acute in light of the recent gains made during FDR's second term. But Roosevelt showed unmistakable signs of a lessening commitment to civil rights. Despite all his alphabetical programs in the Depression years, unemployment and a sluggish recovery still hung over the nation like a cloud. With the elections of 1938 the Republicans had gained political ground. FDR's support was slipping and began to deteriorate perceptibly when his attempt to "pack" the Supreme Court was exposed. The southern contingent of the Democratic party, forced to take a back seat in the earlier years, was now being courted again. Their hawklike interventionist stand was particularly useful to the President, who was seeking support in preparing the country for war.

Receiving little encouragement from the administration, Blacks felt direct action was necessary. Their concerns about discrimination in the defense industries had prompted the formation of such organizations as the Committee for the Participation of Negroes in National Defense and the Allied Committees for National Defense. But it soon became obvious that organizations and rhetoric were getting Blacks nowhere.

The March on Washington

According to the historian Harvard Sitkoff, the idea for a March on Washington to redress discrimination in the defense industries came from a Black woman! Representatives of civil rights organizations were mapping out strategy at a meeting in Chicago when a Black woman said: "Mr. Chairman, we ought to throw fifty thousand Negroes around the White House—bring them from all over the country, in jalopies, in trains, and any way they can get there until we can get some action from the White House." A. Philip Randolph was said to have seconded the proposal, adding: "I agree with the sister. I will be happy to throw [in] my organization's resources and offer myself as a leader of such a movement."[10]

The proposal for a mass march touched a chord among civil rights leaders and, more importantly, among the masses of Blacks. As the idea gained momentum it catapulted Randolph, organizer of the Brotherhood of Sleeping Car Porters, to national stature—a development not wholly appreciated by established civil rights leaders. But the march's momentum kept other leaders in line behind him and prevented any backing down or compromise. Randolph grew more demanding as he threatened that no fewer than 100,000 Blacks were willing to demonstrate in the capital. The ability to mobilize so many Afro-Americans had been demonstrated only once before, and that was during the years of Marcus Garvey's prominence.

The result was the famous Executive Order 8802 in 1941, which forbade discrimination in hiring of workers in the nation's defense industries on the basis of race, creed, color, or national origin. The Federal Employment Practices Commission (FEPC) was also established to act as a watchdog over the execution of the order. Though Black women were concerned that the executive mandate did not include the word *sex,* it was generally taken for granted that the race provision would protect them.

Slowly Black men and women began to trickle into the defense industries. Still, a great deal of discrimination prevailed, and with Black women some of the reasons were particularly bizarre, if unsurprising. For example, a Black newspaper, *The Baltimore Afro-American,* ran a story in 1945 about Black women struggling to be hired by the Naval Ordnance Plant in Macon, Georgia: "The chief opposition to employment of colored women did not come from management or the employees . . . but from white local housewives, who feared lowering the barriers would rob them of maids, cooks, and nurses."[11]

A more common problem was voiced by the vice-president of the Sharon Steel Corporation in Pennsylvania before an FEPC hearing. The absence of Black women in his plant, he said, was the fault of his "women employees [who would] not work with non-Whites."[12]

Black women faced other—and familiar—problems. Where they were allowed to work, they often had the dirtiest and most taxing jobs. In the steel mills they were assigned to the sintering plants as grinders; in the defense industries they were more often than not in custodial positions. One study revealed that although more Black women than ever before were employed in industry, in many cases they simply shifted from private homes to commercial enterprises "without any upgrading or real change in type of work."[13]

Black women fought against discrimination, their relegation to the worst jobs in industrial plants, and unfair wages. Nearly one quarter of all complaints to the FEPC between July 1943 and December 1944 were brought by Black women.

However, the progress of Black women could be characterized as "two steps forward and one step back." In the final analysis, they had made gains in the war years. By 1944, a *Pittsburgh Courier* article stated, they were found in every one of the nation's war industries. The number of Black women in semiprofessional occupations increased dramatically between 1940 and 1947; their number of craftswomen, forewomen, and factory operatives almost quadrupled. The percentage of Black workingwomen earning wages in the industrial sector in 1940 had tripled by 1944, while during the same four years the percentage of domestics dropped from over 60 percent to 45 percent.[14] On other fronts, Black women made a breakthrough in the nation's utilities when Bell Telephone hired the first Black operator in 1945. Thanks to Mary McLeod Bethune, Black women were also poised to become officers in the armed services. As special assistant to the commanding officer of the Women's Auxiliary Corps, Bethune had the responsibility for selecting Black women for the first Officers Training School.

Collectively, these achievements resulted in a precipitous rise in the income of Black women who were working full time. From a median income that was 38 percent that of White women and 51 percent that of Black men in 1939, they would enjoy the greatest percentage increase of any race or sex group in the subsequent decades. That achievement, however, would not be without consequences.

Postwar Developments

The rise of Black women, like that of other Americans, was yoked to that of industry after the war. If industry was to maintain the head of steam generated by lucrative defense contracts in the war years, markets would have to expand accordingly—both at home and abroad. Outside the United States, an interested eye was cast toward the Third World, much of which was clamoring for independence. At home, two groups looked like particularly good prospects to gobble up the coming cascade of manufactured goods: Afro-Americans and women.

The groundwork to prop up Blacks so that they would be in a position to aid the economy by consuming its goods was established in the thirties. In that decade prominent intellectuals espoused the theory that environment, not race, determined intelligence and/or personality. That was the underlying thesis in E. Franklin Frazier's *The Negro Family;* it was what Ashley Montagu and H. J. Muller were writing about; it was what Otto Klineberg's correlations of poverty and I.Q. were all about; it was what Franz Boas had been trying to say since the turn of the century. Environment as the determinant was the message of Richard Wright's *Native Son* and Ann Petry's *The Street.* Scientific racism, even the concept of race was out; social realism, in.

By the 1940's, governmental departments, universities, and institutions such as the Carnegie Corporation underwrote a plethora of research and analysis regarding the plight of Blacks in American life. The culminating *tour de force* of all this activity appeared with the publication of *An American Dilemma* by Gunnar Myrdal, the result of extensive research by sociologists, historians, anthropologists, political scientists, psychologists, economists, and other experts.

According to Ralph Ellison, the views on race relations expressed in *An American Dilemma* revealed another, related, article of social-science faith in a period when racist demagoguery was again on the rise. Racial harmony fostered economic development, and economic development was what the nation's industries needed. This was particularly true in the South. So it was no coincidence that *An American Dilemma,* boiled down, served as a "blueprint for a more effective exploitation of the South's natural, industrial and human resources," in Ellison's words.[15] In the wake of the postwar sociology and economic need, the spirit of interracial cooperation was hoisted once more. In 1944 Black and White Southerners founded the Southern Regional Council, which was, according to John Hope Franklin, a revitalized and expanded Commission of Interracial Cooperation. In the region, interracial goodwill increased and lynching decreased— as much a result of economics as of social conscience. Jessie Daniel Ames commented:

> We have managed to reduce lynchings not because we've grown more law-abiding or respectable but because lynchings became such bad advertising. The South is going after big industry at the moment, and a lawless, lynch-mob population isn't going to attract very much outside capital. And this is the type of attitude which can be turned to advantage much more speedily than the abstract appeal to brotherly love.[16]

Such cynical observations were not in the minds of the majority of Black folk. Most believed that integration into the mainstream of American life was imminent. Social and economic developments seemed to confirm this conviction. Prominent Blacks emerged, were listened to, and even revered by the broader society. And a lot of gates seemed to open. Any cynic would have to explain away the undeniable—if superficial—signs of change. Hadn't Eleanor Roosevelt resigned from the Daughters of the American Revolution in protest when the organization prohibited Marian Anderson from singing in Constitution Hall? Hadn't 75,000 people, including prominent Cabinet members, come to hear Anderson sing at the Lincoln Memorial? Hadn't Jackie Robinson been allowed to add some color to the previously all-White national pastime? Didn't the economic gains speak for themselves? Separate but equal, in theory at least, was no longer relevant. Black civil rights leaders no longer fought for segregated equity but integration.

Yet, "There was no actual integration anywhere," critic Arthur P. Davis declared. "There was surface and token integration in many areas, but the everyday pattern of life for the overwhelming majority remained unchanged. But there was—and this is of utmost importance —the spiritual commitment and climate out of which full integration could develop."[17] Even the Black literature of the forties and early fifties reflected faith in the coming millennium of integration. The protest tradition, Davis wrote, was abandoned for a more universal and introspective tone. Afro-Americans were prompted by a well-calculated message of expectation for the future. Even Black women were confident enough to contribute their share to the baby boom of the postwar era. Although they were not, like White women, backpacking to suburbia or leaving the labor force in great numbers, Black mothers were having more babies than in any previous period, averaging four per family, the highest complete fertility of any group since the decade following the Civil War.*

Faith in the future was confirmed by Black economic gains in the period. It was after World War II that sufficient numbers of Afro-Americans attained middle-class status to form what Frazier dubbed

---

*Childlessness among Blacks also decreased, from 28 percent to 10 percent. Thirty percent of Black women born in the Depression years—between 1930 and 1934—had two children by the time they reached the age of twenty-one; 16 percent had four children by the age of twenty-four; and 10 percent had six children before they reached the grand old age of twenty-seven. Those who had given birth to their first child before they were nineteen averaged five children each. Almost 20 percent of Black women had seven children. However, Black women who lived outside the South, and who reached upper income levels, had fewer children.[18]

the Black Bourgeoisie. And Black gains represented more than the progress of the upper middle class. As E. Franklin Frazier pointed out, the emergence of the Black Bourgeoisie resulted largely from the increase of clerical and kindred occupation workers. Although the actual numbers remained small, from 1940 to 1950, the proportion of Black men in this category rose from one fourth to one half that of White male workers; Black women from one twentieth to one seventh that of White female workers. Additionally, Black men and women increased their percentages as professional and semiprofessional workers. In the meantime the percentage of Black women in domestic service continued to decline. In 1950, 42 percent of Black women were domestics, representing an overall drop of 18 points since 1940.

But economic progress along the lines of the new sociology had its price. With the eclipse of cultural relativism—and its idea that no culture was inferior, just different—the unique heritage of Afro-Americans, so in vogue during the Renaissance, now began to look like something else. "What had been considered warmth and sensual expression, was now emotional inconsistency, and inability to defer gratification," wrote sociologist Nathan Glazer in the preface to a revised edition of Frazier's *The Negro Family*. [19] Such characteristics ran counter to achievement in middle-class terms—and lack of achievement undermined the ability to be a good consumer. So there was pressure to underplay the "African" part of Afro-American, and anyway, as Frazier, Myrdal, and later Daniel Patrick Moynihan and Nathan Glazer stated, there was little—if any—African culture left to save. Upward mobility, and the accumulation of material goods as its measure, became the thing. The trend was also reflected in other parts of the world. In the eyes of many Third World leaders, there was no longer much that was noble about unindustrialized cultures. The United States was looked up to as a model of development—and as a source of manufactured goods to consume.

If Blacks were encouraged to practice the Protestant work ethic, women were encouraged to stay at home and revel in the shower of appliances and household cleaners now inundating the country. "Why is it never said that the really crucial function, the really important role that women serve as housewives is *to buy more things for the house*," asked Betty Friedan in her brilliant polemic *The Feminine Mystique*. [20] It was the housewife, she contended, who was targeted by American business to take up the slack of terminated defense contracts. The

Madison Avenue science of "hidden persuaders" convinced women that they could be given "the sense of identity, purpose, creativity, the self-realization, even the joy they lack—by the buying of things." As with Blacks, women's sense of self had to be whittled away before they could become postulants at the altar of the "new religion." Given their work experience during the war, and the fact that 22 million women—nearly half of them married—were working in 1957, the task would require a formidable array of propaganda.

Recalling the "cult of true womanhood" in the nineteenth century, women were told that their place was in the home, and that a career, if not merely a job to supplement the family income, would have evil consequences for them and for their families.* In the fifties women were told, once again, that careers, assertiveness, and higher education were dangerous chimeras. *Modern Woman: The Lost Sex* by psychiatrist Marynia Farnham and sociologist Ferdinand Lundberg, for example, warned that "careers and higher education were leading to the 'masculinization' of women with enormously dangerous consequences to the home and children." Philip Wylie's *A Generation of Vipers* talked about such women as "female monsters" who had been created by industrialization. They were "narcissistic Moms" who devoured their sons and husbands, drawing from them independence and strength. This was particularly true of the career woman, "whose evil included every desire of the separate self," Friedan wrote. The separate self had frightening sexual connotations, if one believed the fifties' party line. Farnham and Lundberg would have had the reader believe that such assertiveness undermined sexual gratification for women as well as for their husbands. Psychiatrist Helene Deutsch, an adherent of Sigmund Freud (whose theories were recalled with a new vigor in the period), stated that assertive women were suffering from masculinity complexes, penis-envy as Freud called it. Feminism, Lundberg and Farnham concluded, "was at its core a deep illness." The only true and healthy road to a woman's fulfillment was as a housewife; the only means of resolving the fervent wish for the male appendage was impregnation.

The litmus test for feminine salvation was the spurning of higher education, political rights, and fulfilling work. This was not to say that

---

*One consequence of this attitude was that although between 1940 and 1960 the overall percentage of women working outside the home increased, there was a slight but persistent decline in the proportion of professional, technical, and kindred workers.[21]

women didn't have an important role to play. The statesman and diplomat Adlai Stevenson, in a Smith College commencement address in 1955, spelled it out for them. He admitted that "many women feel frustrated and far apart from the great issues and stirring debate for which their education has given them understanding and relish. . . ." But help was on the way:

> The assignment to you, as wives and mothers, you can do in the living room with a baby in your lap or in the kitchen with a can opener in your hand. If you are clever, maybe you can even practice your saving arts on that unsuspecting man while he's watching television. I think there is much you can do about our crisis in the humble role of housewife.[22]

Little wonder that a study of Vassar students in the late fifties concluded that the women were "convinced that the wrongs of society will gradually right themselves with little or no intervention on the part of women college students."[23] Little wonder that another Vassar College study conducted by the Mellon Foundation in 1956 revealed that a typical student's "strong commitment to an activity or career other than housewife was rare. . . . Few plan to continue with a career if it should conflict with family needs."[24] And there were a lot of family needs in the baby boom years. The proportion of women college students declined from 47 percent in 1920 to 35.2 percent in 1958, a trend that made the United States the only country where the proportion of women attaining higher education was decreasing, as Friedan observed with disgust. Not surprisingly, the number of women receiving professional degrees also decreased. There were other things on women's minds: They were marrying younger and having more babies. Friedan estimated that 60 percent of all women college dropouts left school to marry or because they were afraid too much education would be a bar to marriage.

An Afro-American Dilemma

Where did Black women fit in this scheme of things? They shared on the one hand the upwardly mobile achievement ethic of the Black Bourgeoisie, and on the other, the ambivalence toward those aspirations that were felt by women in general. But ambivalent or no, economic necessity and the traditional values of achievement propelled them. The latter was exemplified in a letter written by Mary

McLeod Bethune to Charlotte Hawkins Brown in 1947, congratulating her—and by extension all Black women—on their attainments in recent years.

> My eyes sparkled with glee and my heart vibrated with joy . . . to see your . . . Award for Interracial Advancement. God bless our women. They are reaching forward speedily. . . .
>
> Harriet Tubman, Sojourner Truth, Margaret Washington— all of those who were sowing seeds when it cost so much more than it does now, must rejoice in the Glory Land over the great harvest that is now coming to Negro womanhood in America and throughout the world. . . . The harvest time is bound to come but it is heartening to those of us who have tried so hard, to live sufficiently long to garner in just a little of the harvest while we are still alive.[25]

Eight years before her death, Bethune had much to feel good about. The "harvest" was a rich one and extended into many areas. In the letter, she mentioned Carol Brice, a young singer who made her debut at Town Hall in 1945 and was the first Afro-American to win the coveted Naumburg Award. Brice was one of a number of Black concert singers, including Dorothy Maynor and Lillian Evanti, who reached national acclaim through the door Marian Anderson had opened. In fact, the achievements of Black women in the arts during the forties and early fifties were significant enough to characterize the era as *their* renaissance. Hazel Scott, Billie Holiday, Ella Fitzgerald, and Sarah Vaughn were holding forth in the jazz world. Josephine Baker was preparing to return from Europe; Ethel Waters and Lena Horne were stars on the silver screen. Mahalia Jackson elevated Gospel music to a new standard and appreciation. Elizabeth Prophet, Selma Burke, Augusta Savage, Lois Mailou Jones, and Elizabeth Catlett had become prominent in the art world. Katherine Dunham, Pearl Primus, Mary Hinkson, and Janet Collins were making breakthroughs in dance. Margaret Walker, Gwendolyn Brooks, and Ann Petry won major awards for their writing.

Bethune also mentioned in her letter the unprecedented number of Black women in the colleges. Higher education had always been of great concern to her, and doubtless she was pleased that by 1947, Bethune-Cookman had achieved a Grade A rating as a national senior institution. At a time when White women were beginning to drop out of or not go to college, Black women were attending colleges at a higher rate than either White women or Black men. By 1940, more Black women received B.A. degrees from Black colleges than Black men (3,244 and 2,463 respectively). By 1952–53, the surge of Black women had increased significantly. They received 62.4 percent of all degrees from Black colleges when, in all colleges, the percentage of women graduates was 33.4 percent. The percentage of Black women graduates was in fact just a little below that of *male* graduates in all schools (66.6 percent) and substantially higher than that of Black men (35.6 percent).[26] An important dimension to this was that a large proportion of these women were the first in their families to receive college degrees.

In a study of Black women graduates of this period, educator Jeanne Noble found that of the 412 graduates in her sample, 50 percent belonged to this category. Also, more and more Black women were earning degrees beyond the baccalaureate. In Noble's study, 73 percent had studied beyond their bachelor's degree and 48 percent had received their master's. Over 90 percent of this group also had grade averages of B or better. By the early fifties, more Black women than men had master's degrees, although men still held the edge in Ph.D.'s and M.D.'s by a significant margin.

Increased college attendance translated itself into rising numbers of Black women in the professions, including positions held exclusively by men in the past. Bethune mentioned this in her letter, and she was no doubt thinking of the many prominent Black women who came to the fore in this period. The new generation included women like Crystal Bird Fauset, a member of the Pennsylvania legislature, and racial relations adviser to the federal Office of Civil Defense; Edith Sampson, a judge, and member of the American delegation to the United Nations General Assembly; Anna Arnold Hedgeman, a leader in the YWCA, and the first Black woman to serve as an assistant to the mayor of New York City; and Constance Baker Motley, who was the housing expert on the NAACP legal defense staff that successfully argued the 1954 *Brown* v. *Topeka Board of Education* Supreme Court case, would also become the first Black woman named to the federal bench and to become Manhattan Borough President in New York City.

Beyond such celebrities, the number of Black professional women in general was on the rise: from 4 percent of female professional workers to 6 percent between 1940 and 1950. Many of these women were able to find jobs in the traditional "women's professions"—nursing, teaching, social work—because of the decreasing numbers of White women seeking such work. Largely due to these opportunities in the women's professions, by 1950 a larger percentage of Black women (5.2 percent) were in professional and semiprofessional occupations than were Black men (2.6 percent). Moreover, Noble points out, 30 percent of the younger graduates in her study expressed interest in other than the traditional women's professions, opting for merchandising, reading specialization, or engineering. This drive by Black women to enter the professions resulted in their disproportionate representation within their racial group. By 1950, Black women comprised 58 percent of all Black professional workers, while White women represented 35 percent of all White professional workers. In addition to the traditional race/sex forces pushing Black women into schools and professions, the new wave of Black migration to the North—which began in 1940 and resulted in 4 million Blacks leaving the South in the next three decades—had a telling effect. As had happened in previous migrations, Black women who came to the North tended to be more skilled and better educated than their male counterparts.

If Mary McLeod Bethune was aware of some of the problems attendant on these unprecedented achievements, she didn't mention them in her letter to Charlotte Hawkins Brown. But gains by Black women in a society that was both patriarchal and racist presented difficulties. Black women, positioned as they were on the fulcrum of race and sex, were expected to perform several different—and often conflicting—roles.

Repeating a familiar historical pattern, in periods of racial assertion the contributions of supportive women are heralded. In 1936, a time of racial agitation and economic depression, the Black educator Marion Cuthbert observed: "There is a subtle deference on the part of Negro men to their women." It wasn't a deference of "chivalry," she explained, but one of "comradeship, and a tribute to a great courage. . . . Too many Black men," she continued, "owe part or all of what they are to the toil of mothers; too many men today see wives set forth with them daily to earn bread for their children; too many young, unmarried women gallantly carry on for a whole family group."[27]

When integration and acculturation began to prevail, Black women were seen to have fulfilled still another function. Three years after the publication of E. Franklin Frazier's *The Negro Family* in 1939, which correlated acculturation with Black achievement, *The Crisis* magazine reported:

> Throughout American history colored women have played a most significant role in the development of our civilization. Because their ties with Africa were abruptly severed . . . and because their greater struggle for survival compelled a speedier adaptation to a new life here, they have placed their imprint indelibly on our national life. They are the chief repository of Anglo-Saxon culture. Some students even hold that if every white person were to disappear from the United States, it would continue culturally to be Anglo-Saxon with, of course, the softening and sophisticated touch of Africa.
>
> The colored woman is responsible to a large degree for the rapid adaptation of black folk to American life, for she conveyed to the less favored male what she learned by closer association with the best that the civilized white minority had to offer. Without their economic aid and counsel we would have made little if any progress. Equality of the sexes is an old story in Negro life. Afra-America is even a Matriarchy.[28]

However dubious the "repository" statement, it was true that the economic role of Black women was important, even essential, to the rise of the Black Bourgeoisie. As Frazier had noted, the increased number of clerical and similar workers (a large number of them women) had inspired the emergence of the first Black middle class. On the upper economic levels the Black women's contribution was even more significant. The income of members of the Black Bourgeoisie that Frazier wrote about in the fifties ranged between $2,000 and $2,500; over 60 percent of the *single* women in Jeanne Noble's study made between $2,000 and $3,999.[29]* Whereas only 4 percent of all Black families had a total income as high as $5,000 or above in 1949, of the married women in her survey, 56 percent had family incomes over $6,000. Taking into account that 292 of the 318 married women in the survey worked outside the home,† and half of them had hus-

---

*The figure might be compared to the median income for all men ($2,333) and the median income for women ($1,000) in 1948, and to the average income for all Black women ($676) in 1950.

†Of the 318 married women in the survey, 218 were also employed before marrying.

bands who earned less than they did, one can readily see the contribution women made to swelling the ranks of the Black middle class.

Nevertheless, however proud—and appreciative—men were of their women's achievements, when the number of female college graduates began to exceed that of male graduates, attitudes underwent a change. Cuthbert, who had written so sanguinely of male-female relationships in 1936, observed only six years later: "The increase in Negro women college graduates has caused alarm in some quarters."[30] By the early fifties, Noble would more forthrightly contend that there was "a great deal of tension between Negro men and Negro college women."[31] The tension was exacerbated by the tendency of middle-class Black women to make certain social decisions, no matter what the marriage and baby boom trends of any period. At a time when the median age for women to marry was twenty, and dropping (14 million were engaged by the time they were seventeen), 75 percent of Noble's college graduates tied the nuptial knot between three and four years after graduation; 16 percent waited more than seven years to marry. In a period when the average Black mother had four children and the average White mother had three, 38 percent of the women in Noble's study had one child, 15 percent had two children, and 6 percent had between three and six children. A whopping 41 percent were childless. Noble observed that economics may not have been the sole reason for reduced childbearing: "The constant pressure on the part of the early college pioneers to force the women into the role of a mother 'fit to rear sons' may have caused her to revolt unconsciously and diminish her desire to rear a large family."[32]

Nevertheless, material gain was very much on this generation's mind. In the past, money had been seen as a means to an end—the progress of the race. As late as 1942, a study of Black college women by Marion Cuthbert found that for the students, "Going to college was a desire motivated in larger part by their interpretation of what should be helpful in meeting the grave situation which confronts the Negro."[33] By the mid-fifties, Noble discovered that nearly 90 percent of the students in her study went to college primarily to "prepare for a vocation," straight and simple.[34] Although on the surface their aspirations appear to have been greater than those of White middle-class women, their underlying attitudes were similar. Black women, too, were terribly ambivalent about being ambitious. Although "preparing for a vocation" was at the top of their list, "a better chance to get ahead in the world" was listed among the least important reasons.[35] In addition, Black women were less concerned about a fulfilling career in the professions than about financial reward. "You don't have very many women who really want a career above all else," one of Noble's interviewees revealed. "They want the things that money can buy—a certain place in life."[36] One of the consequences was that women concentrated on areas of study that had a cash value. "I ask students why they don't take courses in philosophy," commented a dean of students. "It is because we as people have been interested in taking those courses that make it possible to fulfill our physical needs."[37]

The attitudes reflected the materialistic ethos of the postwar period and the concomitant decline of racial militancy. The diminution of the protest tradition in literature and politics was further squelched by the "Red Scare," which ensnared such leaders as W.E.B. Du Bois, Paul Robeson, and Black Communist politician Benjamin Davis, with varying degrees of viciousness. It had even caught up with the "team player" Mary McLeod Bethune. In 1942 she was investigated by the FBI for alleged disloyalty to the government, and in 1943 was accused of being a Communist by HUAC. Though Bethune was exonerated on both charges, the accusations showed how wide the Red net was cast.

The deterioration of Black organizations was another factor in the late forties. By 1940 the NAACP, which had eclipsed the National Urban League and the Brotherhood of Sleeping Car Porters as the leading civil rights organization, was itself in eclipse. In that year, according to a report in *Negro Digest,* it lost 168,000 members, which represented a 40 percent drop from the year before.[38] Also in 1949, Bethune resigned from the presidency of the National Council of Negro Women, and the organization floundered. Not only was Bethune's energetic and well-connected leadership a hard act to follow, but the lack of a clear racial and policy direction clouded the NCNW's focus. With the deaths of such leaders as Mary Church Terrell and Bethune in 1954 and 1955 respectively, few veterans of the struggle were left to inspire the membership. The new generation of women within its ranks, with a diminished political orientation to guide them, used women's organizations like the NCNW as outlets for self-expression as much as for group goals. A résumé of a September 4 convention meeting of the NCNW in 1958 reflected the concern of President Dorothy Height about the organization. "Miss Height stated," reads the report, "that the problem we have is that the level of thinking women have about the Council is beneath the level that women should be operating on. They think of it more like a club and if many women saw things that women's organizations were doing like the National Council of Jewish Women, National Council of Catholic Women, United Churchwomen . . . they would have more respect and understanding."

The upshot of these developments was that Black college women, who in the past had made up the ranks of activists, were less likely to be politically involved in the fifties: only 16 percent of Noble's students were affiliated with any political organization. The lack of interest in racial matters also underlined the separation of the middle class from the masses of Blacks. Ironically, the separation was abetted by the increase of college students on Black campuses. As a commentator in Noble's study observed: "By placing the Negro campus in isolation from the cities we have helped students run away from their heritage as Negroes." There was a lack of desire, she said, "to associate with the 'bandana headed' Negro woman."[39]

The absence of group goals also served to throw Black women's personal lives into confusion. With no rationale for achievement save material gain, they worried about how they were perceived as women at a time when their White peers were staying at home, having children, and scanning the shelves for the latest appliances. One of Noble's respondents said: "Sometimes I feel that Negro women feel guilty about the education that they do have. They are more conscious of the fact that accomplishments may prevent them from getting married. I have actually had them ask me how they can put on brakes, to keep from being 'A' students and presidents of clubs, and so forth." Nevertheless, economic exigency and the combined forces of sexism and racism kept propelling Black women forward. As the previous speaker noted: "The fact that they go on to higher degrees is not so surprising. There are so few things that come naturally to the Negro woman to inspire her to be herself. She is forever having to meet requirements for a job in order to make sure that she is in a position to bargain. . . . It is regrettable that she is not free to make a genuine search either for learning or self-fulfillment." The result, she said, was a "lack of a healthy self-concept" which "created a sense of insecurity."[40]

If Black women were insecure about their self-concept, much of their anxiety was due to confusion and guilt concerning their roles.

The status of middle-class housewife/breadwinner was a new experience for most. About 90 percent of the female Black Bourgeoisie came from lower-economic-class backgrounds (compared to 35 percent of comparable White women) and there were few role models to draw upon.[41] "Preparation for marriage and family life" was second only to "preparing for a vocation" as the foremost reason why Black women went to college, according to Noble's findings. One of the respondents expressed their concerns this way:

> The role of the Negro woman has not been defined. She is not adept at combining the role of career woman and homemaker. She is expected to play the subordinate role of "female." I think it is because she is married to a Negro man. . . . Even though she may have a professional job the Negro man expects her to be a buffer for him—to work eight hours a day and come home and keep house. I am sure the Negro woman feels incapable of doing this adequately. For this reason she feels that somebody has let her down. She wants college to give her information on how she can do the impossible.[42]

But, the speaker hastened to conclude, "You cannot blame the Negro man." He was not allowed to be "an integrated human being and give his wife freedom to develop her own personality." Until society allowed him the opportunity to "support his family in the culture that gives him values but excludes him—he is going to have this inferiority and compensate for it by forcing his wife to be a buffer for him. Education must face this,"[43] she said.

Although frustrated by their own situation, Black women were sensitive to the ego needs of men. Another woman said that even if it meant making a sacrifice, wives should not buy the food for the home or pay for the children's education. "I think you take away a man's dignity when he cannot pay for the essentials." Though not in total agreement with that statement, another woman concurred that American society was to blame for having made Negro men second-class citizens. "No Negro man is able to adequately protect his wife at any level," she said. "When he cannot do this you cut into the heart of his relation with his society. The Negro woman demands more than he can give, so she must help, both financially and socially."[44]

Their attitudes toward men also reflected a broad concern about the startling signs of the deterioration of the Black family (by 1940, women headed 20 percent of all such families) and the new direction of sociological inquiry. The emphasis on development and upward mobility shifted the focus of inquiry from the "mother" to the "father." It was the increasing number of father-absent families, according to social scientists like Thomas Pettigrew and E. Franklin Frazier, that was keeping a large segment of Black families "underdeveloped."

This perspective led inevitably to the question: "Why are so many men leaving home?"—a question that tended to put men on the defensive. More often than not, the answer overlooked the broader issues of sexism and racism to zero in on the shortcomings of Black women—especially middle-class women. In content, the criticisms were much like those of Philip Wylie and others who castigated assertive White women. But Black women were more obvious targets, because fewer of them—by necessity—had submitted to "traditional" roles. Black women were caught between the two functions they were expected to fulfill: enhancing the material quality of life for their families, and at the same time behaving like housewives. With E. Franklin Frazier setting the tone in *The Negro Family* and *The Black Bourgeoisie,* Black women were scolded for being too domineering and too insecure; too ambitious and too decadently idle, all in the same breath. Thus, despite the special socioeconomic circumstances faced by Blacks, Black men saw Black women in the same context that White men saw White women. Black magazines like *Ebony* and *Jet,* with articles entitled "Do Career Women Make Good Wives?" or "Do Working Women Make Good Wives?" or "Do Pretty Women Make Good Wives?" were not only male-oriented but beside the point.

The "damned if you do, damned if you don't" syndrome was never more evident than in the period following World War II. E. Franklin Frazier, attempting to explain the rising divorce rate among Blacks, speculated that in many instances, the man, now more acculturated into the society, acquired "new interests and a different outlook on life from that of his wife."[45] In other words, Black wives didn't "grow" with their men, a criticism commonly leveled against them at the time. So, presumably while Black men were becoming worldly and urbane, Black women were "catty," petty, and maintained a "false sense of material values," or so Roi Ottley charged in a *Negro Digest* article, "What's Wrong With Negro Women?"[46]

Material values were a major issue. The single-minded quest for money and possessions was not only predominantly attributed to Black women (as if men were not also materialistic) but also cast males in a subservient role, according to critics. In middle-class families, Frazier wrote, "The husband is likely to play a pitiful role. The greatest compliment that can be paid . . . is that he 'worships his wife' which means that he is her slave and supports all of her extravagances and vanities." Frazier continued: "The conservative and conventional middle-class husband presents a pathetic picture. He often sits at home, impotent physically and socially. . . ."[47] That was, if the husband survived the ordeal at all: "The life of many a 'wealthy' Negro doctor is shortened by the struggle to provide diamonds, minks, and an expensive home for his wife," continued the sociologist.[48] The only way out of the materialistic mire was extramarital affairs, Frazier implied, and this was the cause of many a divorce. "Middle-class men get divorced for running around—not running away," wrote Black sociologist St. Clair Drake in the *Negro Digest* article "Why Men Leave Home."[49]

Though sociologists like Frazier did acknowledge that Black women could be frustrated too, the cause for their dissatisfaction had little to do with what women like the college graduates in Noble's study were talking about. While men's frustrations were largely due to their women, women's frustrations had nothing to do with the men they lived with. "The frustration of the majority of the women among the black bourgeoisie," Frazier concluded, "is probably due to the idle or ineffectual lives which they lead."[50] But those who weren't idlers were guilty of disrupting the nest too. "In other cases," Frazier noted, "the wife may seize an opportunity to enter upon a career of her own and thus destroy the pattern of family life which the man has become accustomed to."[51]

Black middle-class women's ineffectual, narrow-minded lives were no doubt responsible for another of their shortcomings: an "inferiority complex" in relation to White women which Ottley mentioned in his article. The White-woman–Black-man issue was on a lot of minds because of the growing visibility of interracial relationships and some widely publicized interracial marriages. The marriages of the NAACP's executive director Walter White and the organization's administrative assistant Leslie Perry—both of whom married White women in 1950, a time when the association was at a low ebb—were seen to have broad implications. A *Negro Digest* article asked if interracial marriages were "ruining the NAACP," and described how Black women "wailed about [Walter] White," who was, at the time, the most conspicuous Black person in America.

For Frazier and company, the negative reaction arose from nothing other than the Black woman's sense of inferiority. Frazier wrote:

> There is an intense fear of the competition of white women for Negro men. They often attempt to rationalize their fear by saying that the Negro man always occupies an inferior position to the white woman or that he marries much below his "social status." They come nearer to the source of their fear when they confess that there are not many eligible Negro men and that these few should marry Negro women. . . . The middle-class Negro woman's fear of the competition of white women is based often upon the fact that she senses her own inadequacies and shortcomings. . . . The middle-class white woman not only has a white skin and straight hair, but she is generally more sophisticated and interesting because she has read more widely and has a larger view of the world.[52]

Whatever the accuracy of the men's assertions, plainly missing was an introspective, self-critical view of the problem. When women weren't to blame, society was, as St. Clair Drake affirmed in "Why Men Leave Home": "The inescapable conclusion from Frazier's work is that if Negro men are to be kept at home, the first step is to make jobs and housing available to them, so that they can maintain a stable pattern of family relations. When more have a chance to become solidly middle-class, desertion rates will stop. Man must be the provider."[53]

Women of the period may not have disagreed, but they had to contend with the stark and present reality of their lives. Several women writers of the fifties explored the question with the objectivity so lacking in their male counterparts. Dorothy West's *The Living Is Easy* portrays a young protagonist whose zestful spirit is misdirected into getting dollar dole-outs from a good, if boorish, middle-aged husband and furthering her social ambitions. Paule Marshall's *Brown Girl, Brownstones* exposes the ambivalence of a young girl toward her parents' conflicting values. The mother wants to use money inherited by her husband to purchase a brownstone in New York City, while the father dreams of returning to his native Barbados and the past. The most poignant expression of the conflict and dilemma Blacks and Black families faced in this period was Lorraine Hansberry's *Raisin in the Sun.* How is a family to use the insurance money from the deceased father of the family? Will they buy a house in a White neighborhood that spurns them and send the daughter to college, or will they give it to the son who wants to invest it in a liquor store and in his own dream of independence and manhood?

Gwendolyn Brooks's *Maud Martha* brought to the fore the first "ordinary" female protagonist, who perhaps answers the question "Do Pretty Women Make Good Wives?" "I am what he would call —sweet," Maud Martha understands, "but I am certainly not what he would call pretty." Brooks also went against the current with her essay in *Negro Digest* entitled "Why Negro Women Leave Home":

> She may resent, for instance, dollar dole-outs. Perhaps she under-stands that he does this because he feels that he is no very great shakes out there in the world and therefore must be at least a little shake at home. But her understanding does not make her accom-panying shyness, awe or fear any more pleasant to bear.
>
> The woman with an income of her own may have another problem. . . . Her husband, although enjoying the added com-forts in their home, might actually prefer to do without them, because he vaguely feels that his manhood has suffered detrac-tion. As compensation for this, he often makes less of an effort himself. . . .
>
> Others have married men whom they consider inferior, in education or intelligence or in breeding, and the honeymoon is hardly over before they realize that they were in error. . . .
>
> Some working women leave home when they discover that their husbands are gold-diggers. . . . Few are the women willing to take on the full support of able-bodied males. On the other side of the picture . . . there are the young women who leave home because they have married middle-aged or elderly men from whom they expected either early death and resultant insurance benefits . . . or luxurious care. When these are not forthcoming, they withdraw.[54]

The poet and novelist also broached the issue of extramarital affairs: "Among those who do bid farewell for this reason there is a growing number who leave because the 'other' women are white," she asserted. And as far as the materialistic issue was concerned, women were interested in having a well-appointed home, but for a reason the men hadn't thought of. When her husband "stayed out

most or all of the night, she could fret or grieve in prettier surroundings, at least." In conclusion, Brooks wrote that Black women left
home when "they no longer love and/or are loved, or when they
believe that their partners are making less of a contribution . . . than
they are, or when the relationship no longer seems essential to the
happiness of their children."[55]

In many ways, giving Blacks half a loaf in exchange for acculturation into American society had a more dire impact on the Black family
than slavery, war, or racial violence. By the end of the 1950's, 25
percent of all Black families were headed by women, and one out of
every three Black women over the age of fourteen was divorced or
separated. Between 1947 and 1967, Black out-of-wedlock births rose
106.3 percent.[56]

For those reserving an entire loaf for themselves, such statistics
hardly seemed important in the boom of the postwar years. By the
mid-fifties, Americans, who made up 6 percent of the world's population, were creating two thirds of the world's manufactured goods and
consuming one third of the world's goods and services. From 1940
to 1955 the GNP (gross national product) doubled, and the personal
income of Americans rose 293 percent.

But inequality was still festering in the body politic. And Blacks
were the first to notice. After all was said and done about the "progress" of Blacks, statistics showed that the real gains had occurred
between 1942 and 1945; subsequently they had begun to lose
ground. In 1949, Frazier pointed out, the median income of all Black
families ($1,665) was still only 51 percent of the median for White
families ($3,232).[57]

Although a relatively high proportion of Black women were
attending college and working in the professions and although Black
women had been in the labor force longer than White women and
more had jobs outside the home (57 percent versus 37 percent for
White women in 1949), the median income for Black women was 57
percent that of their White counterparts. In 1950 the average Black
woman earned about $13 a week! And although Black women were
represented in a wider variety of professions, the overwhelming majority were still engaged in domestic work, and female sales-force and
managerial positions were more than 90 percent filled by Whites. In
the fifties, one out of six non-White dwellings was dilapidated, compared to one out of thirty-two for Whites; two fifths of Black housing
lacked indoor plumbing.

The situation motivated a number of women civil rights activists in the forties and fifties to lead "Don't Buy Where You Can't Work" campaigns throughout the country. The South, where conditions were worst, again received the focus of attention—especially from the Black women of the NAACP. There was Ruby Hurley, named Youth Director of the organization in 1943, who eight years later went south to organize branches in Alabama, Georgia, Florida, Mississippi, and Tennessee. There was Daisy Bates, who would become president of the NAACP chapter in Little Rock, Arkansas, the scene of the most critical, and probably the most violent, school integration struggles. There was Rosa Parks, one of the first women to join the Montgomery, Alabama, NAACP. In the fifties, membership in that branch was a courageous act in itself, but Parks went on to become an elected officer and secretary to the branch president. Finally there was Ella Baker, who, after being president of the New York branch (where she initiated community action against de facto segregation in the school system), became national director of branches and devoted much of her energy to organizing membership drives in the South. Such women not only had special determination and courage but were imbued with a compelling sense of race. At the end of a membership campaign—one of up to three hundred which often included 12,000 travel-miles within a year—Baker wrote to a legal assistant in 1942: "I am too weary to think; and even if I could think, I could not write. This race saving business is . . . But who am I to weary of the noble task of molding the destiny of 13,000,000?"[58]

There was something else about these women too, something that would become even more evident in the next generation, which they would lead. Walter White recognized that there was a new sensibility of the postwar generation, a generation that saw renewed racial violence, the illusion of racial progress, and the severe repression of progressive leaders in the name of anticommunism. "Young people today are aggressive, analytical, and even skeptical to the point of cynical," White wrote to William Hastie in a prophetic letter about the appointment of Ruby Hurley in 1943. "They are also frankly worried about what the postwar world will bring about. They do not want to be treated as children . . . they want to work in a movement of which they are an integral part rather than be treated as mentally inferior persons to whom the law is laid down from above."[59]

Perhaps as a point of comparison White was thinking of women like Ann Tanneyhill of the National Urban League and Daisy Lampkin in his own organization. Tanneyhill joined the league in 1928 (retiring fifty years later) and was the first woman to acquire professional status in the organization. The National Urban League did not have a significant number of women professionals before the 1940's, and Tanneyhill, who became director of vocational guidance, was among its highest-ranking women. She and Daisy Lampkin, veteran field secretary of the NAACP, were examples of women who performed much of the nuts-and-bolts work of their organizations, yet were hardly expected to gain public recognition or even to be in on major policy decisions. Their high positions did not automatically bring them satisfaction with their roles. "I need not tell you that it was most embarrassing to me not to be able to say that I knew anything about the conference when questions were asked of me," Lampkin wrote White from one of her field trips to Chicago. "One man said to me, 'Oh, you are the only person who helps raise the money!' "[60] A month later Lampkin wrote White again. Her doctor, she told him, warned her to slow down, and as a result she was thinking of quitting. White pleaded with her not to. "I shudder to think of an NAACP without Daisy Lampkin," he wrote.[61]

Not only would the new generation demand to be an integral part of the racial movement, but many would be in its forefront. This was not merely a feminist stand. In the recalcitrant South, it was a necessity. "In the South," Frazier wrote, "the middle-class Negro male is not only prevented from playing a masculine role, but generally he must let Negro women assume leadership in any show of militancy."[62] And, in the first phase of the civil rights movement, women did.

Part III

THE UNFINISHED REVOLUTION

The movement of the fifties and sixties was carried largely by women. . . .
—ELLA BAKER

XV

~ Dress Rehearsal for the Sixties ~

Ironically, it was the *Brown* v. *Topeka* Supreme Court decision of 1954 that brought a simmering discontent to an angry boil. The court's desegregation mandate had prescribed no timetable for compliance with its ruling. It was the first time, as historian Milton Viorst pointed out, that the the Court had vindicated a constitutional right and then "deferred its exercise for a more convenient time."[1] There was no "more convenient time" for southern racists, who dug in their heels. On Capitol Hill the loophole was gleefully welcomed by such senators as Harry Byrd of Virginia, who issued a "Southern Manifesto"—a call for massive resistance—and nineteen senators and twenty-seven House members signed it.

In the South it became clear that the struggle would be a bloody one. Within a year there were the deaths of Reverend George Lee, killed for helping Blacks to vote in Belzoni, Mississippi, and Emmett Till, a fourteen-year-old, lynched for allegedly whistling at a Mississippi White woman. Ruby Hurley was dispatched by the NAACP to investigate the deaths—at great personal risk—and to attempt to gather evidence against the killers.

There was no one more anxious to translate the Court's words into action than E. D. Nixon, president of the Montgomery branch of the NAACP and regional director of the Brotherhood of Sleeping Car Porters. In the wake of the Court decision he attempted to enroll some Black youngsters in a local White school, only to see them turned out by the police. Nixon contacted the NAACP national office —but the racial logjam wasn't going to be broken that way. He was told not to take any direct action, and his frustration lingered—until Friday, December 1, 1955. On that date, Rosa Parks, secretary to E. D. Nixon, boarded the Cleveland Avenue bus in Montgomery. And on that day a movement began. "The Negro revolt is properly dated from the moment Mrs. Rosa Parks said 'No' to the bus driver's demand that she get up and let a White man have her seat," wrote the late Black journalist Louis Lomax.[2]

It was only appropriate that the modern civil rights movement was sparked in just that way. The refusal of Rosa Parks had been spontaneous on her part, but not uncharacteristic. The middle-aged, bespectacled Parks had long been a member of the Montgomery chapter of the NAACP and had served as the organization's elected secretary. For the last twelve years, she had run the office headquarters for E. D. Nixon. Rosa Parks had had similiar confrontations with bus drivers before. She was previously evicted from a bus and sometimes drivers refused to pick her up. And her refusal to be humiliated reflected a historical pattern.

There had always been a tinderbox quality to the ill-treatment of Black women on public conveyances. As early as 1866 the millionaire activist Mary Ellen Pleasant sued the San Francisco Trolley Company after she was prevented from riding on one of its cars. A few years later Sojourner Truth successfully subdued a conductor in Washington, D.C., who tried to physically evict her from a trolley. The abolitionist and newspaper publisher Mary Ann Shadd Cary glared at a trolley driver determined to pass her by with such a "fire-like" gaze that he found himself mysteriously compelled to stop and pick her up. Treatment on the Jim Crow cars had been a catalyst in Ida B. Wells's activist career, had fired up Charlotte Hawkins Brown, and had been an issue Black women had put on the agendas of NAWSA and CIC and NACW. Yes, there was an old and special relationship between Black women and public transportation.

Their treatment on public transportation was probably the most vivid reminder of how they were perceived in a society that was moving forward while most of them were being left behind. Black women needed public vehicles to get to the White part of town to perform the numbing and exploitative work that had been their lot for centuries. They needed the vehicles to return home for precious and fleeting moments with their children before morning, when they had to ride them to work again. Ill-treatment on public transport represented the final insult and humiliation to Black women in a society run by White men.

Riding the buses in Montgomery was especially humiliating. Blacks, who made up the vast majority of riders, were forced to pay their fares at the front of the bus, disembark, and then reenter through the back door. To be required also to give up a seat in the segregated back section of the bus was asking a lot—too much for some. Years before the 1954 decision, a Black woman by the name of Viola White had refused to get up when a bus driver ordered her to. When he attempted to remove her, she "had nearly beaten him to death," according to E. D. Nixon. Viola White was arrested and later sentenced to a term in jail. And though her conviction was appealed, the case languished in the courts for over a decade. White died before she could get a hearing.

Just weeks before Rosa Parks's fateful bus ride, a young Black teenager had refused a bus driver's demand to move to the back of the bus. "Nigger," the driver had commanded, "I told you to move back." The girl replied, "I done paid my dime. I ain't got no right to move."[3] The driver repeated his order; the young girl repeated her answer. Finally the driver stopped the bus in the middle of Dexter Avenue, called the police, and the teenager was taken away in handcuffs. When the girl was jailed, E. D. Nixon believed that this could be the test case he was looking for. Rosa Parks called a meeting of the NAACP youth group to discuss plans for a campaign. But there was an unforeseen hitch. The girl's mother forbade the young girl to appear in court, for her daughter was visibly pregnant—and unmarried.

Rosa Parks was both disappointed and deeply disturbed by the turn of events—not only by the failure of the test case, but also by the personal circumstances of the young girl. She "took [the case] very hard," recalled Virginia Durr, a White activist who had been prominent in the southern interracial movement since the forties. "She felt that the child had been extremely brave and that she had suffered for it; and also that for a fifteen-year-old to get pregnant in that kind of inconsequential way . . . was also a curse of Negro women. . . . She felt that this was a kind of burden that Negro women had to bear for so many generations—you know, of being used."[4] Rosa Parks lived with the consequences of being used. Her husband, according to Durr, was a fair-skinned man whose father had been White. His mother later married a Black man, but she died when Parks was a teenager, and the stepfather turned Parks and his sister out of the house. "Go to the big house and tell your own daddy to feed you," Mr. Parks was told. "I have fed you long enough."[5] Rosa Parks's husband seemed never to recover from the cruelty of his early life. He worked only intermittently, as a barber, and was, said Durr, an alcoholic.

On that December day there was probably a lot on Rosa Parks's mind. There was the frustrating situation in the South; there was the indelible image of the defiant teenager. There were the upcoming Christmas holidays, which meant that she had a heavier load of work than usual. In addition to her duties at Nixon's office, Rosa Parks was employed in a tailor's shop as a seamstress. With her paltry salary of $23 a week, she often did extra work to make ends meet. In fact, she had been doing some sewing for Virginia Durr. On this day, Rosa Parks also had a full bag of groceries. As was her custom, she had done the food shopping, and was undoubtedly looking forward to a quiet weekend at home.

She got on the bus with her groceries and sat down. When the bus filled up, leaving a White man without a seat, the driver demanded that she and three other Blacks get up and stand in the back. The three other passengers reluctantly arose; Rosa Parks remained seated. The bus driver became abusive. "Nigger, move back," he barked. As Rosa Parks subsequently told inquirers, she was tired. But it wasn't just her feet that ached for relief.

Although Rosa Parks's refusal was a spontaneous act, the response of Black women community leaders to her arrest was not. The Women's Political Council, led by Joanne Robinson, had long prepared to transform a singular act of defiance into a citywide demonstration. The council—formed in 1946 by Mary Burke, an instructor at Alabama State College, to provide youths with greater educational opportunities—had been reorganized in 1950, when Robinson became president. The group had adopted a more protest-oriented direction. "It wasn't that we were so militant," said Robinson, "but we felt that the Council should direct itself more toward bringing decency to Black people in Montgomery."[6] The treatment of Blacks on the buses, especially of Black women who utilized them to go to work, was a natural starting point. "Not a week went by where someone wasn't fined or insulted," Robinson recalled.

Well before Parks's arrest, the Women's Political Council had decided a bus boycott would be an effective tactic, "not to just teach a lesson but to break the system," said Robinson. "We knew if the women supported it, the men would go along." Flyers had already been printed to distribute throughout the community: ". . . don't ride the bus to work, to town, to school, or anyplace. . . . Another Negro woman has been arrested and put in jail because she refused to give up her seat," the flyers read. Added to the preprinted leaflets were the date and time for the mass meeting and the boycott. A network had also been put in place for the distribution of the flyers. Key people, mostly students, knew to pick up the packets containing the flyers and post or distribute them in strategic places around the city. At 5:00 P.M. Joanne Robinson heard of the Parks arrest, and within two hours, she said, some fifty thousand leaflets calling for a bus boycott had blanketed the city.

About six o'clock the same evening, E. D. Nixon telephoned Clifford Durr, a White liberal civil rights lawyer and husband of Virginia Durr. Nixon told him that Rosa Parks had been arrested and was in jail, and the Durrs and Nixon went to the police station to post Parks's bond. They knew that the moment had come, that the arrest of Parks would be the rallying point for challenge of the stubborn South. In the first place, Rosa Parks was the perfect symbol for the campaign. "She was morally clean," said Nixon, "and she had a fairly good academic training. . . . She wasn't afraid and she didn't get excited about anything."[7] In addition, the circumstances surrounding the arrest worked in their favor. The Montgomery authorities prosecuted Parks under a segregation ordinance—whose constitutionality could now be challenged—instead of charging her with something like disobeying an officer. This meant the case could be litigated directly through the federal courts instead of having to wind its way through the lethargic and unpredictable state judicial system. Indeed, the civil rights activists now had their test case.

As for Parks, the decision to be the symbol of the challenge to southern segregation must have been difficult—despite her activist background. The road ahead was a dangerous one, and her husband pleaded with her not to take it. "He had a perfect terror of White people," Virginia Durr recalled. "The night we went to get Mrs. Parks from the jail, we went back to her apartment and he was drunk and he kept saying, 'Oh, Rosa, Rosa, don't do it, don't do it. . . . The White folks will kill you.' "[8]

But Parks would go through with it. The movement was on.

E. D. Nixon pulled together a number of community leaders, including prominent ministers like Ralph Abernathy, H. H. Hubbard, and a twenty-six-year-old Ph.D. who had recently come to Montgomery from Atlanta as pastor of the Dexter Avenue Baptist Church: Martin Luther King, Jr. The ministers agreed to support a boycott—anonymously. Their idea was to pass around the leaflets but not to let the White authorities know of their active participation.

Nixon was furious at the suggestion, and accused them of acting like "little boys." "What the hell you talkin' about?" he demanded. "How you gonna have a mass meeting, gonna boycott a city bus line without the White folks knowing it?" Nixon was merciless. He told them: "You guys have went around here and lived off these poor washerwomen all your lives and ain't never done nothing for 'em. And now you got a chance to do something for 'em, you talkin' about you don't want the White folks to know it."9 He then threatened to tell the community that the boycott would be called off because the ministers were "too scared."

Faced with a choice of confronting either the wrath of White racists or those Black women, they chose the safer course. The Montgomery Improvement Association (MIA) was formed, and the young pastor from Atlanta was nominated as president. That seemed to be Nixon's idea. He had been impressed by a speech of King's and perhaps saw some advantage in having a relative outsider lead the boycott. But Martin Luther King, Jr., was not at all sure he wanted the responsibility. Someone suggested in the meeting that perhaps he was scared. King accepted the post.

On Monday, the Montgomery buses, symbols of an age-old indignity, drove along the streets with no Black passengers in them. The one-day boycott was an eloquent testimony of courage and determination. Now the question was, should it continue? The plan was for it to last only for that Monday. But as Robinson said, "It was so wonderful to feel free, no one wanted to go back. We were willing to fight or die for what we believed." But could a boycott be sustained?

The answer was yes, largely because the tactic was an effective way to engage the entire community. Men organized a car pool and alternate transport system. Women, who made up a large part of the Black passengers who rode the city's buses (about three quarters of all passengers who used them were Black), proved to be a firm spine for the boycott. Yancey Martin, a college student who was a car-pool driver, remarked, "We saw the transportation end really kinda being the backbone of the movement. . . . We didn't mind them getting to work late to keep Miss Ann from getting to her job on time, and of course, they was just tellin' Miss Ann, 'We not ridin' the bus, and you can come pick me up, or you can find somebody else to get the job done, or you can quit *yo'* job and stay at home and keep your house and baby yourself.' "10

But participation wasn't just at the grass-roots level in the Montgomery movement. The same student spoke of Montgomery's "Mrs. Middle-Class Black America" who threw in her lot with the others. "She was like the chairman of the board, see. And, when Mrs. West got involved, even the ladies who were not directly involved and directly participating in meetings were supportive."[11]

As the boycott continued (it would last over a year), White authorities stepped up the pressure. People were harassed, threatened, beaten. Attempts were made to disrupt the legal process after the NAACP had persuaded four women to join a complaint in the federal courts. At the last minute, one changed her mind and dropped out—inciting the Montgomery authorities to bar the NAACP attorney on the grounds that he had sought to represent her without permission. Fortunately, E. D. Nixon had tape-recorded the MIA's negotiations with the women, and so had proof of the original intent. The woman who had dropped out of the proceedings, a municipal worker, subsequently told Bayard Rustin: "I had to do what I did, or I wouldn't be alive today."[12]

The bus boycott attracted national attention. Financial support and other kinds of assistance came pouring in from civic groups, civil rights organizations, Black churches, organized labor. One of the Montgomery Improvement Association's staunchest supporters was an organization called In Friendship. Organized in 1955 or 1956 in New York, In Friendship provided financial assistance to southern Blacks who were suffering reprisals for their political activity. In 1956 the organization sponsored a rally in New York's Madison Square Garden to salute the activists, and a large percentage of the funds raised went to the MIA. Three prominent members of In Friendship were the civil rights activist Bayard Rustin (who was one of the first outsiders to offer voluntary assistance to Martin Luther King, Jr., in the early weeks of the boycott), Stanley Levison, and Ella Baker.

In the meantime, the case was making its way through the courts. On June 4, 1956, the federal court ruled in favor of the MIA, and the case headed to the Supreme Court. At that time, Montgomery Whites made a last desperate effort to harass Blacks by attempting to break up the car pools. But the movement had grown too strong, and fifty thousand Black people still refused to ride the buses. On November 13 the Supreme Court confirmed the lower court's ruling, and by December 20, 1956, the court order reached Montgomery, Alabama.

*   *   *

But then everything just stopped. There were no plans for any follow-up and the movement was on the verge of withering away. There was almost "a complete letdown," recalled Ella Baker. "Nothing was happening." There was no "organizational machinery" to continue the fight. The situation was of deep concern to Baker and the other leaders of In Friendship. Even before the Montgomery boycott, she, Levison, and Rustin had been discussing, as Baker put it, "the need for developing in the South a mass force that would . . . become a counterbalance . . . to the NAACP, which was based largely, in terms of leadership, in the North."[13] They had followed the events in Montgomery with keen interest. All the elements were there for a mass movement: a community politicized by a common issue, an active clergy, and a strong coherent base—the Black church. Nevertheless the momentum had been braked.

Baker met with Martin Luther King, Jr., and asked him why he had permitted that to happen. "I irritated [him] with the question," she recalled. "His rationale was that after a big demonstration, there was natural letdown and a need for people to sort of catch their breath. I didn't quite agree," Baker said in understatement. "I don't think that the leadership in Montgomery was prepared to capitalize . . . on [what] . . . had come out of the Montgomery situation. Certainly they had reached the point of developing an organizational format for the expansion of it."[14]

The In Friendship activists *were* prepared to capitalize on it. By January of 1957 the Southern Christian Leadership Conference (SCLC) was founded on the theory that clergymen in various southern cities were ready to assume civil rights leadership in their communities, according to Louis Lomax. With headquarters in Atlanta, SCLC was a loosely structured organization with sixty-five affiliates in various southern cities. The head of SCLC was Martin Luther King, Jr., but the person designated to run its office and do the groundwork of developing the organization was Ella Baker. It would have been difficult to find a better coordinator.

There was probably a great deal of steely will in Ella Baker's genes. Her grandparents were former slaves, and her grandmother had once refused to marry a light-skinned man of her master's choice, preferring a less refined man of darker hue. As a consequence her grandmother, a house slave, was banished to the life of a field hand. The woman's grandchild, Ella Baker, was born in Virginia in 1905, and was brought up in North Carolina, where she attended Shaw University. Like Mary McLeod Bethune, she had ambitions to be a missionary, and like Bethune never had the finances to realize her dream. So Baker settled for sociology and domestic radicalism.

She came to New York City just before the Depression; the times and the suffering made a great impression on her: "With the Depression, I began to see that there were certain social forces over which the individual had very little control," Baker recalled. "It wasn't an easy lesson to learn. . . . I began to identify . . . with the unemployed."[15] She became involved with workers' education, consumer, and community groups, and joined the Young Negroes' Cooperative League before coming to the NAACP. But Baker eventually became dissatisfied with that civil rights organization. When her efforts to bring it "back to the people," as she put it, seemed utterly futile, she went her own way. She had become more and more interested in exploring the area of "ideology and the theory of social change,"[16] and so became associated with In Friendship.

By the time she became SCLC's coordinator, Baker was fifty-two years old and a seasoned activist. She had planned to work with the organization for six weeks, but its lack of funds made it difficult to find a replacement who had the skills and willingness to perform the unglamorous spadework so sorely needed. Baker ended up as SCLC's coordinator for two and a half years.

From that vantage point she watched the movement gain momentum. In May 1957 the largest civil rights demonstration ever staged by Black Americans, "The Prayer Pilgrimage," was held in Washington, D.C. Three months later a civil rights bill was enacted which, though relatively weak, was the first legislation of its kind to be passed since Reconstruction. When the school year began, the school systems in the South, still unintegrated, became the rallying point, and the front lines were largely staffed by Black women. In that year Autherine Lucy became the first Black student to be admitted to the University of Alabama at Tuscaloosa—the first, in fact, in any public school in the state. By her side when she confronted thousands of mob-angry Whites was Ruby Hurley of the NAACP. The challenge, by some accounts, caused some forty thousand new members to join the White Citizens Council. Under similarly violent circumstances, Hamilton Holmes and Charlayne Hunter integrated the University of Georgia, and Vivian Malone, the University of Alabama. The two women became the first Black students to receive degrees from those schools.

But the most savage reactions would come in Little Rock, Arkansas, where Daisy Bates, president of the NAACP chapter, led the integration of Central High School. From the time that the plans to enroll nine Black children there were known, Bates and the children were threatened with violence. In August 1957, before school opened, a rock was hurled through Bates's window with a note tied to it: "Stone this time, dynamite next." The note proved prophetic. Daisy Bates's home was subsequently bombed, and the newspaper that she and her husband published, the *State Press,* was shut down.

As the struggle proceeded, the brutality in Little Rock escalated. Two Black women, not directly connected with the integration effort, were dragged from their cars and beaten. Reporters who came down to cover the event were not exempt from the hysteria either; some were beaten and kicked, their cameras smashed. Most tragically, the young students themselves were surrounded by venomous hatred. Daily they were met by armed and screaming mobs. Inside the school, one child had acid thrown in her face. The National Guard was called in. The governor of Arkansas ordered them to *bar* the children from the school, not protect them. After that, the violence swelled so alarmingly that for the first time in eighty-one years an American President sent troops to protect Blacks in the South. In the end, enough soldiers were dispatched to subdue a small nation: 11,500 men, including 1,000 paratroopers from the 101st Airborne Division, were called upon to safeguard nine schoolchildren in Little Rock.

As leader of the integration effort, Bates was constantly faced with the decision whether to continue or desist. After all, her own life was only one of those threatened, and many supporters had questioned her determination to go on in the face of such peril. But Bates had unshakable faith that the time had come "to decide if it's going to be this generation or never," as she wrote in her autobiography. "Events in history occur when the time has ripened for them, but they need a spark. Little Rock was the spark at that stage of the struggle of the American Negro for justice."[17]

Montgomery and Little Rock in turn would ignite the next spark in the struggle three years later, when four students from North Carolina Agricultural and Technical State University staged a sit-in at a Woolworth lunch counter in Greensboro.

Revolt Within the Revolt: The Student Movement

The events of the late fifties were especially riveting for the children of the Black Bourgeoisie. Most had grown up in material comfort that their parents could scarcely have envisioned in their own adolescence. No wonder that many had come to have a firm faith in the American dream. If Black parents had doubts that the dream was as attainable for *their* children they rarely expressed them for fear of passing on too bitter a cup. "She did not want me to think of guns hidden in drawers or the weeping Black women who had come screaming to our door for help," recalled activist Angela Davis of her mother, who well knew the racial reality of Birmingham, Alabama, "but of a future world of harmony and equality."[18] Along with this knowing silence, the increasing isolation in middle-class enclaves would make some of the younger generation's awakening all the more startling. As they came of age, the shock of realizing that not all Blacks had been lifted upon the wave of postwar affluence was a rude one. Angela Davis, whose mother was a schoolteacher and whose father managed a gas station, recalled such an experience when she became conscious of class differences within her school. "We were the not-so-poor," she observed of her family:

> Until my experiences at school, I believed that everyone else lived the way we did. We always had three meals a day. I had summer clothes and winter clothes, everyday dresses and a few "Sunday" dresses. When holes began to wear through the soles of my shoes, although I may have worn them with pasteboard for a short time, we eventually went downtown to select a new pair.[19]

Jean Smith, who was born in Detroit and who became a field worker for the Student Nonviolent Coordinating Committee (SNCC) in Georgia and Mississippi, spoke of a similar kind of revelation. Her mother, a widow, had managed to send Jean and her sisters through school, and had herself graduated from college at the age of forty. Although the family, in Smith's words, was "upper lower class," she and her sisters grew up feeling that they had or could get anything they really wanted, such as a house, a car, or a trip to Europe. "Thus my personal experiences suggested that there was room for everybody. After all," she said, "I was nobody special and yet I was doing quite well."[20] When such young women did realize that not everyone was doing well, they felt compelled to do something about it. "My job," Smith commented, "was simply to develop the skills I possessed . . . to create for every person a place of comfort and freedom." Angela Davis's earliest experiences involved stealing change from the kitchen cabinet for her schoolmates who couldn't afford school lunches. "Like my mother," she said, "what I did, I did quietly, without fanfare. It seemed to me that if there were hungry children, something was wrong and if I did nothing about it, I would be wrong too."[21]

In the writings of several of the activists, it is apparent that the value of equality, so vital a part of the traditional American dream, was taken to heart. Chicago-born Diane Nash, a Nashville student leader, saw the desegregation battle as bringing "about a climate in which every individual is free to grow and produce to his fullest capacity."[22] The emergence of the Black Bourgeoisie, despite its apolitical notions, created—at least in some—a keen awareness of the have-nots, a need to do something about them, even a sense of guilt. What the war years had set in motion was the dynamic of a discontented middle class, the stuff of which reform and even revolutions are made.

There was also a more negative, if no less significant, side to this discontent. Many children of the Black Bourgeoisie had paid a heavy price for their physical comfort. The energy expended on materialism and the striving for social position had left emotional scars. In 1963 the Black social scientist Hylan Lewis revealed some of the consequences in a study of three Black mothers who felt they had been victimized by their parents' materialism. The women believed they had been "sacrificed" for material things, like a car or a house, new furniture, or moving into a higher-status neighborhood.[23] In another study, interviews with forty-four unmarried Black mothers revealed that twenty-nine had been rejected by their families, not so much for morality's sake as because of the feeling that their out-of-wedlock children "had broken the family's stride toward social mobility."[24]

Preoccupation with social mobility was not confined to Blacks, of course, but some studies suggest that it was more intense with them than among Whites. An analysis of forty-six Black families and twenty-two White families revealed that "getting ahead" meant an improved or new home for almost twice as many Black families (40 percent) as White (22 percent), though both valued security above upward mobility.[25]

As Frazier suggested in *The Black Bourgeoisie,* many Black colleges bred in their students the same values of social mobility that had been so integral to the postwar experience. Many students saw a future of emotional bankruptcy and great frustration. As Frazier implied in a preface to the 1962 edition of his book, the motives of some young leaders of the sit-ins could be attributed to their reluctance to become the kind of people described in *The Black Bourgeoisie.*

Yet as a result of the migration of the forties and fifties and the upward mobility of their parents, more young Blacks shared the life experiences of their White peers. But at the same time they were frustrated by racism in the North and traditionally Black colleges and universities in the South where there were unaccustomed restrictions and conservative—even reactionary—administrators.

Political awareness was also sharpened by the independence movement in Africa, whose most articulate spokesman, Kwame Nkrumah, president of Ghana, had been educated at Lincoln University in Pennsylvania. Finally, the election of John F. Kennedy further stimulated the racial atmosphere. More fundamental than his gesture of phoning Coretta Scott King when her husband was in jail was that the idea of change was given a positive value in his administration.

But to the Black students, at least in the beginning, *change* carried no radical implications. As Carson observed, the activist students were dissatisfied with the *pace* of change (by 1960 only 6 percent of public schools were integrated, and those mostly in Washington, D.C.), not with its assimilationist direction. Southern prejudice was "slowing the region's progress in industrial, political, and other areas," stressed Diane Nash. Except for their willingness to take on the private sector, the perspective of the students was little different from that of the interracialists of the past.

So when four well-dressed students from North Carolina A & T State University almost casually decided to sit in at a Woolworth lunch counter in Greensboro on February 1, 1960, the act was far from revolutionary. Yet the sit-ins not only detonated a movement within a movement but hurled an entire generation onto a radical path. In less than a decade, students would become the catalysts of a movement that forced a nation to examine its most fundamental values.

Few, not even the A & T students themselves, would have predicted the spontaneous reaction to the Greensboro sit-in. Two critical decisions fanned the spark of protest into a flame that would engulf the nation. First, the students immediately realized that outside assistance was needed, and called upon Dr. George Simkins, a dentist, who was president of the local chapter of the NAACP. Yet Simkins bypassed the national office, knowing that the organization was embroiled in a policy debate over the support of mass demonstrations.

Instead he called in the Congress of Racial Equality (CORE)—which had been leading nonviolent demonstrations since the forties—as well as SCLC and the NAACP youth group.

Within a week, sit-ins had spread to 15 southern cities in 5 states. By March, San Antonio had become the first southern city to integrate its lunch counters, and soon after, 4 national chains representing 150 stores in 112 cities announced that they were integrating *their* lunch counters. White students also joined the movement. In less than 2 months, 1,000 demonstrators were arrested. The sit-in movement not only spread through the South but touched northern states as well. All told, the action involved more people than any other civil rights movement in history. Within 18 months, some 70,000 people participated in sit-ins. After more than 3,600 arrests, 101 southern communities desegregated their eating places.

Amid all the excitement, one person grasped the significance of what was happening and moved to do something about it. "The sit-ins had started, and I was able to get the SCLC to sponsor the conference," recalled Ella Baker. Baker realized that the tremendous potential of the student movement was weakened by its lack of coordination. For the first three months of the sit-ins, each campus group was acting autonomously. It was Baker's idea to pull the students together into one organization. She persuaded the SCLC to contribute $800 to underwrite a student conference toward that end. So, in April 1960, more than three hundred students from fifty-six colleges in the South, nineteen northern colleges, fifty-eight southern communities, twelve southern states, and thirteen observer organizations met at Shaw University in Raleigh, North Carolina.

The energy and latent power of the students was not lost on the established civil rights organizations, which were also in Raleigh for the meeting. "The SCLC, the NAACP and CORE wanted us all to become youth wings of their organizations," recalled Julian Bond, who was present at the conference.[26] Undoubtedly the SCLC, because of its role in the conference and because of Baker's influence with the students, believed they had the inside track. Ella Baker suggested, however, that the students form their own independent organization. She was concerned that they maintain not only their zeal, idealism, and independence, but also their inclination "toward group-centeredness, rather than toward a leader-centered group pattern of organization." Their approach, she said, "was refreshing indeed to those of the older group who bear the scars of battle, the frustrations and the disillusionment that come when the prophetic leader turns out to have heavy feet of clay."[27] Thus the Student Nonviolent Coordinating Committee was born, and Ella Baker had become midwife to the two organizations that would have the most far-reaching impact on the civil rights movement: SCLC and SNCC.

XVI

~ SNCC: Coming Full Circle ~

The decision of the students to form an independent organization added a new dimension to the civil rights movement. SNCC's autonomy meant they could—and would—move beyond the operational methods and perspectives of older civil rights groups. Their emphasis on voter registration and the "freedom school" idea took them into the deep, rural South, an area ordinarily bypassed by the other Black organizations. Their "group-centeredness" and lack of a rigid hierarchy allowed individuals to take independent actions. "Everyone was their own leader to some extent," observed SNCC staffer Jean Wiley. "Whoever took it upon themselves to do something, generally did it."[1] Both the structural nature and the goals of SNCC propelled women into the forefront of the struggle in a way that was not possible in more hierarchical male-led organizations.

In a group that depended on individual initiative and doers it was natural that women would play a major part. Whatever the political orientation of their families, most of the young women in SNCC had female doers as role models. At the least their mothers worked, and were usually capable of coping with *any* situation that could affect their children's lives. Additionally, some had politically active mothers and most had seen other Black women in activist roles. Jean Wiley recalled that many of the political activities in her hometown of Baltimore were led by Black women. Angela Davis, who grew up on Birmingham's Dynamite Hill—so named because of the number of Black homes bombed there—had politically involved parents. Her mother had participated in antiracist movements in college in the campaign to free the Scottsboro Boys, and had remained actively associated with the Birmingham NAACP even after it was banned by authorities in the mid-fifties. Despite her mother's conscious decision to downplay racial antipathies, Davis knew she could always count on her parents' moral support. And like many of the young activists, Davis was influenced by a strong-willed grandmother who made a point of talking about slavery so that her grandchildren "did not forget about that." Davis wrote of her, "She had always been a symbol of strength, age, wisdom and suffering."[2]

Many of the Black women coming of age in the sixties not only had such women as models but were encouraged to be independent, to do what had to be done, regardless of prescribed gender roles. "My mother always told me that I could do anything I was big enough to do," recalled Jean Smith.[3] Gloria Richardson, who led one of the most violent SNCC campaigns in Cambridge, Maryland, came from a politically active family, and had also seen her parents casually exchange gender roles. Her mother worked; sometimes her father cooked and performed other domestic duties within the family.

These young Black women activists not only had role models, but also strong convictions, self-confidence, and at least implicit sanction for what they were doing. Few thought themselves incapable of doing anything men could do, including facing physical danger. That Black women were such an integral part of SNCC helped make the organization the most dynamic and progressive in the history of civil rights. In SNCC's most critical moments, women were there.

One important aspect of SNCC's evolution was the "jail, no bail" strategy. During the first year of the sit-ins, demonstrators who were arrested looked toward other organizations, notably the NAACP, or friends and family to pay the bail or fines to get them out of jail. With all the arrests, financial resources were becoming strained and continuing dependence on outside help was compromising SNCC's position. So almost exactly a year after the first sit-in, a new tactic was tried with students from the NAACP and CORE in Rock Hill, South Carolina. After attending a CORE workshop, arrested demonstrators refused to be bailed out of jail.

After the first round of arrests CORE asked for help, and four students from SNCC, including Diane Nash and Ruby Doris Smith, answered the call. Nash, a leader of the Nashville students, was attending Fisk University at the time. Smith, just seventeen years old, was a student at Spelman College in Atlanta. The women, along with SNCC students Charles Sherrod and Charles Jones, served thirty days: a month of hard labor, fragile health, and racial indignities. The "Rock Hill Four," as they came to be known, were among the earliest students willing to spend long periods of time away from school and to subject themselves to such treatment. Ruby Doris Smith contracted a stomach ailment from which she never fully recovered. All had difficult emotional experiences at Rock Hill, and obviously their schoolwork suffered as well. But their tenacity showed the potential effectiveness of the "jail, no bail" strategy. It was less costly, it could put authorities in an awkward position when jails overflowed, and it was inherently dramatic—a strategy to catch the eye and the hearts of the public. The most important lesson of Rock Hill, however, was the personal effect it had on the students. It forged a strong bond among them and made them more determined than ever to devote their lives to the movement. Both Smith and Nash would eventually leave school to work full time for SNCC. Nash became SNCC's first paid field staff member, and in five years Smith would be elected executive secretary of the organization and become, in James Foreman's words, "one of the few genuine revolutionaries in the Black liberation movement."[4]

The "jail, no bail" tactic also fit in with the posture of moral superiority that characterized the early years of the movement. Nash most poignantly illustrated this attitude when she was arrested and jailed in Mississippi. Although pregnant at the time, she refused to appeal her conviction, opting to remain in jail. For despite her circumstances, Nash would not cooperate with the state's "evil" court system. "We in the nonviolent movement have been talking about jail without bail for two years or more," Nash said, explaining her decision. "The time has come for us to mean what we say and stop posting bond. . . . This will be a Black baby born in Mississippi and thus, wherever he is born, he will be born in prison. I believe that if I go to jail now it may help hasten that day when my child and all children will be free—not only on the day of their birth but for all their lives."[5] Initiated by CORE, used and developed by SNCC, and utilized most effectively by Martin Luther King, Jr., the "jail, no bail" stratagem revolutionized the southern movement.

Smith, Nash, and several other young women in SNCC were also crucial to the success of another important innovation: the Freedom Rides. Conceived by James Farmer, head and founder of CORE, the rides challenged the continued segregation of interstate transportation facilities throughout the South. Departing from Washington, D.C., demonstrators would ride buses scheduled to stop in Virginia, South Carolina, North Carolina, Georgia, Alabama, and finally New Orleans, Louisiana. On May 4 the buses were boarded. Many were relieved when the buses proceeded with little incident through the first four states. But then came news of the demonstrators' arrival in Anniston, Alabama.

When the first bus arrived there, a waiting mob broke windows, slashed tires, and hurled a smoke bomb, forcing the demonstrators to evacuate the vehicle. Heavily armed Whites met them as they got out. When the second bus arrived in Anniston, the mob stopped it and several of them boarded the vehicle. They forced the passengers toward the back, savagely beating anyone who resisted. The Freedom Riders managed somehow to pull themselves together and continued to Birmingham. But if Alabama was one of the meanest states in the country, it was largely because Birmingham was one of its meanest cities. From 1957 to 1963 the city had had no less than fifty cross burnings and eighteen racially motivated bombings. Not surprisingly, angry mobs awaited the demonstrators there, assaulting them so viciously that one rider required fifty stitches.

Obviously, federal assistance was needed if the rides were to continue. But though President Kennedy supported the goal of the rides, he was reluctant to intervene. Kennedy didn't like such confrontations, and anyway, he was much more interested in protecting Black voting rights than in integrating public facilities. Blacks agreed, of course, that the vote was important, but at that stage of the struggle, so was ending the indignity of being denied the use of public facilities that Whites took for granted. Yet the violence, undeterred by lukewarm federal support, was just too much. Many of the demonstrators decided to fly to New Orleans, and CORE was talking about calling the rides off.

When Nashville student activists Diane Nash, Lucretia Collins, and Katherine Burke heard that the rides might be discontinued, they were disturbed. They believed, as Daisy Bates had some years earlier, that the moment was critical. If the segregationists stopped them now, it would be a shattering blow to the future of the movement. "We felt that even if we had to do it ourselves [the Freedom Rides] had to continue," explained Collins, who would leave Tennessee State University to join the rides just weeks before her graduation. "We knew we were subject to being killed," she said. "This did not matter to us. There was so much at stake, we could not allow the segregationists to stop us."[6] Several of the prospective riders made out wills, Nash recalled; others gave her sealed letters to be mailed in the event of their death.

With other demonstrators, the students boarded a bus in Nashville and headed for Birmingham, where they would face some of the most harrowing experiences in the history of the movement. The policemen who stopped the bus in Birmingham must have been shaken by Collins's cool questions: "Are you a Christian?" "Do you believe that Jesus Christ died for all people?" She recalled that one of the exasperated officers said, "Look, this is my job." He didn't want to make trouble. He was hungry. And Katherine Burke replied that she was hungry too; why didn't they all go to the bus station and have dinner? All the policemen seemed to be nervous, she remembered: "One was shaking." Finally the decision was made to arrest the demonstrators.[7]

The following evening Sheriff Bull Connor, who had harassed Mary McLeod Bethune thirty years earlier, visited their cell. They would have to return to Nashville, he said. The women resisted, but were forcibly carried out of the jail and driven to a dark, deserted train station. Though they had no idea if they were being watched, or what would happen to them if they didn't board the train, they decided, defiantly: "If we went home . . . it would be exactly what they wanted us to do," said Burke. The riders called Nashville and waited for a coordinator to pick them up by car and take them to the Reverend Fred Shuttlesworth's house in Birmingham, where they prepared for the next leg of the journey to Montgomery.

In Montgomery a small crowd of Whites was waiting, and after they attacked the reporters and cameramen there, all hell broke loose. Lucretia Collins and some of the others were rescued by a Black cabdriver, who with some difficulty was able to pull away from the scene. Collins looked back to see a White protester, James Zweig, being held by the thugs so White women could dig their fingernails into his face. The women even got their children into the act, holding the toddlers up so they could maul him too.

But the Freedom Riders weren't finished yet, and neither were the racists. Later that day the First Baptist Church, where they held a rally, was surrounded by a mob. They were forced to spend the night until federal authorities came to protect them. Astonishingly, their determination had not been broken. The Freedom Riders next boarded a bus for Jackson, Mississippi, where they were relieved this time to be simply arrested and jailed. The Freedom Rides had continued. On September 22, 1961, the Interstate Commerce Commission banned racial discrimination in interstate buses and facilities. And the riders? Lucretia Collins, for one, would have been "willing to do it all over again because I know a new world is opening up."[8]

What Collins and the others would soon discover was that a great deal of that world would be in the deep, rural South. Clayborne Carson wrote that the penetration of SNCC into McComb, Mississippi, and Albany, Georgia, in 1961 was a turning point for the organization. It marked a "transition from its role as coordinator of campus protest activities to one as the vanguard of a broadly based mass struggle in the Deep South." In the process, the children of the Black Bourgeoisie came full circle to touch—and be touched by— those who had been left behind by the great migrations to the urban centers.

Albany was a particularly strategic spot from which to launch this next stage of the struggle. It was the home of Albany State College, and so hundreds of Black students could be mobilized. It was also a town ripe for change. An army base was there and the treatment of Black servicemen had been a sore point for some fifteen years. The Black community of Albany was well organized and politically aware. Local organizations such as the NAACP, the Baptist Ministerial Alliance, and the Federated Women's Clubs were all active and willing to support the students.

In November 1961, students of the NAACP youth chapter attempted to test the Interstate Commerce Commission's antidiscrimination ruling. When they were refused service in an Albany bus terminal, the issue was joined, and began its lethargic process through the courts. But as Louis Lomax noted, Albany was a potential Montgomery—a point not lost on SCLC and SNCC. To the chagrin of the NAACP, which still looked askance at mass protests, SCLC provided funds for SNCC volunteers to apply to their "jail, no bail" strategy —and the result was one of the largest demonstrations of the movement. On the day that five arrested SNCC students were scheduled to go on trial, six hundred people gathered around the city hall to demonstrate. From then on there were massive meetings, demonstrations—and also arrests, sometimes numbering three hundred at a time. But sustaining the momentum of the Albany Movement wasn't a simple matter. There were a number of contesting factions, on both local and national levels. The NAACP was at odds with the tactics of SCLC and SNCC. After the movement had begun to make headlines, many of the local groups were distressed to see SCLC's Wyatt Tee Walker arrive in Albany and with a heavy hand begin directing the demonstrations. And when plans were made to bring in Martin Luther King, Jr., many of the SNCC students were dead-set against his coming. They felt King's presence would elicit a "Messiah Complex": make the unusually high number of local and grass-roots people who were participating in the demonstrations feel "that only a particular individual could save them [so they] would not move on their own."[9]

It would take a special effort to keep the disparate elements of the Albany Movement together, and SNCC discovered a vital key to that unity. That key, which would be used in subsequent SNCC actions, was music. It was song, the heart of Black cultural expression, that provided the cohesive force to hold the different groups together. Albany became known as a "singing movement" and it was the rich, darkly timbred voice of Bernice Reagon, an Albany State College student who joined SNCC, that evoked the resonances of centuries-old memories and strengths. In Albany, the music born out of depths of history tinged with struggle and triumph provided both a common weapon and a shield. "After a song," Reagon recalled, "the differences between us were not so great. Somehow, making a song required an expression of that which was common to us all. . . . This music was like an instrument, like holding a tool in your hand."[10] The instrument inspired a political harmony, as Foreman pointed out: "It was moving to know," he said, "that a community had developed an awareness of social justice to the point that young people, old people, rich people, and poor were able to unite to protest injustice, an awareness that made the community feel what affected one affected all."[11] In Albany, singing was the tool that helped to forge that unity —and the strength to deal with the consequences of Black resistance.

A SNCC student, Bertha Gober, was suspended by Albany State when administrators discovered she had been arrested; a Black woman by the name of Goldie Johnson lost her job for letting SNCC volunteers stay at her home. For some the price was heavier. Mrs. Marion King, wife of one of the local leaders, was knocked unconscious by a deputy sheriff when she brought food to jailed students. She was visibly pregnant at the time and a few months later gave birth to a stillborn child. Still, she felt that more good than bad had come out of the movement in Albany. Her children had witnessed a courageous battle, and Marion King thanked the SNCC workers: "You have given my children something that cannot be taken away from them."[12]

Subsequent to Albany, SNCC field secretaries established permanent projects throughout the South. In the process they came into contact with an impressive array of rural Blacks, who in many ways were the real heroes and heroines of the movement. They were the ones who literally had to live with the consequences of their actions, when others could leave for safer havens. They were the ones for whom oppression was more real than abstract. And they were the ones apt to gain less materially—if not spiritually—from the civil rights movement.

The Black Church was the most cohesive institution in the deep South, capable of reaching large segments of the Black populace, Carson wrote. And women were the most dynamic force within the Church. For this reason, though many courageous men took part in the struggle, SNCC had to rely chiefly on women. Thus, "The movement of the fifties and sixties was carried largely by women, since it came out of the church groups," Ella Baker explained. ". . . It's true that the number of women who carried the movement is much larger than that of the men."[13]

It was Black women who represented both moral and social authority when controversial decisions had to be made. Jean Wiley remembered hearing of several instances of ministers' not wanting to open their churches to the civil rights workers until women insisted that they do so. These women were often looked up to by the whole community because of their wisdom, tenacity, strength, and ability to transcend the oppressive nature of their lives. Wherever the SNCC volunteers stationed themselves in the rural South, such women were invaluable allies. "There is always a 'mama,'" commented project director Charles Sherrod. "She is usually a militant woman in the community, outspoken, understanding, and willing to catch Hell, having already caught her share."[14] At the least, these women could be counted on to welcome SNCC workers into their homes—a courageous act in itself. In Lee County, Georgia, SNCC students stayed with "Mama" Dolly Raines, who was characterized by Sherrod as a "gray-haired old lady of about seventy who could pick more cotton, slop more hogs, plow more ground, chop more wood, and do a hundred more things better than the best farmer in the area."[15] In nearby Terrell County, Raines's counterpart was Mrs. Carolyn Daniels, and in Cleveland, Mississippi, it was Mary Dora Jones.

Those who sheltered the students could expect to be jailed, burned out, or subjected to the crudest violence. Nevertheless, these women adjusted to the situation and did what they had to do. Jean Smith recalled the day Mrs. Johnson of Mississippi was to be jailed—how she got up early enough to fix breakfast for her family and the students before turning herself in.

Muriel Tillinghast, a project director for COFO (Council of Federated Organizations, a coalition of civil rights groups) in Greenville,

Mississippi, recalled the reaction of Mrs. Silas McGhee when Whites shot at her home after she and her husband became involved with the movement: "Mrs. McGhee called the sheriff and told him . . . she knew exactly who was out there shooting at her and that the sheriff should come and tell these here boys to go home, because they were going to be picking up bodies the next time that she called."[16]

The courage of these modern-day Sojourner Truths was deeply embedded in a philosophy of life where fear played a secondary role. "Dyin' is all right," said Mary Dora Jones, who was told that her house would be burned down if she continued to insist on keeping the SNCC workers. "Ain't but one thing 'bout dyin'. That's make sho' you right, 'cause you gon' die anyway. . . . If they had burnt it down, it was just a house burned down."[17]

Although few of the rural Blacks had ever been engaged in organized civil rights activity before, they had seen their parents resist some of the worst exploitation, and many had in one way or another stood up for their rights. Unita Blackwell, for example, remembered her family's first conflict with a Mississippi plantation owner in 1936. She was three years old and the "boss man" wanted her to work in the fields along with the rest of the family. Blackwell's father refused, and took his family away to Memphis. In subsequent years, the family also moved to Florida, Alabama, and Arkansas, following the harvests —and probably their own sense of dignity as well.

Despite the proven determination of rural Blacks, no civil rights organization had paid them much attention—until SNCC arrived. "I found out later they [the NAACP] had been in the state for forty years," Blackwell said, "but we sure hadn't seen 'em." Yet many were eager to become involved in the struggle. She recalled a conversation with one of her neighbors in Mayersville, Mississippi, about the protest activity throughout the state. "I sure do hope that them folks show up here," Blackwell had said. Her neighbor replied, "They're coming to the state, but they ain't coming here."[18]

But SNCC people did go there, and Blackwell described what it was like to see them for the first time: "We were sitting there and here comes these two young mens walking down the street with a new kind of stroll that we weren't used to and they held up their hands and waved and said hi. I said, 'That's them, Corrine.' She said, 'You reckon that's them sure enough?' I said, 'I know that's them. It's strange folks.'"[19] Blackwell described a moment of time that would be repeated throughout these years. A moment of time when history was coming full circle as young urban students and rural folk of the South peered at each other across the generations and a gulf of life-experience. But they found the link to complete the circle, a thing called freedom. And that link led to a common ground. The "strange folks" asked for a place where they could stay. "The white folks done put it out they better not let nobody stay in their homes," said Blackwell. "So my husband stood up and he said, 'Well, they can stay at our house.' "[20] Muriel Tillinghast stayed with the Blackwells. "We thought it would be teacher," Blackwell recalled of her guest. "And she was, that's true. But we were thinking in terms of another kind of teacher."[21]

In contrast to the standard image they expected: "Here, we looked up and here come this nappy-headed child coming down the street," Unita Blackwell remembered. "I thought she had done washed her hair so I said, 'Well, I know a girl that can fix your hair.' She said okay. She turned me off very nice. So, we got her settled down; she come in the house and talked to me and Jerry. That next morning I asked her was she going to church, 'cause we believes in going to church. She said yes. I said, 'Well, we got to get your hair fixed before you go away from here.' And she said, 'Well, that's all right, I'll just tie something on it and go ahead.' So, she went to church with her head look like that."[22]

Things didn't always go so smoothly. Jean Wiley tells a story about Tuskegee Institute, where she tried to teach her students about the need to challenge authority when it came to acting on their convictions. The task was all the more difficult in a college with such a long paternalistic tradition. One day she walked into class with an Afro hairstyle, which so upset the students that they boycotted her class. "Well," she sighed, "at least I was successful in teaching them to challenge authority—even though it was mine."

The youthful cadres taught the people in these communities more than that. They taught them how to fight for their rights in a politically effective way. And they also were open to learning, in turn, from the community people. "We were all excited about these young people," Blackwell concluded, "because they was educated and they treated us so nice. All the educated folk we had known looked at us like we were fools and didn't know nothing, and these here talked to us like we was educating them."[23]

In many ways, of course, the Unita Blackwells of the world *were* educating the young urban people who had come down south, especially those who didn't have the experience and savvy of the SNCC people. The National Council of Negro Women, for example, initiated a number of rural projects to help the cause, but in the beginning seemed to have trouble relating to the people in the rural communities. Blackwell described a meeting she attended with representatives of the NCNW:

> We went to the meeting, and I just couldn't stand it, you know. 'Cause it was just some bunch of little biddies sittin' there, what I call these "highly elites" you know. And they didn't know what in the world was going on in the community, but they was there, you know, talking about flowers and beautification programs and all this other kind of stuff, which you know wasn't even hittin' nowhere what we was talking about. So, I went back to the hotel and went to packing my few clothes.[24]

But Doris Dozier, one of the NCNW members, sought Blackwell out to ask her and some of the other women not to leave. And when she heard Blackwell's complaints, Dozier inquired what was needed in the community and how the council could help. The next day, all took part in workshops, and one of the NCNW programs that came out of it was Project Home, which dealt with the terrible housing situation in Mississippi. "That's how I got involved with the . . . Council," Blackwell said. She also talked about meeting with the organization's president, Dorothy Height, and learning more about the NCNW's history. "I found out it was started by Mary McLeod Bethune," she said. ". . . I had seen her school . . . in Florida, you know, when I was down there in this harvest."[25] In the end, Blackwell became an integral part of the council and consultant to a number of projects. And she grew quite proud of her contribution. "Thirty new sections done developed since I been working with the National Council," she said. She particularly had good feelings about Project Womanpower, which in the sixties brought in a number of young women activitists who in turn involved large numbers of women in the communities.

The best known of the women who both transformed the movement and were transformed by it was Fannie Lou Hamer. She was forty-four years old when, in 1962, she first saw SNCC workers and heard about a voter registration campaign in Ruleville, Mississippi, the home district of Senator James Eastland. Hamer had spent all her years in Sunflower County, Mississippi, not knowing that Black people had the right to register to vote. But when she heard the young civil rights workers, it was as if a whole new vision of the world opened up to her. "Just listenin' at 'em," she recalled, "I could see myself votin' people out of office I know was wrong and didn't do nothin' to help the poor. I said, you know, that's sumin' I wanna be involved in."[26] "Involved" was an understatement. Hamer showed a tenacity and determination few thought possible, given the limits of human suffering.

The idea that Blacks had the right to vote may have been new to Hamer, but courage wasn't. She was one of twenty children of a sharecropping family, and among the lessons her mother had instilled in her were pride and the determination that went along with it. "There weren't many weeks passed that she wouldn't tell me . . . you respect yourself as a Black child, and when you get grown, if I'm dead and gone, you respect yourself as a Black woman; and other people will respect you."[27]

To respect oneself and be a Mississippi sharecropper added up to another emotion: anger. "So as I got older—I got madder," Hamer said. "It's been times that I've been called 'Mississippi's angriest woman' and I have a right to be angry."[28] In her earlier years, much of that anger, and sadness as well, was forged into determination by the life her mother was forced to lead.

By the forties, farming machines that could do the work of field hands were all over the South. Industrialization had forced many farm workers to leave in search of a better life in the cities. For those left behind, work seemed all the more painful and ironic. "I used to watch my mother with tears in my eyes," Hamer recalled, "how she would have to go out where you see all of these big machines clearing up new grounds. . . . I used to see my mother cut those same trees with an axe just like a man. . . . She would carry us out . . . in these areas . . . and we would have to rake up the brush . . . and burn it. . . . The same land that's in cultivation now, that they got closed to us that we can't own, my parents helped to make this ground what it is."[29] Their poverty literally weighed down on them. "As she got older," Hamer said, she saw how her mother's clothes "would be heavy with patches, just mended over and over, where she would mend it and that mend would break, and she would mend it with something else. Her clothes would become very heavy. So, I promised myself if I ever got grown, I would never see her wear a patched-up piece. . . . I began to see the suffering she had gone through."[30]

But when Hamer "got grown," her life was much the same as her mother's. She did manage to be the "time-keeper" of the plantation—and even got a few rebellious licks in. One time she told the proprietor: "I said, you know the thing that shocked me, our people go to the army just like your white people go . . . and then when they come back home, if they say anything, they killed, they lynched, they murdered. . . . I just don't see no reason they should fight." Hamer went on: "You know they would look at me real funny but I was rebelling in the only way I knew how to rebel. I just steady hoped for a chance that I could really lash out, and say what I had to say about what was going on in Mississippi."[31]

When the SNCC people came to town, she got that chance, and she would take advantage of it by the act of "simply" casting a ballot. "The only thing they could do to me was kill me, and it seemed like they'd been trying to do that a little bit at a time ever since I could remember."[32]

In August 1962, she and seventeen others took a bus to the county seat in Indianola and registered to vote. When Hamer returned, the proprietor told her she must withdraw her name from the voter rolls or leave the plantation. She had worked there eighteen years; her husband, thirty. Still, the choice wasn't hard. "I didn't go down there to register for you," she told him. "I went down to register there for myself."[33] In no time she was gone, and stayed with a friend nearby. That evening, marauding Whites shot into the friend's house sixteen times, forcing Hamer to leave the county for several months.

Hamer eventually returned to Ruleville, found a house for herself and her family, and by December was registered to vote. She subsequently became an instructor of a voter-education program run by SNCC. Her determination was partly due to what she termed "just sick and tired of being sick and tired. We just got to stand up as Negroes for ourselves and our freedom," she said, "and if it don't do me any good, I do know the young people it will do good."[34]

The year that Hamer registered, 1963, was the most violent of the civil rights movement. By that spring and summer the protests had intensified, and so had the reaction. The Southern Regional Council estimated that before the year was over, 930 public protest demonstrations had been held on civil rights issues in at least 115 cities within 11 southern states. Voter registration was going on in Greenwood, Mississippi, where Mary Booth was a field secretary, and where one of the SNCC organizers was shot in the head by Whites. Fortunately, he survived. Medgar Evers, the courageous head of that state's NAACP, did not. He was assassinated in front of his home in Jackson. Fannie Lou Hamer and Annelle Ponder were arrested in Winona and viciously beaten with leaded leather straps. Hamer was permanently debilitated by the assault and disfigured so badly that she wouldn't let her family see her for a month. Ponder, one of two SCLC voter-education teachers stationed permanently in Mississippi, was also brutally beaten. Hamer had overheard Ponder's guard in the adjacent cell:

"Cain't you say *yessir,* nigger? Cain't you say *yessir,* bitch?"

Then Ponder's voice: "Yes, I can say *yessir.*"

"Well, say it," the guard said.

"I don't know you well enough," Ponder retorted.

And then Hamer heard the strokes. "She kept screamin', and they kept beatin' her," said Hamer, "and finally she started prayin' for 'em, and she asked God to have mercy on 'em because they didn't know what they was doin'."[35]

Some days later, a SNCC worker went to see Annelle Ponder in jail. Her face was so swollen that she could scarcely talk, the worker reported. "She looked at me and was able to whisper one word: Freedom."[36]

Such events made it plain that federal intervention was necessary. The penetration into the rural South, the courage of everyone involved, and the savagery it called forth had attracted national attention. In the spring of 1963, television cameras recorded unforgettable images: of Blacks turned into human pinwheels by high-pressure streams from fire hoses; of snarling police dogs snapping at Black flesh; of a uniformed cop grinding his heel into the neck of a Black woman who had been felled. To add to the mounting pressure on the federal government, another showdown was taking place not far from the capital: Cambridge, Maryland.

In 1962, the state NAACP asked SNCC to come into Cambridge to challenge the segregation of public accommodations. The result was the Cambridge Movement, which was historic for a number of reasons: It was the first grass-roots movement outside of the deep South; it would be one of the first campaigns to focus on economic rather than just civil rights; the administration intervened on a broader scale than ever before; its leader, Gloria Richardson, was the first woman to be the unquestioned leader of a major movement—and one of the first major leaders to openly question nonviolence as a tactic.

Born in 1922 in Baltimore and reared in Cambridge, where her grandfather had been a member of the city council for fifty years, Richardson had grown impatient with the gradualist tactics of establishment Blacks. She canvassed the Black community to document the consequences of segregated policies in Cambridge, where many Blacks were relegated to seasonal jobs and some 40 to 45 percent had no jobs at all. Segregated housing was a disgrace; schools were inadequate; poverty was glaring. Richardson, who became chairman of the Cambridge Nonviolent Action Committee, submitted a list of desegregation demands to the city council. The council offered a compromise: The demands would be put to a citywide vote. Richardson refused. Black rights, she said, could not be subject to the whim of a hostile majority.

Subsequent protests by Blacks were met by violence and Richardson did not discourage meeting violence with violence when necessary. The result was that Cambridge erupted into a virtual war, a "Wild West duel," according to some accounts. This time, both sides were armed. The National Guard was called in, and martial law installed. Attorney General Robert Kennedy called in Richardson and the mayor and implored them to sign a truce—"Like representatives of a foreign power," journalist Lerone Bennett commented. But the peace didn't last long. When it was announced that presidential candidate George Wallace was going to speak there, Blacks again planned a major protest.

SNCC worker Cleveland Sellers described the confrontation:

> We marched about three blocks before we saw the national guardsmen. I noticed that they were armed with rifles. Each of the rifles had a bayonet attached to the end of its muzzle. . . . I looked at Gloria. We still had time to turn around. . . . It was a crucial moment, the kind that could make or break a movement. We all understood that Gloria was the only one who could decide its outcome. If she had told us to return to the lodge, we would have done so, even though we would not have wanted to.[37]

But there was no turning back. "I'm going through," she said, and from that moment all hell broke loose. Demonstrators were butted and beaten. Though the protesters were prepared for tear gas, the National Guard employed a new weapon, a gas with an even grimmer effect. Sellers describes the awful confusion of Blacks dispersing after it was sprayed, many of them vomiting, defecating, virtually blinded. Before any degree of justice prevailed in Cambridge, such scenes were repeated again and again, with Richardson in the forefront.

As with many other women in the movement, it is difficult to reconcile the soft-spoken, small-framed Richardson who laughs easily, even at herself, with the gun-toting militant of the Cambridge Movement. But determination and the risks of confrontation evoked extraordinary responses from within. Under ordinary circumstances, one senses they would be little different from other mortals. But finding themselves in special circumstances, the women acted with a calm and courageous conviction that was as astonishing as it was inspiring. SNCC organizer Cynthia Washington, for example, found herself in an Alabama county where no civil rights workers had been before. She worked for a long time alone and, finding a car too much of a target, began getting around the county on the back of a mule.[38] There were others, like Annie Pearl Avery, who one day awed six hundred demonstrators in Montgomery. When a White policeman who had been on a head-beating rampage approached her with a club aimed at her head, she reached up, grabbed the club, and said, "Now what you going to do, motherfucker?" The policeman was stunned by the question long enough for her to slip back, unhurt, into the crowd.[39] And no one was more surprised than petite student Judy Richardson herself, who left Swarthmore to join the movement in Cambridge, when she kicked an Atlanta policeman in the groin. "He was mistreating a Black demonstrator, and it forced me to do something," she explained simply.

1963–1964: Losing Faith

If hopes were buoyed when 250,000 people marched on Washington to dream Martin Luther King's eloquent dream, they were dashed by the Birmingham bombing less than a month later. The news that four little Black girls—Addie Mae Collins, Denise McNair, Carole Robertson, and Cynthia Wesley—had been murdered while attending Sunday school sickened the soul.*

---

*In 1983, only one man has been arrested for the bombing. The case remains unsolved.

An awful realization was scorched indelibly on the mind: No one was immune to hateful, irrational violence in America—not even a popular President, it turned out. The dream of racial harmony, the belief that America had a genuine moral conscience that just needed awakening, was cracking around the edges. It would turn to dust by the end of the summer of '64. One of the things that destroyed the idealism which had motivated much of the movement was the failure of the Mississippi Freedom Democratic Party (MFDP) to be seated in that year's Democratic convention.

The MFDP was created to challenge the racist regular Democratic organization in Mississippi. It reflected the breadth of the movement of the sixties. Among the sixty-eight delegates were Fannie Lou Hamer and other Mississippi activists, like Annie Mae King, Victoria Gray (from Hattiesburg, slated to oppose Senator John Stennis for the next election), and Unita Blackwell (who would eventually become mayor of Mayersville). Ella Baker helped organize the party and gave the keynote address. Jean Smith was also there to help put the challenge together. Among the counsel for the MFDP was a woman who would become better known in later years as the head of the Equal Employment Opportunity Commission (EEOC), Eleanor Holmes Norton; and Marian Wright Edelman, who would subsequently head The Children's Defense Fund, one of the most respected advocacy organizations in Washington. Major contributors to the party included Harry Belafonte, who had been a major supporter of the civil rights movement from the fifties, the actor Sidney Poitier, and others. Through the influence of Ella Baker and Robert Moses, the MFDP had managed to retain one of the most powerful figures in Democratic affairs, Joseph Rauh, then vice-president of Americans for Democratic Action, and general counsel for the United Automobile Workers. These and other supporters of the MFDP's effort represented the makings of a formidable coalition. Blacks from every walk of life were a part of the MFDP; the civil rights organizations and powerful liberals supported it. Added to this, Mississippi itself was a potent symbol of Black oppression.

The well-prepared legal case the MFDP presented was good enough to make President Lyndon Johnson edgy. Not only was the technical challenge intact, but testimony from Fannie Lou Hamer, broadcast over the television networks, made their cause even more compelling. She described how she was beaten in Winona, beaten until the first Black man assigned to the task was too tired to continue.

How a second Black tormentor was told to hit her with a blackjack. And how, while this was going on, a White man pulled down her dress, which had risen above her waist; and then he pulled it back up. "All of this on account we want to register," she told the nation, "to become first-class citizens, and if the Freedom Democratic Party is not seated now, I question America."[40]

It was no coincidence that the TV cameras suddenly cut away from Hamer to cover a hastily called presidential press conference. Pressure was coming down on the MFDP to compromise. Johnson could ill afford, like other Presidents before him, to upset southern politicians (a number of whom would openly support the Republican candidate, Senator Barry Goldwater). Nudging the region toward the mid-twentieth century was one thing, but altering its entire power structure was quite another. The Johnson people offered a compromise: The MFDP delegates would have a voice in the proceedings, but no vote. This was utterly rejected. A second compromise was offered: Two of the delegates would have at-large seats, the remainder would be "guests," and future conventions, starting in 1968, would bar any delegation that discriminated on the basis of race.

This was hotly debated within the MFDP. There were those who argued for acceptance. The MFDP was already losing support from the credentials committee as a result of the administration's arm-twisting. In addition, members of the MFDP were being pressured. Rauh reported that one Black woman from California had told him her husband would lose a judgeship if she didn't go along with the administration. Another person said that the Secretary of the Army had threatened his job. There was even word that Hubert Humphrey's vice-presidency depended on his success in resolving the matter. A number of people went over to the administration's side when the second compromise was offered, considering it sufficient for the time being. Most of the Black establishment urged the MFDP to accept the new terms. Civil rights leaders were applying pressure as well. "God bless his soul . . . one of them was Martin Luther King," recalled Unita Blackwell:

> . . . Of course, he didn't understand. . . . We got a lot of people who is big fish so-called, but it look like they don't seem to understand the trick that they be put in, for them to come in and use their own people. Roy Wilkins, I tell you, I just wasn't going to have no more to say to that fellow after I found out what he

done. He got up and told us you all done proved your point. You know, just mad; he got pure "d" hostile with us. He said we were ignorant and we didn't have no sense and he just didn't understand what in the world we were talking about; we should go on and take this compromise and, I think you're lucky that you're getting this. . . .

And poor Aaron Henry [of the Mississippi NAACP] was swallowing and grunting and going around there—that's my brother-in-law. I shouldn't talk about him, but he got me so mad. Of course, he wanted to be "head nigger in charge," and all this kind of stuff.[41]

The national Black leaders and the White liberals were the ones who didn't understand. The MFDP delegates, many of whom had left Mississippi and even their own counties for the first time, were not about to turn back now. "We have been treated like beasts in Mississippi," said an impassioned Annie Devine. "They shot us down like animals. We risk our lives coming up here."[42]

When someone told Unita Blackwell that if they didn't accept the compromise they would be hated back home for not coming away with anything, she replied: "You know, we is going back with something. We're going back with our dignity."[43]

In the end the MFDP refused to accept the administration's terms, much to the delight of the SNCC people involved. Most of the delegates supported the Johnson campaign and continued to work within the Democratic party. By the mid-sixties, the organization had had a number of local political successes, and in 1968 the Mississippi Loyalist Democratic Party, an offshoot of the MFDP, did unseat the state's regular Democrats at the convention.

However, the 1964 experience was a disturbing one, especially for the SNCC people. They had done everything according to the rules, they were morally right, and still they came up short. They knew now, as James Foreman said, that "the federal government would not change the situation in the Deep South."[44]

SNCC people began to understand that without power, effort was useless, no matter how morally justified. They even talked of "seizing" power. Many of the old assumptions were questioned: the efficacy of working with White liberals, their faith in the federal government, and in a broader sense, the meaningfulness of pursuing civil rights laws when Blacks were at such a perennially low economic level. What did integration mean without power? "The kids tried the established methods," said Ella Baker, "and they tried at the expense of their lives. . . . So they began to look for other answers."[45]

By the spring of 1964, Ruby Doris Smith had concluded that civil rights was a dead issue, since it no longer meant anything to Blacks concerned with the "basic necessities of life."[46] Jean Smith wrote that in contrast to her earlier beliefs, she "came to understand that there wasn't room enough in the society for the mass of Black people."[47]

Other elements began to affect SNCC in the year of the Mississippi challenge. In 1964, Foreman explained, "a fundamental struggle had begun to shift the power of decision-making in SNCC from a rural Southern Black base to a Northern, middle-class interracial base."[48] The composition of the organization had been changing accordingly. In the spring of 1963, Whites comprised one third of the participants in the annual SNCC conference. By the fall, the staff itself was 20 percent White. In the summer of '64, SNCC's "Freedom Summer Project" brought White membership up even further. The idea then was to attract attention and force federal intervention in Mississippi by inviting large numbers of White students to come and work in the state. To a great extent the objective was achieved. However, with the publicity surrounding the murders of two White civil rights workers, Michael Schwerner and Andrew Goodman—along with a Black, James Chaney, in Philadelphia, Mississippi, one didn't have to be cynical to observe that civil rights violence aroused more national attention when the victims were White. For many Black martyrs before them had seemed hardly worth the newsprint. The bringing in of northern students—most of whom were from middle-class and upper-middle-class families and attending prestigious schools—created organizational problems as well. It brought out many insecurities, on both sides. The large numbers alone opened the loose, "leaderless" structure of SNCC to new question. Factions began to form. To add to the confusion, the presence of White female students brought another, and sometimes emotional, dimension to the organization's sexual tension. The significance—and even the number—of interracial liaisons varies according to whom one talks to, but in an organizational context the weight of sex/race history was bound to be explosive.

Additionally, the civil rights protests, culminating in the spectacular Selma-to-Montgomery march led by Martin Luther King, Jr., in 1965, had wrung from Congress the Civil Rights Act(s) and the

Voting Rights Act, two major goals of the movement. This success was, in some ways, disconcerting. The federal government had yielded; now what? Others, especially many in the rapidly fragmenting SNCC organization, began to question whether all the blood and the pain were worth it. For what really had changed? As Jean Smith wrote:

> It is a subtle problem to acknowledge that there was some value in having achieved these rights and yet to understand that there was no basic gain. The value was in the way Negroes could feel like real men and women. . . . The value was in the solidification of the Negro community, in our recognition of the possibility that we could work together to build decent lives. But you must see that there was no basic change. I personally resisted this for a long time. I had invested so much of myself in the fight that I didn't want to admit that it came to so little.[49]

Even the vote, which was thought to be the means of relieving poverty, ending exploitation of Black labor, getting better schools, and improving the communities, was, as Smith noted, in the end a shallow victory. For despite legal rights, "In the end we learned that there are a thousand ways for a people who are weaker than the rest to be 'kept in their place.' "[50]

There were those who believed that the incipient women's movement was one of those ways.

XVII

~ The Women's Movement and Black Discontent ~

As far as many Blacks were concerned, the emergence of the women's movement couldn't have been more untimely or irrelevant. Historians trace its roots to 1961 with the President's Commission on the Status of Women chaired by Eleanor Roosevelt. At a time when Black students were languishing in southern jails, when Black full-time working women were earning 57 percent of what their White peers were earning, the commission concentrated its attention on the growing number of middle-class women who were forced to enter the labor market in low-skill, low-paid jobs. In 1963, the year of the March on Washington, the Birmingham bombing, and the assassination of Mississippi civil rights leader Medgar Evers, the report from the commission was published. Although it did not go so far as to challenge the traditional roles of women, its litany of inequities, especially in employment, was telling. President John Kennedy signed the Equal Pay Act, the first federal legislation that prohibited discrimination on the basis of sex.

In the same year, the publication of Betty Friedan's *The Feminine Mystique* added fuel to the fire of a growing feminist discontent. The author spoke to middle-class White women, bored in suburbia (an escape hatch from increasingly Black cities) and seeking sanction to work at a "meaningful" job outside the home. Not only were the problems of the White suburban housewife (who may have had Black domestic help) irrelevant to Black women, they were also alien to them. Friedan's observation that "I never knew a woman, when I was growing up, who used her mind, played her own part in the world, and also loved, and had children" seemed to come from another planet.[1]

In 1964, two developments spurred the women's movement to a new level of intensity. The first of them, the Civil Rights Act, won by blood sacrifice, provided the legal foundation for women's rights —much as the Fourteenth and Fifteenth Amendments had a century earlier. That wasn't what the proponents of the Civil Rights Act had in mind. But when the bill came to the House, Representative Howard Smith of Virginia tacked the word *sex* to Title VII, which prohibited discrimination in employment. Emulating the tactics used after the Civil War, Smith's purpose was to defeat the entire bill. Sex equality in employment would be viewed as so ridiculous, he believed, that even those whose consciences were pricked by the plight of Blacks wouldn't be able to vote for it. There *was* much ribaldry in the Congress; the day Smith made his proposal was called "Ladies Day" in the House. But evidently the good ol' boys were laughing so hard they missed a step. Some of their colleagues, particularly Representative Martha Griffiths of Michigan, were able to marshal forces sufficient to pass the bill—with its sex provision. In fact Griffiths was going to propose the addition of *sex* herself, but when Smith jumped the gun, she withdrew, figuring that his Machiavellian tactics would gain at least one hundred more votes.

Yet it was clear that women had won only a battle, not the war. The Equal Employment Opportunities Commission was the enforcement arm of Title VII and its first director, Herman Edelsberg, made some alarming statements. He characterized the sex provision as a "fluke," one "conceived out of wedlock." Such an attitude would be a direct catalyst for the formation of the National Organization for Women (NOW).

At the same time, the feminist consciousness of White women in the student movement was also reaching a new plateau. This development had a great deal to do with what was happening within SNCC. In the Black organization's formative years, the role of White women activists had not been inconsequential. For example, Jane Stembridge, a White Virginian, was brought to SNCC by Ella Baker and was one of its earliest staff members. She and others who joined the organization were able to perform just about any task in SNCC that they had heart enough to do. With the "group-centered," egalitarian values of SNCC, any activist who worked hard inevitably had some say in policy decisions. Thus many of the White women gained a respect for their own abilities that would not have been possible in other organizations. Additionally, they benefited from seeing Black women as a new kind of role model.

Contrary to Friedan's experience, Black women in SNCC not only performed heroic deeds, but their activism did not preclude many of them from marrying and having children. Most enlightening was the exposure to the rural women who formed the backbone of the southern movement. "I have been thinking about this," wrote Stembridge in her notes. "Mrs. Hamer is more educated than I am. That is—she knows more." What Fannie Lou Hamer knew had little to do with formal education, Stembridge wrote: ". . . She knows something else. . . . She knows that she is good." Stembridge felt she had no such knowledge about herself. "I went into society. I was there. And that is where I learned that I was bad. . . . Not racially inferior, not socially shameful, not guilty as a White southerner . . . not unequal as women . . but Bad."

Perhaps Hamer's isolation from mainstream society had saved her from learning she was bad rather than good, Stembridge speculated. "If she didn't know that, she couldn't get up and sing the way she sings. She wouldn't stand there, with her head back and sing! She couldn't speak the *way* that she speaks and the way she speaks is this: she announces. I do not announce. I apologize." The difference, Stembridge concluded, was that Hamer had not been taught to be ashamed of "herself, her body, her strong voice."[2]

However, the SNCC of 1964–65 was in no position to incubate the development of Whites. In those years SNCC was going through an identity crisis which had left the organization in confusion. Some of that confusion could be traced to the inevitable tensions of interracial liaisons between White women and Black men which reached a pitch during the Freedom Summer. A White activist of the period, Sara Evans, put it this way:

> For Black men, sexual access to White women challenged the culture's ultimate symbol of their denied manhood. And some of the middle-class women whose attentions they sought had experienced a denial of their womanhood in failing to achieve the cheerleader standards of high school beauty and popularity so prevalent in the fifties and early sixties.[3]

Some relationships were constructive, noted Evans, but others had a "chaotic" and "depersonalizing" nature. The more "enthusiastic" White women posed dangers when their activities extended beyond SNCC circles into local southern communities. The sexual tension of White women in SNCC, said Evans, "was key to their incipient feminism" but also "became a divisive and explosive force within the civil rights movement itself."[4]

Many Black activists agreed that Whites were creating more problems in SNCC than solutions. By 1964, the handwriting was on the wall for a separatist movement, and many of the Whites were being "demoted" accordingly. For White women, who were by now budding feminists, this was a painful blow. They had their chance to respond to the developments within SNCC at its Waveland Conference held in 1964. The purpose of the conference was to sort out the problems through discussions and position papers on various issues confronting the organization. Among the papers presented for discussion was one, unsigned, criticizing SNCC for its treatment of women. The paper cited the relegation of women to clerical work and their exclusion from the decision-making process. It complained of the "assumption of male superiority" in SNCC, one "as widespread and deep rooted and every much as crippling to the woman as the assumptions of white supremacy are to the Negro."[5] Amid all of SNCC's other concerns, the position paper on women was either ignored or ridiculed. Of the latter attitude, Stokely Carmichael's rebuttal, "The only position for women in SNCC is prone," was the most infamous.

That Black women in SNCC did not rise en masse against such flagrant sexism reflected a number of factors: First of all, most of them saw the race issue as so pressing that they had little attention to spare for questions of sex. "I'm certain that our single-minded focus on the issues of racial discrimination and the Black struggle for equality blinded us to other issues," remarked Cynthia Washington, a Black project director.[6] Second, Black women such as Muriel Tillinghast, though angered by Carmichael's statement, were not aware of sex discrimination in SNCC at the time. Men usually held the top spots, but the charge that women were shut out from decision-making or leadership positions didn't really hold up. Women like Ruby Doris Smith (who would soon become executive secretary), Diane Nash, and Donna Richards Moses were in SNCC's inner circles. Others, like Tillinghast and Washington, had been assigned the non-sex–stereotyped roles of project directors in the South—by Carmichael himself. In fact, the influence of Black women was actually increasing at the time; it was White women who were being relegated to minor responsibilities, in part because of indiscriminate sexual behavior. If Black women had complaints of their treatment in SNCC, those complaints often centered around the "brothers' "role in their White "sisters' " sexual liberation. All this was not to say that there was no sexual discrimination in SNCC—James Foreman himself admitted there was —but it was not perceived to be as "crippling" as other problems. In any case, by 1964–65 such White women as Casey Hayden and Mary King, the authors of the unsigned position paper, began to look toward the Students for a Democratic Society (SDS), which was predominantly White. So, echoing the scenario of the nineteenth century, White women developed their feminism in a Black organization and then turned the thrust of their activist energies elsewhere. And as had happened a century earlier, the development occurred at a time when both the Black and women's movements were being radicalized.

In 1965, the year that Malcolm X was assassinated and Watts set off a chain reaction of major urban uprisings, the concept of "Women's Liberation"—a step beyond "rights"—was first presented at an SDS conference. It was laughed off the floor.[7] By 1967, the year that Black Power called for Whites to be purged from the movement, radical feminists did succeed in passing a resolution calling for their full participation in SDS. It was nevertheless clear that men had not lost their derisive attitude toward the woman question. The SDS publication, *New Left Notes,* bore on the cover of the issue that contained the resolution a free-hand illustration of a girl in a baby-doll dress holding a sign that said, "We want our rights and we want them now!"[8] When an SDS woman spoke at a demonstration at Richard Nixon's inauguration two years later, she was jeered. "Take her off the stage and fuck her," an SDS man cried out. White women may have had their complaints about SNCC, but the comparison to SDS was revealing. Betty Carmen, a member of both organizations, observed: "As a woman I was allowed to develop and had and was given more responsibility in SNCC than I ever was in SDS. It would have been tougher for me to develop at all in SDS."[9] Despite, or perhaps because of, the ridicule of male radicals, White women's liberation groups began to proliferate throughout the country. In 1966, these relatively radical leftist groups would be joined by another type of women's group: the National Organization for Women.

NOW was composed primarily of "mainstream" women: members of the state commissions on women, employees of various levels of government, trade union representatives, business and professional women. Like the old American Equal Rights Association organized after the Civil War, it sought to develop a coalition with prominent Black women. Among NOW's early Black participants and/or founding members were: Aileen Hernandez, former ILGWU union organizer and an EEOC commissioner; Pauli Murray, an Episcopalian priest and lawyer who helped write the brief for the *White* v. *Cook* case which struck down state laws denying women the right to serve on juries; Fannie Lou Hamer; Representative Shirley Chisholm (D, N.Y.); Addie L. Wyatt, international vice-president of the Amalgamated Meat Cutters Union; and Anna Arnold Hedgeman, former executive director of the National Council for a Permanent Fair Employment Practices Committee and assistant to the administrator of the Federal Security Agency. In fact, the stated purpose of NOW was to act like an "NAACP for women" to ensure the enforcement of the Civil Rights Act. In later years the organization would go through its own identity crisis. There were regional and ideological conflicts, resulting in the more radical contingent pulling out of NOW because of its hierarchical structure, and the more conservative elements withdrawing because of the organization's endorsement of a woman's right to have an abortion. The leadership of NOW also quarreled with the non-mainstream elements within its own ranks. For instance, Betty Friedan, NOW's first president, initiated a campaign to undermine the influence of lesbian advocates.

Although NOW had made some important breakthroughs by the late sixties—notably the prohibition of sex discrimination by holders of federal contracts—its significance was still largely ignored by Blacks. One reason was that the achievements of the women's movement in general were obscured by derisive media on the one hand and by urgent racial events on the other. In 1968 for example—the year of Martin Luther King's assassination and the explosion of urban ghettos, the year of a planned "Poor People's March," which had been conceived by the grass-roots–oriented National Welfare Rights Organization—media attention to the women's movement was concentrated on a bra-burning protest at the Miss America pageant. And throughout the late sixties and into the seventies—a time when Blacks were trying to forge a consensus around Black Power, and Black students were gunned down at Southern, South Carolina, and Jackson State universities—the image of the women's movement ranged from that of middle-class women with little history of racial sensitivity, to a radical fringe that advocated the view that male supremacy rather than White supremacy was the root of oppression.

On August 26, 1970, the women's movement reached a peak. On that day a Liberation Day March commemorated the fiftieth anniversary of the Nineteenth Amendment. Even beyond the women's most optimistic expectations, the march drew thousands of feminists from around the country, and for a change, the media covered the mammoth event as a straight news story. The result was that for "the first time the potential power of the feminist movement became publicly apparent," wrote Jo Freeman in *The Politics of Women's Liberation,* "and with this the movement came of age."[10] But it came of age in a way that alienated Black women, as an incident in the march clearly illustrated.

Taking part in the demonstration was the Third World Women's Alliance, a Black feminist group that was the only SNCC project still functioning successfully. Led by Frances Beal, the Alliance brandished placards about Angela Davis, who had been expelled from her teaching position at the University of California earlier that year, and in August had been charged with first-degree murder, first-degree kidnapping, and conspiracy to commit both.* Fearful that if caught she would be killed in California—where state authorities led by Governor Ronald Reagan had been harassing her—she fled, and became the first Black woman to make the FBI's Ten Most Wanted list. Naturally there was great concern about Davis at a time of increasing violence against Black radicals, but that concern was evidently not shared by some leaders of the feminist movement. "We had signs reading 'Hands Off Angela Davis,'" Frances Beal recalled, "and one of the leaders of NOW ran up to us and said angrily, 'Angela Davis has nothing to do with the women's liberation.'"

"It has nothing to do with the kind of liberation you're talking about," retorted Beal, "but it has everything to do with the kind of liberation we're talking about."[11]

Woman to Woman: Reactions to the Women's Liberation Movement

The movement's coming of age also fixed its image. After 1970 the women's movement was virtually synonymous with NOW—which itself was undergoing a transformation that would further alienate it from the majority of Black women.

The Liberation Day March attracted a new constituency into the National Organization for Women. They were, well, the *daughters* of the women Friedan had written about: younger women who shared many of the values and circumstances of the *Mystique* generation. They were not career-oriented; many of them had attended college but had

---

*The charges arose when Jonathan Jackson and several others attempted to kidnap a judge, several jurors, and the district attorney during the trial of a Black prisoner, James McClain. In the ensuing melee Jackson and the judge were killed, and several were wounded. Although Davis was not at the scene of the shooting, Jackson's guns were allegedly registered in her name.

not graduated. They were white-collar and clerical workers or suburban housewives who were determined not to leave the same empty legacy to their daughters. These women were less concerned with the larger political or economic issues, Jo Freeman observed, than with the "meaning of feminism to their personal lives and personal relationships."[12] Their *modus operandi* tended more to "rap groups" than to head-to-head confrontations with Washington policy makers.

After 1970 they yearned for a women's organization they could identify with. And by that time NOW, largely because of its national orientation, was the most accessible. It was also the most "respectable." To some of the more ideologically and politically minded members of NOW, the new constituency was not a wholly welcome development. Nevertheless, the priorities of this new group had to be catered to—as in the case of southern women and NAWSA in the earlier part of the century. For the neo-*Mystique* generation caused NOW's membership to swell dramatically in the early seventies. Many chapters expanded 50 to 70 percent.[13] And the children of the *Feminine Mystique* fortified NOW's power in several ways: The organization became more homogeneous, thus easing many of the inherent tensions between the older factions, according to Freeman. Consequently, more than ever before, NOW could speak as one, and its constituency promised to be a factor in the 1972 presidential campaign. This potential was exploited by the founding of the National Women's Political Caucus in 1971.

NOW's coffers also grew. In 1967 it had a budget of $6,888.38; in 1972 the budget was $99,505.93, and $293,499 in 1973. By 1974 some $430,000 was budgeted for general expenses, with an additional $140,750 for the ratification of the ERA and $34,900 for reproductive issues.[14] In the same years the number of chapters multiplied from fourteen to seven hundred; its members from one thousand to forty thousand. NOW's tremendous growth also helped oil its legal machinery. The EEOC began receiving more sex-discrimination than race-discrimination complaints.

In the early seventies, sex-discrimination suits became more consequential to both Blacks and women. Most important of these was the successful suit against AT&T, the largest employer of women in the world, which doled out $15 million in back pay to persons who had been denied promotion because of discrimination, and $23 million in immediate pay increases to women and minority males who were underpaid in their job classifications. Some commentators were quick to point out that the AT&T action showed how the women's movement could positively affect the lives of working-class and minority men and women as well as middle-class women. Nevertheless, the ascendency of the women's movement was viewed with a mixture of disdain, distrust, and fear by Blacks in general and Black women in particular. True, actions such as that against AT&T had benefited the working class and minorities. True, minority and working-class concerns were part of NOW's agenda. In fact, in 1970, Aileen Hernandez, a Black woman who was well known as a civil rights activist, replaced Betty Friedan as NOW president. Still, several factors about NOW, and therefore the perception of the women's movement in general, disturbed Black women.

One was the particular group of women who were emerging at the front of the movement. Black commentator Linda La Rue predicted in 1970: "The few radical women in the 'struggle' will be outnumbered by the more traditional middle-class women. This means that the traditional women will be in a position to take advantage of new opportunities that radical Women's Liberation has struggled to win."[15] Of course this holds true for all movements, including the Black movement, but the specter of *traditional* White women, who had historically been the bane of Black women's existence, wielding power over their lives was particularly distressing. Black women "look at White women and see the enemy," wrote Toni Morrison in an article about the liberation movement, "for they know that racism is not confined to white men and that there are more white women than men in this country." That majority, she continued, "sustained an eloquent silence during the times of greatest stress"—or worse: "The faces of those white women hovering behind that black girl at the Little Rock school in 1957 do not soon leave the retina of the mind."[16]

Criticism by Black women during this period was mixed with an undeniable tone of disdain. There was "no abiding admiration of white women as competent, complete people," Morrison declared. Black women regarded them "as willful children, pretty children, mean children, ugly children, but never as real adults."[17] That they were seen as children was because of their social station in life—described by activist Eleanor Holmes Norton as one "sinking in a sea of close-quartered affluence where one's world is one's house, one's peers, one's children, and one's employer, one's husband."[18] That this kind of woman was gaining power was what bothered many Black women—more than the goals of the women's movement or even NOW.

The second disturbing aspect of the women's movement was that its rise coincided with the deterioration of the Black movement. By the early seventies, assassinations, subversion by domestic intelligence, and internal squabbles had left virtually every Black group in disarray. Now it appeared that the predominantly White women's movement was going to reap the benefits that the Black movement had sown. Comparing the status of women to that of Blacks was particularly upsetting. That White women would characterize themselves as "niggers," and even as a minority deserving special favor, enraged many Black women. Morrison saw this as "an effort to become Black without the responsibilities of being Black."[19] Many women felt as La Rue did: "It is time that definitions be made clear," she suggested. "Blacks are oppressed . . . White women are suppressed . . . and there is a difference."[20] Dorothy Height, president of the National Council of Negro Women, pointed up the difference this way: "Fifty years ago women got suffrage . . . but it took lynching, bombing, the civil rights movement and the Voting Rights Act . . . to get it for Black women and Black people."[21]

Indeed, history had offered little comfort to Black women. In the past, White activists had exploited the parallels between White women's and Blacks' oppression, only to betray Black women in the end. "What do Black women feel about Women's Lib?" asked Morrison. "Distrust . . . Too many movements and organizations have made deliberate overtures to enroll Blacks and have ended up by rolling them. They don't want to be used again to help somebody gain power —a power that is carefully kept out of their hands."[22] La Rue agreed: "One can argue that Women's liberation has not only attached itself to the Black movement but has done so with only marginal concern for Black women and Black liberation and functional concern for the rights of White women."[23]

The concerns of Black women also applied to potential economic conflict between Blacks and women. "When white women demand from men an equal part of the pie, we say, 'Equal to what?' " asked Frances Beal. "What makes us think that white women, given the positions of white men in the system, wouldn't turn around and use their white skin for the same white privileges? This is an economy which favors whites."[24] Ida Lewis, publisher of *Encore American and Worldwide News,* though supporting such goals of the movement as equal pay and child-care centers, nevertheless warned:

The Women's Liberation Movement is basically a family quarrel between White women and White men. And on general principles, it's not good to get involved in family disputes. Outsiders always get shafted when the dust settles. . . . Suppose the Lib movement succeeds. It will follow since white power is the order of the day, that white women will be the first hired, which will still leave black men and women outside.[25]

All professed the suspicion, shared by La Rue, that the women's movement "will probably end up having used the black movement as a stepping-stone to opportunities in a highly competitive economy."[26]

A third disquieting aspect of the women's movement was the shrill tone it adopted against men. Inherent in this, of course, was the prevailing attitude among White women that sexism was the enemy. Black women, far more concerned about the impress of racism on their lives, believed that racial oppression was the root of their problems. "Some groups," Frances Beal observed, "come to the incorrect conclusion that their oppression is due simply to male chauvinism." The enemy wasn't Black men, said Joyce Ladner, "but oppressive forces in the larger society."[27]

In many ways the race-versus-sex argument mirrored that of a century before. Although a number of Black feminists, such as the lawyer Flo Kennedy, adopted Sojourner Truth's argument that women needed power to protect themselves from men, most Black women who spoke out reflected Frances Ellen Harper's view that the race must rise in order for Black women to do so. Betty Friedan reported that when she visited the SNCC office to recruit Black women, they told her they were not interested in joining the feminist movement, but rather in helping Black men get the "rights they had been denied so long."[28] As in the past, the thinking was that before they could gain rights as Black women, the rights of Black men had to be assured. In direct contradiction of the attitudes of White feminists, Frances Beal said, "It must be pointed out that at this time Black women are not resentful of the rise of the power of Black men. We welcome it."[29]

With the Black movement now under siege, Black women were also very sensitive about the issue of Black unity. Ida Lewis, then editor-in-chief of *Essence* magazine, said in an interview with Eleanor Holmes Norton: "If we speak of a liberation movement, as a Black woman I view my role from a Black perspective—the role of Black women is to continue the struggle in concert with Black men for the liberation and determination of Blacks."[30]

As it had been a century earlier, unity was important, as a bulwark not just against the society at large but also against the implicit and explicit racism of the White feminists. The implicit racism was evident in the low priority granted to race by the movement. And explicitly, some familiar charges carried echoes of the past. In a scholarly book about rape, *Against Our Will,* Susan Brownmiller came to some of the same conclusions that Susan B. Anthony and Elizabeth Cady Stanton had a century before. As Angela Davis noted in *Women, Race & Class:* "In pretending to defend the cause of women, [Brownmiller] sometimes boxes herself into the position of defending the particular cause of *white* women, regardless of its implications."[31] The implications, of course, have deep historical roots, and Brownmiller's evocation of the crude intentions of fourteen-year-old Emmett Till was revealing. But it must also be pointed out that the sensationalist writings of such Black intellectuals as Calvin Hernton, Imamu Amiri Baraka, and Eldridge Cleaver, advocating the rape of White women as a justifiable political act—and the slowness of Black women to condemn the idea —provided hemp for a lyncher's rope.

Where White women saw Black sexism as essentially a cruder version of that of White males, Black women saw something else. Toni Morrison contended:

> For years in this country there was no one for black men to vent their rage on except black women. And for years black women accepted that rage, even regarded that acceptance as their unpleasant duty. But in so doing they frequently kicked back, and they seem never to have become the true slaves that white women see in their own history. True, the black woman did the housework, the drudgery; true, she reared the children, often alone, but she did all that while occupying a place on the job market, a place her mate could not get or which *his* pride would not accept. . . . So she combined being a responsible person with being a female.[32]

And combining responsibility with being a female was what those in the women's liberation movement were working toward. Black women felt themselves already "superior in terms of their ability to function healthily in the world," Morrison noted. Why join White women when "Black womanhood," in the words of Joyce Ladner, had "always been the very essence of what American womanhood is trying to become."[33]

Before 1973, virtually the only Black women who acknowledged the value of feminism were those ensconced in the women's movement itself. A notable exception to this was Kathleen Cleaver, a Black Panther and the wife of Eldridge Cleaver. She saw women's liberation in the context of the universal plight of women in a male-dominated society: "In order for women to obtain liberation, the struggles are going to have to be united on the basis of being women, not on the basis of being Black women or White women," she wrote.[34] Still, she did not believe that Black and White women could work toward liberation within the same organization. "The relationship," she said, ". . . will have to be on a coalition basis and not on an integrated basis." The reason, Cleaver felt, was the great difference between the relationship of Black women to Black men (who were "colonized") and that of White women to White men (the colonizers).[35] Consequently, she concluded, "Because the problems of Black women and the problems of White women are so completely diverse, they cannot possibly be solved in the same type of organization nor met by the same type of activity."[36]

Dealing with Male Chauvinism

Despite all the sound reasoning about the women's movement and women's liberation in the early seventies, some Black women felt themselves in a dilemma. Although they were clear about their assessment of Whites, their own situation was more complicated.

During the first heady years of the civil rights movement, Black men and women shared a unity of purpose and camaraderie—particularly in the student movement. As is historically true, in periods of racial assertion Black women's feminist reactions tend to be muted. Nevertheless, there was male chauvinism within the movement, and when the movement began to deteriorate after 1964, the intensity of that chauvinism increased. At the same time, with the movement in decline, Black women were less willing to tolerate such attitudes and became more openly critical of men, as they had done a century before. This was particularly true of women who had played prominent roles in organizations like SCLC and SNCC. For example, the highest-ranking female member of SCLC's staff, Dorothy Cotton, had her problems:

> I'm conscious of the fact that I did have a decision-making role, but I'm also very conscious of the male chauvinism which existed within the movement. . . . Historically, where there was a female

sitting, she was always asked to go get the coffee and to take notes. And interestingly enough, it was a male member of our staff who finally protested that, because I was the educational director, I needed to be part of the deliberations.[37]

One would think that Ella Baker, by virtue of her role in the creation of SCLC, would have had a decision-making role. Although she says she did not seek such a position, her observations of the organization are revealing:

> There would never be any role for me in a leadership capacity with SCLC. Why? First, I'm a woman. Also, I'm not a minister. And second . . . I knew that my penchant for speaking honestly . . . would not be well tolerated. The combination of the basic attitude of men, and especially ministers, as to what the role of women in their church setups is—that of taking orders, not providing leadership—and the . . . ego problems involved in having to feel that here is someone who . . . had more information about a lot of things than they possessed at that time . . . This would never have lent itself to my being a leader in the movement there.[38]

According to at least one account, Martin Luther King, Jr., himself was somewhat uncomfortable around assertive women. This was evident when he met with members of the National Welfare Rights Organization. The NWRO was composed of some very forthright women: Beulah Saunders, Johnnie Tillmon, Etta Horn, and others who had had personal experience with welfare and who organized other welfare women. The organization quickly scored a number of impressive victories in gaining better welfare laws and, as importantly, effectively broached the issues of the urban poor and the government's responsibility to them. In one Senate hearing, the presentation of their case was so effective—and so combative—that Senator Russell Long angrily called them "brood mares." (To the surprise of George Wiley, founder of the organization, no civil rights leader responded to the name-calling.)

The NWRO had actually come up with the idea of a poor people's campaign before King did. And the women in that organization were peeved when King started to beat that drum without even acknowledging their efforts—or their knowledge of the issue. Yet King needed the NWRO, which by 1968 was ten thousand strong and had chapters throughout the country. They demanded a meeting with King which took place in Chicago.

After the women introduced themselves, King explained *his* ideas about the Poor People's Campaign and asked for their support. Etta Horn, NWRO's first vice-chairman, then proceeded to ask him his views on P.L. 90–248. He stared at them blankly. Then Mrs. Tillmon, the chairman, explained to King: "She means the Anti-Welfare Bill, H.R. 12080," passed by the Congress on December fifteenth, and signed into law by Lyndon Baines Johnson on January second. "Where were you . . . when we were down in Washington trying to get support for Senator Kennedy's amendments?" she inquired.[39] It was obvious that King didn't know what they were talking about, and he and his staff were getting defensive. Finally Tillmon said, "You know, Dr. King, if you don't know about these questions, you should say you don't know, and then we could go on with the meeting."[40] King was forced to respond that she was right, that he didn't know much about welfare and had come there to learn.

Andrew Young, one of King's assistants at the time, noted King's uneasiness with strong-willed women in general:

> We had a hard time with domineering women in SCLC, because Martin's mother, quiet as she was, was really a strong, domineering force in the family. She was never publicly saying anything but she ran Daddy King, and she ran the church and she ran Martin, and Martin's problem in the early days of the movement was directly related to his need to be free of that strong matriarchal influence. This is a generality, but a system of oppression tends to produce strong women and weak men.[41]

Obviously, King was not alone in that dilemma. Even the March on Washington, in which almost every conceivable faction was represented, only belatedly included Black women. "A week before the March the final program was presented for review and there was no woman listed as speaker," said Anna Arnold Hedgeman, who was on the March committee. "It is significant," she noted, "that not even the rebellious [SNCC] leader thought of the role which women had played" in the movement.[42] Hedgeman wrote a letter to A. Philip Randolph, protesting that it was "incredible" that no woman was listed as a speaker. Some hasty arrangements were made. And on the day of the March, Gloria Richardson, Diane Nash Bevel, and Mrs. Herbert Lee, wife of a slain civil rights worker, were asked to take part.

On the dais were the wives of the "big six" civil rights leaders, and other women. "Mrs. Daisy Bates was asked to say a few words," Hedgeman recalled. "Mrs. Parks . . . was presented, but almost casually. . . . Some of us recognized anew that Negro women are second-class citizens in the same way that white women are, in our culture."[43]

The Masculine Decade

A male-conscious motif ran throughout the society in the sixties. Commentators attribute this to the "male revolt" against the societal expectations of the postwar years. By the late forties and fifties, the ethos of "rugged individualism" had been replaced by that of the corporate man, who was expected to conform and be obsequious to the power above. Postwar manhood demanded a docile breadwinner whose primary role was to support the consumers who were his wife and children. Henpecked, trapped by family responsibilities, pushed around by his boss, he was ripe for rebellion. Preceding the sexist outbursts of the sixties were the "Gray Flannel Dissidents," the "Beats," and *Playboy* magazine—whose message, as Barbara Ehrenreich indicated in her book *The Hearts of Men,* was not so much eroticism as escape. The most subversive implication of the Hugh Hefner philosophy was that one "didn't have to be a husband to be a man." Ehrenreich concluded that this "male revolt," manifested in part by misogyny and the abandonment of family responsibility, was a cause, not a result, of the feminist movement of the sixties.

One need only recall E. Franklin Frazier's pitiable image of the Black Bourgeoisie male, and his "why men leave home" rationale, to understand that Black men shared this ethos too. In addition, Black masculinity was challenged by racial caste and wives who were already competently engaged in the work force. In the beginning, the civil rights movement had served to confirm masculine as well as racial assertiveness, but when it began to break down, that old nightmare of impotence no doubt resurfaced. The evidence of this was found even in SNCC. In 1966, Ruby Doris Smith was elected executive secretary of the organization. The election of Smith, touted for her leadership skills and toughness, at a time when SNCC was on the verge of dissolution, was believed by many to be the last hope for the organization to pull itself together. Even so, she was plagued by chauvinistic attitudes. As James Foreman asserted, "She endured vicious attacks from the SNCC leadership. They also embodied male chauvinism in fighting her attempts as executive secretary to impose a sense of organizational responsibility and self-discipline, trying to justify themselves by the fact that their critic was a woman."

A year later, Smith succumbed to a rare blood disease—though there were those in SNCC who believed she was deliberately killed. Kathleen Cleaver saw her death in other terms:

> Ruby Doris died at the age of twenty-six and she died of exhaustion. . . . I don't think it was necessary to assassinate her. What killed Ruby Doris was the constant outpouring of work, work, work, work with being married, having a child, the constant conflicts, the constant struggles that she was subjected to because she was a woman. . . . She was destroyed by the movement.[44]

By 1966, the movement had taken a decided turn—to the North. There, manhood was measured by wages, oppression had no face, and powerlessness no refuge. And in the North, the exhibitionism of manhood was not mitigated by the strength of Black institutions whose most vital resource was women. Both Black men and radical-chic White men—women, too—applauded the *machismo* of leather-jacketed young men, armed to the teeth, rising out of the urban ghetto. The theme of the late sixties was "Black Power" punctuated by a knotted fist. It sought a common ethos between northern and southern Blacks. Although it may not have been consciously conceived out of the need to affirm manhood, it became a metaphor for the male consciousness of the era. As Floyd McKissick, who replaced James Farmer as head of CORE, explained: "The year 1966 shall be remembered as the year we left our imposed status as Negroes and became Black men."[45]

Two years later, the assassination of Martin Luther King, Jr., renewed the conviction that a violent struggle was inevitable, and Black men proclaimed their willingness to die for it. Black Panther Huey P. Newton wrote a book entitled *Revolutionary Suicide;* Stokely Carmichael announced that in the coming racial war Black people would "stand on our feet and die like men. If that's our only act of manhood," he said, echoing the lines of the Claude McKay poem written a half-century before: "then Goddamnit we're going to die."[46] H. Rap Brown, who headed SNCC at one time and became associated with the phrase *burn, baby, burn,* believed that any lesser action was tantamount to impotence: "One loses a bit of manhood with every stale compromise," he warned.[47]

This desperate need for male affirmation affected the relationship of men and women in Black militant organizations. Angela Davis discovered this when she cut short her studies in Europe to throw her considerable energies into the movement here. While organizing for a rally in San Diego in 1967, she said:

> I ran headlong into a situation which was to become a constant problem in my political life. I was criticized very heavily, especially by male members of [Ron] Karenga's [US] organization, for doing a "man's job." Women should not play leadership roles, they insisted. A woman was to "inspire" her man and educate his children. The irony of their complaint was that much of what I was doing had fallen to me by default.[48]

A year later she confronted similar problems in the newly organized Los Angeles chapter of SNCC. On the original central staff were six men and three women, one of whom was Davis. However, she said, two of the men and all of the women were doing a disproportionate share of the work. Davis wrote:

> Some of the brothers came around only for staff meetings (sometimes), and whenever we women were involved in something important, they began to talk about "women taking over the organization"—calling it a matriarchal coup d'etat. All the myths about Black women surfaced. (We) were too domineering; we were trying to control everything, including the men—which meant by extension that we wanted to rob them of their manhood. By playing such a leading role in the organization, some of them insisted, we were aiding and abetting the enemy, who wanted to see Black men weak and unable to hold their own.[49]

Davis went on to say that these attitudes were particularly unfortunate because the chapter was one of the few organizations in the country where Black women had any kind of significant role at all. Her experiences there seemed to have contributed to her ultimately joining the Communist party. "I was tired of emphemeral ad-hoc groups that fell apart with the slightest difficulty," she wrote, "tired of men who measured their sexual height by women's intellectual genuflection."[50]

Kathleen Cleaver, who was an officer in the Black Panther Party, noted similar problems. She had to "genuflect" when it came to offering her views about how something could be done within the organization.

. . . if I suggested them, the suggestion might be rejected; if they were suggested by a man the suggestion would be implemented. It seemed throughout the history of my working with the Party, I always had to struggle with this. . . . The suggestion itself was never viewed objectively. The fact that the suggestion came from a woman gave it some lesser value. And it seemed that it had something to do with the egos of the men involved. I know that the first demonstration that we had at the courthouse for Huey Newton which I was very instrumental in organizing, the first time we met out on the soundtrucks, I was on the soundtrucks, the first leaflet we put out, I wrote, the first demonstration, I made up the pamphlets. And the members of that demonstration for the most part were women. I've noticed that throughout my dealings in the Black movement in the United States, that the most anxious, the most quick to understand the problem and quick to move are women.[51]

No better example existed of Cleaver's statement than Gloria Richardson, who had led the Cambridge Movement. But at a rally in her hometown in the late sixties, she was shouted down by members of CORE, who called her a "castrator."[52] As Davis concluded, the late sixties and early seventies were "a period in which one of the unfortunate hallmarks of some nationalist groups was their determination to push women into the background. The brothers opposing us leaned heavily on the male supremacist trends which were winding their way through the movement."[53] Ironically, the most "nationalist" groups were also the most sexist, often to the point of downright absurdity.

The Black Muslim organization, led by Elijah Muhammad and thrust into the national spotlight by Malcolm X, had some appealing aspects. It was a highly disciplined group. They had an independent economic base, with Black Muslim-run restaurants, food stores, schools, and a newspaper that they both published and distributed themselves. At least as appealing to some was that the relationship between men and women in the organization was taken care of by fiat. Through their own Muslim ethic, men were the unquestioned leaders and decision makers; women had a decidedly secondary place in the scheme of things. This appeared, at least, to be as true within their families as in the running of the organization.

Black writer Barbara Sizemore declared that in his *Message to the Black Man,* "Elijah Muhammad openly states that women are property." Sizemore went on to quote such passages as: "The woman is man's field to produce his nation." The *Message* also exhorted men to "keep women from the streets," because they are "given to evil and sin while men are noble and given to righteousness." "To become good Muslims," concluded Sizemore, "black women must become chattel once again, with good and loving masters, to be sure, but chattel nevertheless."[54]

Well, that was one way to solve the difficult problem of male-female relationships and assure "Black manhood": revert to nineteenth-century White society's handling of it. However, the irony was lost on many Blacks at the time. C. Eric Lincoln's study *Black Muslims in America* concluded that the organization's most significant achievement was its promotion of men as the dominant force in the family and the mosque.

Black activist and writer Imamu Amiri Baraka infused into most of the activities he was associated with in the period the idea that "Nature had made women submissive, she must submit to man's creation in order for it to exist." His Spirit House in Newark was run along those lines, and at least at one conference he organized the only women allowed to attend were widows of "Black martyrs" and Queen Mother Moore, a Garveyite who shared this philosophy. He was the main thrust behind the Congress of African Peoples, which was billed as the first modern Pan-African Congress. Documents emanating from the CAP meeting of 1970 included position papers on the Black family and the role of women. Amina Baraka, an activist and wife of Amiri, reiterated the teachings of Ron Karenga which proclaimed: "What makes a woman appealing is femininity and she can't be feminine without being submissive."[55] Another position paper disclosed: "We understand that it is and has been traditional that the man is the head of the house. He is the leader of the house/nation because his knowledge of the world is broader, his awareness is greater, his understanding is fuller and his application of this information is wiser."[56]

It was but a short step from this sort of thinking to advocate that women remain politically barefoot and literally pregnant. Another Baraka orchestration, the Black Power Conference held in Newark in 1967, passed an anti–birth-control resolution along with other serious-minded intentions. The idea had a surprisingly wide distribution. A May 1969 issue of *The Liberator* warned, "For us to speak in favor of birth control for Afro-Americans would be comparable to speaking in favor of genocide." A year earlier, an *Ebony* article had published the views of a physician who saw a revolutionary baby boom as a tactical advantage. He believed if Black women kept producing babies, Whites would have to either kill Blacks or grant them full citizenship.

There were protests, though usually belated, from Black women in the face of this anachronistic thinking. Linda La Rue remarked on the irony of "the rebirth of liberation struggles in the sixties with a whole platform of 'women's place' advocates who immediately relegated Black women to home and babies."[57] It was a reflection of "Puritan-Americanism and/or the lack of simplest imagination," she concluded. Frances Beal called the demand to make Black women submissive "counterrevolutionary" and said, "Women who feel that the most important thing that they can contribute to the Black nation is children are doing themselves a great disservice."[58] Beal also reminded the movement that the object of the "revolution was the freeing of all members of the society from oppression." The sexist emphasis of this period was also criticized by Sonia Pressman, writing in *The Crisis:* "When most people talk about civil rights, they mean the rights of Black people. And when they talk about the rights of Black people, they generally mean the rights of Black males."[59]

Some Black intellectuals of the time were not content merely to relegate Black women to the political—or biological—back seat of the movement. Sociologists, psychiatrists, and the male literati accused Black women of castrating not only their men but their sons; of having low self-esteem; of faring badly when compared to the virtues of White women. Black women were unfeminine, they said; how could they expect the unflagging loyalty and protection of Black men?

The castration theme was most vividly postulated by sociologist Calvin Hernton in *Sex and Racism in America.* Poor Hernton was emasculated by the tender age of seven—not by the racist forces in the South where he grew up—but by his grandmother. By his own account, at this young age he fell in love with a little White girl. When his grandmother discovered his hand-holding affection for the girl, she beat him, evidently with much vigor. Her disciplinary action retarded his sexual development, Hernton wrote. For from then on he acted "like a eunuch" around White women because of his "undefined sense of dread and self-mutilation."[60] That an old Black woman, apparently alone, was forced to take on the full responsibility of protecting a young Black boy in the South to ensure that his "dread" *remained* undefined never seemed to occur to him.

In another litany of complaint, the Black psychiatrists William

Grier and Price Cobbs accused Black mothers of inflicting "senseless pain" on their sons. Not only did they inflict severe corporal punishment, they also exhibited unpredictable shifts of mood from permissive to punitive. The Black mother's behavior, the psychiatrists asserted, was motivated by a desire to prepare "their sons for manhood by blunting their assertiveness and aggression." The result was that Black men "develop considerable hostility toward Black women as inhibiting instruments of an oppressive system."[61] One wonders what Black women would have been charged with had they permitted their sons to be lynched extralegally in the South, or legally in the North.

Nevertheless, the charge was supported by Hernton. He recognized his hostility toward his grandmother after he witnessed her deferring to some young, lower-class White girls who pushed in front of her while she was standing in a line. Insensitive to the possible reasons his grandmother had for enduring the humiliation (which probably included the fact that she was the sole charge of this little Black boy), Hernton wrote: "I knew grandmother was a proud, self-willed woman and I could not understand why she belittled herself before those nasty, lying white girls." Although Hernton felt himself a eunuch, he concluded that "it was the Negro female who bowed her head and tucked her tail between her legs like a little Black puppy."[62] "There arose in me," he continued, "an incipient resentment towards my grandmother, indeed, towards all Black women—because I could not help but compare them with White women." This is a strange comparison after describing "nasty, lying white girls," but of course we know what he meant. Hernton was comparing his grandmother—and all Black women—with mythically beautiful White women, the stuff of male dreams. So not only were Black women kowtowing, destructive mothers, they were no roses either. The "reputed virtues of white women smother whatever worth black women may have," explained Hernton: "The Negro male is put to judging his women by what he sees and imagines the white woman is."[63]

The problem here of course is that Black men "imagined" white women to be diametrically different from Black women. In perhaps the most devastating chapter of Eldridge Cleaver's Soul on Ice, "The Allegory of the Black Eunuchs," a Black man says, "The myth of the strong Black woman is the other side of the coin of the myth of the beautiful dumb blonde. The white man turned the white woman into a weak-minded, weak-bodied, delicate freak, a sex pot, and placed her on a pedestal; he turned the Black woman into a strong self-reliant Amazon and deposited her in his kitchen."[64]

It is interesting to note that these Black men seemed to understand that their attitudes were at least as affected by the indoctrination of White values as by anything else. Yet they, and others, continued to rationalize their compulsions by projecting inadequacies on Black women. The lack of Black "femininity" was an often-used rationale. "Femininity is only imperfectly grasped by most black women," submitted Grier and Cobbs.[65] In *Soul on Ice,* Cleaver used the term *subfeminine.*

This lack of femininity, according to the two psychiatrists, had less to do with the texture of Black women's lives than with the texture of their hair. Their negroid features resulted in their self-rejection and in their rejection by the general society and the family as well. Consequently, Black women not only suffered from the Freudian malaise that all women shared, but had an additional burden to bear. Black women, said the psychiatrists, did not experience the "compensatory blossoming of narcissism" found in women of other races. So they stopped competing for male attention, allowed themselves to become overweight, and their "sexual lives became perverted." Even attractive (i.e., more "White-looking") Black women had their problems. Because they were often the sex objects of White men, they recoiled within themselves. Grier and Cobbs summed up: "Black women have a nearly bottomless well of self-depreciation into which they can drop when depressed."[66] (Little wonder.) Hernton believed this self-depreciation principally motivated the alleged physical abuse of children. Corporal punishment, in his view, did not arise from a mother's concern for her children as much as from "simple personal frustration and self-hatred."

With the notable exception of Eldridge Cleaver, Black men failed to draw logical conclusions from their own expositions. Though they accused Black women of a variety of failings, it was Black men who, by their own admission, felt the self-hatred, lacked the qualities generally attributed to their gender, needed to be accepted in White society. These compulsions, not the shortcomings of Black women, made Black men seek the arms of White women. As Hernton put it: "Having the white woman, who is the prize of our culture, is a way of triumphing over a society that denies the Negro his basic humanity."[67] And another political patron saint of the period, Frantz Fanon, poignantly revealed in *Black Skins, White Masks:*

By loving me she [the white woman] proves I am worthy of white love. I am loved like a white man. I am a white man. Her love takes me onto the noble road that leads to total realization. . . . I marry white culture, white beauty, white whiteness. When my restless hands caress those white breasts, they grasp white civilization and dignity and make them mine.[68]

When in the same book Fanon describes a Black woman who says she will marry only a White man, that she loves his blue eyes and blond hair and submits to him in everything because she really wants to be White, it is difficult not to look at that in the context of his own previous statements. When Grier and Cobbs talk about the Black woman's despair because White society does not recognize her womanhood, they seem to use a criterion more appropriate to men. For if anyone was a "Black puppy," it was men confronting the power of the White woman's hold over them. "The Ogre [the White woman] possessed a tremendous and dreadful power over me. . . . I was at its mercy. . . . If I conquered the Ogre and broke its power over me I would be free," Cleaver wrote.[69] Hernton noted that for the Black man, "the White woman symbolized at once his freedom and his bondage."[70] He further illustrated this thesis by quoting a line in Richard Wright's *The Outsider,* where the protagonist, Cross Damon, on his knees, begs of his White woman: "Have mercy on me. . . . Pity me; be my judge; tell me if I am to live or die."[71]

In James Baldwin's *Another Country,* this power, and the love-hate ambivalence toward it, finally drives the character Rufus, whose girlfriend is White, to suicide. These attitudes were even seen as a justification for the rape of women. Hernton indicated that Black men harbored a desire to rape White women; Fanon characterized rape as a political act; and Imamu Amiri Baraka wrote about "raping White girls" in *The Dead Lecturer* and other works. Eldridge Cleaver freely admitted to *actually* doing it—after "practicing" on Black women. Odd behavior for eunuchs.

There is a tragic irony in these views from prominent Black male thinkers. Their chauvinism invested Black women with the same negative qualities that had been perpetrated upon them—and which they had fought against—for centuries. In the age of the cultural Black aesthetic one was hard put to find any positive female character not wrapped in vice and degradation.

Black women had a complicated and sometimes contradictory reaction to this hail of bullets. They criticized the excesses of the male viewpoint, while attempting to accede to Black men's needs, and to maintain a racial rather than a feminist perspective. For example, although Kathleen Cleaver admitted to being "hostile" toward Black men who had "anything to do with any white woman," she rationalized her husband's penchant for White women, including an affair he had with his lawyer. "When Eldridge was an unknown convict," she said, "the only [attorney] who responded to him was a white woman. . . . No Black women came to his assistance. . . . I had to do a lot of thinking myself in order to accept that."[72] And although she talked about the universality of sexism and described the "assertion of Black manhood" as no different from the sexism of White men, although she noted the "violence . . . the brutality, the hostility, the bitterness" that Black men directed toward women, she postulated that colonialism, not men, was to blame.[73]

Toni Morrison wrote of the "bad" relationships that resulted from men's inability "to deal with a competent and complete personality and the Black woman's refusal to be anything less than that," but she also said an important reason for Black women's not joining "women's lib" was that "black men are formidably opposed to their involvement in it—and for the most part the women understand their fears."[74] Joyce Ladner suggested that Grier's and Cobbs's betrayal of the Black man's victimization overemphasized the degree "to which the Black man had been damaged," but still felt that "the scars of emasculation probably penetrated the Black man more deeply than the injustices inflicted upon the woman." She also criticized their assessment of Black women, saying that the sociological study of women in inner-city St. Louis revealed a great deal of feminine pride and positive sense of self, some of which was due to the "Black Is Beautiful" climate of the period. Ladner also described the self-sufficiency of many women, mothers as well as daughters, in female-headed households. Still, she concluded:

> The bold assertion of Black masculinity has required that Black women redefine their roles, especially as they relate to Black men. . . . An alteration of roles between Black males and females must occur. The "traditional strong" Black woman has probably outlived her usefulness because this role has been challenged by the Black man.[75]

Of course, as in Frances Ellen Harper's day, the question of race had to be paramount in the concerns of Black women. This, combined with a lack of respect and trust for the White women who were leading the feminist movement, explains many of the reactions of Black women. But threading through these attitudes there was also a sense of guilt. Many felt that Black women had somehow gotten a better shake from this racist society, that their men suffered more, and that Black women's duty, as Morrison noted, was to absorb their justifiable rage. Black women were proud that they were strong, that they were responsible, but wondered if they were too strong, both for the good of their men and the good of the race. The other side of the coin of the "bad" relationships Morrison described were those *saved* by the Black woman's "unwillingness to feel free when her man was not free."[76] The notion of aiding men's freedom so that women could be free themselves was a historic one. Not putting a "straw" in Black men's way, as Harper had said almost exactly a century before, was valid. But the question was, were Black men on the path to freedom in the misogynous late sixties and seventies? Would Black women's stepping aside, with no strong, organized sense of their sociopolitical role—as they had at the turn of the century—aid that freedom? Were Black women clear about the distinction between general male sexist impulse and that which had its roots in the specific Black experience?

Hovering over these questions like an obfuscating cloud was a Labor Department document entitled "The Negro Family: The Case for National Action," published in 1965. The document, better known as "The Moynihan Report" (after its author, Daniel Patrick Moynihan), perpetuated the misconception that the success of Black women, not racism, was responsible for the problems of Blacks.

XVIII

~ Strong Women and Strutting Men: The Moynihan Report ~

President Lyndon B. Johnson's "War on Poverty," the key to his Great Society program, was unprecedented in its conception. Not only did the federal government support the equality of Blacks as a right and in theory, but it acted to make equality a result and a fact.[1] The War on Poverty was waged at a time when the percentage of Americans living in poverty had reached an all-time high (17.8 percent) and poor urban Blacks were setting cities on fire. It became clear that Black poverty had to be alleviated if legal rights were to mean anything. So an expert set about the study of how to make economic equality a fact.

The first step was to pinpoint the problem. And the conclusion, detailed in the subsequent Moynihan Report, was: "At the heart of the deterioration of the fabric of the Negro society is the deterioration of the Negro family. It is the fundamental cause of weakness in the Negro community. Unless the damage is repaired all the effort to end discrimination, poverty and injustice will come to little."[2]

So the "case for national action" was no longer to concentrate on the external machinery of racism and discrimination, but on the internal problems of the Black family—as if the two were unrelated. Moynihan arrived at this conclusion through the slavery-specific thesis. The problems of the Black family began under slavery, he postulated, and were worsened by continued discrimination and the migration to cities. In the urban environment, Black men had experienced "disastrous" levels of unemployment since World War II. This fact, combined with the already slave-damaged family structure, resulted in abnormal prominence of women. "A fundamental fact of Negro American family life is the often reversed roles of husband and wife," Moynihan noted,[3] citing studies showing that the wife was "dominant" in the majority of Black families while the reverse was true of Whites. This matriarchal pattern "reinforced" itself over the generations through the continued higher educational attainment of Black women and their greater representation in professional and semiprofessional jobs. All of this made Black men very dispirited, said the report. Consequently they were not good prospective marriage partners, and this translated into high rates of desertion, divorce, and female-headed families, then making up one fourth of the Black family population. This in turn added to the high rate of out-of-wedlock births (about a quarter of all Black urban births) which led to a "startling" increase in welfare dependency. Such circumstances, Moynihan observed, borrowing a phrase from Black sociologist Kenneth Clark, led to a "tangle of pathology," inextricably knotted by a matriarchal head of the household.

A question that might arise from these observations was why men, rather than women, seemed less able to fulfill family obligations under the pressure of racism and discrimination. The answer, Moynihan speculated, was that although all Blacks suffered, men suffered more: "It was the Negro male who was the most humiliated. . . . Segregation and the submissiveness it exacts, is surely more destructive to the male than the female personality."[4] The reason for this evidently had to do with the inherent nature of the species: "The very essence of the male animal, from the bantam rooster to the four-star general, is to strut," was his scientific conclusion.[5]

The report drew a storm of protest. Leaders such as George Wiley, founder of the National Welfare Rights Organization, criticized the emphasis on internal problems of the Black family at a time when racism was particularly virulent. William Ryan, a psychologist who offered one of the most detailed responses to the report, suggested that the race factor may have induced Moynihan to exaggerate the increase in female single-headed households (which was 5 percent from 1940 to 1960) and its causes. Furthermore, he challenged Moynihan's conclusion that Blacks were more entangled in pathology than Whites, especially as reflected in the number of out-of-wedlock births. Whites had a greater tendency to use birth control and to abort unwanted pregnancies, Ryan said. And, especially taking discrimination into account, Black families were not deteriorating at an any more alarming rate than White families were.

The most controversial aspect of the report concerned the Black matriarchy. In response, a number of Black sociologists, including Joyce Ladner and Andrew Billingsly, wrote books stressing the strengths of the nontraditional family. The idea had even greater currency at a time when the middle-class family was under general attack in the society. "One must question the validity of the white middle-class life-style from its very foundation because it has already proven itself to be decadent and unworthy of emulation," said Ladner.[6] In any case, Blacks challenged the accuracy of the term *matriarchy,* which implied female dominance and male subordination within the family. What appeared as matriarchy, many argued, was in reality something else. Despite male economic instability, Ladner wrote, "It could indeed be argued that much of the 'strength' of the Black woman comes as a result of the sustained support she receives through her male partner."[7] Even in slavery, Angela Davis asserted, the Black woman was "in no sense an authoritarian figure. . . . On the contrary, she herself had just been forced to leave behind the shadowy realm of female passivity in order to assume her rightful place beside the insurgent male."[8]

Black sociologist Robert Staples called Black matriarchy a myth, suggesting that the Black woman actually had little power over the family or the society. She did make many decisions affecting the family, but that was because men often deferred to her greater knowledge about certain things, especially the bureaucratic structure with which many families had to deal. The tenacity of Black women was something to be proud of, Staples affirmed. "While White women have entered the history books for making flags and engaging in social work, black women have participated in the total black liberation struggle."[9] Furthermore their assertiveness was part and parcel of a history that had deprived Black men of their ability to protect and provide for the family since slavery. But if that assertiveness had been translated into power and dominance, Staples asked, why did Black women earn an annual wage of $2,372 in 1960 compared to $3,410 for white women and $3,789 for Black men?[10] Writer Albert Murray also criticized the report's thesis: "Moynihan's figures provide for more evidence of male exploitation of females, than of females henpecking males. . . . Negro family instability might more accurately be defined as a cycle of illegitimacy, matriarchy, and female victimization by gallivanting males who refuse to or cannot assume the conventional domestic responsibilities of husbands and fathers."[11]

It is likely that no one was more shocked by the reaction to his report than Daniel Patrick Moynihan. He had taken pains to be racially sensitive. For example, he explicitly stated that the report concerned only a certain segment of the Black community and not the race as a whole. In fact, Moynihan cited evidence in the report that middle-class Black families put "a higher premium on family stability and the conserving of family resources than their White counterparts."[12] Moynihan also praised the strength of Blacks as a race. Many other groups would not have survived the centuries-long ordeal they had undergone, he declared. As far as matriarchy was concerned, Moynihan's report stated that there was nothing inherently wrong or pathological about a woman-headed household, only that it was not the norm in the society and thus subject to disadvantage. No doubt Moynihan was put out by the knowledge that strategy for the War on Poverty in general, and aspects of his report in particular, had been "approved" by the civil rights establishment, including King, Roy Wilkins, and Whitney Young, head of the National Urban League. Moynihan had borrowed heavily from established Black sociologists. In fact, Moynihan was less harsh in his evaluation of the nontraditional family structure than E. Franklin Frazier had been in *The Negro Family in the United States.*

Like Frazier's, Moynihan's thesis suffered from myopia. Moynihan's was also particularly untimely, leaving Blacks with no option but to challenge it. Though many took issue with Moynihan's view of the problem, however, few criticized his suggestion for resolving it—which was even more malevolent. Moynihan concluded, as Frazier had done, that Black family stability could be achieved only if Black men could "strut," even, if need be, at the expense of women. This was epitomized in his program for eradicating Black poverty. He believed, as an analysis of the report points out, "that jobs had primacy and the government should not rest until every able-bodied Negro man was working *even if this meant that some women's jobs had to be redesigned to enable men to fulfill them.*"[13] (Emphasis added.) Not *White men's* jobs, mind you—women's jobs. This, despite the growing number of female-headed families, the fact that the average two-income Black family still earned less than one-income White families, that college-educated Black males earned less than high-school–educated Whites, that Black women earned less than Black men, and that because of historical circumstances more urban Black women were prepared to fill positions in an era of increasing credentialism. The thinking seemed to be: Just make Black men the lords of their own castles and everything will be all right. To reach this utopia, of course, Black women would somehow have to slow down, become less achievement-oriented, give up much of their independence. By remaining assertive, they were ruining the family and so ruining the race.

It was a shortsighted thesis, but what could one expect in an era of male revolt, when Black and White men alike targeted the destructiveness of mothers and wives? The Moynihan Report was not so much racist as it was sexist. Although it can't be held responsible for the intense Black male chauvinism of the period, it certainly didn't discourage it, and the report helped shape Black attitudes. In its wake, an *Ebony* article unequivocally stated, "The immediate goal of Negro women today should be the establishment of a strong family unit in which the father is the dominant person."[14] Dorothy Height, head of the NCNW, said, "The major concern of the Negro woman is the status of the Negro man and his need for feeling himself an important person."[15] All well and good, but the question was: At what cost? At what point did making men feel good provide only diminishing returns?

Finding the answer required a change of focus, away from "why men leave home" and toward why Black women, who were fulfilling their responsibilities, were yet the most vulnerable and exploited group in the society. One should have asked why, despite their status, a larger percentage of Black women stayed in school longer, were disproportionately represented in the professions, and (if full-time workers) were experiencing the greatest percentage increase in median income of all race/sex groups. Finding the answers could have alleviated Black women's guilt and ambivalence.

The traditional value of education among Black women was one key to their success. That parents had historically encouraged their daughters to go to school was not just a racial phenomenon but a class one. In an economy where blue-collar men earned as much as or more than white-collar women, sons dropped out of school to support themselves and their families, while daughters *went* to school to do so. They went to school, in most instances, to prepare for traditionally female occupations. This was true among Blacks and Whites alike. The 1960 percentage of the Black female labor force in professional occupations was 7.2, as compared to 3.1 percent of Black men. However, as one analyst noted, if teaching, social work, and other typically feminine occupations were to be subtracted from the total of female professionals, the total number of Black professional men would "appear in a more favorable light."[16] The same holds true for the White population. In the same year, 13.8 percent of White women were in the professions compared to 10.9 percent of men. But the latter figure was conveniently overlooked in the Moynihan Report. Perhaps because to include it would have begged the question of why the difference in professional representation had a greater effect on Black families?

The reason for the disparity was that Black men had been largely excluded from both the most desirable professional occupations and the lucrative blue-collar positions by big business and discriminatory labor unions. It has always been easier for Black women, often more educated and work-experienced than White women, to enter the lower-paying women's professions than it was for Black men to enter the male professions. Historically, when Black women were allowed —or needed—in occupations like nursing, teaching, and government work they moved into them in disproportionate numbers. In 1965, for example, in the Department of Labor, 70 percent of Black employees, compared to 40 percent of Whites, were women. And in positions open to civil servants with modest credentials, Black women outnumbered men four to one.[17]

In the sixties, as in the past, Black women were able to draw strength and advantage from a situation that oppressed them because of their race and their sex. Through collective effort, they struggled to make substantial gains—in a way Black men were unable to do—in those occupational areas relegated to them. An outstanding example of this was the organization of the National Union of Hospital and Health Care Employees in 1969.

The first focal point of the union effort was New York City's voluntary hospitals. Because voluntary hospitals are nonprofit institutions and thus exempt from minimum wage laws, their nonprofessional workers were woefully underpaid and exploited. They had no unemployment insurance or disability insurance. Consequently only the most marginal class of workers sought jobs in the voluntary hospitals: By the late fifties the overwhelming majority of them were Black and Hispanic women. The hospital and nursing home industry is the third largest employer in the country, and in no field are more Black women employed. Its 2.5 million workers, mostly Black women, constitute a group four times larger than the steelworkers.

In the fifties, the first foray came from New York City's Local 1199, which demanded better pay and working conditions, as well as recognition of the union as the workers' bargaining agent. For a decade the struggle continued. The obstinance of voluntary hospital administrators precipitated walkouts, and the increasingly bitter battle drew the attention of such civil rights leaders as Adam Clayton Powell, Jr., A. Philip Randolph, and Martin Luther King, Jr. The confluence of civil rights organizations, other unions, and the determination of the workers resulted in major concessions and pay raises for New York City voluntary hospital workers in 1968. But that was only the first chapter. Their success inspired the formation of a national organizing committee and other hospital workers throughout the country —most notably in Charleston, South Carolina.

When management discovered that women workers in Charleston were attempting to organize, the leaders of the group were immediately fired. The firings prompted a walkout of four hundred workers, leading to the most spectacular of the labor actions of the sixties. SCLC and other civil rights organizations, along with labor unions and the Charleston Black community, were pitted against the southern establishment. The latter included all the anti-union effort that J. P. Stevens—fearful of the implications of a successful strike— could muster. (His instincts were correct. Six years later a J. P. Stevens plant in Virginia voted to unionize, capping decades of struggle to do so. As with the hospital workers, increasing numbers of Blacks—and especially Black women—in the textile industry provided the crucial margin of victory for the pro-union vote.)

Resulting from the hospital workers' strike were massive rallies and massive arrests, the bringing in of the National Guard, "jail, no bail," and predictable violence. The leader of the Charleston workers was a twenty-seven-year-old Black woman named Mary Moultrie. And one of the most visible civil rights leaders participating was Coretta Scott King, who continued to be active on the workers' behalf even after the assassination of her husband. What had impressed her about the strike was not only the determination of the Black workers and the support of the Black community, but "the emergence of black women as a new breed of union leaders." Such women as Moultrie, Emma Hardin, and Rosetta Simmons were "following in the steps of Harriet Tubman, Sojourner Truth, Rosa Parks, Daisy Bates, and Fannie Lou Hamer," she noted.[18]

A turbulent 113 days and 1,000 arrests later, the Charleston hospital strike was settled, with many gains to the workers. By 1969 the national union was established, and in subsequent years 2.5 million workers throughout the country were organized. As a result, Local 1199—now headed by Doris Turner—and the National Union of Hospital and Health Care Workers are counted among the most important unions for Black and Hispanic women in the country.

The relative success of Black women in the desirable "higher" professions, though more visible, was not as great. Although more Black women than Black men were listed under the general category of "professional" when Moynihan published his report, many more Black men than women were physicians, dentists, engineers, and so on. And that trend was continuing. In 1968, three years after the report was published, Black institutions conferred 91 percent of their professional doctoral degrees on men and only 9 percent on women.[19] A 1969 Ford Foundation survey revealed that 94.5 percent of 1,096 Blacks who had attained doctorates (excluding medical degrees) were men and 5.5 percent were women. Furthermore, a good portion of the Black women who received doctorates got them in education (and their percentage was lower than the percentage of women in the total doctoral population).[20] Nevertheless, the relative achievement of Black women seemed startling. The 1960 census showed, for example, that 7 percent of White physicians as opposed to 9.6 percent of Black physicians were women; 8 percent of Black lawyers, compared to 3 percent of White lawyers, were women. The same trend was apparent in a whole range of occupations. As extraordinary as these statistics were, one must keep in mind that they reflected not only the achievements of Black women but the *lack* of achievement of Black men and White women in these occupations.

Still, the disproportionate number of Black women in the professions deserves further study, for it has fueled the charges of Black women's advantage over Black men. In 1972 sociologist Cynthia Fuchs Epstein studied thirty-one Black women professionals, including lawyers, physicians, university professors, journalists, and public relations executives. What prompted her inquiry was the seeming inconsistency of Black women's success in a society that was both racist and sexist. Epstein discovered that achievement had little to do with advantage but a great deal to do with the attitudes of each woman's family, her sense of self-worth, the role of her mother, and her superiors' perception of her.

In virtually every instance, Black women professionals (unlike most of their White counterparts) grew up in homes where their mothers were doers. Of those interviewed, only four had mothers who had never worked (one of these mothers had thirteen children).

Many of the women's mothers were in professional or semiprofessional occupations themselves; they were teachers, professors, nurses, and one was a physician. Fewer (five out of the thirty) fathers of the women were professionals, and many others held stable jobs, such as postal employee or bricklayer. A description of the mother of one of the women was typical: "My mother was not the stronger of my parents but she was the most aggressive, always planning and suggesting ideas to improve the family's situation."[21] The mother, a dressmaker, would often "slip out" and do domestic work if she had to make ends meet, without telling the father, a carpenter who was excluded from the union and laid off periodically.

Not surprisingly, Epstein found that the daughters of such Black women had a tremendous sense of confidence in themselves and their abilities. She cited a 1964 study of Black women college graduates which confirmed that Black women tended to be more confident of their own abilities than did their White peers. When asked if they had personalities suitable to careers as business executives, 74 percent of Black women thought that they did as compared to 49 percent of the Whites.[22] Another study, conducted by the American Council of Education in 1971, noted that 62.1 percent of Black women college freshmen rated themselves "above average to achieve." This was higher than Black male freshmen (59.2 percent), White female freshmen (53.4 percent), *and* White male freshmen (50.6 percent).[23] Mothers of the Black women in Epstein's study encouraged achievement almost without exception. One physician recalled that her goal was to be a nurse but her mother encouraged her to be a doctor. This was in contrast to White families, who had more ambivalence about their daughters' becoming overeducated and thus having difficulty finding husbands.

One can speculate that although some Black women shared these anxieties, their life expectations generally were different from those of most White women. Black women expected to have to work, whether they were married or not. They didn't often think of their careers as "supplemental" to those of their husbands.

Another interesting characteristic of Black women professionals, Epstein found, was that they seemed to have a higher regard for each other than White women professionals had for *their* peers.[24] In a previous study she had found self-hatred among White women lawyers, including negative stereotypes about "aggressive, masculine" women, but Black women professionals had better attitudes toward

each other. Whereas few White women favored other women professionals, Black women "never indicated doubts about the competence
of other women, and some said that they favored women as colleagues
because they were more reliable and more willing to work than the
men they knew."[25]

The attitudes of Black women professionals also affected how
they were perceived by White male employers. Often they were
regarded as more "serious" than White women, because of their
strong career motivation. Black women were also less apt to become
involved in the sexual politics of the office. Nevertheless it is often
heard that Black women's success is due to the fact that they are
perceived as less of a threat to White males. This is true, but that
perception also has its disadvantages, for it indicates that whatever
their abilities, Black women often progress so far and no farther. They
are less apt than their male or White female peers to displace someone
from the executive suite, because they are women and because they
are Black. And the assumption that the most lucrative and favored
positions will fall to men is borne out by statistics.

As we see, for Black women, double discrimination can cut two
ways. On the one hand their status makes them the most apt to be
unemployed and underemployed. As a result, Black women have had
the lowest median income of all groups. On the other hand, the
tremendous effort required to transcend the barriers of race and sex
has catapulted full-time Black women workers into significant gains in
the ever-widening women's sphere of economic activity. The rate of
progress of this group has been startling to some, not because they
threatened to overtake Black men but because of their proximity to
them despite sex *and* race discrimination. Sociologists like Moynihan
believed that the proximity made Black men too dispirited to be
responsible heads of household.

His male-directed solution ignored the fact that Black women's
income and occupational status compared more favorably to Black
men because of the latter's inability to penetrate the more lucrative
job market reserved for White men. The suggestion that Black *women*
brake their progress, rather than eliminating the discrimination that
kept Black men down, ignored the plight of disproportionate numbers of Black poor women, female heads of families, and the necessity
for two decent incomes if Blacks were to have a quality of life comparable even to that of single-income White families.

By failing to isolate the true reasons for some Black women's relative success in the face of double discrimination, both the women's movement and the Black movement failed to benefit from the valuable lessons inherent in that achievement. Consequently, the failure effectively to challenge Moynihan's solution, with all its implications, retarded both movements. This was made abundantly clear by 1972.

XIX

~ A Failure of Consensus ~

The Shirley Chisholm Campaign

The reform movements of the sixties were to be sorely tested in the presidential campaign of 1972. Could the determination of Blacks, women, and youth to put the nation on a more liberal course be translated into practical politics? Could Blacks who could now vote, women who had been politicized, and youths who had stopped the Vietnam War marshal the necessary forces for a national mandate? The emergence of these constituencies made the Democratic party into a kind of liberal Valhalla. Among the hopefuls for the presidential nomination were Eugene McCarthy, George McGovern, John Lindsay—and Shirley Chisholm.

Shirley Chisholm, Congresswoman from New York, was the first Black woman to be elected to Congress. No candidacy better symbolized the "New Politics" of the period. Elected on a reform slate, she was an effective legislator for Black interests, and her "unbossed, unbought" image was appealing to the more than 3 million college students who either identified with or shared many ideas of the New Left. She was also an early member of NOW and the National Women's Political Caucus.

By her own admission, Chisholm's campaign for the presidency was disorganized and underfinanced. Moreover, her announcement that she would run seemed to come as a surprise to the leaders of the constituencies she sought, indicating that she hadn't done some of the groundwork necessary for the campaign. Nevertheless, the evidence of poor support for her candidacy revealed the shortcomings of both the Black and the feminist movements, shortcomings that would be fundamentally damaging to both. Where the feminists were concerned, Chisholm was "surprised" at their "coolness" to her candidacy. Although some local women's groups endorsed her, such as the Berkeley, California, chapter of NOW, the national leaders were much more ambivalent. The central arena for the political face-off that ensued was the National Women's Political Caucus.

The Caucus was organized in 1971 to get more women elected and appointed to public office, and to support women's issues. Its principal architects were New York Representative Bella Abzug, feminist activists Gloria Steinem and Betty Friedan, and Shirley Chisholm. The internecine struggle provoked by Chisholm's candidacy found Abzug and Steinem on one side, Friedan on the other. While Friedan, according to her own account, wanted the Caucus to endorse Shirley Chisholm, Steinem and Abzug had other ideas. Friedan felt that their goal was to take control of the Caucus in order to deliver a bloc vote to George McGovern. In this way they would consolidate their own position as power-brokers between women and the Democratic party. In all the wheeling and dealing that followed, Friedan's efforts were upended: "The meeting of the women delegates which should have been called by the Caucus so that all of us could swing our power behind Shirley Chisholm had been called off evidently at Gloria's suggestion," Friedan wrote. "And she was already organizing, on her own, as a *fait accompli,* a move for Sissy Farenthold as Vice President."[1]

Failing to get its endorsement, Chisholm resigned from the Caucus which was theoretically created to support a candidacy such as hers. In the meantime, Steinem, when asked whom she supported for President, would make coy remarks like "George McGovern is the best of the *male* candidates." After hearing that response a couple of times, Chisholm told Steinem, "I don't need that kind of help," feeling that it would be less damaging if Steinem just openly supported her "male" candidate.[2]

Such behavior can be categorized as just "politics," but other occurrences were more foreboding. Chisholm later recounted an occasion when Bella Abzug insisted on introducing her at a political gathering, only to make equivocal remarks about Chisholm's candidacy. And according to Friedan, within the Caucus's inner circles (where Black women were excluded) the bloc-vote advocates characterized Chisholm's campaign for delegates as "a quixotic joke."[3] In the end, both Friedan and Steinem did run as Chisholm delegates, but only after Eugene McCarthy (whom Friedan supported) and George McGovern proved unworthy of feminist support. Neither candidate demonstrated the capacity to meld an effective coalition; and McGovern angered feminists when he reneged on a promise to support a right-to-abortion plank in the Democratic platform. But the belated support for Chisholm was too slight to have any impact. The lesson that could be learned was that Black women also figured slightly in the priorities of the leaders of the women's movement.

Chisholm's candidacy would suffer even more at the hands of Black leaders, who by the early seventies were almost exclusively men. Black politicos explored several options in 1972. One was to run "favorite sons" in several states; another was to throw support behind McGovern; and a third, to support a single Black candidate. None, however, seemed to include Shirley Chisholm. She became vividly aware of this after hearing the results of a Black strategy meeting that took place outside of Chicago and which included Julian Bond, Percy Sutton, Richard Hatcher, Jesse Jackson, Imamu Amiri Baraka, Roy Innis, Willie Brown, Basil Patterson, and Clarence Mitchell III. The idea of Chisholm's candidacy received a less than enthusiastic response, according to her. "What was really bothering the black males at the meeting," she wrote, "was more directly hinted at by one who told a *Washington Post* reporter (anonymously): 'In this first serious effort of Blacks for high political office, it would be better if it were a man.' "[4]

The opinion was offered more crudely when she visited a Black Expo in Chicago. When Chisholm appeared, two Black men, probably local political types, said loudly enough for her to hear: "There she is—that little Black matriarch who goes around messing things up."[5]

From the beginning, Chisholm recalled, her campaign was plagued—ironically—by charges that she was a "captive of the women's movement." In 1972, association with an organization like NOW was enough to dampen the kind of Black grass-roots enthusiasm she needed to transcend the other obstacles in her campaign. The charge of "captive" may also have been a cover for some Black politicans who were uncomfortable with Chisholm's controversial political stands. When Chisholm publicly supported bail for Angela Davis, she "caught hell" from men "in Congress and leadership positions" who said they couldn't support Davis because it was not "politically expedient," she wrote. (The only major male-led group to endorse her candidacy was the Black Panthers.) In the end she would feel betrayed by Black men, especially after the losing struggle with the Washington, D.C., delegation where Representative Walter Fauntroy reneged on a promise to throw her the District's delegates on the first ballot, according to Chisholm. Instead most went to McGovern. Although one could say, as with the feminists, that she was just on the wrong end of a political maneuver, the sexist attitudes of Black men were especially painful to her. She concluded that the failure of her campaign was due more to sexism than racism, and the realization was tremendously demoralizing. She summed it up:

> I love a good fight and people know I like a good fight. But what hurts me more than anything else . . . is the brothers in politics. . . . If the brothers would only leave me alone, and stop attacking me so much and stop giving out wrong statements about me, I'd continue. If they would even just say, "well, she's half crazy and we can't work with her" and just leave me and let be I wouldn't mind. But they won't get off my back. After all, I'm only human and how much can I take of all this constant pressure and lies?[6]

In 1983 Shirley Chisholm announced that she would not seek another term in the House.

One can argue that the failure of Black and women leaders to give substantive support to Shirley Chisholm was as much a blow to the New Politics as was the disastrous campaign of Democratic nominee George McGovern. The election of Richard Nixon paralleled the demise of the civil rights/Black Power movement that began in the sixties—a demise hastened by the exclusion of Black women from leadership ranks. The seventies would also crush the momentum of the mainstream women's movement—which put its newfound prestige and power on the line for the passage of an Equal Rights Amendment.

The ERA

Historical patterns suggest that just as Black women are vital to Black movements, so Black movements are vital to the progress of feminist movements. Feminism has always had the greatest currency in times of Black militancy or immediately thereafter. This was true in the 1840's and 1850's, in the post-World War I years, and in the 1960's. Conversely, new gains for women become more difficult to attain when Black issues are not high on the national agenda or the national consciousness. This pattern held true for the seventies, the decade of struggle for the Equal Rights Amendment.

The ERA would have had a better chance if its timing had been better. However, it did not pass both houses of Congress until 1972, and within a year a backlash of antifeminist sentiment stopped the momentum of the ERA's drive to be ratified by three fourths of the states. The failure of the ERA can be viewed from many angles. But there is no question that timing was a factor.

Another factor was a misdirected feminist strategy. Instead of reaching out to those constituencies who could have been their most valuable allies, mainstream women leaders courted those women who, in the end, became the amendment's most effective opponents. The two miscalculations—timing and misplacement of lobbying energy—had a common source: race/class myopia. As in the past, a predominantly White, middle-class feminist movement was insensitive to the needs of working-class women and Black women. Instead of forming an effective coalition with these groups, NOW turned inward, among its own, trying to convince the unreconstructed elements of the *Feminine Mystique* to see the ERA light.

NOW's missteps began in 1967, the year the organization proposed a Bill of Rights for Women to be presented to political candidates and parties for the 1968 election. One of the bill's articles included support for the ERA. The ERA proposal put NOW's members from the United Auto Workers Union in an untenable position. They supported the ERA, but their union—as well as other unions—did not. The reason for labor's antipathy to the amendment was a historical one. Ever since the ERA was first proposed in 1923, organized labor and the Women's Bureau had feared the amendment's potentially adverse effect on working-class women.* The amendment, which called for equal rights under the law regardless of sex, would supersede protective legislation. So labor women believed that "the amendment might provide benefits to professional and/or upper-class women by equalizing the laws governing marriage, but would only be detrimental to them."[7]

As in the past, it appeared that the lines of battle over the ERA would remain rigidly drawn. On one side was labor and on the other, the professional membership of NOW. (A sample survey of five hundred NOW members revealed that 66 percent had bachelor's degrees, 30 percent had advanced degrees, and 50 percent were either

---

*However not all of the male union leadership which opposed the ERA had women's best interests in mind. Many, union men as well as male members of the Left, were motivated essentially by chauvinist considerations.

students or professionally employed.)[8] However, since the passage of Title VII of the Civil Rights Act in 1964, the Women's Department of the UAW had been reexamining the issue of protective legislation for women. They were finding that the Civil Rights Act superseded protective legislation, and, anyway, protective laws were in many cases more discriminatory than beneficial for women.

At the time of the Bill of Rights proposal, the UAW Women's Department was in the process of establishing these findings through court cases. Only then could unions and the Women's Bureau support the ERA. But NOW's ERA proposal was premature. The women of the UAW were not yet adequately prepared to bring the amendment case to their union or to organized labor in general. They informed the leaders of NOW that if the feminist organization supported the ERA, they would have to withdraw their active support—support which was crucial to NOW at that time. The feminist organization was working out of the UAW offices and using its clerical services, including those for mailings. But its insistence on the ERA forced NOW to relocate its national offices, "creating administrative chaos in the process," noted Jo Freeman.[9] That chaos was responsible for loss of valuable time and energy.

NOW's premature support for the amendment also slowed its ultimate passage in the Congress because of labor opposition. The AFL-CIO, the Communication Workers of America, the Amalgamated Clothing Workers, the ILGWU, and the Hotel, Restaurant and Bartenders International Union—all having significant female constituencies—testified against the amendment. Consequently, it was not until 1970 that the House passed the ERA, and 1972 that the Senate passed it. That the amendment survived at all was due more to the effort of the UAW women than to that of NOW's leadership. A year after the union members withdrew their active support, they were prepared to justify the amendment to the labor movement. In turn, large labor unions and the Women's Bureau—headed by a Black woman, Elizabeth Koontz—were able to support it for the first time in their histories. But by that time inchoate reactionary forces were gaining strength through a conservative backlash and a slowed economy.

Nevertheless, in the next eight months, twenty-two states ratified the amendment, and before the year was over twenty-eight states had done so. It seemed well on its way to getting the three quarters of the states needed to put it in the Constitution. But in January 1973 it smacked up against a national "Stop ERA" campaign, led by Phyllis Schlafly. A brilliant debater and organizer backed by well-financed right-wing groups, Schlafly proved a formidable opponent. As others had done in the past, she made the idea of equal rights for women synonymous with "man-hating radical frumps." Schlafly masterfully raised the specter of women drafted for combat, of unisex bathrooms and homosexual marriages, of demonic abortionists. ERA was a threat to the family, she averred. At the very least it could threaten alimony payments.

The Stop ERA campaign struck a surprisingly respondent chord. In *The Hearts of Men,* Barbara Ehrenreich explained that women responded to the male revolt by either struggling for economic self-sufficiency (feminism) or binding men more tightly to them (antifeminism). Stop ERA stirred the deep, previously still waters of the latter. These were a group whose backgrounds, origins, and ennui were very much like those of the NOW constituency. But they were women who concluded that rights won at the expense of privilege constituted a perilous trade-off. Schlafly deftly orchestrated their fears. Many state legislators began to receive letters like the one written by a woman in Oklahoma: "I want to remain a woman," she said, "I want to remain on a pedestal, I want to remain a homemaker."[10] Freeman observed, "The kind of constituent pressure that Congress people had felt at the national level, local legislators felt at the state, but for the opposite position."[11]

Even if the Stop ERA campaign had not tapped this vast emotional pool, so neglected by feminists in their campaign, Schlafly, with her mass mailings to rural and southern legislators, her busing in of women lobbyists, her marshaling of effective testimony at ratification hearings, might have prevailed anyway. But the outpouring of antifeminism for all to see seemed a demoralizing and fatal blow to the ERA. NOW advocates, undoubtedly unprepared for this kind of opposition, never seemed able to get on top of the campaign again. By the end of 1974, a period when the conservative backlash was being felt, only five more states had ratified the amendment; and Nebraska and Tennessee actually rescinded their prior ratification.

NOW redoubled its efforts, but one wonders if they channeled them in the right direction. Instead of consolidating the constituencies most responsive to the ERA, they turned to the weakest link: those who had been responsive to the antifeminist position. NOW changed its tune: Homemaking was no longer the curse the organization had first made it out to be. It watered down feminist ideas to make them more palatable to those women who were desperately clinging to their pedestals. Some may have been stunned, for example, by the position taken by NOW president Eleanor Smeal on the Phil Donahue show at a time when pro-ERA fortunes were low. A middle-aged woman in the audience begged Smeal to say something to her daughter, who had decided to be "only" a housewife. Smeal responded that there was nothing wrong with being a housewife and that the mother didn't understand what feminism was all about if she criticized her daughter's wishes. The woman sat down with a dazed expression.

While NOW was wooing the antifeminists, two of its potentially strongest allies were being neglected. NOW made inadequate efforts to dispel the increasing unease of labor women who feared that anti-male, anti-union feminists could use the movement to undermine the trade unions. In addition, despite their earlier public criticism of the women's movement, unmistakable signs that Black women were becoming more responsive to feminism were evident after 1972. Historically, Black women become more overtly feminist when Black militancy is in eclipse—and male chauvinism is on the rise—and this was again true in the seventies. Thus 1973 saw the creation of organizations such as the National Black Feminist Organization (NBFO), which articulated the need for political, social, and economic equality specifically for Black women. "We have been called 'matriarchs' by White racists and Black nationalists," its statement of purpose pointed out.[12] "It took us some time to realize that we had nothing to fear from feminism," acknowledged Eleanor Holmes Norton, one of the organization's founders, "but we could not have emerged amidst the confusions of five or six years ago." But they were emerging now. Within a year of its founding the NBFO had a membership of two thousand women in ten chapters, and other similar groups followed in its wake.[13] Also, in the early seventies, political Black lesbian groups such as the Combahee River Collective, organized in 1974 in New York, emerged.

Even from the less radically minded, Black women's circumstances in the seventies made the question of women's rights compelling. Within the twenty years between 1952 and 1972, Black women had made substantial gains. The gap in median educational attainment between White and non-White women declined from 4.0 to 1.2 years. Since 1963 more Black men than women were attending college, but in terms of median education, women increased their lead over men from .9 year to 1.2 years. And of all race/sex groups of full-time workers, non-White women had shown the greatest percentage increase in their median incomes since 1939. (White women had the lowest.)[14] However, despite their significant leap, Black women were still the most vulnerable group of workers, with a lower median income than any other group; and their families had the lowest median income of all the groups of families in the society. For Black women, the concept of "relative deprivation," which can be defined as unmet expectations, was certainly a factor.

In addition, another disturbing trend was revealed in the early seventies. Largely due to the implementation of policies suggested by Moynihan, as Aileen Hernandez observed, poverty was falling more heavily on the shoulders of female-headed households than ever before. In 1959 approximately 8.3 million American families were classified as in poverty. Of these, 59 percent were headed by White males, 18 percent by non-White males, 15 percent by White females, and 8 percent by non-White females.

By 1972, the numbers of families beneath the poverty level had declined to 5 million. But the new breakdown of the nature of these families was revealing. White males now headed 46 percent; non-White males, 12 percent; White females, 22 percent; and non-White females, 20 percent.[15] Male-directed policies (which failed to add to the cohesiveness of families) were having an alarming impact on all women. For Black women—who had higher unemployment rates, who were more apt to have to fend for themselves and their families alone—the policies were even more devastating.

So, as with the suffrage issue more than a half-century before, Black women had their own reasons to support women's rights in general and the ERA in particular. This was confirmed by a Louis Harris–Virginia Slims poll conducted in 1972. It revealed that 62 percent of Black women favored "efforts to strengthen or change women's status in society," compared with only 45 percent of White women. Even more startling perhaps, 67 percent of Black women expressed "sympathy with efforts of women's liberation groups," compared with only 35 percent of White women![16]

Black women in organizations like the National Council of Negro Women, the labor union movement, the United Methodist Church, and many others came out in open support of the ERA. Position papers written and published by Black women covered the economic, social, and even biblical rationales for the benefits of the ERA to the Black community. However, there was never a ground swell of Black support. One reason was that the ERA was closely associated with NOW, and NOW still had failed to adequately address issues of particular concern to minority women.

As an article in the *San Diego Union* pointed out in 1979, reasons for the continuing gap between NOW and minorities included the organization's emphasis on such issues as abortion and sterilization, which were touchy ones with Hispanics; there was still disagreement over the race-versus-sex issue, and over the disparity between the needs of affluent White women and those of impoverished minorities. Aileen Hernandez and other Black women attempted to bridge the gap by organizing a NOW minority task force to assess minority women's relationship with the feminist organization. Their report made many suggestions, including one that NOW should address the specific concerns of minorities. But subsequent action by the feminist organization, according to Hernandez, was sorely lacking. "NOW has been silent," she said in 1979—the year of the first deadline for ERA ratification—"on almost any issue that deals with the inequity of society more than the inequity of being female." The organization, Hernandez asserted, "cannot afford the luxury of a single issue focus—even when that issue was as important as the ERA."[17]

With tactics reminiscent of the YWCA struggle in the World War I years, the single-mindedness (and arrogance) of NOW steered them in the direction of sponsoring chapters in minority communities rather than dealing with minority issues. This was a "totally inappropriate approach," charged Hernandez, who interpreted it as attempting to 'indoctrinate minority women" on the ERA rather than attracting them to common issues.

To add insult to injury, at the organization's national convention in Los Angeles in September of 1979, an all-White group of officers was elected for the second straight year, although a Black woman, Sharon Parker, who had headed the minority task force, was running for a national secretary position. Nevertheless, Eleanor Smeal, campaigning for reelection, failed to endorse her. "The National President," noted Hernandez, "called for the election of a slate of officers with whom she could work—a slate personally endorsed by her . . and NOW starts this new administration *once again without any minority women* in national leadership positions."[18] For Hernandez and other Black women, such as California State Senator Diane Watson, the election was the proverbial last straw. Hernandez, once the organization's president and defender, accused NOW of being "too White and middle-class." In 1979 she sponsored a resolution saying that

Blacks should quit NOW or refrain from joining the group until it confronted its own racism and that of the larger society. Watson, the first Black woman to be elected to her position, agreed: "If they don't really go after a mixed group of women, we should not support such an organization, and we should dramatize our non-support."[19]

Such an attitude on the part of Black women diminished the kind of grass-roots support NOW needed in the ratification struggle, which had hard-nosed political overtones. A possible consequence was the defeat of the amendment in a crucial state: Illinois. In the state's House of Representatives, the ERA was drawn into a fight between Black legislators from Chicago and the city's Democratic organization over who would represent Black interests in the House leadership the following year. The Black legislators were angry that the city political leaders, without consulting them, had promised to back a candidate loyal to the Democratic political machine in exchange for his support of the amendment. In June 1978, the legislators, who ordinarily voted against the machine's interests, voted against the amendment, and the ERA was defeated by six votes.

Throughout the ERA campaign, NOW always claimed that more Americans supported the ERA than opposed it. This was true in the late seventies, but the statistical breakdown of that support is of interest: A Gallup poll conducted in 1978 found that the amendment was supported by 62 percent of men and 55 percent of women, and was opposed by 29 percent of men and 33 percent of women. In other words a higher percentage of men than women supported the amendment, while more women than men opposed it! There is little question that the softest support and the hardest opposition to the ERA were to be found among the people inspired by Phyllis Schlafly, those whom NOW futilely sought to turn around. As in the suffrage struggle, NOW demonstrated the inability of a predominantly White feminist organization to reach beyond its own White middle-class constituency. Although such organizations have effectively raised the issues of women's rights throughout American history, they have been doomed to fall short of the ultimate goal of empowerment when Black concerns have not been taken seriously.

The lack of consensus in the seventies, symbolized by the Chisholm campaign, revealed a familiar theme. The disarray of the Black movement and the failure of the ERA had at their base a common cause: the diminished participation of Black women. For it is the historical concerns of the Black woman which are at the core of the Black and women's movements. When she is at her lowest ebb, the racial struggle flounders. When she is compelled to articulate her needs and becomes active in their behalf, the Black movement advances.

The fundamental goals of White feminists have been historically defined through the Black movement. This was evident in the abolitionist movement, the southern antilynching and interracial movements, the struggle of Black women to perform dual roles in the forties and fifties, and the civil rights movement.

So, the relationship between race and sex, one linked by the Black woman, means that her role is of the utmost importance. History suggests that it is only when her convictions are firm in this regard can a society—one born in the depths of racism and sexism—be transformed.

XX

As the link between two of the most significant social reform movements in America, Black women have a complex task in the eighties. The decade has seen the election of a conservative President whose views concerning women and Blacks smack of the turn of the century. In fact, the eighties have a number of things in common with that earlier period: Civil rights gains are being rolled back, Black communities and families are in disarray, and the biggest feminist organization largely ignores the priorities and needs of Black women and other women of color. In addition, we are entering, once more, an era of Black assertiveness, one which will trigger historical tensions over the relationship of race and sex.

Perhaps lessons can be drawn. At the turn of the century, Black women initiated social reform in Black communities when government fell short, and they created the means to educate their own. They went toe to toe with White feminists, defended themselves and the race, and did not hesitate to chastise the men who sought to keep them from doing so. In the process, Black women helped launch and sustain the modern civil rights movement. They also exposed the deep core of feminism, which went to the heart of women's rights: over their souls, their bodies, their families, their labor. And in the course of all that, Black women may be said to have provided the means to free everyone.

The Black woman was able to accomplish so much in those years because she had an unshakable conviction: The progress of neither *race nor womanhood* could proceed without her. And she understood the relationship between the two.

Subsequent years saw significant educational and economic gains on the part of employed Black women. But it also saw confusion and guilt as women tried to fulfill the conflicting roles of breadwinner and housewife, as defined by the broader society. Sociology blamed the increasing discord and separation between Black men and women on Black women's assertiveness.

The racial movement of the fifties and sixties brought Black women once again to the forefront of the civil rights struggle. But their specific role as women in the movement was not defined (as that of past activists had been)—a legacy, no doubt, of the barrage of accusations hurled at them in the years following World War II. Thus their full leadership potential got lost amidst White feminism, Black Power, social science, and poverty programs. The consequences of this were made clear on a recent television show when two Black women magazine editors were asked if they believed in Sojourner Truth's homily that only women could "turn the world right side up again." Both responded that they didn't think Black women played any special role in contemporary life. A pity.

Though not all of us may have the faith that "God Is a Black Woman," as *Encore* publisher Ida Lewis only half-humorously wrote, developments of the seventies and eighties suggest that Black women, without apology, turn the world right side up again; or, short of that, become involved in issues that affect their own well-being.

Racism is still the salient issue. This is demonstrated in part by the fact that their comparative earnings do not reflect their occupational and educational gains in the last forty years, nor their traditionally high rates of labor-force participation. Overt forms of racism have declined, only to reveal the entrenched and slippery character called institutional racism. For all the gains of Black women, unemployment still hits them hardest, and they are still the most marginal group in the labor force—with the fewest resources to fall back on. And Black women who have penetrated the professions and the corporate world are facing more competition from like-minded White women of similar sensibilities. As occupations become more sex- and race-integrated, Black women are likely to be the first squeezed out of a shrinking economy.

Racial oppression maintains a heavy heel on the Black family as well. Despite the growth of the Black middle class in the last two decades, the average income for Black families with children is only about 55 percent that of comparable White families. Even among Black families in which both husband and wife work, their median income is about 83 percent that of Whites, according to the 1980 census.

Other statistics, however, indicate that we must be as vigilant about sex discrimination as racial discrimination, that we concentrate our energies on Black women as a distinct group, as we have in the past. The 1980 census shows that one third of Black women, fifteen years of age and older, are married and living with their husbands. That means that *two thirds* are single and have never been married, or are divorced, separated, or widowed. Almost half of Black families are headed by women, and more than four out of ten children are dependent on the incomes of their mothers. These statistics suggest that the employment issue is an essential one for Black women. The average rate of unemployment among them in 1980 (16 percent) was higher than that of Black men, White women, or White men.[1] The significance of these numbers can be gleaned from the fact that it is *unemployed* single mothers who make up such a large proportion of Black families (including half of Black children) in poverty, as distinct from female single-headed households in general. The rate of unemployment for single mothers increased fivefold between 1969 and 1978.[2] This trend is bound to continue: The out-of-wedlock birth rate among Black teenagers is the highest in the world. The world!

In contrast, Black women who are fully employed, year round, have continued to make median income and earnings gains relative to Black men, White women, and White men. This should suggest that special attention be given to Black women's attaining jobs—in other words, some *female-directed* policies and programs. It should also suggest that Black women be as vigilant about sex bias as they are about racial discrimination. Though they have a higher median educational attainment than Black men, the median income of Black men was 41 percent higher than that of Black women in 1980.[3] Black male college graduates earn more than Black female college graduates. Black women working full time earn about 54 percent of what White men earn. At the 1966–70 rate of change for occupational status, Black women will not reach the level of White men for 135 years, while it will take Black men 35 years.[4]

In this regard, the Black woman's investment in the success of the women's movement is a crucial one for the eighties. The women's movement has been responsible for the intense scrutiny of the relationship of Black poverty and progress to the problems and achievements of Black women. One study, for example, has shown that the recent gains Black women have made are due more to the lessening of sex discrimination than of race discrimination![5]

But to talk about the importance of the women's movement often evokes the timeworn arguments of race-versus-sex, or the accusations of having the same values as White middle-class women. But both the past and the present tell us it is not a question of race *versus* sex, but race *and* sex. In a time when so many Black women and children need sufficient income, the concerns about sex are necessary for the progress—indeed the economic survival—of Afro-Americans as a group. Secondly, Black women have always made up their own women's rights agenda, distinct from that of Whites. There is no reason for the concept of feminism to be usurped by others. The women's movement has allowed a greater and healthier consciousness among ourselves, one which must be passed on to other Black women. It is significant, I think, that at the height of Black feminist consciousness at the turn of the century, out-of-wedlock births were at their lowest rate. Of course there were also other factors involved, but one can't underestimate the role of the women's message in that era.

A clear conviction regarding that role could help unleash the potential power of Black women's organizations. In this regard the vision of Mary McLeod Bethune has yet to be fully realized. New organizations like The National Coalition of 100 Black Women, led by Jewell Jackson McCabe, with thirty chapters in twenty states and the District of Columbia, promises to be a valuable addition to the sororities and the professional and religious-affiliated women's organizations. Founded as a national group in 1981, the Coalition has high priorities in the area of voter registration and mobilization. In this election year, and in those to come, it is good for candidates as well as for those seeking their promises to remember that Black women traditionally register in higher numbers than Black men. They have also been an invaluable asset in providing community support systems which, by the way, could also be more often utilized for their own candidacies.

The Coalition has also stressed the concept of alliance, which in the eighties can be a particularly effective political tool. Certainly among the most important organizations of women whose wisdom has not been adequately shared by Black women's groups are those in organized labor. Such organizations as the Coalition of Labor Union Women (CLUW)—established in 1973 to combat sex discrimination within the unions and to organize women workers—could provide a valuable model. Union groups are good examples of interracial organizations in which Black women have a strong voice in policy making. Additionally, their philosophy goes beyond the labor context and can be applied universally: "The active participation of the women strengthens the union," said Addie L. Wyatt, a founder and international vice-president of CLUW, and international vice-president and director of the Civil Rights and Women's Affairs Department of the United Food and Commercial Workers International Union. "Women have brought very special strengths to every institution and organization in which they have been involved. This is a strong tradition, and the labor movement has to draw from this tradition."[6]

On issues of common concern, alliances with predominantly White feminist organizations can be mutually beneficial. And in the 1980's, coalition is more possible than ever before. There is not as wide a gap in the perception or the circumstances of Black and White women as there has been in the past. The median earnings of Black women are about 97 percent those of White women—and both have median earnings which are less than those of all men. The rate of minority and White women's participation in the labor force is virtually even.

These changes have created many more parallels between White and Black women than existed in the past. Since more White women work and are career-bound today, their sensibility has become more akin to that of Black women. Marriage-and-family expert Robert Blood wrote of working women in general: "The employment of women affects the power structure of the family by equalizing the resources of husband and wife. A working wife's husband listens to her more, and she listens to herself more. . . . Thus her power increases and, relatively speaking, the husband's falls."[7] The working mother also makes a significant impression on the next generation. Blood commented: "Daughters of working mothers are more independent, more self-reliant, more aggressive, more dominant, and more disobedient. Such girls are no longer meek, mild, submissive, and feminine like little ladies ought to be."[8]

Black and White women now share many interpersonal concerns, such as the relationship between career-oriented wives and their husbands, women working when their husbands are unemployed, women earning more than their men. A greater number of professional women, both Black and White, are forced to balance career and family (about 55 percent of all women executives are single) and the particular problems that professional women face in choosing and/or keeping mates. When asked why so many articles in *Cosmopolitan* magazine centered around finding and keeping a man, editor Helen Gurley

Brown replied that not only were there more women than men, but the competition was sharpened because fewer men could meet the criteria of upwardly mobile women. It is also significant that divorce rates seem to have increased among Whites as more women have joined the labor force.

This in turn means that Black and White women are experiencing many of the same dislocations. The growth rate is also rapid for White female-headed households (now at about 16 percent); for out-of-wedlock births among White American teenagers (third highest in the world); and for divorce among Whites. In 1982, 45 percent of all poor families were headed by women (with a poverty rate of 56 percent for Blacks, 55 percent for Hispanics, and 28 percent for Whites) and it is predicted that by the year 2000, poverty in the United States will be synonymous with female poverty. All these commonalities, combined with the sexual revolution of the sixties, have muted many of the negative stereotypes projected on Black women as a group. One of the symbolic but significant signs of this was the naming of Black women as both Miss America and the first runner-up in 1983.

But of course an objective analysis of Black women as a group is not enough. We need to see the reflections of our own personal lives to give them meaning, and to assuage our fears. In the seventies and eighties those mirrors have been put in front of us by such authors as Maya Angelou, Alice Walker, Toni Morrison, Gloria Naylor, Toni Cade Bambara, Pearl Cleage, Audre Lorde, Lucille Clifton, Nikki Giovanni, Margaret Walker, Gwendolyn Brooks, Ntozake Shange, Paule Marshall, June Jordan, Judy Simmons, Louise Meriwether, and J. E. Franklin, among others. Their work has been particularly important because, in the words of critic Mary Helen Washington: "The quest of Black men to achieve manhood has always inspired the highest respect, but the equivalent struggle of the Black woman has hardly been acknowledged—except by Black women writers."[9]

Their work is also important because there are still men who try to impose life-limiting views on us. Perhaps the most intimidating—and destructive—of these is the notion that if a woman makes full use of her intelligence and abilities, she is destined to be alone. (It is one thing to be alone, quite another to be *destined* to be alone.) That seemed to be the thesis of an essay written by Black sociologist Robert Staples in 1979. The former hero of *The Myth of the Black Matriarchy* became ruffled by Ntozake Shange's play *For Colored Girls Who Have*

Considered Suicide/When the Rainbow Is Enuf and Michele Wallace's polemic *Black Macho & the Myth of the Superwoman.* He was angry at their criticism of Black male chauvinism, maintaining that Black men were in "no position to be sexist," whether they wanted to be or not.[10] Nevertheless, he offered the opinion that Black men, especially middle-class Black men, disdained "strong" women. "The middle-class Black male, with a wider range of choices, screens out the strong Black woman beforehand in his choice of mates. . . . Anyone who has met the typical middle-class Black wife knows she scores higher on the femininity scale than her unmarried counterpart."[11] Women, he warned, "will not find it easy to carve out an independent career lifestyle and maintain a stable relationship with a man."[12] Of course, he failed to explain why dependent, unemployed Black women were not finding it easy to maintain such a relationship either.

Explaining why the "best" and the "brightest" Black men often marry White women, he observed, "It could be that the most successful Black men have values and lifestyles most in tune with White society. . . . Among those values will exist the one that women should be supportive and subordinate. Whether true or not, many Black men, including those involved with Black women, do not believe Black women fit the model very well."[13]

Finally, still claiming he was not sure what Black male sexism was, Staples concluded that Black men had "the right to choose a woman that meets their perceived needs, even if their exercise of that right limits the life options of women."[14] Though he added that Black women have the same option, the implication was that Black women suffer the greater loss if they don't compromise. But is that true?

That so many Black families are female-headed explains not only much Black and female poverty, but male poverty as well. Divorced, single, and separated men earn less than 60 percent as much as married men of the same age and credentials.[15] Twice as many Black men as White are single. Like single White men, unmarried Black men tend to have shorter life spans.

Additionally, anyone who has single male friends knows that most of them don't live alone very well. Few seem able to develop a sustaining network of friends and family the way single women do. Even single men with good incomes often lead lives that appear vacuous and disorganized. And one could guess that men who lack sound relationships with women are more likely to become drug addicts, alcoholics, prisoners, and the like. In Robert Staples's *Black*

Singles, published after the essay, he remarked a departure from the past, in that more Black women are choosing to be alone rather than involved in a less-than-satisfactory marriage, or with a husband whose income is lower than theirs. Though the sociologist is appalled by this development (as he was by Shange's exhortation for Black women to "love themselves"), the plight of the single man suggests he must learn to distinguish between his "perceived" needs and his real ones.

In the meantime, such attitudes as those put forth by Staples confirm the conviction that male-directed policies—which have already proven to be detrimental to Black women in particular and Blacks in general—are the solution to Black poverty. For example, the intellectual darling of the supply-siders, George Gilder, stated plainly what his predecessors dared only imply. Citing the gains of Black women—who were making three-quarters the wages of Black men by 1970—he wrote: "The earnings of Black men and women are often compared to White earnings, *but what matters is how they compare to each other.*"[16] (Emphasis added.) To Gilder, "three quarters" was just too much for Black men to put up with. (He also added some bizarre twists of his own to the strong-woman–strutting-man theory. A reason for Black women scoring higher on I.Q. tests, he said, was that so many of them had to rear *sons* alone—a task that evidently increased their intellectual thresholds.)

What such attitudes have wrought is evident in the statistics on the poverty and state of the Black family in the eighties. Away with that kind of thinking! Black men and women need each other too much to be separated by such nonsense. It is a need that has economic, racial, and, in a still racially hostile society, emotional implications as well. Black men and women alike must try to lighten the emotional baggage that keeps them estranged from each other.

The concrete reality of the Black situation does suggest, however, that most of the required revisionist thinking must be done by men. Historically, racial necessity has made Black women redefine the notion of womanhood to integrate the concepts of work, achievement, and independence into their role as women. On the male side of the coin, if abandoning a family, or suppressing that feminine spirit (and it is feminine), is considered a male prerogative, then the same necessity compels Black men to redefine manhood. And women have to help them do it.

The challenges for Black women in the eighties are many and

complex. But Black women survived the rigors of slavery to demand the rights of their race and of their sex. They rose above the most demeaning forms of labor and demanded to be called by their last names. Black women forged humane communities out of rough settlements. They converted the rock of double oppression into a steppingstone. They drew upon centuries of moral authority and determination to launch the movement in the sixties, and to strengthen its tenets thereafter. They have extended the meaning of womanhood and personified the central issues of race and feminism. That is why —as Frances Hooks, member of The National Coalition of 100 Black Women, stated at the New York chapter's political workshop in 1983 —it is "Black women who hold the key to the future of America."

The challenge of the eighties may be difficult, but Black women have done more with less. It is time to call a meeting at some Lyric Hall.

SOURCE NOTES

Chapter I

1. Alfreda M. Duster, ed., *Crusade for Justice: The Autobiography of Ida B. Wells* (Chicago and London: University of Chicago Press, 1970, 1972), p. 51.

2. Jacquelyn Dowd Hall, *Revolt Against Chivalry: Jessie Daniel Ames and the Women's Campaign Against Lynching* (New York: Columbia University Press, 1979), p. 132.

3. Dorothy Sterling, *Black Foremothers, Three Lives* (New York: The Feminist Press, 1979), p. 79.

4. Duster, op. cit., p. 52.

5. Ibid., p. 53.

6. Ida B. Wells-Barnett, *On Lynchings* (New York: Arno Press and The New York Times, 1969), p. 23.

7. Duster, op. cit., p. 9.

8. Ibid., p. 25.

9. Sterling, op. cit., p. 70.

10. Ibid., p. 77.

11. Ibid., p. 74.

12. Ibid.

13. Ibid., p. 79.

14. Gerda Lerner, ed., *Black Women in White America: A Documentary History* (New York: Pantheon Books, 1972), p. 177.

15. Duster, op. cit., p. 70.

16. Florette Henri, *Black Migration: Movement North, 1900–1920, The Road from Myth to Man* (Garden City, N.Y.: Anchor Press/Doubleday, 1976), p. 33.

17. Herbert G. Gutman, *The Black Family in Slavery and Freedom, 1750–1925* (New York: Pantheon Books, 1976), p. 536.

18. Ibid., p. 537.

19. "Some Negro Views of the Negro Question," *Harper's Weekly* (June 18, 1904), p. 928.

20. Duster, op. cit., p. 72

21. Ibid., p. 64.

22. Ibid.

23. Wells-Barnett, op. cit., p. 24.

24. Ibid., p. 4.

25. Sterling, op. cit., p. 82.

26. Duster, op. cit., p. 25.

27. Ibid., p. 78.

28. Sterling, op. cit., p. 81.

29. Gutman, op. cit., p. 536.

30. Bettina Aptheker, "Woman Suffrage and the Crusade Against Lynching, 1890–1920" (paper delivered at conference, "Black Women: An Historical Perspective," sponsored by the National Council of Negro Women, Washington, D.C., November 12–13, 1979), p. 13.

Chapter II

1. James C. Ballagh, *A History of Slavery in Virginia* (Baltimore: Johns Hopkins Press, 1902), p. 42.

2. Ronald T. Takaki, *Iron Cages: Race and Culture in 19th-Century America* (Seattle: University of Washington Press, 1979), p. 12.

3. Ibid., p. 142.

4. Ibid., p. 12.

5. Barbara Welter, *Dimity Convictions: The American Woman in the Nineteenth Century* (Athens: Ohio University Press, 1976), p. 12.

6. Winthrop D. Jordan, *White Over Black: American Attitudes Toward the Negro, 1550–1812* (New York: W.W. Norton & Company, 1968), p. 35.

7. A. Leon Higginbotham, Jr., *In the Matter of Color: Race and the American Legal Process, The Colonial Period* (New York: Oxford University Press, 1978), p. 23.

8. Jordan, op. cit., p. 77.

9. Ibid.

10. Ibid.

11. Higginbotham, op. cit., p. 43.

12. Ibid.

13. Ibid., p. 45.

14. John Hope Franklin, *From Slavery to Freedom: A History of Negro Americans* (New York: Vintage Books/Random House, 1969), pp. 80–81.

15. Lorenzo Johnston Greene, *The Negro in Colonial New England* (New York: Atheneum, 1968, 1969, 1971, 1974), p. 154.

16. Herbert Aptheker, *American Negro Slave Revolts* (New York: International Publishers, 1963), p. 145.

17. Sidney Kaplan, *The Black Presence in the Era of the American Revolution: 1770–1800* (New York: New York Graphic Society, 1973), p. 216.

18. Willie Lee Rose, *Slavery and Freedom* (New York and Oxford: Oxford University Press, 1982), p. 21.

19. Ibid., pp. 24–25.

20. Ann Firor Scott, *The Southern Lady: From Pedestal to Politics, 1830–1930* (Chicago and London: Chicago University Press, 1970), p. 17.

21. Margaret Fuller, *Woman in the Nineteenth Century* (New York: W.W. Norton & Company, 1971), p. 33.

22. Linda Brent, *Incidents in the Life of a Slave Girl* (New York and London: Harvest/Harcourt Brace Jovanovich, 1973), p. 26.

23. Ibid.

24. Ibid., p. 27.

25. Ibid., p. 205.

26. Olive Gilbert, *The Narrative of Sojourner Truth* (New York: Arno Press, 1968), p. 24.

27. Ibid., p. 38.

28. *Aunt Sally, Or the Cross, The Way of Freedom* (Cincinnati: American Reform Tract & Book Society, 1858) p. 59.

29. Bethany Veney, *The Narrative of Bethany Veney, A Slave Woman* (Worcester, Mass., 1889), p. 26.

30. Ibid.

31. Brent, op. cit., p. 57.

32. Ibid.

33. Herbert G. Gutman, *The Black Family in Slavery and Freedom, 1750–1925* (New York: Pantheon Books, 1976), p. 393.

34. Ibid., p. 70.

35. Frances Anne Kemble, *Journal of a Residence on a Georgian Plantation in 1838–1839* (New York and Scarborough, Ont.: New American Library, 1961), p. 95.

36. Gutman, op. cit., p. 138.

37. Ibid., p. 81.

38. Ibid.

39. Darlene Hines, "Female Slave Resistance: The Economics of Sex," *The Western Journal of Black Studies,* Vol. 3, No. 2 (Summer 1979), p. 127.

40. Gerda Lerner, *The Majority Finds Its Past: Placing Women in American History* (New York and Oxford: Oxford University Press, 1979), p. 26.

41. Ibid.

42. Sharon Harley, "Northern Black Female Workers: Jacksonian Era," *The Afro-American Woman: Struggles and Images,* Sharon Harley and Rosalyn Terborg-Penn, eds. (Port Washington, N.Y., and London: Kennikat Press, 1978), p. 8.

43. Ibid., p. 10.

44. Lerner, op. cit., p. 57.

45. Dorothy Porter, "The Organized Educational Activities of Negro Literary Societies, 1828–1846," *Journal of Negro Education,* Vol. V, No. 4 (October 1936), p. 572.

46. "Duty of Females," *The Liberator* (May 5, 1832), p. 70 in *Early Negro Writing, 1760–1837.* Dorothy Porter, ed. (Boston: Beacon Press, 1971), p. 124.

47. Benjamin Quarles, *Black Abolitionists* (London, Oxford, and New York: Oxford University Press, 1969), p. 7.

48. Bert James Loewenberg and Ruth Bogin, eds., *Black Women in Nineteenth-Century American Life: Their Words, Their Thoughts, Their Feelings* (University Park and London: Pennsylvania State University Press, 1976), p. 197.

49. Ibid., p. 193.

50. Ibid., p. 189.

51. Ibid., p. 188.

52. Ibid., p. 194.

53. Ibid., p. 187.

54. Ibid., p. 194.

55. Ibid., p. 192.

56. Ibid., p. 190.

57. Ibid., p. 197.

58. Ibid., p. 189.

59. Ibid., p. 198.

60. Ibid.

61. Ibid.

62. Ibid., p. 199.

63. Ibid.

64. Ibid.

65. Ibid., p. 200.

66. Elizabeth Cady Stanton, Susan Anthony, and Mathilda Joslyn Gage, eds., *The History of Woman Suffrage,* Vol. I (Rochester, N.Y., 1881), pp. 115–117.

67. Eleanor Flexner, *Century of Struggle: The Woman's Rights Movement in the United States* (Cambridge, Mass., and London: Belknap Press/Harvard University Press, 1959, 1975, 1979), p. 91.

68. Ibid.

69. Ellen Carol Du Bois, *Feminism and Suffrage: The Emergence of an Independent Women's Movement in America, 1848–1869* (Ithaca, N.Y., and London: Cornell University Press, 1978), p. 32.

Chapter III

1. Herbert G. Gutman, *The Black Family in Slavery and Freedom, 1750–1925* (New York: Pantheon Books, 1976), p. 402.

2. Ibid., p. 410.

3. Ibid., p. 21.

4. William Still, *The Underground Railroad: A Record* (Philadelphia: People's Publishing Company, 1879), p. 801.

5. E. Franklin Frazier, *The Negro Family in the United States* (Chicago and London: University of Chicago Press, 1939, 1948, 1966, 1973), p. 102.

6. Ibid., p. 47.

7. William C. Nell, *The Colored Patriots of the American Revolution* (New York: Arno Publishers, repr. 1968), p. 179.

8. Benjamin Quarles, *Black Abolitionists* (London, Oxford, and New York: Oxford University Press, 1969), p. 178.

9. Lorenzo Johnson Greene, *The Negro in Colonial New England* (New York: Atheneum, 1968, 1969, 1971, 1974), p. 217.

10. Howard Bell, ed., *Proceedings of the National Negro Conventions, 1830–1864* (New York: Arno Press, 1969) p. 33.

11. Ibid., p. 29.

12. Sharon Harley, "Northern Black Female Workers: Jacksonian Era," *The Afro-American Woman: Struggles and Images,* Sharon Harley and Rosalyn Terborg-Penn, eds. (Port Washington, N.Y., and London: Kennikat Press, 1978), p. 12.

13. Ibid.

14. Irene Diggs, "Du Bois, and Women: A Short Story of Black Women, 1910–34," in *A Current Bibliography on African Affairs,* Vol. 7, No. 3 (Summer 1974), p. 260.

15. Gutman, op. cit., p. 388.

16. Ibid.

17. Barbara Christian, *Black Women Novelists: The Development of a Tradition 1892–1976* (Westport, Conn.: Greenwood Press, 1980), p. 14.

18. Frazier, op. cit., p. 54.

19. Ibid., p. 69.

20. Peter Kolchin, *First Freedom: The Response of Alabama Blacks to Emancipation and Reconstruction* (Westport, Conn.: Greenwood Press, 1972), p. 62.

21. Leon F. Litwack, *Been in the Storm so Long: The Aftermath of Slavery* (New York: Vintage Books, 1980), p. 245.

22. Gutman, op. cit., p. 167.

23. Ibid.

24. Litwack, op. cit., p. 244.

25. Gutman, op. cit., p. 167.

26. Litwack, op. cit., p. 245.

27. Gutman, op. cit., pp. 167–168.

28. Philip S. Foner, *Women and the American Labor Movement: From Colonial Times to the Eve of World War I* (New York: Free Press, 1979), p. 119.

29. Ibid., pp. 124–125.

30. Ibid., p. 119.

31. Litwack, op. cit., p. 246.

32. Ibid.

33. Kolchin, Mobile *Daily Register,* July 2, 1868.

34. Still, op. cit., p. 773.

35. Frazier, op. cit., p. 133.

36. Gutman, op. cit., p. 73.

37. Gerda Lerner, ed., *Black Women in White America: A Documentary History* (New York: Pantheon Books, 1972), p. 569.

38. Ibid., pp. 569–570.

39. Ellen Carol Du Bois, *Feminism and Suffrage: The Emergence of an Independent Women's Movement in America, 1848–1869* (Ithaca, N.Y., and London: Cornell University Press, 1978), p. 69.

40. Lerner, op. cit., p. 569.

41. Still, op. cit., p. 773.

42. Rosalyn Terborg-Penn, "Afro-Americans in the Struggle for Woman Suffrage," Ph.D. dissertation, Howard University, 1977 (University Microfilms International, Ann Arbor, Mich.), p. 82.

43. Ibid., p. 90.

44. Ibid., p. 73.

45. Ibid., p. 82.

46. Elizabeth Cady Stanton, Susan Anthony, and Mathilda Joslyn Gage, eds., *The History of Woman Suffrage,* Vol. II (Rochester, N.Y., 1881), p. 382.

47. E. C. Du Bois, op. cit., p. 187.

48. Terborg-Penn, op. cit., p. 77.

49. Stanton et al., op. cit., pp. 391–392.

50. Foner, op. cit., p. 138.

51. Ibid.

52. Terborg-Penn, op. cit., p. 53.

53. Ibid., p. 55.

54. Ibid., p. 60.

55. Still, op. cit., p. 803.

56. Gutman, op. cit., p. 437.

57. Ibid., p. 438.

58. Frances Ellen Harper, "Colored Women of America," *Englishwoman's Review* (January 15, 1878), p. 12.

59. Ibid., p. 13.

60. Ibid., p. 10.

61. Ibid., p. 14.

62. Gutman, op. cit., p. 390.

63. Ibid., p. 393.

64. E. C. Du Bois, op. cit., p. 69.

65. Gutman, op. cit., p. 85.

66. Ibid., p. 82*n*.

Chapter IV

1. Mary Ann Shadd Cary, "The Colored Women's Progressive Association," Mary Ann Shadd Cary Papers (Moorland-Spingarn Research Center, Howard University, Washington, D.C.).

2. Florette Henri, *Black Migration: Movement North, 1900–1920, The Road from Myth to Man* (Garden City, N.Y.: Anchor Press/Doubleday, 1976), p. 34.

3. Anna H. Jones, "The American Colored Woman," *The Voice of the Negro* (October 1905), pp. 692 and 693.

4. Addie Hunton, "Negro Womanhood Defended," *The Voice of the Negro* (July 1904), p. 282.

5. Tullia K. Brown Hamilton, "The National Association of Colored Women, 1896 to 1920," Ph.D. dissertation, Emory University, 1978, p. 27.

6. Carol Hymowitz and Michaele Weissman, *A History of Women in America* (New York: Bantam Books, 1978), p. 227.

7. Ann Firor Scott, *The Southern Lady: From Pedestal to Politics, 1830–1930* (Chicago and London: Chicago University Press, 1970), p. 122.

8. Richard Hofstadter, *Social Darwinism in American Thought* (Philadelphia: University of Pennsylvania Press, 1944, 1955), p. 44.

9. Stephen Jay Gould, *The Mismeasure of Man* (New York: W.W. Norton, 1981), p. 124.

10. Wilbur J. Cash, *The Mind of the South* (New York: Knopf, 1941), p. 86.

11. Gould, op. cit., pp. 104–105.

12. Hymowitz and Weissman, op. cit., p. 224.

13. Cash, op. cit., p. 89.

14. Jacquelyn Dowd Hall, *Revolt Against Chivalry: Jessie Daniel Ames and the Women's Campaign Against Lynching* (New York: Columbia University Press, 1979), p. 151.

15. Anna Julia Cooper, *A Voice of the South* (Xenia, Ohio: Aldine Printing House, 1892), p. 28.

16. Ibid., pp. 144–145.

17. Bert James Loewenberg and Ruth Bogin, eds., *Black Women in Nineteenth-Century American Life: Their Words, Their Thoughts, Their Feelings* (University Park and London: Pennsylvania State University Press, 1976), pp. 3–4.

18. Fannie Barrier Williams, "The Club Movement Among Colored Women of America," *A New Negro for a New Century: An Accurate and Up-to-Date Record of the Upward Struggles of the Negro Race*, Booker T. Washington, ed. (Chicago: American Publishing House, 1900), p. 379.

19. Hamilton, op. cit., p. 13.

20. Eleanor Flexner, *Century of Struggle: The Woman's Rights Movement in the United States* (Cambridge, Mass., and London: Belknap Press/Harvard University Press, 1959, 1975, 1979), p. 191.

21. *The Woman's Era* (March 24, 1894), p. 4.

22. Ibid.

Chapter V
1. Elizabeth L. Davis, *Lifting as They Climb: The National Association of Colored Women* (no publisher, 1933), p. 18.

2. Eleanor Flexner, *Century of Struggle: The Woman's Rights Movement in the United States* (Cambridge, Mass., and London: Belknap Press/Harvard University Press, 1959, 1975, 1979), p. 191.

3. Gerda Lerner, ed., *Black Women in White America: A Documentary History* (New York: Pantheon Books, 1972), p. 165.

4. Ibid., pp. 156–158.

5. Ibid., p. 165.

6. Bert James Loewenberg and Ruth Bogin, eds., *Black Women in Nineteenth-Century American Life: Their Words, Their Thoughts, Their Feelings* (University Park and London: Pennsylvania State University Press, 1976), p. 329.

7. Addie Hunton, "Negro Womanhood Defended," *The Voice of the Negro* (July 1904), p. 281.

8. Anna Julia Cooper Papers (Moorland-Spingarn Research Center, Howard University, Washington, D.C.).

9. Tullia K. Brown Hamilton, "The National Association of Colored Women, 1896 to 1920," Ph.D. dissertation, Emory University, 1978, p. 106.

10. Loewenberg and Bogin, op. cit., p. 274.

11. Ibid.

12. Ibid., p. 246.

13. Ibid., p. 247.

14. Alfreda M. Duster, ed., *Crusade for Justice: The Autobiography of Ida B. Wells* (Chicago and London: University of Chicago Press, 1970, 1972), p. 117.

15. Ibid., pp. 151–152.

16. *The Woman's Era* (July 1895), p. 12.

17. Bettina Aptheker, "Woman Suffrage and the Crusade Against Lynching, 1890–1920" (paper delivered at conference, "Black Women: An Historical Perspective," sponsored by the National Council of Negro Women, Washington, D.C., November 12–13, 1979), p. 30.

18. Fannie Barrier Williams, "The Club Movement Among Colored Women of America," *A New Negro for a New Century: An Accurate and Up-to-Date Record of the Upward Struggles of the Negro Race,* Booker T. Washington, ed. (Chicago: American Publishing House, 1900), p. 397.

Chapter VI

1. Elizabeth L. Davis, *Lifting as They Climb: The National Association of Colored Women* (unpublished, 1933), p. 19.

2. Bert James Loewenberg and Ruth Bogin, eds., *Black Women in Nineteenth-Century American Life: Their Words, Their Thoughts, Their Feelings* (University Park and London: Pennsylvania State University Press, 1976), p. 244.

3. Ibid.

4. Ibid., p. 246.

5. Anna Julia Cooper, *A Voice of The South* (Xenia, Ohio: Aldine Printing House, 1892), p. 121.

6. Fannie Barrier Williams, "The Woman's Part in a Man's Business," *The Voice of the Negro* (November 1904), p. 543.

7. Ibid.

8. Fannie Barrier Williams, "The Club Movement Among Colored Women of America," *A New Negro for a New Century: An Accurate and Up-to-Date Record of the Upward Struggles of the Negro Race,* Booker T. Washington, ed. (Chicago: American Publishing House, 1900), p. 379.

9. Cooper, op. cit., pp. 144–145.

10. Ibid., p. 143.

11. *The Woman's Era* (June 1894), p. 5.

12. Ann Firor Scott, *The Southern Lady: From Pedestal to Politics, 1830–1930* (Chicago and London: Chicago University Press, 1970), p. 128.

13. Mary Church Terrell, "What Role Is the Educated Negro Woman to Play in the Uplifting of Her Race?" *Twentieth Century Negro Literature,* D. W. Culp, ed. (Naperville, Ill.: JL Nichols & Co., 1902), p. 175.

14. Williams, "The Club Movement Among Colored Women," op. cit., p. 382.

15. Terrell, op. cit., p. 175.

16. Williams, "The Club Movement Among Colored Women," op. cit., p. 383

17. Ibid., p. 393.

18. Davis, op. cit., p. 18.

19. Josephine Bruce, "What Has Education Done for Colored Women," *The Voice of the Negro* (July 1905), p. 295.

20. Terrell, op. cit., p. 173.

21. Louis Harlan, ed., *The Booker T. Washington Papers,* Vol. 2 (Urbana, Chicago, and London: University of Illinois Press, 1972), p. 305.

22. Fannie Barrier Williams, "The Club Movement Among Negro Women," *Progress of a Race or The Remarkable Advancement of the Colored American,* J. W. Gibson and W. H. Crogman, eds. (Naperville, Illinois: JL Nichols & Co., 1902, 1912), p. 199.

23. Harlan, op. cit., pp. 301–302.

24. Ibid., p. 302.

25. Bruce, op. cit., p. 297.

26. Terrell, op. cit., p. 175.

27. Bruce, op. cit., p. 296.

28. Harlan, op. cit., p. 301.

29. Terrell, op. cit., p. 174.

30. Ibid., p. 175.

31. Ibid.

32. Loewenberg and Bogin, op. cit., p. 330.

33. Jeanne L. Noble, "The Negro Woman's College Education," Ph.D. dissertation, Columbia University (New York: Columbia University, Bureau Publications, 1956), p. 45.

34. Ibid., p. 22.

35. Terrell, op. cit., p. 176.

36. Nannie H. Burroughs, "Negro Women and Their Homes," *What Do You Think?* n.d., Lincoln Heights and Washington, D.C., p. 79.

37. *The Woman's Era* (April 1895), p. 14.

38. *The Woman's Era* (November 1895), p. 14.

39. Noble, op. cit., p. 23.

40. *The Woman's Era* (November 1895), p. 9.

41. Louis H. Harlan, ed., *The Booker T. Washington Papers,* Vol. 3 (University of Illinois Press, 1974), p. 444.

42. Benjamin Quarles, *The Negro in the Making of America* (New York: Collier Books, 1964), p. 167.

43. Ibid., p. 171.

44. Ibid., p. 169.

45. John Hope Franklin, *From Slavery to Freedom: A History of Negro Americans* (New York: Vintage Books/Random House, 1969), p. 442.

46. August Meier, *Negro Thought in America, 1880–1915* (Ann Arbor: University of Michigan Press, 1966), p. 240.

47. Ibid.

48. Louis H. Harlan and Raymond Smock, eds., *The Booker T. Washington Papers,* Vol. 7 (University of Illinois Press, 1977), p. 533.

49. Tullia K. Brown Hamilton, "The National Association of Colored Women, 1896 to 1920," Ph.D. dissertation, Emory University, 1978, p. 53.

50. Lawson Andrew Scruggs, *Women of Distinction: Remarkable in Works and Invincible in Character* (Raleigh, N.C.: L.A. Scruggs, 1893), p. xi.

51. Loewenberg and Bogin, op. cit., p. 324.

52. *The Woman's Era* (March 1894), p. 4.

53. Loewenberg and Bogin, op. cit., p. 324.

54. Scruggs, op. cit., p. 14.

55. Louis H. Harlan, ed., *The Booker T. Washington Papers,* Vol. 1 (University of Illinois Press, 1972), p. 302.

56. Scruggs, op. cit., p. 14.

57. Noble, op. cit., p. 23.

58. Ibid.

59. Dorothy Sterling, *Black Foremothers, Three Lives* (New York: The Feminist Press, 1979), p. 134.

60. Alfreda M. Duster, ed. *Crusade for Justice: The Autobiography of Ida B. Wells* (Chicago and London: University of Chicago Press, 1970, 1972), p. 244.

61. Ibid., p. 102.

62. Ibid., p. 101.

63. Ibid., p. 251.

64. Ibid.

65. "The Three Wives of Booker T. Washington," *Ebony* magazine (September 1982), p. 32.

66. Ibid.

67. Ibid.

68. Williams, "The Woman's Part in a Man's Business," op. cit., p. 545.

69. Loewenberg and Bogin, op. cit., p. 325.

70. Cooper, op. cit., p. 29.

71. Williams, "The Woman's Part in a Man's Business," op. cit., p. 382.

72. Fannie Barrier Williams, "The Colored Girl," *The Voice of the Negro* (June 1905), p. 403.

73. Nannie H. Burroughs, "Not Color But Character," *The Voice of the Negro* (July 1904), p. 277.

74. Ibid., p. 278.

75. Cooper, op. cit., p. 32.

76. Ibid.

77. Burroughs, "Not Color But Character," op. cit., p. 108.

78. Gerda Lerner, ed., *Black Women in White America* (New York: Pantheon Books, 1972), pp. 156–158.

79. Williams, "The Colored Girl," op. cit., p. 402.

80. Ibid.

81. Ibid., p. 403.

82. Duster, op. cit., p. 44.

83. Williams, "The Colored Girl," op. cit., p. 403.

84. Ibid., p. 402.

85. Ibid., p. 403.

86. Burroughs, "Not Color But Character," op. cit., p. 277.

87. Ibid.

88. Alfred A. Moss, Jr., *The American Negro Academy: Voice of the Talented Tenth* (Baton Rouge and London: Louisiana State University Press, 1981), p. 55.

89. Burroughs, "Not Color But Character," op. cit., p. 278.

90. Sterling, op. cit., p. 75.

91. Alexander Crummell, "The Black Woman of the South, Her Neglects and Her Needs," in *Africa and America: Addresses and Discourses* (Springfield, MA: Willey & Company, 1891), p. 71.

92. Loewenberg and Bogin, op. cit., p. 327.

93. Moss, op. cit., p. 41.

94. *The Woman's Era* (June 1894), p. 5.

95. Cooper, op. cit., p. 135.

96. Sterling, op. cit., p. 106.

97. Rosalyn Terborg-Penn, "Black Male Perspectives on the Nineteenth-Cen-

tury Woman," *The Afro-American Woman: Struggles and Images,* Sharon Harley and Rosalyn Terborg-Penn, eds. (Port Washington, N.Y., and London: Kennikat Press, 1978), p. 42.

Chapter VII

1. Aileen S. Kraditor, *The Ideas of the Woman Suffrage Movement, 1899–1929* (Garden City, N.Y.: Anchor Books, 1971), p. 18.

2. R. E. Wall, "Shall Our Girls Be Educated?" *The A.M.E. Church Review* (1888), p. 45.

3. *The Woman's Era* (September 1894), p. 8.

4. Cynthia Neverdon-Morton, The Black Woman's Struggle for Equality in the South," *The Afro-American Woman: Struggles and Images,* Sharon Harley and Rosalyn Terborg-Penn, eds. (Port Washington, N.Y., and London: Kennikat Press, 1978), p. 53.

5. Mary Church Terrell, "The Justice of Woman Suffrage," *The Crisis,* 7 (September 1912), p. 243.

6. W.E.B. Du Bois, "Votes for Women: A Symposium by Leading Thinkers of Colored America," *The Crisis, 10* (August 1915), p. 176.

7. Nannie H. Burroughs, "Black Women and Reform," *The Crisis, 10* (August 1915), p. 187.

8. Anna H. Jones, "Woman Suffrage and Reform," *The Crisis, 10* (August 1915), p. 235.

9. Rosalyn Terborg-Penn, "Afro-Americans in the Struggle for Woman Suffrage," Ph.D. dissertation, Howard University, 1977 (University Microfilms International, Ann Arbor, Mich.), p. 140.

10. William Still, *The Underground Railroad: A Record* (Philadelphia: People's Publishing Company, 1879), p. 803.

11. Terborg-Penn, op. cit., p. 159.

12. Anna Julia Cooper. *A Voice of the South* (Xenia, Ohio: Aldine Printing House, 1892), pp. 139–140.

13. Frances Ellen Harper, *Sketches of a Southern Life* (Philadelphia: Ferguson Brothers, 1893).

14. Burroughs, op. cit., p. 187.

15. Cooper, op. cit., p. 139.

16. Burroughs, op. cit., p. 187.

17. Terborg-Penn, op. cit., p. 169.

18. Senator Ben Tillman to editor of *Maryland Suffrage News,* November 17, 1914 (NAACP files, Suffrage, Library of Congress, Washington, D.C.).

19. Kraditor, op. cit., p. 107.

20. Ibid., p. 110

21. Bert James Loewenberg and Ruth Bogin, eds., *Black Women in Nineteenth-Century American Life: Their Words, Their Thoughts, Their Feelings* (University Park and London: Pennsylvania State University Press, 1976), p. 246.

22. Ibid., p. 245.

23. Kraditor, op. cit., p. 114.

24. Terborg-Penn, op. cit., p. 285.

25. Kraditor, op. cit., p. 143.

26. *The Crisis* (April 1913), p. 298.

27. Herbert Aptheker, ed., *The Correspondence of W.E.B. Du Bois,* Volume I (No city: University of Massachusetts Press, 1973), p. 127.

28. *The Woman's Era* (November 1894), p. 13.

29. Terborg-Penn, op. cit., p. 225.

Chapter VIII

1. Gerda Lerner, ed., *Black Women in White America: A Documentary History* (New York: Pantheon Books, 1972), p. 130.

2. Helen Armstead Johnson, "Some Late Information on Some Early People," *Encore American & Worldwide News* (June 1975), p. 12.

3. James Weldon Johnson, *Black Manhattan* (New York: Knopf, 1930), p. 99.

4. Margaret Just Butcher, *The Negro in American Culture* (New York: Knopf, 1972), p. 220.

5. Carol Watson, "The Novels of Afro-American Women: Concerns and Themes, 1891–1965," Ph.D. dissertation, George Washington University (1978), p. 8.

6. W.E.B. Du Bois, *The Gift of Black Folk,* (Boston: Stratford Press, 1924), p. 259.

7. Landon Y. Jones, *Great Expectations: America and the Baby Boom Generation* (New York: Ballantine Books, 1980), pp. 36–37.

8. Jessie S. Bernard, *Marriage and Family Among Negroes* (Englewood Cliffs, N.J.: Prentice-Hall, 1966), p. 2.

9. Elizabeth L. Davis, *Lifting as They Climb: The National Association of Colored Women* (unpublished, 1933), p. 80.

10. Emmett J. Scott, *Negro Migration During the War* (New York: Arno and The New York Times, 1969), p. 21.

11. Philip S. Foner, *Women and the American Labor Movement: From World War I to the Present* (New York: Free Press, 1980), p. 67.

12. Ibid., p. 66.

13. Ibid., p. 67.

14. Ibid.

15. Ibid., p. 10.

16. Scott, op. cit., p. 39.

17. Ibid., p. 65.

18. Foner, op. cit., p. 11.

19. Sadie T.M. Alexander, "Negro Women in Our Economic Life," *Opportunity* (July 1930), p. 201.

20. Elise Johnson McDougald, "The Double Task: The Struggle of Negro Women for Race and Sex Emancipation," *Survey Graphic* (March 1925), p. 689.

21. Ibid.

22. Foner, op. cit., p. 14.

23. McDougald, op. cit., p. 690.

24. Alexander, op. cit., p. 301.

25. Elizabeth Ross Haynes, "Two Million Negro Women At Work," *Southern Workman* (February 1922), p. 70.

26. McDougald, op. cit., p. 690.

27. Ibid.

28. Ibid.

29. Ibid.

30. Ibid.

31. Ibid.

32. Ibid., p. 691.

33. Georgia Douglas Johnson, *The Heart of a Woman* (Boston: Cornhill Company, 1918), p. 62.

34. McDougald, op. cit., p. 689.

35. Ibid., p. 691.

36. Ibid., p. 689.

37. Marcia Guttentag and Paul Secord, *Too Many Women? The Sex Ratio Question* (Beverly Hills: Sage Publications, 1983).

38. Grace Abbott, "A Message to Colored Women," *The Crisis,* Vol. 39, No. 10 (October 1932), p. 311.

39. Irene Graham, "The Negro Family in a Northern City," *Opportunity* (February 1930), p. 49.

40. Ibid.

41. Abbott, op. cit., p. 311.

42. Graham, op. cit., p. 50.

43. Ibid.

44. McDougald, op. cit., p. 691.

45. Ibid.

Chapter IX

1. Arthur P. Davis, *From the Dark Tower: Afro-American Writers 1900–1960* (Washington, D.C.: Howard University Press, 1974), p. 39.

2. Zora Neale Hurston, "The Hue and Cry About Howard University" *The Messenger* (September 1925), p. 315.

3. Philip S. Foner, *Women and the American Labor Movement: From World War I to the Present* (New York: Free Press, 1980), p. 131.

4. Jacquelyn Dowd Hall, *Revolt Against Chivalry: Jessie Daniel Ames and the Women's Campaign Against Lynching* (New York: Columbia University Press, 1979), p. 83.

5. Ibid., p. 84.

6. Gerda Lerner, ed., *Black Women in White America: A Documentary History* (New York: Pantheon Books, 1972), p. 482.

7. Ibid., pp. 479–480.

8. Hall, op. cit., p. 84.

9. Ibid., p. 85.

10. Ibid.

11. Ibid.

12. Ibid.

13. Ibid., p. 86.

14. Rosalyn Terborg-Penn, "Afro-Americans in the Struggle for Woman Suffrage," Ph.D. dissertation, Howard University, 1977 (University Microfilms International, Ann Arbor, Mich.), p. 293.

15. *New York World,* February 18, 1919 (NAACP files, Suffrage, Library of Congress, Washington, D.C.).

16. *Branch Bulletin,* March 30, 1919 (NAACP files, Suffrage, Library of Congress, Washington, D.C.).

17. Terborg-Penn, op. cit., p. 298.

18. Moorfield Storey to John R. Shillady, May 20, 1919 (NAACP files, Suffrage, Library of Congress, Washington, D.C.).

19. *New York World,* March 1, 1919 (NAACP files, Suffrage, Library of Congress, Washington, D.C.).

20. Ida Husted Harper to Elizabeth C. Carter, March 18, 1919 (NAACP files, Suffrage, Library of Congress, Washington, D.C.).

21. Elizabeth C. Carter to Ida Husted Harper, April 10, 1919 (NAACP files, Suffrage, Library of Congress, Washington, D.C.).

22. Carrie Chapman Catt to John R. Shillady, May 6, 1919 (NAACP files, Suffrage, Library of Congress, Washington, D.C.).

23. Alice Paul to Mary White Ovington, March 31, 1919 (NAACP files, Suffrage, Library of Congress, Washington, D.C.).

24. Mary White Ovington to Alice Paul, July 9, 1920 (NAACP files, Suffrage, Library of Congress, Washington, D.C.).

25. Terborg-Penn, op. cit., p. 304.

26. Ibid., p. 305.

27. Ibid., p. 310.

28. February 11, 1921 (NAACP files, Suffrage. Library of Congress, Washington, D.C.).

29. Addie Hunton to A. H. Grimké, January 29, 1921 (NAACP files, Suffrage, Library of Congress, Washington, D.C.).

30. Addie Hunton to Hallie Q. Brown, February 7, 1921 (NAACP files, Suffrage, Library of Congress, Washington, D.C.).

31. Addie Hunton to James Weldon Johnson, February 7, 1921 (NAACP files, Suffrage, Library of Congress, Washington, D.C.).

32. Addie Hunton to James Weldon Johnson, February 15, 1921 (NAACP files. Suffrage, Library of Congress, Washington, D.C.).

33. Ibid.

34. Resolutions Re: National Woman's Party, February 15–18, 1921 (NAACP files, Suffrage, Library of Congress, Washington, D.C.).

35. Addie Hunton to Maggie Walker, February 23, 1921 (NAACP files, Suffrage, Library of Congress, Washington, D.C.).

36. Coralie Cook to Mary White Ovington, January 21, 1921 (NAACP files, Suffrage, Library of Congress, Washington, D.C.).

Chapter X

1. Ralph Ellison, "An American Dilemma: A Review," *The Death of White Sociology*, Joyce A. Ladner, ed. (New York: Vintage Books, 1973), pp. 86–87.

2. Jacquelyn Dowd Hall, *Revolt Against Chivalry: Jessie Daniel Ames and the Women's Campaign Against Lynching* (New York: Columbia University Press, 1979), p. 86.

3. Ibid., p. 87.

4. Ibid., p. 88.

5. Ibid.

6. Ibid., p. 98.

7. Ibid., p. 88.

8. Ibid., p. 89.

9. Charlotte Hawkins Brown, "What the Negro Woman Asks of White Women in North Carolina," Charlotte Hawkins Brown Papers (Schlesinger Library, Radcliffe College, Cambridge, Mass.: May 1920).

10. Hall, op. cit., p. 93.

11. Ibid., p. 96.

12. Ibid.

13. Ibid.

14. Ibid., p. 99.

15. Ibid., p. 166.

16. Ibid., p. 93.

17. Ibid., p. 100.

18. Charlotte Hawkins Brown, "What the Negro Youth Expects of the White Youth in Their Tomorrow," address to Berea College, Kentucky, Charlotte Hawkins Brown Papers (Schlesinger Library, Radcliffe College, Cambridge, Mass.).

19. Hall, op. cit., p. 97.

20. Mary Church Terrell to Jane Addams, March 21, 1921, Mary Church Terrell Papers (Library of Congress, Washington, D.C.).

21. Alfreda Duster, ed., *Crusade for Justice: The Autobiography of Ida B. Wells* (Chicago and London: University of Chicago Press, 1970, 1972), p. 51.

22. Ibid., pp. 327–328.

23. Elizabeth L. Davis, *Lifting as They Climb: The National Association of Colored Women* (unpublished, 1933), p. 187.

Chapter XI

1. Geoffrey Perrett, *America in the Twenties: A History* (New York: Simon & Schuster, 1982), p. 164.

2. Elise Johnson McDougald, "The Double Task: The Struggle of Negro Women for Race and Sex Emancipation," *Survey Graphic* (March 1925), p. 691.

3. Philip S. Foner, *Women and the American Labor Movement: From World War I to the Present* (New York: Free Press, 1980), p. 100.

4. Chandler Owen, "Black Mammies," *The Messenger* (April 1923), p. 670.

5. Perrett, op. cit., p. 158.

6. Ibid., p. 159.

7. McDougald, op. cit., p. 689.

8. Jervis Anderson, "A Cultural Portrait of Harlem," *The New Yorker* (July 13, 1982), p. 68.

9. Helene Johnson, *"Poem" and "In Magalu,"* Sturdy Black Bridges: Visions of Black Women in Literature, Roseann P. Bell, Bettye J. Parker, and Beverly Guy-Shettall, eds. (Garden City, N.Y.: Anchor Press/Doubleday, 1979), p. 80.

10. Jill Nelson, "The Fortune That Madame Built," *Essence* magazine (June 1983), pp. 85–86.

11. Ibid., p. 154.

12. George S. Schuyler, "Madame C. J. Walker," *The Messenger* (July 1924), p. 257.

13. Ibid., p. 264.

14. Ibid., p. 256.

15. McDougald, op. cit., p. 689.

16. Florette Henri, *Black Migration: Movement North, 1900–1920, The Road from Myth to Man* (Garden City, N.Y.: Anchor Books/Doubleday, 1976), p. 333.

17. Barbara Christian, *Black Women Novelists: The Development of a Tradition, 1892–1976* (Westport, Conn., and London: Greenwood Press, 1980), p. 41.

18. Arthur P. Davis, *From the Dark Tower: Afro-American Writers, 1900–1960* (Washington, D.C.: Howard University Press, 1974), p. 92.

19. Ibid., p. 96.

20. Alice Walker, ed., *I Love Myself When I Am Laughing . . . And Then Again When I Am Looking Mean and Impressive* (New York: The Feminist Press, 1979), p. 15.

21. Christian, op. cit., p. 60.

22. Mark D. Matthews, " 'Our Women and What They Think': Amy Jacques Garvey and *The Negro World,"* Black Scholar (May–June 1979), p. 5.

23. Ibid.

24. Ibid., p. 11.

25. Ibid.

26. Ibid.

27. Bert James Loewenberg and Ruth Bogin, eds., *Black Women in Nineteenth-Century American Life: Their Words, Their Thoughts, Their Feelings* (University Park and London: Pennsylvania State University Press, 1976, 1978), p. 197.

28. Matthews, op. cit., p. 12.

29. *The Messenger* (July 1923), p. 757.

30. McDougald, op. cit., p. 691.

31. Sadie T.M. Alexander, "Negro Women in Our Economic Life," *Opportunity* (July 1930), p. 202.

32. Ibid.

33. Ibid.

34. W.E.B. Du Bois, *The Gift of Black Folk* (Boston: Stratford Press, 1924), p. 259.

35. W.E.B. Du Bois, *Darkwater: Voices from Within the Veil* (New York: Schocken Books, 1920, 1929), p. 180.

36. Ibid., p. 181.

37. Ibid., p. 164.

Chapter XII

1. *National Notes* (September 1924), p. 1.

2. Mary McLeod Bethune to Charlotte Hawkins Brown, June 12, 1947, Charlotte Hawkins Brown Papers (Schlesinger Library, Radcliffe College, Cambridge, Mass.).

3. Mary McLeod Bethune to Mary Church Terrell, June 5, 1925, Mary Church Terrell Papers (Library of Congress, Washington, D.C.).

4. Mary McLeod Bethune to Mary Church Terrell, January 29, 1930, Mary Church Terrell Papers (Library of Congress, Washington, D.C.).

5. Mary McLeod Bethune to Mary Church Terrell, March 15, 1930, Mary Church Terrell Papers (Library of Congress, Washington, D.C.).

6. Bettye Collier-Thomas, *N.C.N.W. 1935–1980* (Washington, D.C: The National Council of Negro Women, 1981), p. 1.

7. *National Notes,* "Message from the President," 1930.

8. Mary McLeod Bethune, "A Century of Progress of Negro Women," June 30, 1933, Mary McLeod Bethune Papers (Amistad Research Center, Dillard University, New Orleans, La.).

9. Nannie H. Burroughs, *The Louisiana Weekly,* November 23, 1933.

10. Collier-Thomas, op. cit., p. 2.

11. Ralph Ellison, *Shadow and Act* (New York: Signet Books, 1966), p. 297.

12. Ibid.

13. Jaquelyn Dowd Hall, *The Revolt Against Chivalry: Jessie Daniel Ames and the Women's Campaign Against Lynching* (New York: Columbia University Press, 1979), p. 161.

14. Ibid., p. 164.

15. Ibid., p. 156.

16. Ibid., p. 196.

17. Ibid., p. 108.

18. Ibid., p. 164.

19. Ibid

20. Gerda Lerner, ed., *Black Women in White America: A Documentary History* (New York: Pantheon Books, 1972), p. 474.

21. Ibid.

22. Ibid.

23. Ibid., p. 475.

24. Hall, op. cit., p. 244.

25. Lerner, op. cit., p. 477.

26. Minutes, NCNW meeting, November 26, 1938 (National Archives for Black Women's History, Mary McLeod Bethune Memorial Museum, Washington, D.C.).

27. W.E.B. Du Bois, "Separation and Self-Respect," *The Crisis* (March 1935), p. 85.

28. W.E.B. Du Bois, "Segregation," *The Crisis* (January 1934), p. 20.

29. Harvard Sitkoff, *A New Deal for Blacks,* Vol. I (Oxford and New York: Oxford University Press, 1978), p. 238.

30. Minutes, NCNW meeting, July 1935, loc. cit.

31. *New York Age* (December 28, 1929), p. 6.

32. Minutes, NCNW meeting, December 5, 1935, loc. cit.

33. Adam Clayton Powell, Sr., to Mary McLeod Bethune, June 6, 1935, Mary McLeod Bethune Papers (Amistad Research Center, Dillard University, New Orleans, La.).

34. Minutes, NCNW meeting, December 5, 1935, loc. cit.

35. Ibid.

36. William Pickens to Charlotte Hawkins Brown, 1932, Charlotte Hawkins Brown Papers (Schlesinger Library, Radcliffe College, Cambridge, Mass.).

37. Minutes, NCNW meeting, December 5, 1935, loc. cit.

Chapter XIII

1. Harvard Sitkoff, *A New Deal for Blacks,* Vol. I (Oxford and New York: Oxford University Press, 1978), p. 38.

2. Ibid., p. 40.

3. Madame Cantacuzene-Grant to Jon Hamilton, January 21, 1936, Mary Church Terrell Papers (Library of Congress, Washington, D.C.).

4. Joseph P. Lash, *Love, Eleanor: Eleanor Roosevelt and Her Friends* (Garden City, N.Y.: Doubleday, 1982), p. x.

5. Gerda Lerner, ed., *Black Women in White America: A Documentary History* (New York: Pantheon Books, 1972), pp. 476–477.

6. B. Joyce Ross, "Mary McLeod Bethune and the National Youth Administration: A Case Study of Power Relationships in the Black Cabinet of Franklin D. Roosevelt," *The Journal of Negro History* (January 1975), p. 2.

7. Elaine M. Smith, "Mary McLeod Bethune and the National Youth Administration," *Clio Was a Woman: Studies in the History of American Women,* Mabel E. Deutrich and Virginia C. Purdy, eds. (Washington, D.C: Howard University Press, 1980), p. 152.

8. Edward Lawson, "Straight from the Capitol," January 23, 1937, Associated Negro Press.

9. Ross, op. cit., p. 2.

10. Ibid, p. 12.

11. Ibid., p. 6.

12. Smith, op. cit., p. 166.

13. Ibid., p. 165.

14. Minutes, NCNW meeting, November 26, 1938 (National Archives for Black Women's History, Mary McLeod Bethune Memorial Museum, Washington, D.C.).

15. Smith, op. cit., p. 157.

16. Minutes, NCNW meeting, November 26, 1938, loc. cit.

17. Ross, op. cit., p. 5.

18. Minutes, NCNW meeting, November 26, 1938, loc. cit.

19. Ibid.

20. Smith, op. cit., p. 149.

21. Ibid.

22. Ibid., p. 159.

23. Minutes, NCNW meeting, November 26, 1938, loc. cit.

Chapter XIV

1. Philip S. Foner, *Women and the American Labor Movement: From World War 1 to the Present* (New York: Free Press, 1980), p. 258.

2. Ibid., p. 183.

3. Marion Cuthbert, "Problems Facing Negro Young Women," *Opportunity* (February 2, 1936), p. 48.

4. Foner, op. cit., p. 344.

5. Ibid., p. 262.

6. Cuthbert, op. cit., pp. 48–49.

7. Foner, op. cit., p. 320.

8. Harvard Sitkoff, *A New Deal for Blacks,* Vol. I (Oxford and New York: Oxford University Press, 1978), p. 170.

9. Foner, op. cit., p. 344.

10. Sitkoff, op. cit., p. 314.

11. Foner, op. cit., p. 347.

12. Ibid., p. 346.

13. Ibid., p. 396.

14. Ibid., p. 345.

15. Joyce A. Ladner, ed., *The Death of White Sociology* (New York: Vintage Books, 1973), p. 92.

16. Jacquelyn Dowd Hall, *Revolt Against Chivalry: Jessie Daniel Ames and the Women's Campaign Against Lynching* (New York: Columbia University Press, 1979), p. 169.

17. Arthur P. Davis, *From the Dark Tower: Afro-American Writers, 1900–1960* (Washington, D.C.: Howard University Press, 1974), p. 138.

18. Landon Y. Jones, *Great Expectations: America and the Baby Boom Generation* (New York: Ballantine Books, 1980), p. 37.

19. Nathan Glazer, Preface to E. Franklin Frazier, *The Negro Family in the United States* (Chicago and London: University of Chicago Press, 1939, 1948, 1966, 1973), p. xii.

20. Betty Friedan, *The Feminine Mystique* (New York: Dell, 1963, 1974), p. 197.

21. Sara Evans, *Personal Politics: The Roots of Women's Liberation in the Civil Rights Movement and the New Left* (New York: Vintage Books, 1980), p. 10.

22. Friedan, op. cit., p. 54.

23. Ibid., p. 143.

24. Ibid.

25. Mary McLeod Bethune to Charlotte Hawkins Brown, June 12, 1947, Charlotte Hawkins Brown Papers (Schlesinger Library, Radcliffe College, Cambridge, Mass.).

26. Jeanne L. Noble, "The Negro Woman's College Education," Ph.D. dissertation, Columbia University (New York: Columbia University, Bureau Publications, 1956), p. 29.

27. Cuthbert, op. cit., p. 48.

28. *The Crisis* (September 1942), p. 287.

29. Noble, op. cit., p. 41.

30. Marion Cuthbert, "Education and Marginality," Ph.D. dissertation, Teacher's College, Columbia University, 1942.

31. Noble, op. cit., p. 162.

32. Ibid., p. 40.

33. Cuthbert, "Education and Marginality," op. cit., p. 28.

34. Noble, op. cit., p. 46.

35. Ibid., p. 74.

36. Ibid., p. 97

37. Ibid.

38. Franklin Fosdick, "Is Intermarriage Wrecking the NAACP?" *Negro Digest* (May 1950), p. 53.

39. Noble, op. cit., p. 104.

40. Ibid., p. 105.

41. Jessie Bernard, *Marriage and Family Among Negroes* (Englewood Cliffs, N.J.: Prentice-Hall, 1966), p. 45.

42. Noble, op. cit., p. 98.

43. Ibid., p. 99.

44. Ibid., p. 98.

45. E. Franklin Frazier, op. cit. (see Note 19), p. 288.

46. Roi Ottley, "What's Wrong with Negro Women?" *Negro Digest* (December 1950), p. 71.

47. E. Franklin Frazier, *The Black Bourgeoisie: The Rise of a New Middle Class in the United States* (New York: Collier Books, 1962), p. 182.

48. Ibid., p. 181.

49. St. Clair Drake, "Why Men Leave Home," *Negro Digest* (April 1950), p. 27.

50. Frazier, *The Black Bourgeoisie,* op. cit., p. 183.

51. Frazier, *The Negro Family in the United States,* op. cit., p. 288.

52. Frazier, *The Black Bourgeoisie,* op. cit., p. 180.

53. Drake, op. cit., p. 26.

54. Gwendolyn Brooks, "Why Negro Women Leave Home," *Negro Digest* (March 1951), pp. 26–28.

55. Ibid.

56. Bernard, op. cit., p. 7.

57. Frazier, *The Black Bourgeoisie,* op. cit., p. 48.

58. Ella Baker to legal research assistant, March 25, 1942 (NAACP files, Library of Congress, Washington, D.C.).

59. Walter White to William Hastie, March 8, 1943 (NAACP files, Library of Congress, Washington, D.C.).

60. Daisy Lampkin to Walter White, October 28, 1943 (NAACP files, Library of Congress, Washington, D.C.).

61. Walter White to Daisy Lampkin, November 12, 1943 (NAACP files, Library of Congress, Washington, D.C.).

62. Frazier, *The Black Bourgeoisie,* op. cit., p. 182.

Chapter XV

1. Milton Viorst, *Fire in the Streets: America in the 1960's* (New York: Simon & Schuster, 1979), p. 26.

2. Louis Lomax, *The Negro Revolt* (New York: Signet Books, 1962, 1963), p. 92.

3. Virginia Durr, interview, 1968, The Civil Rights Documentation Project (Moorland Spingarn Collection, Howard University, Washington, D.C.), p. 62.

4. Ibid., p. 63.

5. Ibid., p. 58.

6. Joanne Robinson, interview, November 1983.

7. Howell Raines, *My Soul Is Rested: Movement Days in the Deep South Remembered* (New York: G.P. Putnam's Sons, 1977), p. 43.

8. Durr, loc. cit., p. 58.

9. Raines, op. cit., p. 49.

10. Ibid., p. 60.

11. Ibid.

12. Viorst, op. cit., p. 47.

13. Ella Baker, interview, 1968, The Civil Rights Documentation Project (Moorland-Spingarn Collection, Howard University, Washington, D.C.), p. 8.

14. Ibid., p. 9.

15. Ibid., p. 4.

16. Ibid.

17. Daisy Bates, *The Long Shadow of Little Rock: A Memoir* (New York: David McKay, 1962), p. 221.

18. Angela Davis, *Angela Davis: An Autobiography* (New York: Random House, 1974), p. 79.

19. Ibid., p. 89.

20. Jean Smith, "I Learned to Feel Black," *Black Power Revolt,* Floyd Barbour, ed. (Boston: Porter Sargent, 1968), pp. 208–209.

21. Davis, op. cit., p. 89.

22. Clayborne Carson, *In Struggle: SNCC and the Black Awakening of the 1960's* (Cambridge, Mass., and London: Harvard University Press, 1981), p. 61.

23. Jesse Bernard, *Marriage and Family Among Negroes* (Englewood Cliffs, N.J.: Prentice-Hall, 1966), p. 35.

24. Ibid., p. 51.

25. Ibid., p. 35.

26. Paula Giddings, "Julian Bond: From Candidate to Commentator," *Encore American & Worldwide News* (January 16, 1978), p. 11.

27. James Foreman, *The Making of Black Revolutionaries* (New York: Macmillan, 1972), p. 218.

Chapter XVI

1. Jean Wiley, interview, March 2, 1982.

2. Angela Davis, *Angela Davis: An Autobiography* (New York: Random House, 1974), p. 62.

3. Jean Smith, interview, June 23, 1982.

4. James Foreman, *The Making of Black Revolutionaries* (New York: Macmillan, 1972), p. 475.

5. Sara Evans, *Personal Politics: The Roots of Women's Liberation in the Civil Rights Movement and the New Left* (New York: Vintage Books, 1980), p. 40.

6. Foreman, op. cit., p. 145.

7. Ibid., p. 151.

8. Clayborne Carson, *In Struggle: SNCC and the Black Awakening of the 1960's* (Cambridge, Mass., and London: Harvard University Press, 1981), p. 38.

9. Foreman, op. cit., p. 225.

10. Carson, op. cit., p. 63.

11. Foreman, op. cit., p. 253.

12. Carson, op. cit., p. 62.

13. Gerda Lerner, ed., *Black Women in White America: A Documentary History* (New York: Pantheon Books, 1972), p. 351.

14. Carson, op. cit., p. 75.

15. Ibid.

16. Ibid., p. 122.

17. Howell Raines, *My Soul Is Rested: Movement Days in the Deep South Remembered* (New York: G.P. Putman's Sons, 1977), p. 280.

18. Unita Blackwell, interview, The Civil Rights Documentation Project (Moorland-Spingarn Collection, Howard University, Washington, D.C.), p. 4.

19. Ibid.

20. Ibid., p. 8.

21. Ibid.

22. Ibid.

23. Ibid.

24. Ibid., p. 28.

25. Ibid., p. 31.

26. Raines, op. cit., p. 249.

27. Fannie Lou Hamer, interview, The Civil Rights Documentation Project (Moorland-Spingarn Collection, Howard University, Washington, D.C.), p. 3.

28. Ibid.

29. Ibid., p. 1.

30. Ibid., p. 3.

31. Ibid., p. 5.

32. Carson, op. cit., p. 73.

33. Raines, op. cit., p. 251.

34. Carson, op. cit., p. 74.

35. Raines, op. cit., p. 253.

36. Evans, op. cit., p. 75.

37. Cleveland Sellers with Robert Terrell, *The River of No Return: An Autobiography of a Black Militant and the Life and Death of SNCC* (New York: William Morrow, 1973), p. 70.

38. Evans, op. cit., p. 74.

39. Ibid.

40. Carson, op. cit., p. 125.

41. Blackwell, loc. cit., p. 16.

42. Carson, op. cit., p. 125.

43. Blackwell, loc. cit., p. 16.

44. Carson, op. cit., p. 91.

45. Ella Baker, interview, The Civil Rights Documentation Project (Moorland-Spingarn Collection, Howard University, Washington, D.C.), p. 65.

46. Carson, op. cit., p. 105.

47. Jean Smith, "I Learned to Feel Black," *Black Power Revolt*, Floyd Barbour, ed. (Boston: Porter Sargent, 1968), p. 208.

48. Foreman, op. cit., p. 402.

49. Smith, op. cit., p. 211.

50. Ibid., p. 212.

Chapter XVII

1. Betty Friedan, *The Feminine Mystique* (New York: Dell, 1963, 1974), p. 68.

2. Jane Stembridge, "Some Notes on Education," N.D.

3. Sara Evans, *Personal Politics: The Roots of Women's Liberation in the Civil Rights Movement and the New Left* (New York: Vintage Books, 1980), p. 79.

4. Ibid., p. 78.

5. Ibid., p. 86.

6. Clayborne Carson, *In Struggle: SNCC and the Black Awakening of the 1960's* (Cambridge, Mass., and London: Harvard University Press, 1981), p. 148.

7. Jo Freeman, *The Politics of Women's Liberation* (New York and London: Longman, 1975), p. 57.

8. Ibid., p. 58.

9. Evans, op. cit., p. 108.

10. Freeman, op. cit., p. 84.

11. Charlayne Hunter, "Many Blacks Wary of 'Women's Liberation' Movement," *The New York Times* (November 17, 1970), p. 60.

12. Freeman, op. cit., p. 85.

13. Ibid.

14. Ibid., p. 91.

15. Linda J.M. La Rue, "Black Liberation and Women's Lib," *Trans-Action* (November–December 1970), p. 61.

16. Toni Morrison, "What the Black Woman Thinks About Women's Lib," *The New York Times Magazine* (August 22, 1971), p. 15.

17. Ibid., p. 64.

18. Eleanor Holmes Norton, "For Sadie and Maude," *Sisterhood Is Powerful: An Anthology of Writings from the Women's Liberation Movement*, Robin Morgan, ed. (New York: Vintage Books, 1970), p. 400.

19. Morrison, op. cit., p. 64.

20. La Rue, op. cit., p. 61.

21. Hunter, op. cit., p. 47.

22. Morrison, op. cit., p. 15.

23. La Rue, op. cit., p. 60.

24. Hunter, op. cit., p. 60.

25. Morrison, op. cit., p. 15

26. La Rue, op. cit., p. 64.

27. Norton, op. cit., p. 393.

28. Betty Friedan, *It Changed My Life: Writings on the Women's Movement* (New York: Random House, 1963, 1975), p. 96.

29. Frances M. Beal, "Double Jeopardy: To Be Black and Female," *Sisterhood Is Powerful,* op. cit. (see Note 18), p. 386.

30. Ida Lewis, "Conversation: Ida Lewis and Eleanor Holmes Norton," *Essence* magazine (July 1970), p. 15.

31. Angela Davis, *Women, Race & Class* (New York: Random House, 1981), p. 198.

32. Morrison, op. cit., p. 63.

33. Joyce A. Ladner, *Tomorrow's Tomorrow: The Black Woman* (Garden City, N.Y.: Doubleday, 1971), p. 239.

34. Julia Herve, *"Black Scholar* Interviews Kathleen Cleaver," *Black Scholar* (December 1971), p. 56.

35. Ibid., p. 59.

36. Ibid., p. 56.

37. Howell Raines, *My Soul Is Rested: Movement Days in the Deep South Remembered* (New York: G.P. Putnam's Sons, 1977), p. 432.

38. Ella Baker, interview, The Civil Rights Documentation Project (Moorland-Spingarn Collection, Howard University, Washington, D.C.), pp. 34–35.

39. Nick Kotz and Mary Kotz, *A Passion for Equality: George Wiley and the Movement* (New York: W.W. Norton & Company, 1977), p. 249.

40. Ibid.

41. Ibid., p. 252n.

42. Anna Arnold Hedgeman, *The Trumpet Sounds: A Memoir of Negro Leadership* (New York: Holt, Rinehart & Winston, 1964), p. 178.

43. Ibid., p. 180.

44. Julia Herve, op. cit., p. 55.

45. Harvard Sitkoff, *The Struggle for Black Equality, 1954–1980* (New York: Hill & Wang, 1981), p. 215.

46. Carson, op. cit., p. 288.

47. Ibid., p. 289.

48. Angela Davis, *Angela Davis: An Autobiography* (New York: Random House, 1974), p. 161.

49. Ibid., p. 181.

50. Ibid., p. 187.

51. K. Cleaver, op. cit., p. 56.

52. Gloria Richardson, interview, June 28, 1982.

53. Davis, *Angela Davis: An Autobiography,* p. 181.

54. Barbara A. Sizemore, "Sexism and the Black Male," *Black Scholar* (March–April 1973), p. 6.

55. Bibi Amina Baraka, "Coordinator's Statement," *African Congress: A Documentary of the First Modern Pan-African Congress,* Imamu Amiri Baraka, ed. (New York: William Morrow, 1972), p. 177.

56. Akiba ya Elimu, "The Black Family," *African Congress,* ibid., p. 179.

57. La Rue, op. cit., p. 61.

58. Beal, op. cit., p. 386.

59. Sonia Pressman, "Job Discrimination and the Black Woman," *The Crisis* (March 1970), p. 103.

60. Calvin Hernton, "The Negro Male," *The Black Male in America: Perspectives on His Status in Contemporary Society,* Doris Y. Wilkinson and Ronald Taylor, eds. (Chicago: Nelson-Hall, 1977), p. 246.

61. William H. Grier and Price M. Cobbs, *Black Rage* (New York: Bantam, 1968), p. 51.

62. Hernton, op. cit., p. 247.

63. Ibid.

64. Eldridge Cleaver, *Soul on Ice* (New York: McGraw-Hill, 1968), p. 162.

65. Grier and Cobbs, op. cit., p. 40.

66. Ibid., p. 9.

67. Hernton, op. cit., p. 260.

68. Frantz Fanon, *Black Skins, White Masks* (New York: Grove Press, 1967), p. 63.

69. E. Cleaver, op. cit., p. 6.

70. Hernton, op. cit., p. 251.

71. Ibid., p. 261.

72. Julia Herve, op. cit., p. 56.

73. Ibid., p. 59.

74. Morrison, op. cit., p. 66.

75. Ladner, op. cit., p. 279.

76. Morrison, op. cit., p. 66.

Chapter XVIII

1. Lee Rainwater and William L. Yancey, *The Moynihan Report and the Politics of Controversy* (Cambridge, Mass.: M.I.T. Press, 1967), p. 24.

2. Ibid., p. 5.

3. Ibid., p. 77.

4. Ibid., p. 16.

5. Ibid.

6. Joyce A. Ladner, *Tomorrow's Tomorrow: The Black Woman* (Garden City, N.Y.: Doubleday, 1971), p. 273.

7. Ibid., p. 35.

8. Angela Davis, "Reflections on the Black Woman's Role in the Community of Slaves," *Black Scholar* (December 1971), p. 14.

9. Robert Staples, "The Myth of the Black Matriarchy," *Black Scholar* (November–December 1981), repr., p. 32.

10. Ibid., pp. 29–30.

11. Albert Murray, "White Norms, Black Deviation," *The Death of White Sociology,* Joyce A. Ladner, ed. (New York: Vintage Books, 1973), p. 104.

12. Rainwater and Yancey, op. cit., p. 52.

13. Ibid., p. 29.

14. Carolyn Bird, "Woman Power," in *New York* magazine, March 1969, p. 38.

15. Ibid.

16. Wilbur Bock, "Farmer's Daughter Effect: The Case of the Negro Female Professionals," *Phylon* (Spring 1979), p. 21.

17. George Gilder, *Wealth and Poverty* (New York: Basic Books, Inc., 1981), p. 50.

18. Philip S. Foner, *Women and the American Labor Movement: From World War I to the Present* (New York: Free Press, 1980), p. 442.

19. "Minority Women and Higher Education," #1 (Project on the Status and Education of Women, Association of Women's Colleges, 1974), p. 3.

20. Ibid.

21. Cynthia Fuchs Epstein, "Positive Effects of the Double Negative: Explaining the Success of Black Professional Women," *The American Journal of Sociology* (1972), p. 919.

22. Ibid., p. 922.

23. "Minority Women and Higher Education," op. cit., p. 3.

24. Epstein, op. cit., p. 932.

25. Ibid.

Chapter XIX

1. Betty Friedan, *It Changed My Life: Writings on the Women's Movement* (New York: Random House, 1963, 1975), p. 178.

2. Shirley Chisholm, *The Good Fight* (New York: Harper & Row, 1973), p. 77.

3. Freidan, op. cit., p. 177.

4. Chisholm, op. cit., p. 31.

5. Ibid., pp. 31–32.

6. Shirley Chisholm, interview, The Civil Rights Documentation Project (Moorland-Spingarn Collection, Howard University, Washington, D.C.), p. 29.

7. Jo Freeman, *The Politics of Women's Liberation* (New York and London: Longman, 1975), p. 211.

8. Ibid., p. 91.

9. Ibid., p. 80.

10. *The New York Times* (March 21, 1979), p. 24.

11. Freeman, op. cit., p. 221.

12. "Black Feminism: A New Mandate," *Ms.* magazine (May 1974), p. 99.

13. Philip S. Foner, *Women and the American Labor Movement: From World War I to the Present* (New York: Free Press, 1980), p. 489.

14. Freeman, op. cit., p. 39.

15. Aileen Hernandez, "Small Change for Black Women," *Ms.* magazine (August 1974), p. 16.

16. Freeman, op. cit., p. 38.

17. "Ex-President of NOW Calls Group 'Racist,' " *The San Diego Union* (October 21, 1979).

18. Ibid.

19. Ibid.

Chapter XX

1. Barbara A.P. Jones, "Economic Status of Black Women," *The State of Black America 1983* (The National Urban League, January 19, 1983), p. 132.

2. Robert B. Hill, "Black Families in the 1970's," *The State of Black America 1980* (The National Urban League, January 22, 1980), p. 55.

3. Jones, op. cit., p. 125.

4. Phyllis A. Wallace, *Black Women in the Labor Force* (Cambridge, Mass., and London: M.I.T. Press, 1980), p. 50.

5. Ibid., p. 67.

6. Philip S. Foner, *Women and the American Labor Movement: From World War I to the Present* (New York: Free Press, 1980), p. 572.

7. Jo Freeman, *The Politics of Women's Liberation* (New York and London: Longman, 1975), p. 34.

8. Ibid.

9. Mary Helen Washington, ed., *Midnight Birds: Stories of Contemporary Black Women Writers* (Garden City, N.Y.: Anchor Books/Doubleday, 1980), p. xv.

10. Robert Staples, "The Myth of Black Macho: A Response to Angry Feminists," *Black Scholar* (March–April 1979), p. 24.

11. Ibid., p. 28.

12. Ibid., p. 29.

13. Ibid., pp. 28–29.

14. Ibid.

15. George Gilder, *Wealth and Poverty* (New York: Basic Books, 1981), p. 133.

16. Ibid., p. 151.

SELECTED BIBLIOGRAPHY

Books

Aptheker, Herbert. *American Negro Slave Revolts*. New York: International Publishers, 1963.

Barbour, Floyd, ed. *The Black Power Revolt*. Boston: Porter Sargent, 1968.

Bates, Daisy. *The Long Shadow of Little Rock: A Memoir*. New York: David McKay, 1962.

Bell, Howard, ed. *Proceedings of the National Negro Conventions, 1830–1864*. New York: Arno Press, 1969.

Bell, Roseann P., Bettye J. Parker, and Beverly Guy-Sheftall, eds. *Sturdy Black Bridges: Visions of Black Women in Literature*. Garden City, N.Y.: Anchor Press/Doubleday, 1979.

Bennett, Lerone. *The Shaping of Black America*. Chicago: Johnson Publishing Company, 1975.

Brent, Linda. *Incidents in the Life of a Slave Girl*. New York: Harcourt, Brace, Jovanovich, 1861, 1973.

Butcher, Margaret Just. *The Negro in American Culture*. New York: Knopf, 1972.

Carson, Clayborne. *In Struggle: SNCC and the Black Awakening of the 1960's*. Cambridge, Mass., and London: Harvard University Press, 1981.

Chisholm, Shirley. *The Good Fight*. New York: Harper & Row, 1973.

Christian, Barbara. *Black Women Novelists: The Development of a Tradition, 1892–1976*. Westport, Conn., and London: Greenwood Press, 1980.

Cooper, Anna J. *A Voice of the South*. Xenia, Ohio: Aldine Publishing House, 1892.

Davis, Angela. *Angela Davis: An Autobiography*. New York: Random House, 1974.

————. *Women, Race & Class.* New York: Random House, 1981.

Davis, Elizabeth. *Lifting as They Climb: The National Association of Colored Women.* Unpublished, 1933.

Davis, George, and Gleg Watson. *Blacks in Corporate America.* Garden City, N.Y.: Doubleday, 1983.

Du Bois, Ellen Carol. *Feminism and Suffrage: The Emergence of an Independent Women's Movement in America, 1848–1869.* Ithaca, N.Y., and London: Cornell University Press, 1978.

Du Bois, W.E.B. *Darkwater: Voices from Within the Veil.* New York: Schocken Books, 1920, 1969.

Duster, Alfreda, ed. *Crusade for Justice: The Autobiography of Ida B. Wells.* Chicago and London: University of Chicago Press, 1970, 1972.

Ellison, Ralph. *Shadow and Act.* New York: Signet, 1966.

Evans, Sara. *Personal Politics: The Roots of Women's Liberation in the Civil Rights Movement and the New Left.* New York: Vintage Books, 1979.

Foner, Philip S. *Women and the American Labor Movement.* New York: Free Press, 1979.

Freeman, Jo. *The Politics of Women's Liberation.* New York and London: Longman, 1975.

Gibson, J. W., and W. H. Crogman. *Progress of a Race or the Remarkable Advancement of the Colored American.* Naperville, Ill.: J.L. Nichols and Company, 1902, 1912.

Gilbert, Olive. *The Narrative of Sojourner Truth.* New York: Arno Press, 1968.

Greene, Lorenzo J. *The Negro in Colonial New England.* New York: Atheneum, 1968, 1969, 1971, 1974.

Gutman, Herbert. *The Black Family in Slavery and Freedom, 1750–1925.* New York: Pantheon, 1976.

Hall, Jacquelyn Dowd. *Revolt Against Chivalry: Jessie Daniel Ames and the Campaign Against Lynching.* New York: Columbia University Press, 1979.

Harley, Sharon, and Rosalyn Terborg-Penn, eds. *The Afro-American Woman: Struggles and Images.* Port Washington, N.Y., and London: Kennikat Press, 1978.

Hedgeman, Anna Arnold. *The Trumpet Sounds: A Memoir of Negro Leadership.* New York: Holt, Rinehart and Winston, 1964.

Henri, Florette. *Black Migration: Movement North 1900–1920, The Road from Myth to Man.* Garden City, N.Y.: Anchor Press/Doubleday, 1976.

Higginbotham, A. Leon. *In the Matter of Color: Race and the American Legal Process, The Colonial Period.* New York: Oxford University Press, 1978.

Kaplan, Sidney. *The Black Presence in the Era of the American Revolution: 1770–1800.* New York: New York Graphic Society, 1973.

Kolchin, Peter. *First Freedom.* Westport, Conn.: Greenwood Press, 1972.

Kotz, Nick, and Mary Kotz. *A Passion for Equality.* New York: W.W. Norton, 1977.

Kraditor, Aileen. *The Ideas of the Woman Suffrage Movement, 1899–1929.* Garden City, N.Y.: Anchor Books/Doubleday, 1971.

Ladner, Joyce. *Tomorrow's Tomorrow: The Black Woman.* Garden City, N.Y.: Doubleday, 1971.

———, ed. *The Death of White Sociology.* New York: Vintage Books, 1973.

Lerner, Gerda. *The Majority Finds Its Past: Placing Women in American History.* Oxford and New York: Oxford University Press, 1979.

———, ed. *Black Women in White America: A Documentary History.* New York: Pantheon Books, 1972.

Litwack, Leon. *Been in the Storm So Long: The Aftermath of Slavery.* New York: Vintage Books, 1979.

Loewenberg, Bert, and Ruth Bogin, eds. *Black Women in Nineteenth-Century Life: Their Thoughts, Their Words, Their Feelings.* University Park and London: Pennsylvania State University Press, 1976.

Lomax, Louis. *The Negro Revolt.* New York: Signet Books, 1962, 1963.

Noble, Jeanne. *Beautiful, Also, Are the Souls of My Black Sisters: A History of the Black Woman in America.* Englewood Cliffs, N.J.: Prentice-Hall, Inc., 1978.

Quarles, Benjamin. *The Negro in the Making of America.* New York and London: Collier Books, 1964.

Raines, Howell. *My Soul Is Rested: Movement Days in the Deep South Remembered.* New York: G.P. Putnam's Sons, 1977.

Rose, Willie Lee. *Slavery and Freedom.* New York and Oxford: Oxford University Press, 1982.

Scott, Anne Firor. *The Southern Lady: From Pedestal to Politics 1830–1930.* Chicago: University of Chicago Press, 1972.

Scruggs, Lawson. *Women of Distinction: Remarkable in Works and Invincible in Character.* Raleigh, N.C.: L.A. Scruggs, 1893.

Sitkoff, Harvard. *A New Deal for Blacks.* New York and Oxford: Oxford University Press, 1978.

Sterling, Dorothy. *Black Foremothers, Three Lives.* New York: The Feminist Press, 1979.

Still, William. *The Underground Railroad: A Record.* Philadelphia: People's Publishing Company, 1879.

Takaki, Ronald T. *Iron Cages: Race and Culture in 19th-Century America.* Seattle: University of Washington Press, 1979.

Veney, Bethany. *The Narrative of Bethany Veney: A Slave Woman.* Worcester, Mass., 1889.

Walker, Alice, ed. *I Love Myself When I Am Laughing . . . : A Zora Neale Hurston Reader.* New York: The Feminist Press, 1979.

Wallace, Phyllis. *Black Women in the Labor Force.* Cambridge, Mass., and London: M.I.T. Press, 1980.

Washington, Booker T. *A New Negro for a New Century.* Chicago, 1900.

Wells-Barnett, Ida. *On Lynchings.* New York: Arno Press, 1969.

Manuscript Collections

Mary Ann Shadd Cary Papers, Moorland-Spingarn Research Center, Howard University, Washington, D.C.

Anna Julia Cooper Papers, Moorland-Spingarn Research Center, Howard University, Washington, D.C.

The Civil Rights Documentation Project, Moorland-Spingarn Research Center, Howard University, Washington, D.C.

NAACP Files, Library of Congress, Washington, D.C.

Mary Church Terrell Papers, Library of Congress, Washington, D.C.

Charlotte Hawkins Brown Papers, Schlesinger Library, Radcliffe College, Cambridge, Mass.

The Black Woman Oral History Project, Schlesinger Library, Radcliffe College, Cambridge, Mass.

Unpublished Materials

Bettina Aptheker, "Woman Suffrage and the Crusade Against Lynching, 1890–1920," Paper delivered at the First Scholarly Research Conference on Black Women, "Black Women: An Historical Perspective," sponsored by the National Council of Negro Women, Washington, D.C., November 12–13, 1979.

Marion Cuthbert, "Education and Marginality," Ph.D. dissertation, Columbia University, 1942.

Tullia K. Brown Hamilton, "The National Association of Colored Women, 1896 to 1920," Ph.D. dissertation, Emory University, 1978.

Jeanne L. Noble, "The Negro Woman's College Education," Ph.D. dissertation, Columbia University, 1956.

Rosalyn Terborg-Penn, "Afro-Americans in the Struggle for Woman Suffrage," Ph.D. dissertation, Howard University, 1977.

Index